CHEVROLET PARTS
INTERCHANGE MANUAL

Paul A. Herd

Motorbooks International
Publishers & Wholesalers ®

First published in 1995 by Motorbooks International Publishers & Wholesalers, PO Box 2, 729 Prospect Avenue, Osceola, WI 54020 USA

Motorbooks International books are also available at discounts in bulk quantity for industrial or sales-promotional use. For details write to Special Sales Manager at the Publisher's address

All drawings and illustrations in this book are the copyrighted property of General Motors Corporation. They are reproduced under license from the General Motors Corporation.

Library of Congress Cataloging-in-Publication Data
Herd, Paul A.
   Chevrolet parts interchange manual, 1959–1970/
      Paul A. Herd.
         p. cm.
   Includes index.
   ISBN 0-7603-0016-X
   1. Chevrolet automobile—Parts—Catalogs. I. Title.
TL215.C5H47   1995
629.222—dc20   94-44216

On the front cover: The pristine 402ci-powered 1971 Chevelle on the cover is a Canadian car restored from the frame up by owner Norm Dubord with the help of his sons, Richard and Larry. *Don Lyons*

Printed and bound in the United States of America

Contents

Acknowledgments

This book would not have been possible without the assistance of the following individuals: Melissa Garman and Nancy Finey of Chevrolet Public Relations who gracefully provided the original model photos; very special thanks to Barbara Hillick and all those at YEAR ONE, who went out of their way to provide additional photos of reproduction parts; thanks also to K.C. Winston and Mike and Ed at R & R Auto Salvage.

Also, a big thank you to Lisa Finch and those at Special Events for providing press passes to the car shows. And finally a thank you to all those car owners who allowed me to photograph their vehicles.

YEAR ONE offers a vast supply of original an reproduction parts to suit your Chevrolet. Contact them at Box 129, Tucker, GA or 1-800-950-9503.

Preface

When your classic Chevrolet was brand new it had both specialty and line, or interchangeable, parts. Specialty parts are those designed specifically for a certain model. Line, or interchangeable, parts are those used in several different model types and model years. These interchangeable parts allowed the manufacturer to keep production costs down, and gave you an affordable method of transportation.

Now, several years later, you most likely view your Chevrolet in a different light. You—and legions of other collectors—consider it a piece of automotive history. Fortunately, the ability to use interchangeable parts still exists.

That brings us to the purpose for writing this book. By referring to the book *before* you go looking for used parts at the salvage yard or swap meet, you will be able to find the correct part that will fit your car, even though the part may or may not have come from the same model as yours. The book can also be a guide to buying reproduction parts.

Many times, a part from a Camaro may be cheaper than, say, a part for a Nova, even though they are the same exact part!

In most cases the interchange in this manual is based on part number, meaning that the same part number was used for all models listed. However, there are cases where a different part number will fit while appearing and performing the same as the original unit. Also, when different colors are offered (for example, in seatbelts) there is no color listed in the interchange. Instead, interchange is based on the premise that the same part was used for *all* of the models and that either you will find the correct color or change it to suit your needs.

In researching this manual, I used the GM Master parts catalog for Buick, Chevrolet, Pontiac, and Oldsmobile. I also consulted assembly manuals for the models covered in this guide and for related parts available over the counter.

Introduction

How to Use This Book

The book is divided into sixteen chapters, which are further organized into sections covering specific components. For example, chapter 1 (engines) is broken down into eleven sections, or categories. These sections cover everything related to the engine, from cylinder blocks to crankshafts to valve covers. Each section is on a particular part and includes a model identification chart that give, you interchange numbers. The chart will look similar to this:

Door, Front

Model Identification

Camaro ....Interchange Number
1967 1
1968...2
1969...3
1970...4

Look for your model and year of car. That will give you the interchange number for the model(s) on which that particular part can be found. Then skim through the following pages, still in the same section, to find the interchange chart, which gives interchange numbers and any other information you are looking for. The interchanges are listed in numerical order. The chart will look something like this:

Interchange

Interchange Number: 1
Part Number(s): RH, 7645892; LH, 7645893
Usage: 1967 Camaro; 1967 Pontiac Firebird

Interchange Number: 2
Part Number(s): RH, 7742292; LH, 7742293
Usage: 1968 Camaro; 1968 Pontiac Firebird

Interchange Number: 3
Part Number(s): RH, 8723785; LH, 8723786
Usage: 1969 Camaro; 1969 Pontiac Firebird
Notes: Right-hand door only on Firebird. Left-hand door slightly different on Firebird due to way mirror mounts. Still will fit 1969 Camaro if Pontiac mirror is used.

Part numbers, if listed, are either the original or original replacement numbers. Also listed are the models that the part was used on (under "Usage"). "Notes" include things to watch for during interchange, such as bodystyle restrictions or modifications that can be done to make other parts fit. And, like the example, it may cross-reference another interchange that will also fit.

Decoding VIN Tag

The various letters and numbers that make up a car or truck's Vehicle Identification Number, or VIN, help to identify such things as engine type, place and year of manufacture, and other factors.

1959

For 1959 Chevrolet models, the VIN tag is riveted to the left-front-door hinge pillar. It begins with the code D59 (A59 if a six-cylinder), which is for the engine type and model year. That is followed by a code letter representing the location of the assembly plant.
These are the plant locations and codes:
A–Atlanta, GA
B–Baltimore, MD
F–Flint, MI
J–Janesville, WI
K–Kansas City, MO
L–Los Angeles, CA
N–Norwood, CA
O–Oakland, CA
S–St. Louis, MO
T–Tarrytown, NY
W–Willow Run, MI

The last digits in the VIN represent the serial number, which begins at 10001 at each plant.

1960–64

For 1960–64 Chevrolets, the VIN tag was located in the same place as in 1959, but the codes changed in 1960. The ID number now began with the last digit of the model year: 0–60, 1–61, 2–62, 3–63, 4–64. This was followed by a two-digit code indicating a six-cylinder or V-8, according to model.

For example Impala used the code 17 for cars with a six-cylinder, and the code 18 for cars with a V-8. The exception was the 1963–64 Impala SS (SS, for Super Sport), which used the code 13 for six-cylinders and code 14 for the more common V-8 equipped cars. Chevy II Nova (including Nova SS) used the code 04 for six-cylinders while the low-ball Chevy 100 used the code 02. A four-cylinder Chevy II 100 used the code 01.

Chevelle became available in 1964 and, because of the vast array of models available, many different codes were used.

Model/Engine Type	Code
Chevelle 300 six-cylinder	53
Chevelle 300 V-8	54
Malibu six-cylinder	55
Malibu V-8	56
Malibu SS six-cylinder	57
Malibu SS V-8	58

The next two digits were for body type, regardless of the model. The following codes were used; however, not all bodystyles were available in all models.

Body Type	Code
Two-door sedan	11
Four-door hardtop	39
Two-door hardtop	37
Convertible	67
El Camino	80

The sixth symbol is a letter that signifies the assembly plant. The following codes were used:

A–Atlanta, GA
B–Baltimore, MD
F–Flint, MI
J–Janesville, WI
K–Kansas City, MO
L–Los Angeles, CA
N–Norwood, CA
O–Oakland, CA
S–St. Louis, MO
T–Tarrytown, NY
W–Willow Run, MI

The last six digits form the sequential number built that model year at that plant.

1965–70

On the 1959–67 models the tag is located in the same location that the 1959–64 models were. But from 1968 on, the tag is located on the driver's side of the instrument panel and can be read through the windshield.

The 1965–70 VIN begins with the number 1 regardless of model, as it stands for Chevrolet. The next two digits are for model. The following codes were used:

Model/Engine Type	Code
Camaro six-cylinder	23
Camaro V-8	24
Camaro (Deluxe) six-cylinder	25
Camaro (Deluxe) V-8	26
Chevelle 300 six-cylinder	31
Chevelle 300 V-8	32
Chevelle Deluxe six-cylinder	33
Chevelle Deluxe V-8	34

Malibu six-cylinder	35
Malibu V-8	36
Chevelle Concours six-cylinder	37
Chevelle SS 396 or Concours V-8	38
Chevy II four-cylinder	11
Chevy II 100 six-cylinder	13
Chevy II Nova six-cylinder	15
Chevy II Nova V-8	16
Nova SS V-8	17
Impala six-cylinder (except SS)	63
Impala V-8 (except SS)	64
Impala SS V-8 or Caprice V-8	66
Impala SS six-cylinder	67

The fourth and fifth digits designate bodystyle. The following codes were used for bodystyle:

Body Type	Code
Two-door sedan	11
Four-door hardtop	69
Two-door hardtop, depending on model and year	39, 17, 37, or 87
Convertible	67

Notes: The Impala Custom and Caprice two-door for 1968–70 used the code 47; the Nova two-door for the same years was listed as 27.

The sixth digit in the VIN represents the last digit of the vehicle's model year. For example, 5–65, 6–66, 7–67, 8–68, 9–69, and 0–70.

The seventh symbol, a letter, signifies the assembly plant. The following were used:

A–Atlanta, GA
B–Baltimore, MD
D–Doraville
F–Flint, MI
G–Farmingham, MA
J–Janesville, WI
K–Kansas City, MO
L–Los Angeles, CA
N–Norwood, CA
O–Oakland, CA
R–Arlington, TX
S–Southgate, CA
S–St. Louis, MO
T–Tarrytown, NY
U–Lordstown, OH
W–Willow Run, MI
Y–Wilmington, DE
Z–Freemount, CA
1–Ontario, Canada

Remaining digits make up the sequential number built at that plant for that model year. Each plant and each year begins at 100001 for most models. Exceptions include the Camaro, which began at 300001 in 1968, and 500001 in 1969; the Nova, which began at 200001 in 1968 and 400001 in 1969; the Chevelle, which began at 300001 in 1969; and the Impala, which began at 000001 in 1969. Otherwise, all models began at 100001 regardless of model year.

Chapter 1

Engine

Engine

As explained in the introductory pages, this chapter is divided into sections of parts that make up the engine as a whole. As a complete unit, engines are pretty much interchangeable.

If your car was available from the factory with a particular engine, that engine will probably fit in your car. For example, your 1970 Chevelle came with a 307ci. That car was available from the factory with a 454ci engine, so it is likely that a big block will fit (in this case, you will have to change the motor mounts).

When making such drastic changes, components like transmission, suspension, and rear end may have to be changed to accommodate the heavier and more powerful engine.

Cylinder Block

Cylinder blocks are identified by their casting number. On small-blocks, this number is located at the back of the block on the passenger's side of the flywheel flange. On big-blocks, it is located on boss near the top of the bell housing on the driver's side. (Note that this interchange is limited to a bare block only. Short-blocks can use the same block on a low-powered passenger car and a special high-performance Camaro V-8.)

When it comes to early (1964–67) Chevy II V-8 cylinder blocks, remember that they are unique to this model only. Due to clearance problems, the oil filter mount was moved forward about 2.5in. Thus, these blocks *are not interchangeable* with other models or later (1968–70) Chevy II models—nor are other blocks interchangeable with the 1964–67 Chevy II.

Model Identification

283ci	Interchange Number
1959–61	1
1962–64, all but Chevy II	2
1965–67, all but Chevy II	3
1964–65 Nova SS	4
1966–67 Chevy II	5

302ci	Interchange Number
1967	6

Engine identification pad is at the front of the engine, just below the passenger's side cylinder head. *Year One*

Cylinder heads are identified by their casting number which typically is stamped as shown. This head casting number 3986839 is for the 1968–74 307 or 350ci powerplant.

The 1969–70 Z-28 Camaro used aluminum cast valve covers.

When installed in a muscle car, the 396 and 427 used chrome-plated valve covers.

Interchange

Interchange Number: 1
  Casting Number(s): 3556519, 3737739, 3849852
  Usage: 1959–61 full-size Chevrolet
  Notes: Castings 3556519 and 3737739 were used only with 4bbl carburetors these years

Interchange Number: 2
  Casting Number(s): 3789935, 3849852, 3864812
  Usage: 1962–64 full-size Chevrolet; 1964 Chevelle

Interchange Number: 3
  Casting Number(s): 3849852, 3849935, 3896944
  Usage: 1965–67 full-size Chevrolet; 1965–67 Chevelle

Interchange Number: 4
  Casting Number(s): 3790721
  Usage: 1964–65 Chevy II
  Notes: No other interchange

Interchange Number: 5
  Casting Number(s): 3862194
  Usage: 1966–67 Chevy II
  Notes: No other interchange

Interchange Number: 6
  Casting Number(s): 3892657
  Usage: 1966–67 Chevelle with 327/360hp; 1967 Camaro Z-28
  Notes: No special block was used for the 302ci powerplant. Instead, the high-performance 327ci block was used. Note, though, that special engine ID code was used for this engine. So a 327ci V-8 block is not a 100 percent interchange.

Interchange Number: 7
  Casting Number(s): 3932386, 3970010
  Usage: 1968–69 Camaro Z-28
  Notes: No special block was used for this powerplant. Instead, the high-performance 350ci four-bolt block was used. Note, though, that special engine ID code was used for this engine. So a 350ci V-8 block is not a 100 percent interchange.

Interchange Number: 8

Casting Number(s): 3959512, 3782870, 3789817, 3794460, 3852174, 3858180

Usage: 1962–64 full-size Chevrolet; 1964 Chevelle

Notes: Not interchangeable with 1964–67 Chevy II. Casting 3959512 used in 1962–63 only.

Interchange Number: 9

Casting Number(s): 3782870, 3789817, 3903352, 3852174, 3892657

Usage: 1964–67 Chevelle; 1965–67 full-size Chevrolet; 1967 Camaro

Notes: Not interchangeable with 1965–67 Chevy II. Some casting numbers carry over from other years. Used with all outputs.

Interchange Number: 10

Casting Number(s): 3791362

Usage: 1965–67 Chevy II/Nova

Notes: No other interchange.

Interchange Number: 11

Casting Number(s): 3970041, 3814660, 3970010, 3914678, 3932386, 3955618

Usage: 1968 Chevelle; 1968 Nova; 1968–69 Camaro

Interchange Number: 12

Casting Number(s): 3732755, 3755011, 3798962, 3771705

Usage: 1959–61 full-size Chevrolet

Notes: Casting numbers 3755011 and 3771705 were used in both standard and high-performance applications.

Interchange Number: 13

Casting Number(s): 3855961, 3932388, 3958618, 3970014

Usage: 1968–79 Nova; 1968–70 full-size Chevrolet; 1968–79 Camaro; 1969–77 Chevelle

Notes: All blocks have two-bolt mains. Not used in high-performance applications in Chevelle or Camaro.

Interchange Number: 14

Casting Number(s): 3956618, 3970010, 3932386

Usage: 1968–69 Chevelle (300hp+); 1968–70 Camaro (300hp+); 1969–70 Nova (300hp+)

Notes: Also used in later model Z-28 and Corvette. Block is also found on Chevrolet and GMC trucks.

Interchange Number: 15

Casting Number(s): 3855962

Usage: 1965 Chevelle SS 396; 1965 Impala

Notes: High-performance block.

Interchange Number: 16

Casting Number(s): 3855961 (325 & 360hp)

Usage: 1966 Chevelle SS 396; 1966 Impala

Notes: Two-bolt mains not used with 375hp version.

Interchange Number: 17

Casting Number(s): 3873858

Usage: 1966 Chevelle SS 396

Notes: High-performance block four-bolt mains used this model only.

Interchange Number: 18

Casting Number(s): 3902406

Usage: 1967 Chevelle SS 396; 1967 Camaro SS 396; 1967 Impala

Notes: Used with both two- and four-bolt mains. The 375hp used four-bolt mains not found in Impala.

Interchange Number: 19

Casting Number(s): 3916323

Usage: 1968 Chevelle SS 396; 1968 Camaro SS 396; 1968 Impala; 1968 Nova SS 396

Interchange Number: 20

Casting Number(s): 3935440

Usage: 1969 Chevelle SS 396; 1969 Camaro SS 396; 1969 Impala; 1969 Nova SS 396

Notes: Late 1969 blocks were overbored to 402ci displacement. It used a different casting number. See 402ci V-8.

Interchange Number: 21

Casting Number(s): 3955272

Usage: 1969 Chevelle SS 396; 1969 Impala; 1969 Camaro SS 396

Notes: Overbored 396ci block. Still referred to as 396ci V-8.

Interchange Number: 22

Casting Number(s): 3969854

Usage: 1970 Camaro SS 396; 1970 Nova SS 396; 1970–71 Chevelle SS 396; 1970–71 Monte Carlo

Notes: Still referred to as 396ci V-8 in 1970; referred to as 400ci V-8 in 1971. *Warning:* A small-block 400ci was also available in Impala and 1970 Monte Carlo. Small-block has 2bbl, big-block 4bbl. Do not confuse the two.

Interchange Number: 23

Casting Number(s): 3788068

Usage: 1962–63 full-size Chevrolet

Notes: Used with all output levels in 1962; used with 340hp output in early 1963 only.

Interchange Number: 24

Casting Number(s): 3830814

Usage: Late 1963–65 full-size Chevrolet

Notes: Note for 400 or 425hp outputs. Used in later 1963 models; took place of 3788068.

Interchange Number: 25

Casting Number(s): 3844422

Usage: 1964–65 full-size Chevrolet

Interchange Number: 26

Casting Number(s): 3869942

Usage: 1966–67 Impala SS 427; 1967 Corvette

Interchange Number: 27

Casting Number(s): 3904351

Usage: 1967 Impala SS 427; 1967 Corvette

Interchange Number: 28

Casting Number(s): 3916321

Usage: 1968 Impala SS 427; 1968 Corvette

Notes: Four-bolt mains only

Interchange Number: 29
> Casting Number(s): 3963512
> Usage: 1969 Impala SS 427; 1969 COPO Camaro; 1969 COPO Chevelle
> Notes: This block was also used on the 1970–71 Chevelle SS 454 with the LS-5;1970–71 GMC Sprint; 1970–71 Impala police car package; 1970–71 Monte Carlo SS 454. (COPO stood for Central Office Production Order.)

Short Block

A short-block is a complete engine without the induction system, cylinder heads, exhaust system, or oil pan. To be interchangeable the block must have the same inner components; that is, the same engine identification code.

The engine identification code is a system of letters and numbers that indicate where the engine was built, the date it was built, the model(s) it will fit, and the horsepower it will generate. The code can be found on the passenger's side cylinder head. A typical code will look like this: T 10 10 MQ. This particular engine was manufactured at the Tondawanda engine plant (T), on October 10 (10 10), and the MQ indicates that it was originally installed in a 1967–68 396ci/375hp V-8 in a Camaro.

Engine identification codes are included in the Interchange chart for short-blocks. Note that these engines were built at the Flint (F) engine plant. Part numbers are also given.

Model Identification

Interchange

Interchange Number: 1
> Horsepower: All
> Carburetor: 2bbl and 4bbl
> Compression Ratio: 9.25:1
> Crankshaft Type: (1)
> Part Number(s): Short-block, 3970164
> Usage: 1962–64 full-size Chevrolet; 1964 Chevelle
> Engine ID Codes:
> *Manual:*
> 190hp:
> Chevelle three-speed: J for 1964; four-speed: JA for 1964 Impala three-speed: C for 1962–64
> *Automatic:*
> 190hp:
> Chevelle: JD for 1964
> Impala: D

Interchange Number: 2
> Horsepower: 290
> Carburetor: 4bbl
> Compression Ratio: 11:1
> Crankshaft Type: Forged
> Part Number(s): Short-block, 3937290; engine, 3916355
> Usage: 1967 Camaro Z-28
> Engine ID Codes: Four-speed only: MO; MP with AIR*
> Notes: No interchange. See cylinder block.

Interchange Number: 3
> Horsepower: 290
> Carburetor: 4bbl
> Compression Ratio: 11:1
> Crankshaft Type: Forged
> Part Number(s): Short-block, 3931639; engine

Usage: 1968–69 Camaro Z-28
Engine ID Codes:
Four-speed only: DZ
*AIR stands for Air Injection Reactor, an air pump and delivery system.

Interchange Number: 4
Horsepower: 210
Carburetor: 2bbl
Compression Ratio: 8.75:1
Crankshaft Type: Nodular
Part Number(s): Short-block, N/A; engine, 3908989
Usage: 1967–69 Camaro
Engine ID Codes:
Manual: MA, MB with AIR
Powerglide: ME, MF with AIR
Notes: No interchange; no other model used this engine. Base V-8.

Interchange Number: 5
Horsepower: 275/300hp
Carburetor: 4bbl
Compression Ratio: 10:1
Crankshaft Type: Nodular
Part Number(s): Short-block, N/A
Usage: 1966–67 Chevelle; 1966–67 full-size Chevrolet; 1966–67 Corvette; 1967–69 Camaro
Engine ID Codes:
Manual:
Camaro: MK, ML with AIR for 1967; EA for 1968
Chevelle: EA, EB with AIR
Impala: HA, MB with AIR
Powerglide:
Camaro: MM, MN with AIR
Chevelle: EC, EE with AIR
Impala: HC, HF with AIR
Turbo Hydra-matic 350:
Impala: KL without AIR, KM with AIR for 1967;
Powerglide: ME, MF with AIR

Interchange Number: 6
Horsepower: 300
Carburetor: 4bbl
Compression Ratio: 11:1
Crankshaft Type: Nodular
Part Number(s): Short-block, N/A; engine
Usage: 1964–65 Chevelle; 1964–65 Impala
Engine ID Codes:
Manual:
Chevelle: JR for 1964, EB for 1965
Impala: RB for 1964, HB for 1965
Powerglide:
Chevelle: SS for 1964, EF for 1965
Impala: SB for 1964, HD for 1965

Interchange Number: 7
Horsepower: 360
Carburetor: 4bbl
Compression Ratio: 11:1
Crankshaft Type: Forged
Part Number(s): Short-block, N/A; engine 3863145
Usage: 1964–65 Corvette; 1965 Chevelle

Engine ID Codes:
Manual: EC, ED with transistor ignition for 1965: Corvette: RR (365hp); RT (365hp), RU (365hp), RX (375hp) for 1964; HK (365hp), HL (365hp), HM (365hp), HN (375hp)
Notes: No automatic transmission interchange.

Interchange Number: 8
Horsepower/Carburetor: 250 4bbl, 300 4bbl
Compression Ratio: 10.5:1
Crankshaft Type: Cast
Usage: 1965–66 Chevy II
Engine ID Codes:
Manual:
250hp: ZA, ZE with a/c for 1965
270hp: ZA, ZB with AIR, ZE with a/c, ZC with AIR& a/c for 1966
300hp: ZB, ZF with a/c for 1965
Powerglide:
250hp: AK, ZM with a/c for 1965
270hp: ZD with AIR, ZM with a/c, ZF with AIR & a/c, ZK for 1966
300hp: ZL, JN with a/c for 1965
Notes: This is a Chevy II block only. Will not fit any other model.

Interchange Number: 9
Horsepower: 350
Carburetor: 4bbl
Compression Ratio: 11:1
Crankshaft Type: Forged
Usage: 1966–67 Chevy II
Engine ID Codes:
Manual: ZG with AIR, ZH with AIR & a/c, ZI without AC, ZJ with a/c for 1966–67
Notes: Will not fit any other model.

Interchange Number: 10
Horsepower: 250/280
Compression Ratio: 11:1
Crankshaft Type: Cast
Part Number(s): 3774977
Usage: 1959–61 full-size Chevrolet
Engine ID Codes:
Manual:
250hp: F for 1959–61
280hp: FA for 1959–61
Powerglide:
250hp: G for 1959–61;
280hp: GB for 1959–61;
Notes: 280hp has three 2bbls; 250hp has single 4bbl.

Interchange Number: 11
Horsepower: 315/305/320/345
Compression Ratio: 11.25:1
Crankshaft Type: Forged
Part Number(s): 3782012
Usage: 1959–61 full-size Chevrolet
Engine ID Codes:
Manual:
305hp: FD for 1959–61
315hp: FB for 1959

320hp: FG for 1959–61
345hp: FE for 1959–61
Powerglide:
GD for 1959–61 (305hp only)
Notes: 315 and 345 ratings are with three 2bbl carbs; others are single 4bbls. 305 and 315 ratings are high-performance; other two are special high-performance

Interchange Number: 12

Horsepower: 295
Carburetor: 4bbl
Compression Ratio: 10.25:1
Crankshaft Type: Cast
Usage: 1967–70 Camaro; 1968–70 Nova;
  1969–70 (300hp); Chevelle; 1969–70 (300hp) Impala; 1969–70 (300hp) Corvette; 1970 Monte Carlo (300hp)
Engine ID Codes:
Manual:
Camaro: MS for 1967–68; MT with AIR for 1967 only; HA (300hp) for 1969; CNJ (300hp) for 1970
Chevelle: HA, HD with heavy-duty clutch for 1969; CNJ for 1970 Corvette: HY for 1969; CTL for 1970
Impala: HG, HD with heavy-duty clutch for 1969; CNQ for 1970
Nova: MS for 1968; HA, HP with heavy-duty clutch for 1969; CNJ for 1970
Monte Carlo: See 1970 Chevelle
Powerglide:
Camaro: MU, MV with AIR for 1967 only–67–68; HE (300hp); CNK (300hp) for 1970
Chevelle: H3 for 1969; CNK for 1970
Corvette: N/A
Impala: HK for 1969; CNS for 1970
Nova: HE for 1969; CNK for 1970
Monte Carlo: See 1970 Chevelle
Turbo Hydra-Matic 350:
Camaro/Chevelle/Nova: HB for 1969; CRE for 1970 (all 300hp)
Corvette: N/A
Impala: HN for 1969; CNR (CNT for Police) for 1970
Monte Carlo: See 1970 Chevelle
Notes: All 1968 Camaro codes are for the 300hp version.

Interchange Number: 13

Horsepower: 250
Carburetor: 2bbl
Compression Ratio: 9:1
Crankshaft Type: Cast
Usage: 1969–70 Camaro; 1969–70 Chevelle; 1969–70 Impala; 1969–70 Nova; 1970 Monte Carlo
Engine ID Codes:
Manual:
Camaro/Chevelle/Nova/Monte Carlo: HC for 1969; CNI for 1970 Impala: HI for 1969; CND (CNP for police) for 1970
Powerglide:
Camaro/Chevelle/Nova: HF for 1969; CNM for 1970
Impala: HL for 1969; CNM for 1970

Interchange Number: 14

Horsepower: 255
Carburetor: 2bbl
Compression Ratio: 10.25:1
Crankshaft Type: Cast
Usage: 1969 Camaro;1969 Chevelle;1969 Impala; 1969 Nova
Engine ID Codes:
Manual:
Camaro/Chevelle/Nova/: HQ for 1969 Impala: HT for 1969
Powerglide:
Camaro/Chevelle/Nova: HR for 1969
Impala: HU for 1969
Turbo Hydra-Matic 350:
Camaro/Chevelle/Nova: HS for 1969
Notes: This engine output level was offered just this one year only, but the 300hp version is the same block inside. The heads are different, though.

Interchange Number: 15

Horsepower: 300
Carburetor: 4bbl
Compression Ratio: 10.25:1
Crankshaft Type: Cast
Usage: 1969–70 Camaro; 1969–70 Chevelle;
  1969–70 Corvette; 1969–70 Impala; 1969–70 Nova; 1970 Monte Carlo
Engine ID Codes:
Manual:
Camaro: HA for 1969; CNJ for 1970
Chevelle: HA, HD with heavy-duty clutch for 1969; CNJ for 1970
Corvette: HY for 1969; CTL for 1970
Impala: HG, HD with heavy-duty clutch for 1969; CNQ for 1970
Nova: MS for 1968; HA, HP with heavy-duty clutch for 1969; CNJ for 1970
Monte Carlo: See 1970 Chevelle
Powerglide:
Camaro: HE for 1969; CNK for 1970
Chevelle: HE for 1969; CNK for 1970
Impala: HK for 1969; CNS for 1970
Nova: HE for 1969; CNK for 1970
Monte Carlo: See 1970 Chevelle
Turbo Hydra-Matic 350:
Camaro/Chevelle/Nova: HB for 1969; CRE for 1970
Impala: HN for 1969; CNR (CNT for Police) for 1970
Monte Carlo: See 1970 Chevelle
Notes: Same compression ratio and short-block was used with the 255hp block above and the 295hp 350ci V-8.

Interchange Number: 16

Horsepower: 360
Carburetor: 4bbl

Turbo Hydra-Matic 350:
Camaro/Chevelle/Nova: HD for 1969; CNN for 1970
Impala: HM for 1969; CNV (CNX for police) for 1970
Notes: 1968 blocks will fit, but a 1968 intake must be used. However, it will be incorrect visually.

Compression Ratio: 11:1
Crankshaft Type: Forged
Usage: 1970 Camaro Z-28; 1970 Corvette
Engine ID Codes:
Manual: (four-speed) CTB for Camaro; CTV for Corvette
Turbo Hydra-Matic 400: CTC for Camaro; CTR for Corvette
Notes: This is a powerful small-block V-8. It was used only in these two models, but in the Corvette it was rated at 370hp. It was made this year only.

Interchange Number: 17
Horsepower: 325
Carburetor: 4bbl
Compression Ratio: 10.25:1
Crankshaft Type: Cast
Usage: 1966 Chevelle; 1966 Impala
Engine ID Codes:
Manual:
Chevelle: ED, EH with AIR
Impala: IA, IB with AIR
Powerglide:
Chevelle: EK, EM with AIR
Impala: IG, IC with AIR

Interchange Number: 18
Horsepower: 360
Carburetor: 4bbl
Compression Ratio: 10.25:1
Crankshaft Type: Cast
Usage: 1966 Chevelle
Engine ID Codes:
Manual:
Chevelle: EF, EJ with AIR
Powerglide: EL, EN with AIR

Interchange Number: 19
Horsepower: 325/350
Carburetor: 4bbl
Compression Ratio: 10.25:1
Crankshaft Type: Cast
Casting Number: 3902406
Usage: 1967–68 Impala (325hp); 1967 to mid-1969 Camaro; 1967 to mid-1969 Chevelle; 1968 to mid-1969 Nova
Engine ID Codes:
Manual:
325hp:
Camaro: MW, MX with AIR (1967 only) for 1967–68; JU for 1969
Chevelle: ED, EH with AIR (1967 only) for 1967–68; JA for 1969
Impala: IA
350hp:
Camaro: EI, EY with AIR for 1967–68; KA with heavy-duty clutch, JF for 1969
Chevelle: EF, EG with AIR (1967 only) for 1967–68; JC for 1969
Nova: MX for 1968; JF for 1969
Powerglide:

325hp:
Camaro: MW for 1967–68; JB for 1969
Chevelle: EK for 1967–68
Impala: IG, IC with AIR (1967 only) for 1967–68
Nova: JU for 1969
Turbo Hydra-Matic 400:
325hp:
Camaro: MY, MZ with AIR (1967 only) for 1967–68; JG for 1969
Chevelle: ET, EV with AIR (1967 only) for 1967–68; KH for 1969
Impala: IV for 1967–68
Nova: JM for 1969
350hp:
Camaro: EQ for 1967; MR for 1968; JI for 1969
Chevelle: EU, EW with AIR (1967 only) for 1967–68; JE for 1969
Nova: MR for 1968; JI for 1969
Notes: Late in the 1969 model year a change was made to 402ci. The above codes are for true 396ci blocks.

Interchange Number: 20
Horsepower: 375
Carburetor: 4bbl
Compression Ratio: 11:1
Crankshaft Type: Forged
Usage: 1966 Chevelle
Engine ID Codes:
Manual: EG

Interchange Number: 21
Horsepower: 375
Carburetor: 4bbl
Compression Ratio: 11:1
Crankshaft Type: Forged
Usage: 1967 to mid-1969 Camaro; 1967 to mid-1969 Chevelle; 1968 to mid-1969 Nova
Engine ID Codes:
Manual:
Camaro: MQ, MR with AIR (1967 only) for 1967–68; MT for 1968; JH, KC with heavy-duty clutch, JJ for 1969
Chevelle: EG, EX with AIR (1967 only) for 1967–68; KD, KG, KI for 1969 Nova: MQ for 1968; JH, KC (with heavy-duty clutch) for 1969
Turbo Hydra-Matic 400:
Camaro/Nova: JL for 1969
Chevelle: KF
Notes: (1) Changed to 402ci blocks in late 1969. These are true 396ci blocks. (2) JJ, KG, and KI models were equipped with aluminum heads, but the short-block is the same.

Interchange Number: 22
Horsepower: 325/350
Carburetor: 4bbl
Compression Ratio: 10.25:1
Crankshaft Type: Cast
Usage: Late 1969–70 Camaro; late 1969–70 Chevelle; late 1969–70 Nova; 1970 Monte Carlo
Engine ID Codes:
Manual:

325hp:

Camaro: CJU for 1969

Chevelle: CJA, CJV with heavy-duty clutch for 1969

350hp:

Camaro/Chevelle/Nova: CJF for four-speed for 1969; CTX for 1970

Powerglide:

325hp:

Camaro: CJB for 1969

Turbo Hydra-Matic 400:

325hp:

Camaro: CJG for 1969

Chevelle: CJK for 1969

350hp:

Camaro/Nova: CJI for 1969; CTW for 1970 Chevelle: CJE for 1969;CTW for 1970

Notes: (1) Some 1970 Camaros used the late 1969 codes. (2) In 1970 the 325hp block was rated at 330hp, but codes are the same as in late 1970s.

Interchange Number: 23

Horsepower: 375

Carburetor: 4bbl

Compression Ratio: 11:1

Crankshaft Type: Forged

Usage: Late 1969–70 Camaro; late 1969–70 Chevelle; late 1969–70 Nova

Engine ID Codes:

Manual:

Camaro/Nova: CJH for 1969; CKO for 1970 Chevelle: CJD for 1969; CKO, CKT, CKQ with heavy-duty clutch for 1970

Turbo Hydra-Matic 400:

Camaro/Nova: CJL for 1969; CTY for 1970

Chevelle: CJF for 1969; CTY for 1970

Notes: Codes CKP for the Turbo Hydra-Matic 400, CKT, and CKU for the manual are the same block but were equipped with aluminum heads. Code CKU-W/heavy-duty clutch.

Interchange Number: 24

Horsepower: all outputs

Compression Ratio: 11.0:1

Crankshaft Type: forged

Part Number(s): 3839752

Usage: 1961–63 full-size Chevrolet

Engine ID Codes:

Manual:

380hp: Q for 1961; QA for 1962

Interchange Number: 25

Horsepower: 390

Carburetor: 4bbl

Compression Ratio: 10.25:1

Crankshaft Type: Modular

Usage: 1966–68 full-size Chevrolet

Engine ID Codes:

Manual: IH, II with AIR for 1966–68 (all but SS 427); SS 427 only IE, IX with AIR for 1967–68

Turbo Hydra-Matic 400: IJ, IO with AIR for 1966–68 (all but SS 427); SS 427 only IS, IF with AIR for 1967–68

Notes: The 1967–68 SS 427 included a heavy-duty clutch.

Interchange Number: 26

Horsepower: 425

Carburetor: 4bbl

Compression Ratio: 11:1

Crankshaft Type: Forged

Usage: 1966–69 full-size Chevrolet; 1966–69 Corvette

Engine ID Codes:

Manual:

Impala: ID, IK with AIR for 1966–68

Corvette: IK, IP for 1966; IT, IU, JA with AIR JE for 1967; IR, IT, IU for 1968; LR, LT, LO, LU for 1969

Turbo Hydra-Matic 400:

Impala: IO for 1968; LS for 1969

Corvette: LX for 1969

Notes: Codes IU and LU are with aluminum heads. The 1968–69 Corvette is rated at 435hp.

Interchange Number: 27

Horsepower: 360

Carburetor: 4bbl

Compression Ratio: 10.25:1

Crankshaft Type: Cast

Usage: 1970 Chevelle; 1970 Impala (390hp); 1970 Corvette (390hp); 1970 Monte Carlo

Engine ID Codes:

Manual:

Chevelle/Monte Carlo: CRN, CRT for 1970

Corvette: CZU

Impala: CGU, CGT for police

Turbo Hydra-Matic 400:

Chevelle/Monte Carlo: CRQ

Corvette: CGW

Notes: This powerplant was available on the Chevelle and Monte Carlo only when the SS 454 packages were ordered. Also, note that there is a 345hp 454 on the Impala. This is not the same as the above.

Interchange Number: 28

Horsepower: 450

Carburetor: 4bbl

Compression Ratio: 11:1

Crankshaft Type: Forged

Usage: 1970 Chevelle; 1970 Monte Carlo

Engine ID Codes:

Manual:

Chevelle/Monte Carlo: CRV

Turbo Hydra-Matic 400:

Chevelle/Monte Carlo: CRR, CRS

Notes: This was the most powerful production V-8 ever installed in a muscle car. It was made in 1970 only. The Turbo Hydra-matic 400 was installed only when the SS 454 option and the LS-6 engine option were checked off. Code CRS was equipped with aluminum heads; short-block was same as CRR.

Crankshaft

Chevrolet crankshafts are available in two different materials: cast nodular iron and forged steel. The first type came standard in most engines, and therefore are the most common.

A couple of cautions:

(1) When converting from a manual transmission to an automatic, be sure to remove the clutch pilot bushing.

(2) A forged crankshaft can be used in place of a nodular unit, but a nodular crank must *never* be used in place of a forged unit.

Model Identification

Interchange

Interchange Number: 1

Part Number(s): 3815827
Casting Number(s): 3735236, 3815822, 3836266
Usage: 1957–67 except with Turboglide
Crankshaft Type: Nodular

Interchange Number: 2

Part Number(s): 3727449
Casting Number(s): 3735236, 3815822

Usage: 1957–61 Impala Turboglide
Crankshaft Type: Nodular

Interchange Number: 3

Part Number(s): 3917265
Casting Number(s): 6764, 3876764
Usage: 1967 Camaro Z-28
Crankshaft Type: Forged/Tuftrided
Notes: Small journals, balanced for 11:1 compression ratio. Will *not fit* 1968–69 blocks.

Interchange Number: 4

Part Number(s): 3941176
Casting Number(s): 1178, 3279, 3923278
Usage: 1968–69 Camaro Z-28
Crankshaft Type: Forged/Tuftrided
Notes: Large journals, balanced for 11:1 compression ratio.
Will *not fit* 1967 blocks.

Interchange Number: 5

Part Number(s): 3889304
Casting Number(s): 4577, 3782680, 3734627, 3941172
Usage: 1962–67, all models
Crankshaft Type: Cast
Notes: Used in under 300hp applications only.

Interchange Number: 6

Part Number(s): 3838495
Casting Number(s): 2680
Usage: 1965–67 Chevelle; 1966–67 Chevy II
Crankshaft Type: Forged
Notes: Used in over 300hp applications only. Unit is also Tuftrided and balanced for 11:1 compression ratio. Has small journals.

Interchange Number: 7

Part Number(s): 3830809
Casting Number(s): 391101A
Usage: 1968 full-size Chevrolet, Chevelle, or Nova
Crankshaft Type: Cast
Notes: This same shaft was used in the 1968 307ci V-8. This unit *will not fit* earlier or later engines. (See note 1 at front of section.)

Interchange Number: 8

Part Number(s): 3914681
Usage: 1968 Chevelle or Nova
Crankshaft Type: Forged
Notes: Large journal, Tuftrided, balanced for 11:1 compression ratio. *Will not fit* any other year.

Interchange Number: 9

Part Number(s): 3941172
Casting Number(s): 3911001, 3914681, 3941172
Usage: 1969 Camaro
Crankshaft Type: Cast
Notes: Also used in the 1969–73 307ci V-8 and will interchange. Used with all horsepower outputs.

Interchange Number: 10

Part Number(s): 3760427
Casting Number(s): 3732692

Usage: 1959–61 Impala 348ci
Crankshaft Type: Cast
Notes: Originally installed with manual transmission, but can be adapted to cars with automatic by removing clutch pilot bushing.

Interchange Number: 11
Part Number(s): 3828475
Casting Number(s): 3732692, 3741642
Usage: 1959–61 Impala high-performance 348ci with Powerglide

Interchange Number: 12
Part Number(s): 3741640
Casting Number(s): 3732692, 3741640
Usage: 1959–61 Impala 348ci with Turboglide
Crankshaft Type: Cast

Interchange Number: 13
Part Number(s): 3912335
Casting Number(s): 310514
Usage: 1967–68 Camaro; 1968 Chevelle, Chevy II, or Impala
Crankshaft Type: Cast
Notes: Used this two years only; small journals. Will not fit 1969–up models. (See note 1 at front of section.)

Interchange Number: 14
Part Number(s): 3932444
Casting Number(s): 1182, 2690, 3912335, 3932442, 3932444, 3941184
Usage: 1969–72, all Chevrolets
Crankshaft Type: Cast
Notes: Will not fit 1967–68 block. (See note 1 at front of section.)

Interchange Number: 15
Part Number(s): 3941184
Casting Number(s): 3941184
Usage: 1970–72 Camaro Z-28; 1970–72 Corvette
Crankshaft Type: Forged
Notes: Large journals, balanced. (See note 1 at front of section.)

Interchange Number: 16
Part Number(s): 3887114
Casting Number(s): 5140
Usage: 1965 Chevelle SS 396; 1965 Impala
Crankshaft Type: Forged

Interchange Number: 17
Part Number(s): 3882848
Casting Number(s): 3856223
Usage: 1966–70, all but 375hp
Crankshaft Type: Forged
Notes: Should never be used in 375hp (L-78) engines.

Interchange Number: 18
Part Number(s): 3882841
Casting Number(s): 6223
Usage: 1966–70 Camaro or Chevelle; 1968–70 Nova
Crankshaft Type: Forged
Notes: Trifled, cross-drilled used originally in 375hp versions only. Can fit lesser powered versions, but will

be incorrect. Better performance, though.

Interchange Number: 19
Part Number(s): 3833147
Casting Number(s): 3795589, 3829027, 3838416
Usage: 1962–65 full-size Chevrolet
Crankshaft Type: Forged

Interchange Number: 20
Part Number(s): 3882849
Casting Number(s): 6223
Usage: 1966–68 Impala SS 427; 1969 Impala Police sedan
Crankshaft Type: Forged
Notes: Good performance crankshaft. Not for use in 425hp version. Nor 1969 regular production 427 in Impala. (See note 1 at front of section.)

Interchange Number: 21
Part Number(s): 3882842
Usage: 1966–69 Impala SS 427; 1969 COPO
Crankshaft Type: Forged
Notes: Cross-drilled, trifled. For use in 425hp version. Balanced for 11:1 compression ratio.

Interchange Number: 22
Part Number(s): 3937739
Usage: 1969 Impala 335hp
Crankshaft Type: Cast
Notes: This engine only. Do not use in 390 or 425hp versions.

Interchange Number: 23
Part Number(s): 3967463
Usage: 1970 Chevelle SS 454; 1970 Monte Carlo SS 454
Crankshaft Type: Cast
Notes: Originally used with automatic only.

Interchange Number: 24
Part Number(s): 3975945
Usage: 1970 Chevelle SS 454; 1970 Monte Carlo SS 454
Crankshaft Type: Cast
Notes: Originally used with manual only. Can be used with automatic if pilot bushing is removed.

Interchange Number: 25
Part Number(s): 3963523
Usage: 1970 Chevelle SS 454; 1970 Monte Carlo SS 454
Crankshaft Type: Forged
Notes: Used only with LS-6 engine. Excellent performance crankshaft and can fit LS-5 block. Used with both automatic and manual (See note 1).

Flywheel, with Ring Gear

Model Identification

SMALL-BLOCK (283, 302, 327, 348, 350, 409)

Manual ....*Interchange Number*
1959–64 Impala, all but twin 4bbl 409..............................4

1965–67 283ci, all but models with 11-inch clutch..........1
1967–69 Camaro Z-28 1
1965–69 327, except special high-performance 1
1965–68 327ci special high-performance 1
1967–69 350ci, all but models with 11-inch clutch..........1
1965–69, all with 11-inch clutch 2
1970 Camaro Z-28, Chevelle 350ci 330hp V-8.................3

Powerglide ....*Interchange Number*
1959–70, all engines...5

Turbo Hydra-Matic
1965–68, all models, all engines 6
1969 Chevelle, Camaro, Impala with Turbo Hydra-Matic 400
....7, 8
1970, all but Camaro Z-28 8
1970 Camaro Z-28......................................9, 10

BIG-BLOCK (396, 427, 454)

Manual..*Interchange Number*
1965–70 396; 1966–69 427ci...........................11
1970 Chevelle SS 454..12

Powerglide ....*Interchange Number*
1965–66 Chevelle; Impala 396ci 13

Turbo Hydra-Matic ....*Interchange Number*
1966–69 Impala, Chevelle, Nova 16
1970 Chevelle, Impala, Nova, Camaro 14
1970 Chevelle SS 454 LS-6 15

Interchange

Interchange Number: 1
Part Number(s): 3973452
Casting Number(s): 3791021
Type: Solid used without heavy-duty clutch
Usage: 1964–69 327ci V-8; 1964–70 230ci and 250ci
six-cylinder; 1965–67 283ci V-8; 1967–69 302ci V-8;
1968–71 Buick Special six-cylinder; 1968–72 307ci
V-8; 1969 Impala 350ci V-8; 1970–74 250ci Camaro
and Pontiac Firebird; 1973–74 Buick Apollo six-cylinder

Interchange Number: 2
Part Number(s): 3998281
Type: Solid used with heavy-duty 11-inch diameter
clutch
Usage: All except 302ci V-8

Interchange Number: 3
Part Number(s): 3899668
Type: Solid used with super heavy-duty clutch
Usage: 1970 Z-28; 1970 Chevelle 350ci 330hp V-8

Interchange Number: 4
Part Number(s): 3739423
Casting Number(s): 3729004
Usage: 1959–64 Impala 283, 348, and 409ci, except
425hp
Notes: Used with 10-inch diameter clutch

Interchange Number: 5
Part Number(s): 3789821

Type: Spoke type with six 2-inch diameter holes
Usage: All with Powerglide, including 409ci V-8

Interchange Number: 6
Part Number(s): 3991401
Type: Spoke type; uses one mounting bolt
Usage: 1965–68, all with Turbo Hydra-Matic
Notes: Some 1968 models used part number 3937736;
this unit has two mounting bolts. Both units are 11-
1/2 inches in diameter. However, they are not inter-
changeable due to the mounting holes.

Interchange Number: 7
Part Number(s):3991402
Usage: 1969, all 327ci with Turbo Hydra-Matic 400
Notes: Part number 3991403 was used with this setup
also.

Interchange Number: 8
Part Number(s): 3991403
Usage: 1969, all 327ci with Turbo Hydra-Matic 400;
1970–72 350ci V-8, all but Z-28

Interchange Number: 9
Part Number(s): 3937736
Usage: with automatic transmission
1971–72 Z-28

Interchange Number: 10
Part Number(s): 3973453
Usage: 1970 350ci Z-28; 1970 Corvette 350ci V-8

Interchange Number: 11
Part Number(s): 3998281
Type: Used with 11-inch clutch
Usage: 1965–70 396ci; 1966–69 427ci
Notes: See type above also used with 1965–67 327,
350, and 360hp versions.

Interchange Number: 12
Part Number(s): 3993827
Usage: 1970–72, all 454ci V-8

Interchange Number: 13
Part Number(s): 3868806
Type: Spoke type with 2-15/32 inch center hole
Usage: 1965–66 Chevelle SS 396 or Impala 396ci V-8

Interchange Number: 14
Part Number(s): 3992069
Usage: 1970–72 Chevelle SS 454, all but 1970–71 LS-6;
1970–72 Impala police cruiser

Interchange Number: 15
Part Number(s): 3992070
Usage: 1970–71 Chevelle SS 454 (LS-6); 1970–71
Corvette 454ci LS-7

Interchange Number: 16
Part Number(s): 3991401
Type: Spoke type; uses one mounting bolt
Usage: 1967–68, all with Turbo Hydra-Matic 400
Notes: Some 1968 models used part number 3937736;
this unit has two mounting bolts. Both units are 11-
1/2 inches in diameter. These are not interchange-
able.

Connecting Rods

Model Identification

Interchange

Interchange Number: 1
Part Number(s): 3703525
Forging Number(s): rod, 3703527; cap, 3703526
Usage: 1955–61 265ci V-8; 1959–61 283ci V-8
Notes: These rods have oil "spit holes" to lubricate the bearings.

Interchange Number: 2
Part Number(s): 3864881
Usage: 1962–67 283ci V-8; 1962–67 327ci V-8; 1967 302ci V-8
Notes: Used with small journals. Some early 1968 327s used these rods.

Interchange Number: 3
Part Number(s): 3973386
Usage: Early 1968 302ci V-8; 1970–72 350 Z-28
Notes: This unit is used with a pressed-in pin; rod is shot peened.

Interchange Number: 4
Part Number(s): 3946841
Usage: Late 1968–69 302ci Z-28 V-8; 1969 Corvette 350ci 370hp V-8
Notes: Used with full floating pins.

Interchange Number: 5
Part Number(s): 3916396
Usage: 1968–82 small-blocks, all but special high-performance
Notes: Will not fit early blocks.

Interchange Number: 6
Part Number(s): 3774771
Usage: 1959–61 348ci V-8
Notes: This rod is 6-1/8 inches in length.

Interchange Number: 7
Part Number(s): 3933174
Usage: 396ci; 427ci V-8 except special high-performance versions
Notes: Rod has orange stripe. Do not use in 396ci 375hp or 427ci 425hp versions.

Interchange Number: 8
Part Number(s): 3856240
Usage: 396ci; 427ci V-8 special high-performance only
Notes: Can be used in low-performance version for a stronger engine.

Interchange Number: 9
Part Number(s): 3814126
Forging Number(s): rod, 3795624; cap, 3732717
Usage: 1962–65 409ci V-8, all but Z-11
Notes: Z-11 option used special stressed rods.

Interchange Number: 10
Part Number(s): 3933174
Usage: 1970–72 454ci V-8, all but LS-6 special high-performance
Notes: Do not use in LS-6. Rod has orange mark.

Interchange Number: 11
Part Number(s): 3963552
Usage: 1970–72 454ci V-8 LS-6 special high-performance
Notes: Rod has white marks.

Pistons
Piston size—if given—is diameter by height.

Model Identification

Interchange

Interchange Number: 1
Part Number(s): 3734627
Size: 3 7/8x3 23/64
Compression Ratio: All
Usage: 1959–61 283ci V-8
Notes: Part number 3860407 will fit.

Interchange Number: 2
Part Number(s): 3860407
Size: 3 7/8x3 51/64
Compression Ratio: All
Usage: 1962–67 283ci V-8
Notes: Earlier style will not fit. 1962–70 230ci six-cylinder and 1962–70 153ci four-cylinder pistons will interchange.

Interchange Number: 3
Part Number(s): 3927177
Usage: 1967–68 302ci V-8
Notes: No interchange; use only with earlier style rod.

Interchange Number: 4
Part Number(s): 3946876
Usage: Late 1968–69 302ci V-8
Notes: Use with floating rod only.

Interchange Number: 5
Part Number(s): 3799491
Size: 4 x3 17/32
Usage: 1962–69 327ci V-8
Notes: Use in all 327ci V-8s except those with special high-performance.

Interchange Number: 6
Part Number(s): 3871208
Size: 3 7/8x3 23/64
Usage: 1964–68 327ci with special high-performance
Notes: Can fit lesser powered 327, but be careful with valve clearance.

Interchange Number: 7
Part Number(s): 3769731
Usage: 1959–61 348ci V-8

Notes: Use with non-high-performance or special high-performance.

Interchange Number: 8
Part Number(s): 3769731
Usage: 1959–61 343ci V-8
Notes: Can be used with high-performance and special high-performance.

Interchange Number: 9
Part Number(s): 3911020
Usage: 1967–70 350ci V-8, all but 1970 Z-28
Notes: Do not use in 360hp V-8.

Interchange Number: 10
Part Number(s): 3989048
Usage: 1970 Camaro Z-28 350ci V-8
Notes: No interchange.

Interchange Number: 11
Part Number(s): RH, 38781228; LH, 3878227
Size: 4 3/32x 3 1/2
Compression Ratio: 10.25:1
Usage: Early 1965 to 1969 396ci V-8, all but 375hp; 427ci V-8, all but 425hp
Notes: Fits true 396ci V-8; will not fit 402ci V-8. Unique to each bank.

Interchange Number: 12
Part Number(s): 3878231
Size: 4 3/32x 3 43/64
Compression Ratio: 11:1
Usage: Early 1965 to 1969 396ci 375hp V-8; 427ci 425hp V-8
Notes: Fit all cylinders. If used with lesser powered blocks, special high-performance crankshaft must be used.

Interchange Number: 13
Part Number(s): RH, 399982; LH, 3999981
Compression Ratio: 10.25:1
Usage: Late 1969 to 1970 402ci V-8, all but 375hp
Notes: Will not fit true 396 block.

Interchange Number: 14
Part Number(s): 3969989
Compression Ratio: 11:1
Usage: Late 1969 to 1970 396ci 375hp
Notes: Will not fit true 396ci block.

Interchange Number: 15
Part Number(s): cylinders 1 & 5, 3834141; cylinders 2 & 6, 3834143; cylinders 3 & 7, 3834145; cylinders 4 & 8, 3834147
Size: 4 5/16x2 1/4
Compression Ratio: 11:1
Usage: 1962–65 340hp 409ci V-8
Notes: Do not use in 400hp or 425hp versions. Will not swap positions.

Interchange Number: 16
Part Number(s): cylinders 1, 4, 5, & 8, 3819577; cylinders 2, 3, 6, & 7, 3819577 3819577
Size: 4 5/16x3 63/64
Compression Ratio: 11:1

Usage: 1963–65 409ci with 400hp or 425hp
Notes: Unique placement pistons will not swap with each other.

Interchange Number: 17

Part Number(s): RH, 3976016; LH, 3976015
Compression Ratio: 10.25:1
Usage: 1970 454ci LS-5 V-8
Notes: Do not use in 1970 LS-6. Each bank is unique and will not swap.

Interchange Number: 18

Part Number(s): 3976013
Compression Ratio: 11.25:1
Usage: 1970 454 LS-6
Notes: 1971 pistons will not fit.

Camshaft

Model Identification

Interchange

Interchange Number: 1

Part Number(s): 3896929
ID Number(s): 3896930
Specifications:
Lift: 0.390 inch intake, 0.410 inch exhaust
Duration: 195 degree intake, 202 degree exhaust
Type: Hydraulic lifters
Usage: 1959–67 283ci V-8; 1962–69 327ci V-8 (all but special high-performance); 1967–72 350ci V-8 (all but 1970 Z-28 350); 1968–73 307ci V-8; 1970 400ci 2bbl V-8
Notes: Often called a 350ci 300hp cam.

Interchange Number: 2

Part Number(s): 3972178
ID Number(s): 3849347
Specifications:
Lift: 0.458 in intake, 0.485 inch exhaust
Duration: 229 degree intake, 237 degree exhaust
Type: Solid lifters
Usage: 1964 327ci 360hp V-8 Chevelle; 1967–69 302ci V-8; 1970–72 350ci Camaro Z-28

Interchange Number: 3

Part Number(s): 3863151
ID Number(s): 3849347, 3863152
Specifications:
Lift: 0.447 inch intake and exhaust
Duration: 221 degree intake and exhaust
Type: Hydraulic lifters
Usage: 1965–68 327 with special high-performance. Called a 327 350hp cam.

Interchange Number: 4

Part Number(s): 3755946
ID Number(s): 3755947
Usage: 1959–61 348ci V-8 with high-performance and special high-performance

Interchange Number: 5

Part Number(s): 3744901
ID Number(s): 3744430
Usage: 1959–61 348ci V-8, all but high-performance or special high-performance; 1962–65 409ci 340hp V-8

Interchange Number: 6

Part Number(s): 3830690
ID Number(s): 3822930
Usage: 1962–65 409ci V-8 with high-performance
Notes: First design; used in blocks coded before T118OB. Not for use with 1962 Z-11 option.

Interchange Number: 7

Part Number(s): 3837735
ID Number(s): 7736
Usage: 1962 Z-11 option; 1963–65 409ci V-8 with high-performance or dual 4bbl
Notes: Second design; used only in blocks coded after T1118QA or T1118QB. Use with valve springs part number 3858367.

Interchange Number: 8

Part Number(s): 3874872
ID Number(s): 3874874
Specifications:
Lift: 0.461 inch intake, 0.480 inch exhaust
Duration: 350 degree intake, 352 degree exhaust

Type: Hydraulic lifters
Usage: 1965–70 396ci 325hp (330hp in 1970)

Interchange Number: 9
Part Number(s): 3883986
Specifications:
Lift: 0.460 inch intake, 0.488 inch exhaust
Duration: 213 degree intake, 217 degree exhaust
Type: Hydraulic lifters
Usage: 1966–69 427ci 390hp; 1966–70 396ci 350hp
(360hp in 1966); 1970 454ci 360hp; 1971 454ci
365hp

Interchange Number: 10
Part Number(s): 3863143
ID Number(s): 3863143
Specifications:
Lift: 0.520 inch intake and exhaust
Duration: 242 degree intake and exhaust
Type: Solid lifters
Usage: 1965 396ci 425hp; 1965–70 396ci 375hp;
1966–69 427ci 425hp; 1970 454ci 450hp V-8

Timing Chain and Sprockets
Small-blocks used two different chains; both were early link type. From 1962 to 1967, part number 3704150 was used. It housed an eighteen-tooth steel sprocket, part number 3759980, and an iron sprocket, part number 3865964 and casting number 3704214.

After 1967, the chain was listed as part number 3896961. It used an eighteen-tooth steel sprocket, listed as part number 3896959, and an iron sprocket, part number 3896960. These parts were used on all small-blocks regardless of horsepower output or camshaft type.

Big-blocks also used two different sets of components. But here, the difference was the camshaft. All but those with special high-performance used a chain listed as part number 3902428 while those with special high-performance versions used part number 3902428. High-performance outputs of 396ci/350hp (360hp in 1966 only), 427ci/390hp, and 454ci/360hp did not use this chain. Only the 396ci/375hp, 396ci/425hp, 427ci/425hp, and 454ci/450hp versions used it.

Sprockets also differed according to output. Regular and high-performance engines used a steel 3 1/2 inch diameter sprocket (part number 3902422) with nineteen teeth. The special high-performance powerplants used part number 3860035. That gear was 3 1/32 inches in diameter.

A thirty-eight-tooth sprocket made of aluminum was also used with both types—but the part number is different. All except the special high-performance engines used part number 330815; it was cast as 3856356. Special high-performance engines used part number 330814 (it has no casting number).

The 348 and 409ci V-8s used the same chain (part number 3704150). It, too, is an early link type. A steel eighteen-tooth 2 7/8 inch diameter sprocket (part number 3759980) was used on the 409. The 348 used a twenty-seven-tooth sprocket stamped "71." Both used a thirty-six-tooth iron sprocket, listed as part number 3704214.

Main Bearing Caps
The change in main bearing caps for small-blocks is the difference in journal size. Those made in 1967 or before used

small journals, while those coming after used larger journals.

Also, some high-performance engines made between 1968 and 1969—the 302 and 350ci V-8s—used four-bolt mains.

The big-block's special high-performance block used four-bolt mains as well. All are interchangeable within each engine family. In other words, those from a 350 four-bolt will fit a 302ci V-8 with four-bolt mains, and a 396ci with four-bolt mains will fit an LS-6 454 V-8.

Small-Block Main Bearing Caps

Two-bolt	Front	Rear
1962–67	3970194*	3911052
1968–72	3956688	3911007

*Has light blue stripe.

Four-bolt	Front	Rear
1968–70	3956686	3911007
400ci 2bbl	6259412	3973308

Big-Block Main Bearing Caps

	Front	Rear
Two-bolt	3877462	3877464
Four-bolt	3877470	3877464

Cylinder Head
Chevrolet used many different sets of cylinder heads. But, two basic styles are most commonly found: the standard-duty passenger type and the high-performance type. The high-performance heads were sometimes cast in aluminum; however, aluminum heads normally don't have much of a flow advantage over the cast-iron types. They are a great weight savings, though.

Heads are generally identified by their casting number. Care should be used when inspecting heads to look for cracks and warpage. A good way to check for warpage is by laying a straight-edge (like a ruler) across the head.

Model Identification

283ci V-8	Interchange Number
Early 1959 4bbl	1, 2
Late 1959–60 4bbl	3, 4
1961–67	5, 6

302ci V-8	Interchange Number
1967–68	9
1969	10

327ci V-8	Interchange Number
1962–67, all but special high-performance	5, 6
1964–67 with special high-performance	9
1968–69	7, 8

348ci V-8	Interchange Number
1959–60 with high-performance	26
1960–61 without high-performance or multi-carbs	27

350ci V-8	Interchange Number
1967–68 4bbl	10
1969–70 4bbl	11
1969–70 2bbl	12
1970 Camaro Z-28	13

Interchange

Interchange Number: 1

Casting Number(s): 3760116

Type: Iron; high-performance & special high-performance

Usage: Early-built 1959 283ci V-8 with single 4bbl or fuel injection

Interchange Number: 2

Casting Number(s): 3755550

Type: Iron; high-performance & special high-performance

Usage: Early-built 1959 283ci V-8 with single 4bbl or fuel injection in Corvette

Notes: Both this and 3760116 head are interchangeable. Both were the first design, and used special valve covers.

Interchange Number: 3

Casting Number(s):3767754

Type: Iron; high-performance & special high-performance

Usage: Late-built 1959–60 283ci V-8 with single 4bbl or fuel injection in Corvette

Notes: Second design took the place of heads listed in interchange number 2.

Interchange Number: 4

Casting Number(s): 3767792

Type: Iron; high-performance & special high-performance

Usage: Late-built 1959–60 283ci V-8 with single 4bbl or fuel injection in Corvette

Notes: Second design. Interchangeable with casting number 3767754.

Interchange Number: 5

Casting Number(s): 3795896

Part Number(s): 3817680

Type: Iron; high-performance

Usage: General use small-block head. Used on 1961–67 283, and 327ci V-8 without special high-performance. Was used with 250–300hp 327ci V-8.

Notes: This head will fit earlier blocks if its valve cover is used. This cover will be visually incorrect for 1959–60 Impalas.

Interchange Number: 6

Casting Number(s): 3836842

Type: Iron; high-performance

Usage: General use small-block head. Used on 1961–67 283, and 327ci V-8 without special performance. Was used with 250–300hp 327ci V-8.

Notes: This head will fit earlier blocks if its valve cover is used. This cover will be visually incorrect for 1959–60 Impalas.

Interchange Number: 7

Casting Number(s): 3927185

Part Number(s): 3958602

Type: Iron; no high- or special high-performance

Usage: General use small-block head. Used on 1969–72 307ci V-8, and 1969 327ci V-8 only.

Interchange Number: 8

Casting Number(s): 3917293

Part Number(s): 3958607

Type: Iron; high-performance Usage: Low-octane cylinder head used in 1968 327ci V-8

Interchange Number: 9

Casting Number(s): 3782461

Type: Iron; special high-performance

Usage: 1964–67 327ci V-8 with special high-performance (over 300hp); 1967 302ci Z-28 Camaro

Interchange Number: 10

Casting Number(s): 3917291

Part Number(s): 3987376

Type: Iron; special high-performance

Usage: 1969 302ci Z-28; 1969 350ci 350hp V-8 in Corvette

Notes: Uses threaded rocker studs. Will fit 1964–67 327ci V-8.

Interchange Number: 11

Casting Number(s): 3947041

Part Number(s): 3958603

Type: Iron; high-performance

Usage: 1969–70 350ci 4bbl V-8 with up to 300hp

Notes: Not for use on 1970 Z-28 Camaro.

Interchange Number: 12

Casting Number(s): 3958606

Part Number(s): 3932441

Type: Iron; no high- or special high-performance

Usage: 1969–70 350ci 2bbl V-8

Interchange Number: 13

Casting Number(s): 3987376
Part Number(s): 3927186
Type: Iron; special high-performance
Usage: 1970 350ci 4bbl V-8 in Camaro Z-28; 1970 Corvette
Notes: No other interchange. The 1968 327ci special high-performance heads will fit, but use a different casting number.

Interchange Number: 14

Casting Number(s): 3856206 and 3856208
Type: Iron; special high-performance
Usage: 1965 396ci with either 375hp or 425hp

Interchange Number: 15

Casting Number(s): 3872702
Type: Iron; high-performance
Usage: 1966 396ci 325hp and 360hp; 1966 427ci 390hp V-8
Notes: Pushrod guides differ between 396 and 427ci V-8s. This unit used oval-shaped ports.

Interchange Number: 16

Casting Number(s): 3916323
Type: Iron; high-performance
Usage: Late 1966–67 396ci with 325 or 350hp; late 1966–67 427ci V-8 with 390hp
Notes: Pushrod guides differ between 396 and 427ci V-8s. This unit used oval-shaped ports.

Interchange Number: 17

Casting Number(s): 3917215
Type: Iron; high-performance
Usage: 1968 396ci V-8 with 325 or 350hp; 1968 427ci V-8 with 390hp
Notes: Pushrod guides differ between 396 and 427. Unit has oval-shaped ports. Will fit earlier models, but temperature sending hole will have to be plugged. This will be visually incorrect.

Interchange Number: 18

Casting Number(s): 3931063
Type: Iron; high-performance
Usage: Late 1969 396ci with 325 or 350hp; late 1969 427ci V-8 with 390hp
Notes: Pushrod guides differ between 396 and 427. Unit has oval-shaped ports. Will fit 1967 and earlier models, but temperature sending hole will have to be plugged. This will be visually incorrect.

Interchange Number: 19

Casting Number(s): 3964290
Type: Iron; high-performance
Usage: 1970 396ci with 330 or 350hp; 1970 LS-5 454ci 360hp V-8

Interchange Number: 20

Casting Number(s): 3964292
Type: Iron; special high-performance
Usage: 1970 LS-6 454ci 450hp V-8; 1970 375hp 396ci V-8

Interchange Number: 21

Casting Number(s): 3873858
Type: Iron; special high-performance
Usage: 1966 396ci 375hp and 427ci 425hp
Notes: Pushrod guides differ between 396 and 427. Unit has rectangular-shaped ports.

Interchange Number: 22

Casting Number(s): 3904391
Type: Iron; special high-performance
Usage: 1967 396ci 375hp and 427ci 425hp
Notes: Pushrod guides differ between 396 and 427. Unit has rectangular-shaped ports.

Interchange Number: 23

Casting Number(s): 3919840
Type: Iron; special high-performance
Usage: 1968–69 396ci 375hp and 427ci 425hp
Notes: Pushrod guides differ between 396 and 427. Unit has rectangular-shaped ports. Will fit 1967 and earlier blocks, but temperature sender hole will have to be plugged. Will be visually incorrect.

Interchange Number: 24

Casting Number(s): 3919842
Type: Aluminum; special high-performance
Usage: 1969 396ci 375hp and 427ci 425hp
Notes: Pushrod guides differ between 396 and 427. Unit has rectangular-shaped ports. Called L-89 option.

Interchange Number: 25

Casting Number(s): 3946074
Type: Aluminum; special high-performance
Usage: 1970 396ci 375hp

Interchange Number: 26

Casting Number(s): 3758379 and 3767738
Part Number(s): 3785086
Type: Iron; high-performance and special high-performance
Usage: 1959–60 348ci V-8 with high-performance

Interchange Number: 27

Casting Number(s): 3830817
Part Number(s): 3839747
Type: Iron; no high- or special high-performance
Usage: 1960 348ci V-8 without high-performance or multi-carburetion. Also used on 1963–65 409/340hp V-8
Notes: Do not use on 400hp or multi-carburetor 409ci V-8.

Valve Cover

Model Identification

Interchange

Interchange Number: 1

Part Number(s): 3853411
Usage: 1959–65 348 or 409ci
Notes: Unique design, fits either side.

Interchange Number: 2

Part Number(s): 3910298
Usage: 1962–67 327ci; 1965–67 283ci;
Notes: Painted steel; not for use special high-perfor-
mance.

Interchange Number: 3

Part Number(s): 3850049
Usage: 1959–64 283ci V-8
Notes: Not for use on later styles; has even holes.

Interchange Number: 4

Part Number(s): 3910297
Usage: 1964–67 327 with special high-performance;
1967 302ci Z-28

Interchange Number: 5

Part Number(s): 3923226
Usage: 1968 327 with special high-performance; 1968
302ci Z-28
Notes: Had chrome-plated steel covers.

Interchange Number: 6

Part Number(s): RH, 3965542; LH, 3965541
Usage: 1969 302ci Z-28; 1970 Camaro Z-28
Notes: Made of cast aluminum. Unique fit to each side
because RH cover used an ID emblem part number
3946860. Used on high-performance 350 V-8 up to
1976.

Interchange Number: 7

Part Number(s): 6272227
Usage: 1968–69 327, all but special high-performance;
1968–72 307; 1968–72 350, all but 1970 Z-28;
1970 400 (small-block)
Notes: Generic small-block cover. Stamped steel painted Chevrolet Orange. Was used up to 1973 on all
350ci V-8s except the special high-performance versions and 1971–73 400 2bbl V-8s.

Interchange Number: 8

Part Number(s): RH, 338262; LH, 338261
Usage: 1965–69 396ci V-8 without special high-perfor-
mance in Impala only; 1966–69 427ci 390hp, all but
Impala SS; 1970 Chevelle, all 396 (RH only)
Notes: Painted steel covers. Not for use on Impala
425hp, or in Impala SS with any 427ci V-8.

Interchange Number: 9

Part Number(s): RH, 325174; LH, 325169
Usage: 1965–69 Chevelle 396 V-8; 1967–70 Camaro
396; 1968–70 Nova SS; 1968–69 Impala SS 427ci
425hp and 390hp; other Impalas with the 427ci
390 or 335hp used painted steel covers.
Notes: Chrome-plated valve covers. Not for use in Impala, except in 1965 with 425hp. Not for use with
aluminum heads.

Interchange Number: 10

Part Number(s): RH, 3902390; LH, 3908923
Usage: 396ci 375hp; 427ci 425hp with aluminum
heads

Interchange Number: 11

Part Number(s): 3993841, LH only
Usage: 1970 Chevelle 396; LH side only
Notes: See interchange number 8 for RH cover.

Chapter 2

Fuel System

Fuel Tank

Model Identification

Interchange

Interchange Number: 1
Part Number(s): 3912377
Capacity: 18 gallons
Usage: 1967–68 Camaro; 1967–68 Pontiac Firebird
Notes: Sending units differ between Chevrolet and Pontiac.

Interchange Number: 2
Part Number(s): 3953844
Capacity: 18 gallons
Usage: 1969 Camaro; 1969 Pontiac Firebird
Notes: Sending units differ between Chevrolet and Pontiac.

Interchange Number: 3
Part Number(s): 6263025
Usage: 1970 Camaro without EEC; 1970 Pontiac Firebird without EEC
Notes: This tank was used in all states in 1970 except California. Sending units differ between Chevrolet and Pontiac.

Interchange Number: 4
Part Number(s): 6272127
Capacity: 18 gallons
Usage: 1970 Camaro with EEC; 1970 Pontiac Firebird with EEC; 1971–72 Camaro; 1971–72 Firebird
Notes: Sending units differ between Chevrolet and Pontiac.

Interchange Number: 5
Part Number(s): 3867745
Capacity: 20 gallons
Usage: 1964–67 Chevelle, all but El Camino and station wagon; 1965–66 full-size Chevrolet, all but station wagon

Interchange Number: 6
Part Number(s): 3857231
Usage: 1964–67 El Camino; 1965–67 Chevelle station wagon; 1964 Chevelle station wagon with two seats only
Notes: 1964 Chevelle station wagon with three seats will not interchange.

Interchange Number: 7
Part Number(s): 3940133
Usage: 1968–69 Chevelle, except pickup and station wagon

Interchange Number: 8
Part Number(s): 393080
Capacity: 18 gallons
Usage: 1968–70 El Camino

Notes: For 1970 tanks except those in California. Station wagon tanks will no longer interchange due to filler neck location.

Interchange Number: 9
Part Number(s): 3998309
Capacity: 20 gallons
Usage: 1970 Chevelle, all but station wagon or El Camino, without EEC
Notes: No other interchange.

Interchange Number: 10
Part Number(s): 3998310
Capacity: 20 gallons
Usage: 1970 Chevelle, all but station wagon or El Camino; 1970 Monte Carlo, all with EEC
Notes: Although part numbers are different, the 1971–72 Chevelle fuel tank will fit 1970 models with EEC.

Interchange Number: 11
Part Number(s): 3775654
Capacity: 20 gallons
Usage: 1959–60 full-size Chevrolet, all but El Camino or station wagon
Notes: El Camino used part number 3764265, which was also used in six-passenger station wagon.

Interchange Number: 12
Part Number(s): 3777685
Capacity: 20 gallons
Usage: 1961–64 full-size Chevrolet, except station wagon

Interchange Number: 13
Part Number(s): 3930952
Usage: 1967 full-size Chevrolet, all except station wagon
Notes: No other interchange.

Interchange Number: 14
Part Number(s): 3968731
Capacity: 25 gallons

The 1967–68 Camaro SS used a gas cap that doubled for model identification.

The 1967–68 Camaro with RS package used this gas cap. *Year One*

Usage: 1968–70 Impala without EEC, all except station wagon

Interchange Number: 15
Part Number(s): 3982841
Usage: 1970 Impala with EEC, all except station wagon
Notes: The EEC tank was used mostly in California cars in 1970. No interchange.

Interchange Number: 16
Part Number(s): 3793946
Capacity: 16 gallons
Usage: 1962–67 Chevy II/Nova, all except three-seat station wagon
Notes: Two-seat station wagon used the same fuel tank and will interchange.

Interchange Number: 17
Part Number(s): 3998317
Usage: 1968–70 Chevy II/Nova, all without EEC

Interchange Number: 18
Part Number(s): 3995720
Usage: 1970 Chevy II/Nova with EEC; 1971–72 Nova; 1971–72 Pontiac Ventura II
Notes: EEC used in California only in 1970, and in all states in 1971–72.

Fuel Cap

Model Identification

Camaro	Interchange Number
1967–68 without RS or SS	1
1967–68 with RS	2
1967–68 with SS	3

Interchange

Interchange Number: 1
Part Number(s): 3910043
Usage: 1967–68 Camaro, all but RS or SS
Notes: Painted to match car.

Interchange Number: 2
Part Number(s): 3910189
Usage: 1967–68 Camaro RS, all but SS
Notes: SS/RS Camaros used an SS cap.

Interchange Number: 3
Part Number(s): 3910045
Usage: 1967–68 Camaro SS, or RS and SS with 350 4bbl or 396ci V-8
Notes: Has SS lettering on cap.

Interchange Number: 4
Part Number(s): 3931449
Type: Vented
Usage: *Chevrolet:* 1968–69 Chevelle station wagon and El Camino; 1968–70 Impala station wagon; 1969–70 Camaro; 1970 Nova; 1970 Chevelle.
Pontiac: 1961–62 Tempest; 1964 Tempest; 1965–69 Tempest station wagon; 1967–69 Firebird; 1970 station wagon, all except with EEC.
Buick: 1957–63, all but station wagon; 1964 LeSabre or Wildcat; 1965 Riviera; 1965–69 station wagon;
Oldsmobile: 1968–69 Vista Cruiser

Interchange Number: 5
Part Number(s): 405373
Type: Non-vented
Usage: *Chevrolet:* 1964–69 Chevelle, all but El Camino or station wagon; 1964–70 full-size Chevrolet, all but station wagon;
Buick: 1966–70 Skylark, all but station wagon; 1966–70 full-size except station wagon. *Pontiac:* 1965–70 Le-Mans, except station wagon;
1969 Firebird; 1965–67 full-size, all but station wagon.
Oldsmobile: 1966–67 full-size, except station wagon; 1966–70 Cutlass, except station wagon

Interchange Number: 6
Part Number(s): 3814439
Type: Vented

Usage: 1959–63 full-size Chevrolet, all except station wagon or El Camino

Interchange Number: 7
Part Number(s): 3792252
Type: Chrome plated
Usage: 1962–64 Chevy II

Interchange Number: 8
Part Number(s): 3867853
Type: Chrome plated
Usage: 1965–67 Chevy II

Interchange Number: 9
Part Number(s): 3914863
Type: Vented
Usage: *Chevrolet:* 1968–69 Nova.
Buick: 1970 LeSabre station wagon with EEC.
Pontiac: 1970 station wagon, all with EEC

Fuel Pump

Model Identification

Interchange

Interchange Number: 1
Part Number(s): 6415824
Stamped: 4701
Usage: 1959–63 full-size Chevrolet 283ci 2bbl

Interchange Number: 2
Part Number(s): 6415824
Stamped: 6942 or 40510
Usage: 1964–66, all models with 283ci 2bbl

Interchange Number: 3
Part Number(s): 6416712
Stamped: 40503
Usage: early 1967 327ci; early 1967 Camaro 350ci; 1967 283ci; 1968–72 307ci

Interchange Number: 4
Part Number(s): 6415616
Stamped: 4432, 4656, 4657, 4662
Usage: 1959–62 348ci 4bbl (except high-performance or special high-performance); 1959–66 283ci 4bbl; 1962–66 327ci 4bbl (except 350 or 360hp); 1962–65 409ci (all outputs)

Interchange Number: 5
Part Number(s): 6470422 (AC 40524 or 40725)
Stamped: 40524 or 40725
Usage: 1967–68 302ci; late 1967–68 327ci V-8; 1967–68 350ci V-8

Interchange Number: 6
Part Number(s): 6470779 (AC 40669)
Stamped: 40669
Usage: 1969 302ci; 1969 350ci; 1969 327ci

Interchange Number: 7
Part Number(s): 6415563
Stamped: 40148
Usage: 1965 327ci 350hp
Notes: No interchange.

Interchange Number: 8
Part Number(s): 5621718
Stamped: 4799
Usage: 1959–61 348ci with high-performance or multi-carburetion

Interchange Number: 9
Part Number(s): 6470310
Stamped: 40777
Usage: 1970 350 300hp or 360hp; 1973–74 350ci 4bbl V-8

Interchange Number: 10
Part Number(s): 6470779
Stamped: 40726, 1970–72
Usage: 1970–72 350ci, except 300hp in 1970; 1970–72 400ci small-block

Interchange Number: 11
Part Number(s): 6415961
Stamped: 40193
Usage: 1965–66 396, except 375hp or 425hp in 1965; 1966 390hp 427ci V-8

Interchange Number: 12
Part Number(s): 6416245
Stamped: 6415325
Usage: 1965 Chevelle SS 396 (Z-16); 1965 Impala 425hp

Interchange Number: 13
Part Number(s): 6416459
Stamped: 40358
Usage: 1966 Chevelle 427ci 360 or 375hp; Impala 425hp

Interchange Number: 14
Part Number(s): 6470424
Stamped: 40468 for 1967–68; 40470 for 1967–69; 40727 for 1970–72
Usage: 1967–69 427ci, except 396ci 330hp in 1970; 1967–70 396ci; 1970 454ci 450hp

Interchange Number: 15
Part Number(s): 6470307
Stamped: 40768
Usage: 1970 402ci 330hp; 1970 454ci 360hp

Intake Manifold

Model Identification

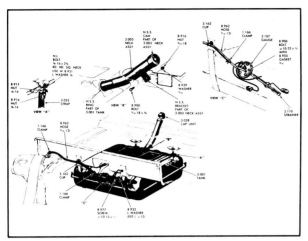

1959-60 passenger gasoline tanks. *Chevrolet*

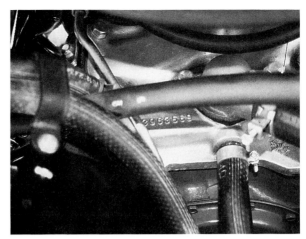

Intake manifolds are identified by a casting number located on one of the runners.

Interchange

Interchange Number: 1
Part Number(s): 3852568
Casting Number(s): 3746829
Usage: 1958–64 283ci; 1962–64 327ci, except special high-performance

Interchange Number: 2
Part Number(s): 3870394
Usage: 1965 283 and 327ci 4bbl, except high-performance or special high-performance

Interchange Number: 3
Part Number(s):3888886
Usage: 1966 283ci 4bbl; 1966 327ci 4bbl except special high-performance

Interchange Number: 4
Part Number(s): 3958622
Usage: 1967 302ci V-8 with aluminum intake

Interchange Number: 5
Part Number(s): 3958627
Usage: 1968–69 302ci V-8 with aluminum intake

Interchange Number: 6
Part Number(s): 3931575
Usage: 1967–68 327ci 4bbl, except special high-performance; 1967–68 350ci 4bbl

Interchange Number: 7
Part Number(s): 3987361
Usage: 1969–70 350ci, except Z-28 in 1970

Interchange Number: 8
Part Number(s): 3972114
Usage: 1970 (aluminum) Z-28; 1970 Chevelle 330hp; 1970 Corvette 330hp

Interchange Number: 9
Part Number(s): 3852569
Usage: 1962–63 327ci 300hp

Interchange Number: 10
Part Number(s): 3852569
Usage: 1964–65 327ci with high-performance, except special high-performance versions

Interchange Number: 11
Part Number(s): 3852570
Casting Number(s): 3795397
Usage: 1965 327ci 360hp (aluminum)

Interchange Number: 12
Part Number(s): 3760436

Usage: 1958–61 348ci without multi-carb and without high-performance

Interchange Number: 13
Part Number(s): 3770084
Usage: 1958–60 348ci with high-lift cam

Interchange Number: 14
Part Number(s): 3797775
Casting Number(s): 3797776
Usage: 1958–61 348ci with special high-performance but without multi-carburetion; 1961 409ci with single 4bbl (aluminum)

Interchange Number: 15
Part Number(s): 3844462
Usage: 1962–65 409ci with high-performance, with single 4bbl

Interchange Number: 16
Part Number(s): 3876818
Casting Number(s): 3966948
Usage: 1965–67 396ci V-8 with Holley carb, except 375hp; 1966–67 427ci 390hp V-8

Interchange Number: 17
Part Number(s): 3957996
Casting Number(s): 3883948
Usage: 1966–67 396ci, except 375hp with Rochester carb; 1966–67 427ci with Rochester carb

Interchange Number: 18
Part Number(s): 3947084
Casting Number(s): 3866963
Usage: 1965 396ci 425hp in Impala, and 375hp in Chevelle (aluminum intake)

Interchange Number: 19
Part Number(s): 3947084
Casting Number(s): 3805069
Usage: 1966–67 396ci 375hp and 427ci 425hp

Interchange Number: 20
Part Number(s): 3947996
Casting Number(s): 3883948, 3931063
Usage: 1968–69 396ci, all but 375hp; 1968–69 427ci, except 425hp

Interchange Number: 21
Part Number(s): 3947084
Casting Number(s): 3885069, 3931063
Usage: 1968–69 396ci 375hp; 1968–69 427ci 425hp (aluminum intake)

Interchange Number: 22
Part Number(s): 3977608
Casting Number(s): 3955287
Usage: 1970–72 396ci (also 402ci), except 375hp; 1970–72 454ci 360hp

Interchange Number: 23
Part Number(s): 3977609
Casting Number(s): 3963569
Usage: 1970 396ci 375hp; 1970–71 LS-6 454ci V-8 (aluminum intake)

Interchange Number: 24
Part Number(s): 3814880
Usage: 1961–64 409ci twin 4bbl

Interchange Number: 25
Part Number(s): 3764018
Casting Number(s): 374998
Usage: 1958–61 348ci with multi-carbs
Notes: Has bypass hose.

Carburetor

Carburetors differ in a number of ways: engine size, engine output, type of transmission, emission controls, and in some cases, options installed on the car.

Three different brands of carburetors were used on Chevrolet models. The most popular was the Rochester, next was Holley, and then Carter. Interchange is based on the same part number and, or model number. Due to the lack of interest, 2bbl carbs have been deleted to save space.

Rochester Carburetor

Typically, the Rochester ID number is found stamped on a metal tag. Location of this tag varies with carb model. For example, on 4GC models the tag is triangular in shape and attached to the top of the air horn. For 4MV models (Quadrajet), the tag is round and is fixed to the lower body assembly of the carburetor, usually just in front of the throttle control.

Model Identification

MANUAL TRANSMISSION

283ci V-8..........................Interchange Number
1959–61 4bbl 1
1964 4bbl 2
1965–66 4bbl 3

327ci V-8..........................Interchange Number
1966–67 4bbl
except special high-performance........................4
1968 4bbl 5

350ci V-8..........................Interchange Number
1967 4
1968–69 5
1970, all except Z-28...6

396ci V-8..........................Interchange Number
1966–67 325hp 7
1968–69 325hp or 350hp 8
1970 330hp 9
1970 350hp 10

AUTOMATIC TRANSMISSION

293ci V-8..........................Interchange Number
1964–66 4bbl 11

327ci V-8..........................Interchange Number
1964–66 250hp 11
Late 1966–67 12
1968 13

350ci V-8..........................Interchange Number

Interchange

Interchange Number: 1
Usage: 1959–61 283ci 4bbl V-8
Model: 4GC
ID Number(s): 7013004, 7013010, 7015907

Interchange Number: 2
Usage: 1964–65 327ci 250hp; 1964–66 283ci 4bbl
Model: 4GC
ID Number(s): 7024125, 7024225

Interchange Number: 3
Usage: 1965 327ci 250hp; 1965–66 283ci
Model: 4GC
ID Number(s): 7025127, 7025121

Interchange Number: 4
Usage: 1966–67 327ci 275hp; 1967 350ci 4bbl
Model: 4GC
ID Number(s): 7027203, 7702713

Interchange Number: 5
Usage: 1968 327ci 4bbl V-8; 1968–69 350ci 4bbl
Model: 4MC
ID Number(s): 7028213, 7049203

Interchange Number: 6
Usage: 1970 350ci 4bbl, all except Z-28 Camaro
Model: 4MC
ID Number(s): 7040502, 7040503, 7040513

Interchange Number: 7
Usage: 1966–67 396ci 325hp;1966–67 427ci 390hp
Model: 4MC
ID Number(s): 7027201, 7027211
Notes: California cars used special carburetors not listed.

Interchange Number: 8
Usage: 1968–69 396ci 350hp; 1968–69 427ci 390hp;
    1968–69 396ci 350hp; 1968–69 427ci 335hp
Model: 4MC
ID Number(s): 7028209, 7028211, 7028217,
    7029201, 7029215

Interchange Number: 9
Usage: 1970 396ci 330hp
Model: 4MC
ID Number(s): 7040200, 7040201, 7040221,

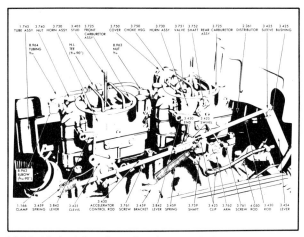

1956–62 dual four-barrel carburetor linkage. *Chevrolet*

    7040500, 7040501, 7040521
Notes: For use on both manual and automatic transmissions.

Interchange Number: 10
Usage: 1970 396ci 350hp; 1970 454ci 390hp
ID Number(s): 7040204, 7040205, 7040504, 7040505

Interchange Number: 11
Usage: 1964–66 283ci 4bbl; 1964–66 327ci 250hp
Model: 4GC
ID Number(s): 7008737, 7009846, 7011108,
    7012126, 7012128, 7013975, 7015004, 7015006,
    7015010, 7015012, 7019004, 7019006, 7019010,
    7019014, 7020006, 7020012, 7020022, 7023006,
    7023012, 7024121, 7024122, 7024220, 7024226,
    7025121, 7025122, 7025126, 7025128
Notes: Some models will have provisions for smog controls (AIR) that were used in California-sold cars.

Interchange Number: 12
Usage: Late 1966–67 327ci 275hp;
1967 350ci Camaro
Model: 4MC
ID Number(s): 7072702, 7027212, 7027218,
    7036210, 7036202, 7036210, 7037202, 7037212,
    7037218
Notes: Some models will have provisions for smog controls (AIR) that were used in California-sold cars.

Interchange Number: 13
Usage: 1968–69 350ci 4bbl
Model: 4MC
ID Number(s): 7028202, 7028212, 7029202, 2029212

Interchange Number: 14
Usage: 1966–67 396ci 325hp; 1966–67 427ci 390hp
Model: 4MC
ID Number(s): 7026200, 7027200, 7027210,
    7027216, 7036204, 7036200, 7037200, 7037216

Interchange Number: 15
Usage: 1968–69 396ci 325hp; 1968–69 427 335hp
Model: 4MC
ID Number(s): 7028210, 7029200

Interchange Number: 16
Usage: 1968–69 396ci 350hp; 427ci 390hp
Model: 4MC
ID Number(s): 7029204, 7028216, 7028218

Holley Carburetor

The Holley 4bbl is identified by its Holley part number, which is stamped on the outer side of the air horn.

Model Identification

MANUAL

302ci V-8	Interchange Number
1967	4
1968–69	5

327ci V-8	Interchange Number
1965 360hp	1
1967 350hp	9

350ci V-8	Interchange Number
1970 Z-28	11

396ci V-8	Interchange Number
1965 375hp, 425hp	2
1965–66 325hp	3
1966–67 360hp	6
1966 375hp	7
1967 375hp	4
1968–69 375hp	5
1970 375hp	8
1967 325 or 350hp	10

AUTOMATIC

327ci V-8	Interchange Number
1966 275hp	12

396ci V-8	Interchange Number
1966–67 360 or 350hp	13

Interchange

Interchange Number: 1
Usage: 1965 327ci 350hp V-8
Model: 4150
ID Number(s): R-3043

Interchange Number: 2
Usage: 1965 396ci V-8 with 375 or 425hp V-8
Model: 4150
ID Number(s): R-3123, R-3124

Interchange Number: 3
Usage: 1965–66 396ci 325hp; 1966 327ci 275hp (optional)
Model: 4160
ID Number(s): 3139, 3140

Interchange Number: 4
Usage: 1967 302ci Z-28; 1967 396ci 375hp; 1967 427ci 425hp
Model: 4150
ID Number(s): R-4815, R-3911, R-3910

Interchange Number: 5
Usage: 1968–69 302ci Z-28; 1968–69 396ci 375hp;
1968–69 427ci 425hp
Model: 4150
ID Number(s): 4346, 4053

Interchange Number: 6
Usage: 1966–67 396ci 350hp (360hp in 1966)
Model: 4160
ID Number(s): 3839, 3837, 3609, 3419, 3420
Notes: Some have provisions for smog controls (AIR) for sale in California.

Interchange Number: 7
Usage: 1966 396ci 375hp; 1966 427ci 425hp
Model: 4150
ID Number(s): 3246, 3613

Interchange Number: 8
Usage: 1970 396ci 375hp; 1970 454ci 450hp
Model: 4150
ID Number(s): 4557, 4559, 4581 without EEC; 4491, 4493, 4558 with EEC

Interchange Number: 9
Usage: 1967 327ci 350hp V-8
Model: 4150
ID Number(s): 3807, 3607

Interchange Number: 10
Usage: 1967 396ci 325 or 350hp V-8; 1967 427ci 390hp optional
Model: 4160
ID Number(s): 3839, 3609, 3837
Notes: ID number 3837 is with AIR smog control only.

Interchange Number: 11
Usage: 1970 350ci Camaro Z-28
Model: 4150
ID Number(s): 4489, 4488
Notes: ID number 4488 is with EEC emissions.

Interchange Number: 12
Usage: 1966 327ci 275hp
Model: 4160
ID Number(s): 3230

Interchange Number: 14
Usage: 1966–67 396ci 360 or 350hp
Model: 4160
ID Number(s): 3838, 3608

Carter Carburetor

Identification of the Carter carburetor is found stamped on a metal tag attached to the top of the bowl, or the Carter part number is stamped into the base.

Model Identification

327ci V-8	Interchange Number
1962–65 300hp	1
1962–64 250hp	3
1966 275hp	2

409ci V-8	Interchange Number
1962–65 high-performance	4
1962–64 twin 4bbl	5

Interchange

Interchange Number: 1
   Usage: 1962–65 327ci 300hp V-8
   Model: AFB
   ID Number(s): 3269, 3461, 3720, 3721

Interchange Number: 2
   Usage: 1966 327ci 275hp V-8
   Model: AVS
   ID Number(s): 4027

Interchange Number: 3
   Usage: 1962–64 327ci 250hp V-8 Impala
   Model: WCFFB
   ID Number(s): 3190 for 1962; 3500 for 1963; 3696 for
       1964

Interchange Number: 4
   Usage: 1962–65 409ci 400hp V-8
   Model: AFB
   ID Number(s): 3270 for 1962, 3345 for 1963; 34990
       for 1964; 3783 for 1965

Interchange Number: 5
   Usage: 1962–64 409ci twin 4bbl
   Model (front): AFB
   ID Number(s): 3361, all years
   Model (rear): AFB
   ID Number(s): 3362 for 1962–63; 3804 for 1964
   Notes: The later 1964 was phased into production
       around October 7,1963, and will fit earlier models.

Air Cleaner

Model Identification

283ci V-8..Interchange Number
1959–62 4bbl 1
1963–65...5
1966 4bbl 6

302ci V-8..Interchange Number
1967–68 3

Several different engine sizes used the chrome open element air cleaner.

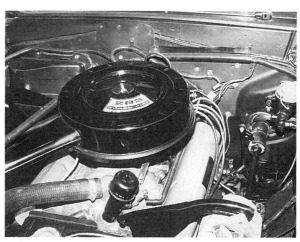

The 283 and 327ci engines used a single-snorkel air cleaner.

1969 without cowl hood 4

327ci V-8..Interchange Number
1962 4bbl 1
1963–65 4bbl, all except special high-performance 5
1965 special high-performance 8
1966–67, all except special high-performance..................6
1966 special high-performance 9
1967 Chevy II special high-performance..........................10
1968 4bbl, all except special high-performance 7

348ci V-8..Interchange Number
1959–61 triple 2bbl 2

350ci V-8..Interchange Number
1967 17
1968 4bbl 18
1969 4bbl Impala or Chevelle 19
1969 4bbl Camaro or Nova without cowl hood.............20
1969 Camaro with cowl hood 33
1970 4bbl Impala or Chevelle 21
1970 4bbl Camaro or Nova, all except Z-28 22
1970 Z-28...23

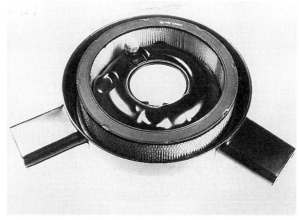

The 1970 Camaro Z-28 used this air cleaner. *Year One*

A unique air cleaner was used with cowl induction.

Single four-barrel 348ci and 409ci engines used an air cleaner of this type.

Interchange

Interchange Number: 1
Part Number(s):1553997
Type: Single-snorkel
Usage: 1959–61 343ci 4bbl V-8; 1959–62 283ci 4bbl

Interchange Number: 2
Part Number(s):1553998
Type: Special dual-snorkel
Usage: 1959–61 348ci with triple 2bbl carburetion

Interchange Number: 3
Part Number(s): 6423907
Type: Chrome open element
Usage: 1967–68 302ci Z-28; 1967–68 396ci 375hp; 1968 427ci 425hp; 1968–69 396ci 350hp

Interchange Number: 4
Part Number(s): 6423272
Type: Chrome open element
Usage: 1969 302ci; 1969 396ci 375hp; 1969 427ci 425hp
Notes: Used on Z-28 only without cowl induction hood.

Interchange Number: 5
Part Number(s): 6420903
Type: Single-snorkel
Usage: 1964–65 283ci 4bbl; 1964–65 327ci 4bbl, except special high-performance

Interchange Number: 6
Part Number(s): 6421966
Type: Single-snorkel
Usage: 1966–67 327ci; 1966 283ci 4bbl California cars used part number 6484410. It can be recognized by the provisions in the base for the emission hoses.

Interchange Number: 7
Part Number(s) (automatic): 6484220
Type: Single-snorkel
Usage: 1968 327ci 4bbl automatic
Part Number (manual): 6484221
Usage: 1968 327ci 4bbl manual, except special high-performance

Interchange Number: 8
Part Number(s): 6420857
Type: Dual-snorkel
Usage: 1965 327ci 350hp with special high-performance

Interchange Number: 9
Part Number(s): 6421964
Type: Dual-snorkel
Usage: 1966 Chevelle and Chevy II 327 special high-performance L-79
Notes: Odd looking; has side-mounted snorkels at a 90 degree angle.

Interchange Number: 10
Part Number(s): 6423506
Type: Chrome open element
Usage: 1967 Chevy II 327ci special high-performance
Notes: California cars used part number 6423507, which has provision for emission hose.

Interchange Number: 11
Part Number(s): 5648090
Type: Dual-snorkel
Usage: 1961–62 409ci single 4bbl

Interchange Number: 12
Part Number(s): 5649859
Type: Dual-snorkel
Usage: 1963 409ci single 4bbl

Interchange Number: 13
Part Number(s): 6419511
Type: Single-snorkel
Usage: 1964–65 409ci 340hp

Interchange Number: 14
Part Number(s): 6419509
Type: Dual-snorkel
Usage: 1964–65 409ci 400hp

Interchange Number: 15
Part Number(s): 5648706
Type: Special dual-snorkel
Usage: 1962 409ci twin 4bbl

Interchange Number: 16
Part Number(s): 6419512
Type: Special dual-snorkel
Usage: 1963 409ci with twin 4bbl
Notes: Part number 6419512 will fit 1962 models, but lid is incorrect due to ID badges used. Earlier style can fit 1963 models, but holes will have to be drilled to attach the ID badges.

Interchange Number: 17
Part Number(s): 6424486
Type: Single-snorkel
Usage: 1967 Camaro SS 350
Notes: California cars used part number 6484493.

Interchange Number: 18
Part Number(s) (automatic): 6484222
Type: Single-snorkel
Usage: 1968 350ci 4bbl automatic
Part Number(s) (manual): 6484223
Usage: 1968 350ci 4bbl manual

Interchange Number: 19
Part Number(s) (automatic): 6485240
Type: Single-snorkel
Usage: 1969 350ci 4bbl automatic
Part Number(s) (manual): 6484581
Usage: 1969 350ci 4bbl V-8 manual
Notes: Used with Chevelle or Impala only.

Interchange Number: 20
Automatic:
Part Number(s): 6484583
Type: Single-snorkel
Usage: 1969 350ci 4bbl V-8

Manual:
Part Number: 6484674
Notes: Used in Nova or Camaro models only without cowl duct hood.

Interchange Number: 21
Part Number(s): 6485240
Type: Single-snorkel
Usage: 1970–72 350ci 4bbl V-8
Notes: In Chevelle or Impala models only.

Interchange Number: 22
Part Number(s): 6485242
Type: Single-snorkel
Usage: 1970–72 350ci 4bbl V-8, except Z-28
Notes: In Camaro or Nova models only.

Interchange Number: 23
Part Number(s): 6485242
Type: Dual-snorkel
Usage: 1970 350ci Z-28 Camaro
Notes: No other interchange.

Interchange Number: 24
Part Number(s): 6421214
Type: Dual-snorkel
Usage: 1965 Chevelle SS 396; 1965 Impala 396ci 425hp
Notes: Uses Special ID emblem.

Interchange Number: 25
Part Number(s): 6484411
Type: Single-snorkel
Usage: 1966–67 Chevelle 396ci 325hp

Interchange Number: 26
Part Number(s): 6485252
Type: Dual-snorkel
Usage: 1970 396ci 330hp; 1970 LS-5 454 (360hp)
Notes: Used without cowl hood.

Interchange Number: 27
Part Number(s): 6421970
Type: Dual-snorkel
Usage: 1966 Impala 427ci 425hp

Interchange Number: 28
Part Number(s): 6421773
Type: Single-snorkel
Usage: 1966–67 Impala 427ci 390hp, all except 1967 Impala SS
Notes: Super Sport models used part number 6424482.

Interchange Number: 29
Part Number(s): 6483663
Type: Single-snorkel
Usage: 1968 Impala 427ci 390 or 335hp

Interchange Number: 30
Part Number(s): 6484593
Type: Single-snorkel
Usage: 1969 427ci 390hp V-8

Interchange Number: 31
Part Number(s): 6485257
Type: Open element
Usage: 1970 396ci 350 or 375hp; 1970 454ci in Chevelle

Notes: Used without cowl hood.

Interchange Number: 32

Part Number(s): 6485235

Type: Single-snorkel.

Usage: 1969 Camaro; 1970–71 Chevelle SS 396 or 454ci V-8, with cowl induction (RPO ZL-2) hood

Interchange Number: 33

Part Number(s): 6485232

Type: Single-snorkel

Usage: 1969 Camaro 350ci four-speed with cowl induction (RPO ZL-2) hood

Part Number(s): 6485234

Usage: 1969 Camaro 350ci 4bbl automatic with cowl induction (RPO ZL-2) hood

Chapter 3

Oil and Cooling System

Oil Pump

Model Identification

1959–70, ALL MODELS

283; 327; 348; 350; 409ci V-8 ....Interchange Number
except with high-performance or multi-carbs; all except
    1970 Z-28 1
1970 Camaro Z-28 2

302ci V-8..Interchange Number
1967–69 2

396ci V-8..Interchange Number
1965–70, all except 375 or 425hp....................................3
1965–70 375 or 425hp 4

409ci V-8..Interchange Number
1962–65 high-performance or with multi-carbs 2

427ci V-8..Interchange Number
1966–69, all except 425hp...3
1966–69 425hp 4

454ci V-8..Interchange Number
1970, all except 450hp (LS-6) 3
1970 450hp (LS-6) 4

Interchange

Interchange Number: 1
    Part Number(s): 3821979
    Usage: All small-blocks, but only some high-perfor-
        mance or special high-performance. Not for use
        with multi-carb 409ci or 302ci V-8s. Used in special
        high-performance 327ci versions.
    Notes: Replacement part number 3764547 also fits.

Interchange Number: 2
    Part Number(s): 3848907
    Usage: High-performance or special high-performance
        small-blocks. Includes 1962–65 409ci with high-per-
        formance or with multi-carbs; 1967–69 302ci;
        1970–72 350ci Z-28

Interchange Number: 3
    Part Number(s): 3904827
    Usage: All 1965–74 big-blocks except special high-per-
        formance

Interchange Number: 4
    Part Number(s): 3904826
    Usage: Big-blocks with special high-performance. In-
        cludes 396ci 375hp; 396ci 425hp; 427ci 425hp;
        454ci 450hp.

Oil Pan

Model Identification

Camaro ....Interchange Number
1967–69
    302ci...6
    327ci...7
    350ci...7
    396ci...12
1970
    350ci, all except Z-28..7
    350ci Z-28..6
    396ci...12

Chevelle ....Interchange Number
1964–66
    283ci...2
    327ci...2
    396ci...10
1967–70
    283ci...2
    327ci...7
    350ci...7
    396ci...12
    427ci...12
    454ci...12

Impala..Interchange Number
1959–64
    283ci...1
1959–61

Interchange

Interchange Number: 1
Part Number(s): 3788816
Usage: 1959–64 full-size Chevrolet 283 or 327ci

Interchange Number: 2
Part Number(s): 3830089
Usage: 1964–67 Chevelle 283 or 327ci

Interchange Number: 3
Part Number(s): 3790722
Usage: 1964–66 Chevy II 283 or 327ci
Notes: Interchange Number 4 will fit.

Interchange Number: 4
Part Number(s): 3869920
Usage: 1967 Chevy II 283 or 327ci

Interchange Number: 5
Part Number(s): 3854788
Usage: 1965–67 full-size Chevrolet 283 or 327ci
Notes: Interchange number 7 will fit.

Interchange Number: 6
Part Number(s): 3974251
Usage: 1967–74 Camaro Z-28 302 (1967–69) or 350ci
(1970–74)

Interchange Number: 7
Part Number(s): 3974252
Usage: 1967 Camaro 327 or 350ci; 1968–72 Camaro

327 or 350ci, except Z-28; 1968–72 Chevelle 327 or
350ci; 1968–72 Impala 327 or 350ci; 1968–72
Nova 327 or 350ci; 1969–72 307ci, all models

Interchange Number: 8
Part Number(s): 3859937
Usage: 1965–66 396 or 427ci, except Impala 425hp

Interchange Number: 9
Part Number(s): 3871282
Usage: 1965–66 Impala with the following engines:
396ci 425hp; 396ci 375hp; 427ci 425hp

Interchange Number: 10
Part Number(s): 3872762
Usage: 1965–66 Chevelle 396ci V-8, all outputs
Notes: Interchange number 12 will fit.

Interchange Number: 11
Part Number(s): 3974328
Usage: 1967–70 Impala 396, 427, or 454ci

Interchange Number: 12
Part Number(s): 3985999
Usage: 1967–72 Chevelle SS 396, 427, or 454ci V-8;
1967–74 Camaro; 1968–72 Nova SS; 1971–74 Impala 402 or 454ci

Interchange Number: 13
Part Number(s): 3758927
Usage: 1958–61 348ci Impala

Interchange Number: 14
Part Number(s): 3799873
Usage: 1962–65 409ci, except high-performance or
twin 4bbl
Notes: Standard sump. Interchange number 15 will fit if
dipsticks are swapped.

Interchange Number: 15
Part Number(s): 3816322
Usage: 1962–65 409ci high-performance or with twin
4bbl
Notes: Deep sump.

Radiator

Model Identification

Camaro Interchange Number

Chevelle Interchange Number

Interchange

Interchange Number: 1

Part Number(s): 3010181
ID Number(s): UU; UW; UX
Dimensions: 17x23x1 1/4 and 17x23x2 inches
Type: Heavy-duty
Usage: 1967 to early 1968 327 and 350ci V-8 4bbl; 1968 Pontiac Firebird 350 or 400ci (except with Ram Air); all automatic

Interchange Number: 2

Part Number(s): 3010179
ID Number(s): UE; UR; US
Dimensions: 17x20 3/4x1 1/4 and 17x20 3/4x2 inches
Usage: 1967–68 six-cylinder automatic; 1967–69 327 or 350ci with heavy-duty cooling or a/c; 1967–69 302ci; 1967–69 Pontiac Firebird with six-cylinder automatic; late 1968–69 327ci 4bbl; 1969 six-cylinder with heavy-duty cooling

Interchange Number: 3

Part Number(s): 3010175
ID Number(s): UG; UT
Dimensions: 17x20 3/4x1 1/4 inches
Usage: 1967 Pontiac Firebird six-cylinder with heavy-duty cooling; 1967–68 six-cylinder manual; 1967–69 327 and 350ci V-8 manual without a/c or heavy-duty cooling

Interchange Number: 4

Part Number(s): 3016689
Dimensions: 17x23x1 1/4 and 17x23x2 5/8 inches
Usage: 1967–68 Camaro with 396ci

Interchange Number: 5

Part Number(s): 3010176
Usage: 1969 Camaro with six-cylinder automatic without heavy-duty cooling; 1969 327 automatic without a/c or heavy-duty cooling

Interchange Number: 6

Part Number(s): 3017838
Usage: 1969 Camaro SS 396 without heavy-duty cooling or a/c; 1968–70 Nova SS 396

Interchange Number: 7

Part Number(s): 3018623 :
Usage: 1969 396ci V-8 Turbo Hydra-Matic 400 with a/c or heavy-duty cooling

Interchange Number: 8

Part Number(s): 3018624
Usage: 1969 396ci V-8 manual with a/c or heavy-duty cooling

Interchange Number: 9

Part Number(s): 3016670
ID Number(s): VB
Usage: 1970 six-cylinder; 1970–71 Camaro 307 or 350ci except Z-28

Interchange Number: 10
Part Number(s): 3021301
ID Number(s): LG
Usage: 1970–71 350ci Z-28 and all Camaros with heavy-duty cooling or a/c, except 396ci

Interchange Number: 11
Part Number(s): 3021385
ID Number(s): LN
Usage: 1970–71 396ci (402) without heavy-duty cooling or a/c

Interchange Number: 12
Part Number(s): 3021775
ID Number(s): LS
Usage: 1970–71 396ci with heavy-duty cooling or a/c

Interchange Number: 13
Part Number(s): 3159110
ID Number(s): 619A
Dimensions: 15 1/2x23.02x1.26 inches
Type: Without cooler
Usage: 1964–65 Chevelle 283ci manual

Interchange Number: 14
Part Number(s): 3002011
ID Number(s): 611A
Dimensions: 15 1/2x25.22x1.985 inches
Type: Without cooler
Usage: 1964–65 Chevelle 283ci manual with a/c or heavy-duty cooler

Interchange Number: 15
Part Number(s): 3159118
ID Number(s): 619A
Dimensions: 15 1/2x25.22x1.26 inches
Type: With cooler
Usage: 1964 Chevelle 283ci Powerglide

Interchange Number: 16
Part Number(s): 3002019
ID Number(s): 619A
Dimensions: 15 1/2x25.22x1.985 inches
Usage: 1964–65 Chevelle 283ci Powerglide with a/c
Notes: This unit was used as a service part and will fit 1964–65 283ci Chevelles with any type of transmission

Interchange Number: 17
Part Number(s): 3004518
ID Number(s): 10
Dimensions: 15 1/2x23.02x1.26 inches
Type: With cooler
Usage: 1965 Chevelle 283ci Powerglide without a/c; 1965 Chevelle 327ci manual or Powerglide, all except special high-performance

Interchange Number: 18
Part Number(s): 3004519
ID Number(s):
Dimensions: 15 1/2x25.22x1.985 inches
Type: With cooler
Usage: 1965 Chevelle 283 or 327ci Powerglide with a/c; late 1967 Chevy II 327ci Powerglide with a/c and heavy-duty cooling

Notes: Service part will fit 1964–65 Chevelle, all applications.

Interchange Number: 19
Part Number(s): 3003616
Dimensions: 15 1/2x23.02x1.75 inches
Type: Without cooler
Usage: 1965 Chevelle 327ci 360hp V-8 (special high-performance)
Notes: No other interchange.

Interchange Number: 20
Part Number(s): 3007610
Dimensions: 15 1/2x23x1 1/4 inches
Type: Without cooler
Usage: 1966–67 283ci Chevelle manual without AIR emissions, a/c, or heavy-duty cooling

Interchange Number: 21
Part Number(s): 3007618
Dimensions: 15 1/2x23.02x1.26 inches
Type: With cooler
Usage: 1966–67 Chevelle 283ci six-cylinder with Powerglide; 1967 Chevelle 327ci Powerglide with AIR, but without a/c

Interchange Number: 22
Part Number(s): 3007620
Dimensions: 15 1/2x25.25x2.00 inches
Type: Without cooler
Usage: 1965–66 Chevelle SS 396 manual with or without heavy-duty cooling and a/c

Interchange Number: 23
Part Number(s): 3007621
Dimensions: 15 1/2x25 1/4x2.00 inches
Type: With cooler
Usage: 1966 Chevelle SS 396ci Powerglide

Interchange Number: 24
Part Number(s): 3012212
Dimensions: 15 1/2x23x1 1/4 inches
Type: Without cooler
Usage: 1966–67 Chevelle 283ci manual in California; 1967 Chevelle 283ci manual for all states

Interchange Number: 25
Part Number(s): 3012519
Dimensions: 16x25.1/4x1.3/4 inches
Type: With cooler
Usage: 1966–67 Chevelle 283ci or 327ci Powerglide with a/c

Interchange Number: 26
Part Number(s): 3012213
Dimensions: 15 1/2x23x1 1/4 inches
Type: Without cooler
Usage: 1967 Chevelle 327ci 275hp V-8 manual

Interchange Number: 27
Part Number(s): 3012241
Dimensions:15 1/2x23x1 1/4 inches
Type: With cooler
Usage: 1966–67 Chevelle 327ci automatic

Interchange Number: 28
Part Number(s): 3012137

Dimensions: 15 1/2x25.1/4x1 3/4 inches
Type: Without cooler
Usage: 1966–67 Chevelle SS 396 325hp manual

Interchange Number: 29
Part Number(s): 3010209
Dimensions: 15 1/2x25 1/4x2 5/8 inches
Type: With cooler
Usage: 1966–67 Chevelle SS 396ci automatic with heavy-duty cooling or a/c

Interchange Number: 30
Part Number(s): 3013424
Dimensions: 16x25.25x1.75 inches
Type: With cooler
Usage: 1967 Chevelle SS 396 automatic without a/c or heavy-duty cooling

Interchange Number: 31
Part Number(s): 3007620
Dimensions: 15.50x25.25x2.00 inches
Type: Without cooler
Usage: 1966 Chevelle 327ci 325hp manual with heavy-duty cooling or a/c; 1966–67 Chevelle 396ci 375hp
Notes: Interchange number 32 will fit.

Interchange Number: 32
Part Number(s): 3007621
Dimensions:15.50x25.25x2.00 inches
Type: With cooler
Usage: 1967 Chevelle SS 396ci with Turbo Hydra-Matic 400

Interchange Number: 33
Part Number(s): 3022040
ID Number(s): VB
Dimensions: 17x20.75x1.25 inches
Type: Without cooler
Usage: *Chevrolet:* 1968 Nova 327ci or six-cylinder; 1968–70 Chevelle 327 or 350ci without heavy-duty cooling or a/c; 1968–70 Chevelle six-cylinder with heavy-duty cooling; 1969–71 Nova 307 or 350ci V-8; 1970–71 Camaro 307 or 350ci except Z-28; 1970–71 Monte Carlo 350ci V-8 without a/c or heavy-duty cooling
Buick: 1966–67 Skylark 340ci V-8 without a/c; 1968–69 Skylark six-cylinder without a/c
Oldsmobile: 1966–69 Cutlass (except 442) 350 or 455ci automatic without a/c
Pontiac: 1969–71 LeMans six-cylinder without a/c; 1971 LeMans 400ci V-8 without a/c; 1971 Ventura 307ci V-8

Interchange Number: 34
Part Number(s): 3017258
Dimensions: 17x28 3/8x1 1/4 and 17x28 3/8x2 inches
Usage: *Chevrolet:* 1968 Chevelle SS 396 manual without a/c or heavy-duty cooling; 1968–69 Chevelle 307, 327, or 350ci with a/c and heavy-duty cooling; 1970–71 Monte Carlo V-8 with heavy-duty cooling; 1971 Chevelle 307 or 350ci V-8 with a/c and heavy-duty cooling; all with manual
Buick: 1970–71 LeSabre 350ci V-8 without a/c.

Oldsmobile: 1971 442 455ci without a/c; 1971 Cutlass 350ci V-8 with a/c

Interchange Number: 35
Part Number(s): 3014609
Dimensions: 17x28 3/8x1 1/4 and 17x28 3/8x2 inches
Usage: *Chevrolet:* 1968 Chevelle 396ci with a/c and heavy-duty cooling; 1968 Chevelle SS 396 automatic without a/c or heavy-duty cooling
Oldsmobile: 1968 full-size 350 or 455ci without a/c or heavy-duty cooling

Interchange Number: 36
Part Number(s): 3019205
ID Number(s): BR
Dimensions: 17x28x8x1 1/4 and 17x28x8x2 inches
Usage: *Chevrolet:* 1969–70 396ci (402) 375hp; 1969–71 396ci automatic with heavy-duty cooling or a/c; 1970 Monte Carlo 402ci V-8 automatic with a/c; 1970–71 Chevelle SS 454 LS-6; 1970–71 Monte Carlo SS 454
Pontiac: 1968 Tempest 400 2bbl or 350 4bbl; 1968–69 Tempest 350 without a/c; 1969 Bonneville 428ci V-8; 1969 Pontiac Grand Prix 400 or 428ci V-8; 1969 Tempest 400 2bbl with heavy-duty cooling; 1970 GTO 400 with RAM AIR III but without a/c or heavy-duty cooling; 1970 Tempest 400 with a/c but without RAM AIR; 1970 GTO 455 without a/c or heavy-duty cooling; 1970–71 Tempest 350 automatic with a/c or heavy-duty cooling; 1970–71 Pontiac Grand Prix 455 without a/c; 1970–71 Bonneville 350 or 400ci V-8 with a/c or heavy-duty cooling; 1971 Tempest 455ci 335hp without a/c
Notes: Part number is listed as 3020143 in Pontiac, but will fit the Chevelle.

Interchange Number: 37
Part Number(s): 3016908
Usage: *Chevrolet:* 1969–70 Chevelle 396, except for 375hp or with heavy-duty cooling or a/c; 1970 Monte Carlo 402 four-speed; 1971 Chevelle SS 402 with a/c
Pontiac: 1970 Tempest 350ci manual without a/c; 1970 Bonneville 350 or 400ci manual without a/c

Interchange Number: 38
Part Number(s): 3017248
Usage: *Chevrolet:* 1970 Chevelle 454ci with heavy-duty cooling or a/c; 1970 402ci with heavy-duty cooling and a/c
Pontiac: 1968–69 Tempest 350 with a/c and heavy-duty cooling; 1968 Tempest 400 2bbl or 350hp 4bbl; 1969 Pontiac Grand Prix 400 or 428ci V-8; 1969 Bonneville 428ci V-8; 1969 Tempest 400 2bbl with heavy-duty cooling; 1970 GTO 400ci with RAM AIR III with a/c and heavy-duty cooling or heavy-duty cooling; 1970 Tempest 400ci with a/c but without RAM AIR; 1970 GTO 455 with a/c and heavy-duty cooling, or just heavy-duty cooling; 1970–71 Tempest 350 automatic with a/c or heavy-duty cooling; 1970–71 Grand Prix 455ci with a/c and heavy-duty cooling; 1970–71 Bonneville 350 or 400ci V-8 with

a/c or heavy-duty cooling; 1971 Tempest 455ci 335hp with a/c and heavy-duty cooling

Interchange Number: 39
Part Number(s): 3141951
ID Number(s): 1
Dimensions: 25-1/4x15-1/2x1-3/4 inches
Usage: 1959 Impala 283ci manual
Notes: Interchange number 42 will fit. Those with automatic will also fit.

Interchange Number: 40
Part Number(s): 3141804
Dimensions: 25-1/4x15-1/2x1-3/4 inches
Type: With cooler
Usage: 1959 Impala 283ci Powerglide

Interchange Number: 41
Part Number(s): 3141953
ID Number(s): 5
Usage: 1959 Impala 283ci Turboglide

Interchange Number: 42
Part Number(s): 3146506
ID Number(s): 6
Dimensions: 25-1/4x17x1-3/4 inches
Usage: 1959 Impala 343ci manual; 1959–60 Impala 283ci with heavy-duty cooling

Interchange Number: 43
Part Number(s): 3144709
Usage: 1959 Impala 343ci Powerglide

Interchange Number: 44
Part Number(s): 3141954
ID Number(s): 7
Usage: 1959–60 Impala 343ci Turboglide

Interchange Number: 45
Part Number(s): 3147101
Dimensions: 23x15.5x1.75 inches
Usage: 1960 Impala 283ci manual

Interchange Number: 46
Part Number(s): 3147103
Dimensions: 23x15.5x1.75 inches
Usage: 1960 Impala 283ci Powerglide

Interchange Number: 47
Part Number(s): 3147105
Dimensions: 23x15.5x1.75 inches
Usage: 1960 Impala 283ci Turboglide

Interchange Number: 48
Part Number(s): 3148513
Dimensions: 25.25x17x1.75 inches
Usage: 1960–61 Impala 343ci manual with a/c

Interchange Number: 49
Part Number(s): 3148518
Dimensions: 25 1/4x17-7/8x2 inches
Usage: 1960-61 Impala 343ci automatic and a/c

Interchange Number: 50
Part Number(s): 3149703, 3149705, 3144709, 3151107
Dimensions: 23x15.5x1.25 inches
Usage: 1961 Impala 283ci automatic without a/c

Interchange Number: 51
Part Number(s): 3149701 and 3149702
Dimensions: 23x15.5x1.25 inches
Usage: 1961–62 Impala six-cylinder 283ci manual; 1962 327ci manual; both without a/c

Interchange Number: 52
Part Number(s): 3153503, 3153511
ID Number(s): R11
Dimensions: 23x15.5x1.25 inches
Usage: 1962 Impala 283 and 327ci Powerglide without a/c

Interchange Number: 53
Part Number(s): 3153507
Dimensions: 25-1/4x17x1-3/4 inches
Usage: 1962 Impala 283 and 327ci Powerglide with a/c

Interchange Number: 54
Part Number(s): 315305, 3153513
Dimensions: 25-1/4x17x1-3/4 inches
Usage: 1962 Impala 283 and 327ci manual with a/c but without heavy-duty cooling

Interchange Number: 55
Part Number(s): 3150018
ID Number(s): 3150018
Dimensions: 25-1/4x17-3/8x2 inches
Usage: 1962–63 Impala 283 and 327ci manual without a/c

Interchange Number: 56
Part Number(s): 3153517
ID Number(s): 3153517 or R18
Dimensions: 25-1/4x17-3/8x2 inches
Usage: 1962–63 Impala 409ci Powerglide with a/c; 1962–63 Impala 327ci with heavy-duty cooling

Interchange Number: 57
Part Number(s): 3156015
Usage: 1962–63 Impala 409ci manual with a/c

Interchange Number: 58
Part Number(s): 3158909
ID Number(s): 9
Dimensions: 17x25.22x1.75 inches
Usage: 1964 Impala 283 or 327ci three-speed or over-drive
Notes: Interchange number 59 will also fit.

Interchange Number: 59
Part Number(s): 3158910
ID Number(s): 10
Dimensions: 17x25.22x1.75 inches
Usage: 1964 Impala 283 and 327ci automatic

Interchange Number: 60
Part Number(s): 3158918
Dimensions: 17.4x25.22x1.985 inches
Usage: 1964 Impala 409ci manual without a/c

Interchange Number: 61
Part Number(s): 3158919
Dimensions: 17.4x25.22x2.62 inches
Usage: 1964 Impala 409ci manual with a/c

Interchange Number: 62
Part Number(s): 3003178

Dimensions: 17.4x25.22x1.985 inches
Usage: 1964 Impala 409ci Powerglide without a/c

Interchange Number: 63
Part Number(s): 3158915
Dimensions: 17.4x25.22x2.62 inches
Usage: 1964 Impala 409ci Powerglide with a/c

Interchange Number: 64
Part Number(s): 3002310
Dimensions: 17x25.22x1.75 inches
Usage: 1965 Impala 283 or 327ci Powerglide

Interchange Number: 65
Part Number(s): 3002309
Dimensions: 17x25.22x1.75 inches
Usage: 1965 Impala 283 or 327ci manual

Interchange Number: 66
Part Number(s): 3002317
Dimensions: 17x25.22x1.985 inches
Usage: 1965 Impala 409ci Powerglide without a/c; 1965 Impala 327ci high-performance

Interchange Number: 67
Part Number(s): 3002318
Dimensions: 17x25.22x1.985 inches
Usage: 1965 Impala 409ci four-speed without a/c

Interchange Number: 68
Part Number(s): 3002319
Dimensions: 17x25.22x2.62 inches
Usage: 1965 Impala 409ci four-speed with a/c

Interchange Number: 69
Part Number(s): 3002315
Dimensions: 17x25.22x2.62 inches
Usage: 1965 Impala 409ci Powerglide with a/c

Interchange Number: 70
Part Number(s): 3007705
Usage: 1966 Impala 283 or 327ci manual

Interchange Number: 71
Part Number(s): 307707
Usage: 1966 Impala 283 or 327ci Powerglide

Interchange Number: 72
Part Number(s): 3007711
Usage: 1966 Impala 396ci manual

Interchange Number: 73
Part Number(s): 3007704
Usage: 1966 Impala 396ci automatic

Interchange Number: 74
Part Number(s): 3007717
Usage: 1966 Impala 427ci automatic

Interchange Number: 75
Part Number(s): 3007718
Usage: 1966 Impala 427ci manual

Interchange Number: 76
Part Number(s): 3014454
Dimensions: 17x25-1/4x1-3/4 and 17-3/8x25-1/4x2 inches
Usage: 1967 Impala 396 or 427ci manual with AIR; 1968 Impala 396 or 427ci manual; 1968 307 or

327ci manual with a/c or heavy-duty cooling

Interchange Number: 77
Part Number(s): 3016801
Dimensions: 15-1/2x23x1-1/4 inches
Usage: 1967 Impala 283ci manual with AIR but without a/c; 1968 Impala 307ci manual

Interchange Number: 78
Part Number(s): 3014455
Dimensions: 17x25-14x1-3/4 inches
Usage: 1967 Impala 283 or 327ci automatic with AIR or heavy-duty cooling; late 1967 to early 1968 Impala 427ci with a/c or heavy-duty cooling; 1968 Impala 307ci automatic with a/c or heavy-duty cooling; 1968 Impala 396ci automatic without a/c; 1968 Impala 427ci automatic without a/c or heavy-duty cooling

Interchange Number: 79
Part Number(s): 3012203
Dimensions: 15-1/2x23x1-1/4 and 17x25-1/4x1-3/4 inches
Usage: 1967 Impala 283 or 327ci automatic with AIR, but without a/c or heavy-duty cooling

Interchange Number: 80
Part Number(s): 3012415
Dimensions: 17x25-1/4x1-3/4 inches
Usage: 1967 Impala 327ci manual with AIR, but without a/c or heavy-duty cooling

Interchange Number: 81
Part Number(s): 3012343
Dimensions: 17x25-1/4x1-3/4 inches
Usage: 1967 Impala 396 or 427ci automatic with AIR, but without a/c or heavy-duty cooling

Interchange Number: 82
Part Number(s): 3011407
Dimensions: 15-1/2x23x1-1/4 inches
Usage: 1967 Impala 283 or 327ci automatic without AIR and without a/c or heavy-duty cooling

Interchange Number: 83
Part Number(s): 3011405
Dimensions: 17x23x 1-1/4 inches
Usage: 1967 Impala 283 or 327ci manual without AIR

Interchange Number: 84
Part Number(s): 3012411
ID Number(s): CM
Dimensions: 17x25-1/4x1-3/4 inches
Usage: Early 1967 Impala 396ci manual without AIR; 1967 Impala 427ci 390hp V-8 manual without AIR

Interchange Number: 85
Part Number(s): 3012404
ID Number(s): CE
Dimensions: 17x25-1/4x1-3/4 inches
Usage: 1967 Impala 427ci automatic without AIR; early 1967 396ci automatic with or without AIR

Interchange Number: 86
Part Number(s): 3012349
ID Number(s): CI
Dimensions: 17x25-1/4x1-1/4 inches

Usage: Late 1967 Impala 396ci automatic without AIR

Interchange Number: 87
Part Number(s): 3012719
Dimensions: 17x25-1/4x1-3/4 inches
Usage: 1967 Impala 427ci 425hp manual without AIR

Interchange Number: 88
Part Number(s): 3012348
ID Number(s): CG
Dimensions: 17-1/2x25-1/4x1-1/4 inches
Usage: Late 1967 Impala 396ci manual without AIR

Interchange Number: 89
Part Number(s): 3017031
Dimensions: 17-3/8x23x1-1/4 inches
Usage: 1968 Impala 307 or 327ci automatic without a/c or heavy-duty cooling

Interchange Number: 90
Part Number(s): 3007641
Dimensions: 15-1/2x23x1-1/4 inches
Usage: Late 1968 Impala 427ci manual without a/c or heavy-duty cooling

Interchange Number: 91
Part Number(s): 3016819
Usage: Late 1968 Impala 427ci manual with a/c or heavy-duty cooling

Interchange Number: 92
Part Number(s): 3016804
Usage: Late 1968 Impala 427ci automatic with a/c or heavy-duty cooling

Interchange Number: 93
Part Number(s): 3018027
Usage: 1969 Impala 327ci manual, and late 1969 350ci 255hp manual; both without a/c

Interchange Number: 94
Part Number(s): 3018008
Usage: 1969 Impala 327ci automatic; 1969 350ci 255hp automatic; both without a/c or heavy-duty cooling

Interchange Number: 95
Part Number(s): 3018004
Usage: early 1969 350ci 255hp manual without a/c; 1969 Impala 350ci 2bbl manual

Interchange Number: 96
Part Number(s): 3018028
Usage: 1969 Impala 350ci 300hp manual without a/c or heavy-duty cooling

Interchange Number: 97
Part Number(s): 3018026
Usage: 1969 Impala 350ci 300hp automatic; 1970 Impala 350ci 4bbl; both without a/c

Interchange Number: 98
Part Number(s): 3018035
Usage: 1969 Impala 396 or 427ci with a/c; 1970 Impala 454ci automatic with a/c

Interchange Number: 99
Part Number(s): 3018026
Usage: 1969 Impala 350ci 300hp automatic without a/c or heavy-duty cooling; 1970 Impala 350ci 4bbl automatic without a/c

Interchange Number: 100
Part Number(s): 3018035
Usage: 1969 Impala 396 or 427ci with a/c or heavy-duty cooling; 1970 Impala 454ci with a/c or heavy-duty cooling

Interchange Number: 101
Part Number(s): 3018015
Usage: 1969 Impala 327 or 350ci with a/c or heavy-duty cooling; 1969 Impala 396ci without a/c; 1970 Impala 350 or 400ci with a/c; 1970 Impala 454ci without a/c

Interchange Number: 102
Part Number(s): 3022526
Usage: 1970 Impala 350 or 400ci (small-block) with heavy-duty cooling

Interchange Number: 103
Part Number(s): 3001411
ID Number(s): 111A
Dimensions: 15.5x23.02x1.75 inches
Usage: 1964–65 Chevy II 283ci manual

Interchange Number: 104
Part Number(s): 3001419
ID Number(s): 119B
Dimensions: 15.5x23.02x1.75 inches
Usage: 1964–65 Chevy II 283ci automatic with a/c

Interchange Number: 105
Part Number(s): 3154118
Dimensions: 15.5x23.02x1.75 inches
Usage: 1964–65 Chevy II 283ci automatic without a/c
Notes: Interchange number 104 will fit, but radiator hoses will have to be rerouted from their original position.

Interchange Number: 106
Part Number(s): 3007661
Usage: 1966 to early 1967 Chevy II 283ci manual with a/c or heavy-duty cooling

Interchange Number: 107
Part Number(s): 3007659
Usage: 1966 Chevy II 283ci automatic with a/c

Interchange Number: 108
Part Number(s): 3014511
Dimensions: 15.5x23x2.00 inches
Usage: Late 1967 Chevy II 283ci automatic with a/c

Interchange Number: 109
Part Number(s): 3007652
Dimensions: 15.5x23x1.25 inches
Usage: Early 1967 Chevy II 283ci manual with AIR, but without a/c

Interchange Number: 110
Part Number(s): 3007660
Dimensions: 15.5x23x1.25 inches
Usage: Early 1967 Chevy II 283ci manual without a/c; 1967 Chevy II 327ci manual without a/c; late 1967 Chevy II 327ci manual with AIR, but without a/c

Interchange Number: 111
> Part Number(s): 3013605
> Dimensions: 15.5x23x1.25 inches
> Usage: Late 1967 Chevy II 283ci manual without a/c

Interchange Number: 112
> Part Number(s): 3007668
> Dimensions: 15.5x23x1.25 inches
> Usage: 1967 Chevy II 283 or 327ci automatic without a/c

Interchange Number: 113
> Part Number(s): 3007635
> Dimensions: 15.5x23x1.25 inches
> Usage: 1967 Chevy II 327ci manual with a/c

Interchange Number: 114
> Part Number(s): 3007578
> Dimensions: 15-1/2x23x2-5/8 inches
> Usage: 1967 Chevy II 327ci automatic with a/c or heavy-duty cooling

Fan Blades

Fan blades are identified by their diameter and number of blades, along with the type of drive that was used. Interchange involves the bare fan assembly, without the drive or spacers. The interchange rule for fans is, more blades are okay, but fewer are not. For example, you can replace a five-blade fan with a seven-blade unit, but you would *never* replace a seven-blade fan with a five-blade unit.

Model Identification

Interchange

Interchange Number: 1
> Part Number(s): 3839282
> No. of Blades: Four
> Diameter: 17 5/8 inches
> Type: Spacer
> Usage: *Chevrolet:* 1959–68, all with 283, 327, 348ci; 409 or 350ci except special high-performance or with a/c
> *Pontiac:* 1961–62 LeMans V-8 without a/c; 1964–66 LeMans six-cylinder

Interchange Number: 2
> Part Number(s): 3990936
> Diameter: 18 inches
> Type: Clutch drive
> Usage: 1959–68 Impala 283, 327, 348, or 409ci; 1964–68 Chevelle 283 or 327ci; 1966–67 Chevy II 283 or 327ci; 1966–68 Impala 396 or 427ci without a/c, except special high-performance; 1967–68 Camaro 327, 350, 396ci, all except 396ci 375hp; 1968 Nova 307 or 350ci, all with a/c or heavy-duty cooling
> Notes: Originally a five-blade fan. Replaced by a seven-blade fan.

Interchange Number: 3
> Part Number(s): 3931002
> No. of Blades: 7
> Diameter: 18 inches
> Type: Clutch drive
> Usage: 1962–65 409ci; 1967 Camaro 396ci; 1965–68 Impala 396 or 427ci with a/c; 1965–68 Chevelle 396ci, except 375hp; 1968 Chevelle, all with a/c except 327 or 396ci special high-performance

Interchange Number: 4
> Part Number(s): 3871276
> No. of Blades: 5
> Diameter: 18 inches
> Type: Clutch drive
> Usage: 1965–68 396ci 375hp; 1966–67 Chevelle six-cylinder with a/c; 1966–68 Impala 396 or 427ci special high-performance; 1967–68 302ci; 1968, all six-cylinders with a/c
> Notes: Interchange number 5 can fit, if swapped with drive.

Interchange Number: 5
> Part Number(s): 393996
> No. of Blades: 7
> Diameter: 18 inches
> Type: Clutch drive
> Usage: 1969 302ci; 1969 427ci 425hp; 1969 Chevelle V-8 with a/c; 1969–70 Nova with 350ci and a/c; 1969–70 396ci 375hp; 1970 350ci Z-28; 1970 454ci 450hp; 1970, all with V-8 and a/c

Interchange Number: 6
> Part Number(s): 3927791
> No. of Blades: 4
> Diameter: 17 5/8 inches
> Type: Standard

Usage: 1969–72, all models and engines except for 1970 350ci Z-28, 1970 454ci 450hp, 1969–70 396ci 375hp, and 1969 302ci
Notes: Used only without a/c or heavy-duty cooling.

Fan Drive

Model Identification

Model ....Interchange Number
1967–68 302ci...2
1969 302ci..3
1969–70 327ci & 350ci except 1970 Z-28.......................4
1970 350ci Z-28..3
1965–67 396ci...1
1968–70 396ci, all except 375hp................................4
1968–70 396ci 375hp..3
1966–67 427ci...1
1968–69 427ci, all but 425hp..................................4
1968–69 427ci 425hp...3
1970 454ci, all except 450hp..................................4
1970 454ci 450hp..3

Interchange

Interchange Number: 1
Part Number(s): 3916141
Usage: 1962–65 409ci; 1964–66 Chevy II with heavy-duty cooling; 1965 327ci 300hp (first design); 1965–67 396 or 427ci; 1965–67 six-cylinder with a/c or heavy-duty cooling; 1967 Chevy II 327ci with a/c; 1968 Nova 327ci with a/c
Notes: Stamped CK.

Interchange Number: 2
Part Number(s): 3927103
Usage: 1967–68 427ci 425hp; 1967–68 396ci 375hp; 1967–68 302ci

Interchange Number: 3
Part Number(s): 3991430
Usage: 1969 302ci; 1969 427ci 425hp; 1969, all models with V-8 and a/c; 1969 police car (Impala or Chevelle); 1969–70 396ci 375hp; 1970 454ci 450hp; 1970–71 Z-28 Camaro; 1970–71 Monte Carlo with a/c, all except 454ci
Notes: Some are stamped CV.

Interchange Number: 4
Part Number(s): 3946050
Usage: 1969–70, all six-cylinders or V-8s with fan drive (clutch), except for 396ci 375hp, 427ci 425hp, 302ci, or 1970 Z-28 350ci

Water Pump

Model Identification

Model ....Interchange Number
1959–67 283ci, all except 1966–67 Impala or 1965 Chevelle or 1966–67 Chevy II 1

1965 Chevelle 283ci 3
1966–67 Chevy II 283ci......................................2
1967 302ci 3
1968 302ci 1
1969 302ci 4
1962–67 327ci, all but 1966–67 Impala, Chevelle, or Chevy II, or 1965 Chevelle with special high-performance 1
1965 Chevelle 327ci 360hp 3
1966–67 Impala 327ci 3
1966–67 Chevelle 327ci 3
1966–67 Chevy II 327ci 2
1968 327ci 3
1969 327ci 4
1967–68 350ci 3
1969–70 350ci 4
1959–61 348ci 5
1962–64 409ci 5, 6
1964–65 409ci 6
1965–68 396ci 7
1969–70 396ci 8
1966–68 427ci 7
1969 427ci 8
1970 454ci 8

Interchange

Interchange Number: 1
Part Number(s): 3998207
Casting Number(s): 3738493
Usage: 1959–67 283, 307, 327, 350ci V-8; 1968 302ci. All models except: 1966–67 Impala; 1965 Chevelle with 283ci or 327/360hp; 1967 Camaro; 1966–67 Chevy II V-8

Interchange Number: 2
Casting Number(s): 3839175
Usage: 1964–67 Chevy II V-8
Notes: Has two outlets 1/2 and 3/4 inch diameter used with external bypass hose.

Interchange Number: 3
Part Number(s): 39982206
Casting Number(s): 3890017
Usage: 1964–67 Chevy II V-8; 1965 Chevelle 283ci or 327ci 360hp; 1966–67 Impala; 1967 Camaro; 1968, all except 302ci Camaro

Interchange Number: 4
Part Number(s): 6272157
Casting Number(s): 3998198
Usage: 1969–72 302, 307, 327, 350ci V-8, all models; also used on 400ci small-block

Interchange Number: 5
Part Number(s): 3774213
Casting Number(s): 3755797
Usage: 1959–61 348ci; 1962 to approximately 10-1-63, except for Z-11
Notes: Has bypass hose.

Interchange Number: 6
Part Number(s): 3857853

Casting Number(s): 3850145
Usage: After approximately 10-1-63 to 1965, all 409ci

Interchange Number: 7
Part Number(s): 3990993
Casting Number(s): 3856284
Usage: 1965–68 396 or 427ci

Interchange Number: 8
Part Number(s): 6272159
Casting Number(s): 3969811
Usage: 1968–72 396 (402ci); 1970–74 454ci

Chapter 4

Exhaust System

Exhaust Manifold

Exhaust manifolds are greatly interchangeable within their own family group. But certain restrictions do apply. Emissions systems—specifically the Air Injection Reactor, or AIR, system—greatly influence the interchange process. Transmission type may also affect certain applications. If any restrictions apply, they appear in the "Notes" section of each interchange entry.

Model Identification

The 1970 Z-28 exhaust manifolds will fit all small-blocks and add performance. *Year One*

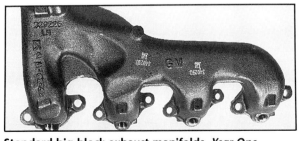

Standard big-block exhaust manifolds. *Year One*

Interchange

Interchange Number: 1

Part Number(s): RH, 3872730; LH, 3892683

Casting Number(s): RH, 3750556; LH, 3749965

Usage: With AIR only: 1966–67 Chevelle 283 or 327ci; 1967–68 Camaro 302, 327, 350ci small-block, all; 1968 Chevelle 307ci; 1968 Nova 307, 327, or 350ci manual

Notes: All manifolds use no choke tube. Can be used on non-AIR cars if holes are plugged. Was done this way at factory at year end.

Interchange Number: 2

Part Number(s): RH, 3817806; LH, 3749965

Casting Number(s): replacement RH, 3750556; replacement LH, 3749965; original RH, 37470387, 3750556, or 3747042; original LH, 3749965 or 3846558

Usage: 1959–64 full-size Chevrolet 283 or 327ci, all except high-performance or special high-performance 327ci V-8

Notes: Care should be used when swapping manifolds from a car without a/c to a car with it. While a car with a/c will fit a car without a/c the opposite is not true.

Interchange Number: 3

Part Number(s): RH, 3814970; LH, 3797901

Casting Number(s): RH, 3797902; LH, 3797901

Usage: 1962–63 Corvette 327ci special high-performance and fuel injection; 1962–64 Impala 327ci high-performance

Notes: These free-flowing manifolds will fit a regular 327ci with little or no modification.

Interchange Number: 4

Part Number(s): RH, 3817806; LH, 3855163

Casting Number(s): RH, 3750556; LH, 3749965

Usage: 1965–68 Impala small-block without AIR; 1967–68 Chevrolet or GMC C-10 truck 283, 327, or 307ci

Notes: The RH unit can be found in 1962–64 Impala with small-block (except with high-performance), but the RH unit is unique to these model years. Those in 1968 (including pickup) are for automatic only.

Interchange Number: 5

Part Number(s): RH, 3932461; LH, 3932469

Usage: 1968–69 Impala 307, 327, 350ci V-8 manual; 1968–69 Chevrolet or GMC pickup (C-10 to C-30) manual

Interchange Number: 6

Part Number(s): RH, 3989036; LH, 3989055

Usage: 1968–69 Impala small-block automatic

Interchange Number: 7

Part Number(s): RH, 3989055; LH, 3989036

Usage: 1970 Impala 307, 350, or 400ci (small-block)

Interchange Number: 8

Part Number(s): RH, 3890424; LH, 3790729

Usage: 1964–67 Chevy II 283 or 327ci V-8

Notes: Without AIR only in 1966–67 models.

Interchange Number: 9

Part Number(s): RH, 3872738; LH, 3872723

Usage: 1966–67 Chevy II V-8 with AIR emissions

Interchange Number: 10

Part Number(s): RH, 3893608; LH, 3892679

Usage: 1964–68 Chevelle 283 or 327ci without AIR; 1967–68 Camaro 302, 327, or 350ci without AIR

Interchange Number: 11

Part Number(s): RH, 3872730; LH, 3892683

Usage: 1967–68 Chevelle small-block with AIR; 1967–68 Camaro small-block with AIR

Interchange Number: 12

Part Number(s): RH, 3986330; LH, 3989041

Usage: 1969 Chevelle, Nova, Camaro small-block V-8 with manual; 1970 Camaro Z-28 350ci

Notes: The LH unit was used in 1972–73 Impala with small-block, with NB2 emissions package.

Interchange Number: 13

Part Number(s): RH, 3932376; LH, 3367706

Usage: 1969 Chevelle, Nova, Camaro 307, 327, or 350ci V-8 with automatic

Interchange Number: 14

Part Number(s): RH, 336708; LH, 336706

Usage: 1969–72 Chevelle, Camaro, Nova 307, 327, or 350ci V-8

Notes: Will not fit 1970 Z-28; used with 4bbl V-8 (except 302ci) in 1969 only.

Interchange Number: 15

Part Number(s): RH, 3768000; LH, 3767583

Casting Number(s): RH, 3768000; LH, 3767583

Usage: 1959–61 348ci high-performance (without high-lift cam); 1961 409ci special high-performance.

Interchange Number: 16

Part Number(s): RH, 3750304; LH, 3732793

Casting Number(s): RH, 3750304; LH, 3732793

Usage: 1959–61 348ci without high-performance or special high-performance; 1961 343ci with high-lift cam; 1962–64 409ci without high-performance

Interchange Number: 17

Part Number(s): RH, 3822924; LH, 3722923 or 3822925

Casting Number(s): RH, 3822926; LH, 3822925

Usage: 1961–64 409ci high-performance or twin 4bbl

Interchange Number: 18

Part Number(s): RH, 3867962; LH, 3855161

Usage: 1965 409ci

Interchange Number: 19
    Part Number(s): RH, 3884504; LH, 3904399
    Usage: 1965–67 Impala 396ci (except 425 or 375hp) or
        427ci 390hp
    Notes: Without AIR in 1966–67 models.

Interchange Number 20
    Part Number(s): RH, 3879898; LH, 3880833
    Usage: 1965 Impala 396ci 425hp

Interchange Number 21
    Part Number(s): RH, 3880834; LH, 3880827
    Usage: 1966 Impala 396ci 375hp or 427ci 425hp

Interchange Number 22
    Part Number(s): RH, 3884504; LH, 3904399
    Usage: 1967 Impala 396 or 427ci with AIR emission

Interchange Number 23
    Part Number(s): RH, 3969910; LH, 3969909
    Usage: 1965–66 Chevelle 396ci; without AIR in 1966.

Interchange Number 24
    Part Number(s): RH, 3989312; LH, 3989345
    Usage: 1967–69 Chevelle, Camaro SS 396, 1968–69
        Impala 396 or 427ci; 1968–70 Nova SS 396ci; 1970
        Impala 454ci

Interchange Number: 25
    Part Number(s): RH, 3989312; LH, 3975921
    Usage: 1967–69 Chevelle or Camaro 396; 1968–69
        Nova SS
    Notes: Normally used with automatic.

Interchange Number: 26
    Part Number(s): RH, 353028; LH, 3989343
    Usage: 1970 Chevelle or Camaro 396 (402ci) V-8; 1970
        454ci, except 450hp in Chevelle SS
    Notes: LH exhaust is also found in 1971–72 models with
        402 or 454ci (except 425hp
    in 1971).

Interchange Number: 27
    Part Number(s): RH, 353028; LH, 3989345
    Usage: 1970 Chevelle SS 454ci 450hp; 1970 Chevelle
        SS 396ci 375hp

Muffler

Model Identification

Camaro ....*Interchange Number*
1967
    All but models with deep tone exhaust 16
    All models with deep tone exhaust...........................17
1968–69
    327 or 350ci...1
    With deep tone exhaust...17

Chevelle ....*Interchange Number*
1964–65
    283 or 327ci, all except special high-performance...12, 13
    327ci special high-performance................................11
1965–67
    396ci except 375hp 14
    396ci 375hp..7

1968–69
    All engines with dual exhaust except chambered ex-
        haust or 396ci 375hp 4
    396ci 375hp...2

Impala....................................*Interchange Number*
1959–62
    All engines except high-performance 8
1959–64
    348 or 409ci high-performance.................................9
1962–64
    327ci, all except special high-performance...............10
    327ci special high-performance 9
1968 427ci 425hp 3
1969 427ci 425hp...4, 5
1970 454ci..6

Chevy II/Nova ....*Interchange Number*
1965–67 283 or 327ci...15, 18
1968–70
    327 or 350ci..1
    With deep tone exhaust...17

Interchange

Interchange Number: 1
    Part Number(s): 3981951 (fits either side)
    Usage: 1968–69 Camaro or Nova 327 or 350ci V-8 with
        dual exhaust, except with deep tone exhaust

Interchange Number: 2
    Part Number(s): RH, 3866582; LH, 3904077
    Usage: 1968–69 Impala or Chevelle with dual exhaust
        with 327, 350, 396, or 427ci, except with special
        high-performance

Interchange Number: 3
    Part Number(s): RH, 3884800; LH, 3928215
    Usage: 1968 Impala 427ci 425hp V-8

Interchange Number: 4
    Part Number(s): 3930752 (fits either side)
    Usage: 1968–69 Chevelle 327ci 325hp or 396ci 375hp
        V-8; 1969 Impala 427ci 425hp
    Notes: LH side only. See interchange number 5 for RH
        unit.

Interchange Number: 5
    Part Number(s): RH, 3884800
    Usage: 1969 Impala 427ci 425hp
    Notes: RH side only. See interchange number 4 for LH
        unit.

Interchange Number: 6
    Part Number(s): RH, 3976484; LH, 3976483
    Usage: 1970 Impala 454ci

Interchange Number: 7
    Part Number(s): 3983320
    Usage: 1965–67 Chevelle 396ci V-8

Interchange Number: 8
    Part Number(s): 3981945
    Usage: 1959–62 Impala, all with dual exhaust, except
        for high-performance

Interchange Number: 9
Part Number(s): RH, 385810; LH, 38352809
Usage: 1959–64 327, high-performance 348, and all 409ci

Interchange Number: 10
Part Number(s): 3830468 (fits either side)
Usage: 1962–64 327ci, except special high-performance

Interchange Number: 11
Part Number(s): 3952874 (fits either side)
Usage: 1964 Chevelle 327ci 350hp V-8; 1965–67 Impala 327, 396, or 409ci station wagon

Interchange Number: 12
Part Number(s): RH, 3851352; LH, 3851351
Usage: 1964 Chevelle 283 or 327ci (except 327ci 350hp) V-8 with dual exhaust

Interchange Number: 13
Part Number(s): RH, 3866582; LH, 3866583
Usage: 1965–67 Chevelle 327ci, except special high-performance for 1965–66; 1965–67 Impala 327ci coupe or sedan with dual-exhaust

Interchange Number: 14
Part Number(s): RH, 3884800; LH, 3930752
Usage: 1965–66 Impala 396, except 425ci 375hp; 1965–67 Chevelle SS 396; 1966 Chevelle 327ci, all except 350hp

Interchange Number: 15
Part Number(s): RH, 3872286; LH, 3908399
Usage: 1965–67 Nova V-8; 1967 Nova, LH side only

Interchange Number: 16
Part Number(s): 3981951
Usage: 1967–68 Camaro with dual exhaust except with deep tone

Interchange Number: 17
Part Number(s): 3910566
Usage: 1967–68 Camaro dual exhaust with deep tone
Notes: Use if deep tone pipes are swapped.

Interchange Number: 18
Part Number(s): 3914830
Usage: 1967 Nova RH side, dual exhaust

Tail Pipe

Interchange

Interchange Number: 1
Part Number(s): RH, 3934874; LH, 3932747
Usage: 1967–68 Camaro, all with dual exhaust; 1968–69 Nova with dual exhaust
Notes: RH side pipe used on models with single exhaust

Interchange Number: 2
Part Number(s): RH, 3961397; LH, 3958459
Usage: 1969 Camaro, all with dual exhaust except 302 or 396ci with chamber exhaust option
Notes: These tailpipes have no chrome tip. Were used until 6-12-69. For models built after that date, see interchange number 3.

Interchange Number: 3
Part Number(s): RH, 3974213; LH, 39655627
Usage: 1969 Camaro, all with dual exhaust except 302 or 396ci with chamber exhaust
Notes: These units replaced the above units (see interchange number 2) on late 1969 models. Was used on those 1969 Camaros that were considered 1970 models.

Interchange Number: 4
Part Number(s): RH, 3984570; LH, 3984569

Usage: 1970 Camaro 350 or 396ci, both with dual exhaust

Interchange Number: 5
Part Number(s): RH, 3901732; LH, 3901731
Usage: 1966–67 Chevelle SS 396

Interchange Number: 6
Part Number(s): RH,3925104; LH, 3925103
Usage: 1968–69 El Camino or station wagon with dual exhaust

Interchange Number: 7
Part Number(s): RH, 3928266; LH, 3928265
Usage: 1968 Chevelle coupe or convertible with dual exhaust

Interchange Number: 8
Part Number(s): RH, 3956758; LH, 3956757
Usage: 1969 Chevelle coupe or convertible with dual exhaust, except with chamber exhaust

Interchange Number: 9
Part Number(s): RH, 3956752; LH, 3956751
Usage: 1969 Chevelle with 396ci and chamber exhaust

Interchange Number: 10
Part Number(s): RH, 3973828; LH, 3973857
Usage: 1970–72 Chevelle SS 396 or 454ci coupe or convertible
Notes: The tailpipes used built-in resonators. Monte Carlo uses a similar type tailpipe, but will not interchange due to difference in resonator shape.

Interchange Number: 11
Part Number(s): RH, 3983388; LH, 3983387
Usage: 1970–72 El Camino or station wagon with dual exhaust

Interchange Number: 12
Part Number(s): RH, 3869356; LH, 3869355
Usage: 1959–64 (1959–60 RH side) Impala V-8 with dual exhaust, except high-performance or 327ci

Interchange Number: 13
Part Number(s): RH, 3815626; LH, 3815625
Usage: 1962–64 Impala 327ci, except high-performance
Notes: Pipes are stamped with part number.

Interchange Number: 14
Part Number(s): RH, 3861854; LH, 3859817
Usage: 1965 Impala 327ci coupe; 1965 396, 409, or 327ci station wagon with dual exhaust

Interchange Number: 15
Part Number(s): RH, 3934022; LH, 3934021
Usage: 1965 Impala 396ci 425hp; 1966 396 or 427ci 425hp

Interchange Number: 16
Part Number(s): RH, 3930704; LH, 3930703
Usage: 1967 Impala 427 with 425hp

Interchange Number: 17
Part Number(s): RH, 3884862; LH, 3874241
Usage: 1966–67 Impala small-block V-8 with dual exhaust

Interchange Number: 18
Part Number(s): RH, 3930708; LH, 3934023
Usage: 1968 Impala 327 or 396ci with dual exhaust, all but station wagon
Notes: Units have resonators built in.

Interchange Number: 19
Part Number(s): RH, 3930706; LH, 3934013
Usage: 1968 Impala 427ci 390hp with dual exhaust
Notes: Units have built-in resonators.

Interchange Number: 20
Part Number(s): RH, 3930704; LH, 3934021
Usage: 1968 Impala 427ci 425hp V-8
Notes: Pipes do not have resonators.

Interchange Number: 21
Part Number(s): RH, 3954674; LH, 3954673
Usage: 1969 Impala 350, 396, or 427 335hp and 390hp V-8, all but station wagon
Notes: Units have built-in resonators.

Interchange Number: 22
Part Number(s): RH, 3954686; LH, 3954685
Usage: 1969 Impala 427ci 425hp
Notes: Units do not have resonators.

Interchange Number: 23
Part Number(s): RH, 3972514; LH, 3972513
Usage: 1970 Impala with dual exhaust, all engine sizes

Interchange Number: 24
Part Number(s): RH, 3863962; LH, 3863961
Usage: 1964–65 Chevelle 283 or 327ci, all except station wagon or El Camino
Notes: Interchange number 26 will fit.

Interchange Number: 25
Part Number(s): RH, 3857388; LH, 3857387
Usage: 1964–67 283 or 327ci El Camino or station wagon

Interchange Number: 26
Part Number(s): RH, 3876306; LH, 3876305
Usage: 1966–67 Chevelle 283 or 327ci, except El Camino or station wagon

Interchange Number: 27
Part Number(s): RH, 3798474; LH, 3798473
Usage: 1959–61 Impala 348ci high-performance; 1962–64 Impala 327ci high-performance; 1962–64 409ci

Interchange Number: 28
Part Number(s): RH, 3884862; LH, 3884861
Usage: 1966 Chevy II
Notes: Used with 327ci originally, but can fit those with 283ci. Also, Interchange Number 29 may fit. Can be adapted to fit 1964–65 Chevy II.

Interchange Number: 29
Part Number(s): RH, 3909984; LH, 3909983
Usage: 1967 Chevy II, all engines

Emission Control System AIR Pump

Model Identification

Model ....Interchange Number
1966–67, all except 327ci 4bbl, Chevelle SS 396, Camaro SS
    396, and Chevy II 1
1966–67 327ci 4bbl 2
1966–67 SS 396 3
1966–67 Chevy II 5
1968–70, all models, all engines 4

Interchange

Interchange Number: 1
Part Number(s): 5696104
Usage: 1966 Impala 283, 396, or 427ci; 1966 Pontiac
    Tempest or LeMans V-8; 1966–67 Chevelle 283 or
    327ci; 1966–67 Nova V-8 without a/c; 1966–67 C-
    10 V-8 Chevrolet/GMC pickup; 1966–67 full-size
    Buick; 1966–67 Buick Skylark; 1966–67 Olds Cutlass
    V-8 with a/c; 1967 Camaro 327ci

Interchange Number: 2
Part Number(s): 5696468
Usage: 1966–67 Impala 327ci 4bbl; 1966–67 Chevelle
    327ci 4bbl; 1967 Camaro 327ci 4bbl

Interchange Number: 3
Part Number(s): 7800308
Usage: 1967 Chevelle SS 396; 1967 Camaro SS 396

Interchange Number: 4
Part Number(s): 7806686
Usage: 1968–71 Chevelle; 1968–71 Camaro; 1968–71
    Impala; 1968–71 Nova; 1969–70 C-10 to C-30
    Chevrolet or GMC truck with V-8; 1970–71 Monte
    Carlo
Notes: (1) Special modification must be made when us-
    ing on a small-block 1968 car with manual trans-
    mission. The red relief valve must be used. (2) The
    1972–74 pump will fit these but is slightly different
    in design and part number.

Interchange Number: 5
Part Number(s): 5697527
Usage: 1966–67 Chevy II V-8 with a/c

Chapter 5

Transmission

Transmission

There are many ways to identify a transmission. One way is by its design or type, or by the manufacture and build date codes. Although this will not tell you what model of car the transmission came out of, it *will* tell you the assembly plant and the date the transmission was built. Another ID code was painted or stamped on the transmission for identification at the factory. However, note that the interchange here is based on the part number and the physical characteristics of the unit. Thus, many different code numbers can be used in the interchange.

Manual Transmission

To conserve space and due to a general lack of interest, three-speed manual transmissions have been left out of this book. Only four-speeds and automatics are listed. The 1959–60 Turboglide is not listed for the same reasons.

The Saginaw design is a general-duty four-speed that saw wide usage. It has a cast-iron case and extension, and a seven-bolt cover with three shift rods.

The Muncie four-speed is a high-performance transmission that also was widely used. There are two versions: wide-ratio and close-ratio. Wide ratio has twenty-four teeth on the input shaft; close-ratio has twenty-six teeth on shaft. Both versions have a seven-bolt cover with two shift rods. The case is aluminum.

There is also a low-performance four-speed Muncie unit that was used in a number of cars. It has a cast-iron case but is not as desirable for performance applications as the aluminum case units.

A transmission's assembly plant and build date code location varied with the manufacturer. The 1959–63 Warner four-speed ID was positioned on the cover side rear flange, where it began with the letter "W" for the Warner assembly plant. In 1963, when the Muncie transmission was first used, the build date code was stamped on the cover side of the case and began with the letter "P."

Both the Warner and Muncie codes were followed by the calendar build date of month and day. For example: "2 22" stood for February 22. The later letter code indicated the shift on which the part was made, "D" for Day or "N" for Night.

All 1964–65 four-speeds were stamped on the top right-hand side of the flat area on the case assembly. From 1966 to 1968 the build date appeared on the right-hand

side of the case, just ahead of the extension. On 1970 models, the ID can be found on a machined surface on the left-hand side of the case, just below the side cover for light-duty units. On ID on high-performance applications, the ID was stamped vertically on the right-hand side of the case, just ahead of the extension.

Muncie transmissions still used the "P" letter code and Warner used the "W," with the addition of the letter "R" to indicate the Saginaw plant. Build date code was the same as in earlier years—except for the Warner plant, which used a single letter to indicate the month ("A" for January to "M" for December), with the letter "I" not being used. Also, following the build day was the last digit of the year. Thus, the Code WC217 would translate as March 21, 1967. Also, the particular shift was represented by a single number (1–3).

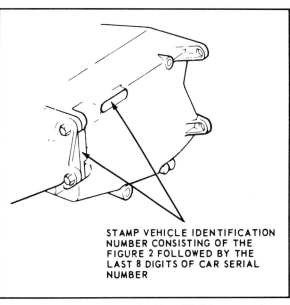

STAMP VEHICLE IDENTIFICATION NUMBER CONSISTING OF THE FIGURE 2 FOLLOWED BY THE LAST 8 DIGITS OF CAR SERIAL NUMBER

Manual transmissions can be identified by a two-letter code marked in yellow paint that is stamped on the right-hand side of the transmission case (as shown).

Four-Speed Manual Transmission

Model Identification

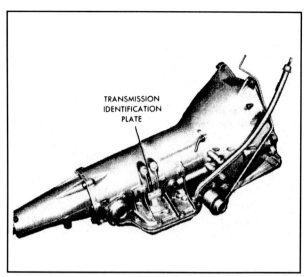

Turbo Hydra-matic transmissions are marked with an identification code on a plate mounted to the right-hand side of the transmission (as shown). *Chevrolet*

Interchange

Interchange Number: 1
Part Number(s): Chevrolet, 3867265
Usage: 1963–65 full-size Chevrolet; 1964 Corvette; 1964–65 Chevelle; 1964–65 Olds Cutlass
Notes: Has 2.56:1 ratio. Muncie-built.

Interchange Number: 2
Part Number(s): Chevrolet, 3964502
ID Codes: P, FM, FF, HP
Usage: 1964–67 Chevy II; 1964–68 full-size Chevrolet; 1965–68 Chevelle; 1965–68 Olds Cutlass, except 442; 1967–68 Camaro; 1967–68 Buick Skylark; 1967–68 Pontiac Firebird; 1968 Nova
Notes: Has 2.52:1 ratio. Muncie-built.

Interchange Number: 3
Part Number(s): Chevrolet, 3964506
ID Codes: N, HF, FX, FN
Usage: 1965–68 Chevelle; 1965–68 full-size Chevrolet; 1965–68 Olds Cutlass 442; 1966–67 Chevy II; 1967–68 Camaro; 1967–68 Buick Skylark; 1967–68 Pontiac Firebird; 1968 Nova
Notes: Has 2.20:1 ratio, cast-iron case, close-ratio transmission, excellent high-performance transmission. Muncie-built.

Interchange Number: 4
Part Number(s): Chevrolet, 3964503
ID Codes: P, FM, FF, HP
Usage: 1965–68 Chevelle; 1965–68 full-size Chevrolet; 1965–68
Olds Cutlass, except 442; 1966–67 Chevy II; 1967–68 Camaro; 1967–68 Buick Skylark; 1967–68 Pontiac Firebird; 1968 Nova
Notes: Has 2.52:1 ratio, cast-iron case. Used same codes as aluminum unit and was identified by case. Muncie-built.

Interchange Number: 5
Part Number(s): Chevrolet, 3964505
ID Codes: N, HF, FX, FN
Usage: 1965–68 Chevelle; 1965–68 full-size Chevrolet; 1965–68 Olds Cutlass, except 442; 1966–67 Chevy II; 1967–68 Camaro; 1967–68 Buick Skylark; 1967–68 Pontiac Firebird; 1968 Nova
Notes: Has 2.20:1 close-ratio, aluminum case. Muncie-built.

Interchange Number: 6
Part Number(s): Chevrolet, 3884603
Usage: 1966 Chevy II; 1966 Chevelle; 1966 full-size Chevrolet; all with 327ci, except high-performance or special high-performance applications
Notes: Saginaw unit cast-iron case, 2.54:1 ratio.

Interchange Number: 7
Part Number(s): Chevrolet, 3916103
Usage: 1966 Chevy II; 1966 Chevelle; 1966 full-size Chevrolet; all with 283ci, except with 3.55 or 3.70 rear axle ratios
Notes: Saginaw unit cast-iron case, 3.11:1 ratio.

Interchange Number: 8
Part Number(s): Chevrolet, 3964508
Usage: 1965–67 Impala; 1966–68 Chevelle; 1967–68 Camaro; 1968 Nova; all with heavy-duty Rock Crusher transmission
Notes: Not used with 3.07 or 3.31 rear axle ratios. Super performance transmission; cast-iron case; Muncie-built.

Interchange Number: 9
Part Number(s): Chevrolet, 3964507
Usage: 1966–68 Chevelle; 1967–68 Camaro; 1968 Nova; 1968 Olds Cutlass; 1968 Pontiac Firebird; 1968 Corvette; all with heavy-duty Rock Crusher transmission
Notes: With aluminum case. Muncie-built.

Interchange Number: 10
Part Number(s): Chevrolet, 3933853
ID Codes: R, FS, FH
Usage: 1967–68 Nova, Camaro, or Chevelle 327ci; 1969 Nova, Chevelle 350ci; not with high-performance
Notes: Saginaw-built.

Interchange Number: 11
Part Number(s): Chevrolet, 3946797
ID Codes: P
Usage: 1969 Chevelle, Camaro, Nova with 3.55, 3.73, and 4.10 rear axle ratios
Notes: General performance standard transmission built in Muncie. 2.52:1 gear ratio in first gear.

Interchange Number: 12
Part Number(s): Chevrolet, 3946798
ID Codes: N, XF, XD
Usage: 1969 Chevelle, Camaro, Nova with 3.55, 3.73, and 4.10 rear axle ratios
Notes: General performance standard transmission built in Muncie. 2.20:1 gear ratio in first gear.

Interchange Number: 13
Part Number(s): Chevrolet, 3950316
Usage: 1969 Chevelle, Camaro, Nova with 3.07 or 3.31 rear axle ratios
Notes: Has 2.20:1 first gear ratio.

Interchange Number: 14
Part Number(s): Chevrolet, 3950376
Usage: 1969 Camaro, except with 2.73 rear axle ratio
Notes: Has 2.85:1 first gear ratio. Saginaw-built. Due to high first gear ratio, not a great performance transmission.

Interchange Number: 15
Part Number(s): Chevrolet, 3950379
ID Codes: R, FH
Usage: 1969 Camaro 327 or 350ci with 2.73 ratio
Notes: Saginaw-built. Has 2.54:1 first gear ratio.

Interchange Number: 16
Part Number(s): Chevrolet, 3952658
Usage: 1970 Chevelle 350ci; 1970 Nova 350 or 396ci; 1970 Camaro
Notes: Saginaw-built. Will fit 1969 models if cover is changed.

Interchange Number: 17
Part Number(s): Chevrolet, 6271516
ID Codes: P, WB
Usage: 1970 Camaro, Chevelle, Impala, Nova; 1970 Olds Cutlass; 1970 Pontiac Firebird
Notes: Muncie wide-ratio 2.52:1 first gear ratio. Will fit 1969 models if cover is changed.

Interchange Number: 18
Part Number(s): Chevrolet, 6271517
Codes: P, WC
Usage: 1970 Camaro, Chevelle, Impala, Nova; 1970 Olds Cutlass; 1970 Pontiac Firebird
Notes: Muncie close-ratio 2.20:1 ratio. Will fit 1969 models if cover is changed.

Interchange Number: 19
Part Number(s): Chevrolet, 3792621
ID Codes: AA
Usage: 1959–63 Impala
Notes: Warner-built; has nine-bolt cover.

Interchange Number: 20
Part Number(s): Chevrolet, 3831819
Usage: 1959–63 Impala, except 409ci
Notes: Muncie-built.

Interchange Number: 21
Part Number(s): Chevrolet, 3820271
Usage: 1962–63 Impala 409ci
Notes: Warner-built.

Interchange Number: 22
Part Number(s): Chevrolet, 3831821
Usage: 1962–63 Impala 409ci
Notes: Muncie-built.

Interchange Number: 23
Part Number(s): Chevrolet, 3820268
Usage: 1963 Impala 409ci
Notes: Warner-built. Will fit 1962 models. Close-ratio.

Interchange Number: 24
  Part Number(s): Chevrolet, 3831823
  Usage: 1963 Impala 409ci
  Notes: Muncie-built. Will fit 1962 models. Close-ratio.

Automatic Transmission

Chevrolet used three types of automatic transmissions: Powerglide, which has two forward speeds, and Turbo Hydra-Matic 350 and 400, both of which have three forward speeds. The transmissions can be identified by their visual characteristics.

Powerglide came in either a cast-iron or aluminum case with a flat, smooth, or rounded ridge top. A quick way to identify the transmission is to look for the word "POWERGLIDE" stamped into the case. A popular transmission, the Powerglide was used extensively until 1969 when Chevy began to phase it out in favor of the Turbo Hydra-Matic 350.

The Powerglide is an excellent drag-racing transmission, even better than the Turbo Hydra-Matic. If you chose it for this purpose, opt for the aluminum case unit, as it is much lighter.

Turbo Hydra-matics (both 350 and 400) are easily identified by their two-part (converter/transmission housing and extension) design. They can be further classified by their pan design. The Turbo Hydra-Matic 350 uses a square-shaped oil pan that has a notched corner and is held on with thirteen bolts. The down-shift cable connector is located on the right-hand side of the unit.

The Turbo Hydra-Matic 400 has an oil pan that is also secured with thirteen bolts, but the pan is longer and has no uniform shape. The down-shift cable is located on the left-hand side of the unit and is controlled electronically. The Turbo Hydra-Matic 400 appeared in 1965 models. Be careful, though, because other GM makes (Pontiac, Buick, and Oldsmobile) also used Turbo Hydra-Matic 350 and 400 and have the same visual markings. In some cases an example from a Pontiac will fit, but a unit from a Buick uses a different bolt pattern that will not fit in a Chevrolet model. For the safest interchange, a Chevrolet unit is the best bet.

The Turbo Hydra-Matics are also identified by their code letters. These codes are found stamped on the servo cover on the right-hand side of the transmission. For the Turbo Hydra-Matic 400, the code can be found on a tag riveted to either the right-hand or the left-hand side of the case, depending on the model. The code can be helpful in locating a heavy-duty unit from a standard passenger car unit. You can use a heavy-duty unit in a non-high-performance car, but you really should not place a lighter duty unit behind the engine of a high-performance car. However, you can rebuild a standard-duty unit and make it a heavy-duty unit.

Model Identification

POWERGLIDE

TURBO HYDRA-MATIC

Interchange

POWERGLIDE

Interchange Number: 1
  Part Number(s): Chevrolet, 3966981
  ID Codes: C or T
  Usage: 1959–64 full-size Chevrolet 283ci, all except 1962–64 Impala SS

Interchange Number: 2
  Part Number(s): Chevrolet, 3831949
  ID Codes: C or T
  Usage: 1962–64 full-size Chevrolet 327ci

Interchange Number: 3
  Part Number(s): Chevrolet, 3832581
  ID Codes: C, T, or E
  Usage: 1962–65 full-size Chevrolet 409ci
  Notes: Not for use with special high-performance.

Interchange Number: 4

Part Number(s): Chevrolet, 3977622

ID Codes: C, T, or E

Usage: 1964–67 Chevelle 283ci except with 3.55 or 3.70 axle ratios; 1965–67 Chevy II 283ci V-8; 1965–67 full-size Chevrolet 283ci; 1967 Camaro 396ci with floor console; 1968 Chevelle 307ci with column shift; 1968 Nova with floor shift and a/c or with 307ci; 1968 full-size Chevrolet 307ci

Interchange Number: 5

Part Number(s): Chevrolet, 6258385

ID Codes: C , T, or E

Usage: 1965–68 full-size Chevrolet 327ci; 1965–68 Chevelle 327ci; 1966–67 Chevy II 327ci; 1967–68 Camaro 327ci; 1968 Nova with floor console and a/c or with 327ci, except with 3.55 rear axle ratio

Interchange Number: 6

Part Number(s): Chevrolet, 3895797

ID Codes: C, T, or E

Usage: 1967 Camaro 350ci

Interchange Number: 7

Part Number(s): Chevrolet, 3887076

ID Codes: C ,T, or E

Usage: 1965–67 full-size Chevrolet 396ci; 1966–67 Chevelle SS 396

Interchange Number: 8

Part Number(s): Chevrolet, 3919344

ID Codes: C , T, or E

Usage: 1968 full-size Chevrolet 396ci

Interchange Number: 9

Part Number(s): Chevrolet, 3919342

ID Codes: C , T, or E

Usage: 1968 Chevelle SS 396 with column shift

Interchange Number: 10

Part Number(s): Chevrolet, 3919339

ID Codes: C, T, or E

Usage: 1968 Chevelle SS 396 with floor shift

Interchange Number: 11

Part Number(s): Chevrolet, 3946749, 3967319

ID Codes: C, T, or E

Usage: 1968–69 Chevelle; 1968–70 full-size Chevrolet; 1969–72 Camaro; 1969–72 Nova; 1970–72 Pontiac Firebird; 1970–72 Pontiac LeMans; 1971–72 Pontiac Ventura II; 1971–72 GMC Sprint; all with V-8

TURBO HYDRA-MATIC 350

Interchange Number: 12

Part Number(s): Chevrolet, 332564

ID Codes: B, X , or Y

Usage: 1968–69 Chevelle, Camaro, Nova, all 2bbl (307 or 350ci) small-block

Interchange Number: 13

Part Number(s): Chevrolet, 6261554

ID Codes: B, X, or Y

Usage: 1968 Camaro, Chevelle, Nova 327ci 2bbl; 1969 full-size Chevrolet, Camaro, Chevelle, Nova, all 350ci 2bbl with 3.078 or 3.08 rear axle ratios

Interchange Number: 14

Part Number(s): Chevrolet, 340662

ID Codes: B, X, or Y

Usage: 1968 Camaro, Chevelle, Nova, full-size Chevrolet 327ci 4bbl or with a/c; 1969–71 Camaro, Chevelle, Nova, full-size Chevrolet 2bbl 350ci

Interchange Number: 15

Part Number(s): Chevrolet, 325108

ID Codes: B, X, or Y

Usage: 1969–70 Camaro, Chevelle, Nova, full-size Chevrolet 350ci 4bbl; 1970 full-size Chevrolet or Monte Carlo 400ci (small-block)

TURBO HYDRA-MATIC 400

Interchange Number: 16

Part Number(s): Chevrolet, 8626648

ID Codes: CA

Usage: 1965–70 full-size Chevrolet 350, 396, 327 or 400ci 2bbl (small-block), all with three-speed automatic

Interchange Number: 17

Part Number(s): Chevrolet, 8626005

ID Codes: CA, PV, PS, PH

Usage: 1967–68 Chevelle; 1967–68 Camaro (late 1967 style)

Notes: 1966–68 Pontiac big-block transmission will interchange, but extension may need to be changed to Chevrolet unit.

Interchange Number: 18

Part Number(s): Chevrolet, varies with usage

ID Codes: CA

Usage: 1969–74 Chevelle, Camaro, Nova

Notes: The part number range interchanges. But note that the larger the engine or the more horsepower it has, the more heavy duty the unit is. A lighter duty unit such as a 350 2bbl should not be used behind, say, a 396ci Chevelle; however, the reverse would work well and even provide a stronger transmission. Also note that cars with a trailer package used a stronger transmission than those without the package.

Gearshift

Gearshift interchange is based on original part numbers. In most cases, it is for the entire lever assembly (lower mechanism and upper lever). Some models used different shift levers according to the type of seating arrangement used.

Model Identification

MANUAL FLOOR SHIFT

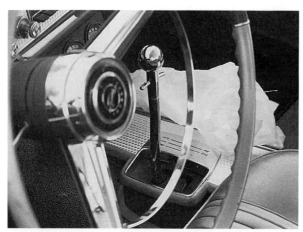

Models with a console may use a different shifter than those without one. This is the 1964 Impala unit.

1968	10, 11, 12
1969	11, 12
1970	13, 14, 15

Impala	Interchange Number
1959–63, all except SS	1
1962–63 SS	2
1964	3
1965–68	4, 5
1969	6

Chevy II/Nova	Interchange Number
1962	20
1963, all except SS	21
1963 Nova SS	22, 23
1964	24
1965–66, all except SS	25
1965 Nova SS	26
1966 Chevy II 283ci, all but SS	27
1966 Chevy II 327ci, all but SS	25
1966 Nova SS 283ci	28
1966 Nova SS 327ci	26
1967, all but SS	29
1967 Nova SS	30
1968–70 without console	16
1968–70 with console	18

Interchange

Interchange Number: 1
Part Number(s): 3828658
Usage: 1959–63 full-size Chevrolet, except 1962–63 Impala SS

Interchange Number: 2
Part Number(s): 3828659
Usage: 1962–63 Impala SS
Notes: Unit is dabbed with yellow paint.

Interchange Number: 3
Part Number(s): 3841472
Usage: 1964 full-size Chevrolet

Interchange Number: 4
Part Number(s): 3859883
Usage: 1965–68 full-size Chevrolet with bench seats

Interchange Number: 5
Part Number(s): 3879740
Usage: 1965–68 full-size Chevrolet with bucket seats

Interchange Number: 6
Part Number(s): 3922514
Usage: 1969 full-size Chevrolet
Notes: A rare find!

Interchange Number: 7
Part Number(s): 3853137
Usage: 1964–66 Chevelle SS

Interchange Number: 8
Part Number(s): 3853134
Usage: 1964–66 Chevelle, except SS 396
Notes: Has more arc than the SS unit in interchange number 7. Will fit SS 396 (was replacement unit) but is visually incorrect.

Interchange Number: 9
Part Number(s): 3903077
Usage: 1967 Chevelle

Interchange Number: 10
Part Number(s): 3922522
Usage: 1968 Chevelle M20 four-speed with bench seats
Notes: Upper lever is the same unit used with 1968 three-speed; lower unit must be changed.

Interchange Number: 11
Part Number(s): 3922523
Usage: 1968 Chevelle M21 or M22 four-speed with bench seats; 1969 Chevelle, all four-speeds, with bench seats

Interchange Number: 12
Part Number(s): 3922524
Usage: 1968–69 Chevelle with bucket seats
Notes: Used as a replacement shifter for the 1968–69 Chevelle, regardless of seat type.

Interchange Number: 13
Part Number(s): 3973865
Usage: 1970–72 Chevelle with bench seats

Interchange Number: 14
Part Number(s): 3973864
Usage: 1970 Chevelle with bucket seats without console

Interchange Number: 15
Part Number(s): 3973866
Usage: 1970–72 Chevelle with console, except 1971–72 SS 350

Interchange Number: 16
Part Number(s): 6264025
Usage: 1967–68 Camaro; 1968–72 Nova without console; 1972 Pontiac Ventura II without console

Interchange Number: 17
Part Number(s): 9792437
Usage: 1968–69 Pontiac Firebird; 1969 Camaro
Notes: With Hurst shifter

Interchange Number: 18
Part Number(s): 6264024
Usage: 1968–72 Nova; 1968–72 Pontiac Ventura II with console

Interchange Number: 19
Part Number(s): 3992596
Usage: 1970–72 Camaro

Interchange Number: 20
Part Number(s): 3791135
Usage: 1962 Chevy II

Interchange Number: 21
Part Number(s): 3793880
Usage: 1963 Chevy II, except SS (see interchange number 22)

Interchange Number: 22
Part Number(s): 3937019
Usage: 1963 up to 11-30-62; Nova SS

Interchange Number: 23
Part Number(s): 3839256
Usage: Beginning 12-1-62; 1963 Nova SS
Notes: Has straighter design than non-SS models.

Interchange Number: 24
Part Number(s): 3853134
Usage: 1964 Chevy II

Interchange Number: 25
Part Number(s): 3859343
Usage: 1965 Chevy II except SS; 1966 Chevy II 327ci except SS

Interchange Number: 26
Part Number(s): 3859344
Usage: 1965 Nova SS; 1966 Nova SS 327ci

Interchange Number: 27
Part Number(s): 3886572
Usage: 1966 Chevy II 283ci, except Nova SS

Interchange Number: 28
Part Number(s): 3886582
Usage: 1966 Nova SS 283ci

Interchange Number: 29
Part Number(s): 3857524
Usage: 1967 Chevy II, all engines, all models except Nova SS

Interchange Number: 30
Part Number(s): 3845895
Usage: 1967 Nova SS, all engines

AUTOMATIC ON THE COLUMN

Interchange

Interchange Number: 1
Part Number(s): 3779638
Usage: 1959–65 full-size Chevrolet (up to 5-20-65)
Notes: Overall length 9-13/32 inches.

Interchange Number: 2
Part Number(s): 3882906
Usage: 1966 full-size Chevrolet
Notes: Overall length 8-15/32 inches.

Interchange Number: 3
Part Number(s): 3904087
Usage: 1966–67 Chevelle; 1967 full-size Chevrolet
Notes: A few late-built 1966 models may have used this unit. Interchange numbers 4 and 5 will fit.

Interchange Number: 4
Part Number(s): 3928319
Usage: 1968 full-size Chevrolet; 1968 Chevelle

Interchange Number: 5
Part Number(s): 3914815
Usage: 1967 Chevy II; 1975 Nova; 1975 Pontiac Ventura; 1975 Buick Apollo; 1975 Olds Omega
Notes: Replacement unit for 1964–67 Nova or 1964–67 Chevelle.

Interchange Number: 6
Part Number(s): 3939741
Usage: 1969–74 full-size Chevrolet, Chevelle, Camaro
Notes: Interchange number 5 will fit.

Interchange Number: 7
Part Number(s): 3792499
Usage: 1962–65 Chevy II
Notes: Some early 1962 (built in the first month) models used an additional lever. The difference is only slight and both will interchange.

Interchange Number: 8
Part Number(s): 3879746
Usage: 1966 Chevy II automatic or three-speed manual on the column
Notes: Both transmissions used the same chrome lever.

Interchange Number: 9
Part Number(s): 3905551
Usage: 1967 Pontiac Firebird; 1967–68 Camaro; 1968–71 Nova; 1971–72 Pontiac Ventura II

Interchange Number: 10
Part Number(s): 383836
Usage: 1964 Olds Cutlass three-speed manual on the column; 1964–65 Chevelle

Interchange Number: 11
Part Number(s): 3879746
Usage: 1966 Chevelle automatic or three-speed manual on the column
Notes: Interchange numbers 3, 5, and 12 will fit.

Interchange Number: 12
Part Number(s): 3904085
Usage: 1967 Chevelle automatic or manual shift on the column
Notes: Interchange numbers 3, 5, and 11 will fit.

Interchange Number: 13
Part Number(s): 3832568
Usage: 1963–65 full-size Chevrolet

Interchange Number: 14
Part Number(s): 3888724
Usage: 1966 full-size Chevrolet

Interchange Number: 15
Part Number(s): 3900565
Usage: 1967 full-size Chevrolet; 1967 Chevelle
Notes: Interchange number 16 will fit.

Interchange Number: 16
Part Number(s): 3928239
Usage: 1968 full-size Chevrolet; 1968 Chevelle
Notes: Was used for replacement unit on 1967 models.

Interchange Number: 17
Part Number(s): 3832568
Usage: 1964–65 Chevelle

Interchange Number: 18
Part Number(s): 3884849
Usage: 1966 Chevelle

Interchange Number: 19
Part Number(s): 3895210
Usage: 1967 Camaro; 1967 Pontiac Firebird

Interchange Number: 20
Part Number(s): 3928325
Usage: 1968 Camaro

Interchange Number: 21
Part Number(s): 7806159
Usage: 1969 Chevelle; 1969 full-size Chevrolet

Interchange Number: 22
Part Number(s): 3962727
Usage: 1969–72 Camaro; 1969–72 Nova; 1970–72 Chevelle; 1970–72 Monte Carlo; 1970–72 Impala; 1971–72 GMC Sprint; 1971–72 Pontiac Ventura

AUTOMATIC ON THE FLOOR

Interchange with the automatic floor-shift component involves the lever and the mounting bracket, and is available for 1964 and up. Early models used two different levers, one for the two-speed Powerglide and another for the three-speed Turbo Hydra-Matic. Later models from 1968 and up (except for the Nova) used a single horseshoe-shaped lever with all transmissions.

Model Identification

Camaro ....*Interchange Number*
1967 Powerglide 8
1967 Turbo Hydra-Matic 9
1968–69 11
1969 Sport shifter 15
1970 14

Chevelle ....*Interchange Number*
1964–65 5
1966–67, all but Turbo Hydra-Matic 6
1967 Turbo Hydra-Matic 400 7
1968–70 12
1969 Sport shifter 15

Impala ....*Interchange Number*
1964 1
1965–66 3
1967 ....-
1968–69 10

Chevy II/Nova ....*Interchange Number*
1964 2
1965–67 4
1968–70 Powerglide...8
1968 Turbo Hydra-Matic 9
1969–70 Turbo Hydra-Matic 13

Interchange

Interchange Number: 1
Part Number(s): 3843124
Usage: 1964 full-size Chevrolet

Interchange Number: 2
Part Number(s): 3832016
Usage: 1964 Chevy II
Notes: Unique design looks like a four-speed shifter.

Interchange Number: 3
Part Number(s): 3879742
Usage: 1965–67 full-size Chevrolet
Notes: Part number for Powerglide. Two-speed and three-speed automatic shifter differ.

Interchange Number: 4
Part Number(s): 3862911
Usage: 1965–67 Chevy II

Interchange Number: 5
Part Number(s): 3843285
Usage: 1964–65 Chevelle

Interchange Number: 6
Part Number(s): 3880851
Usage: 1966–67 Chevelle Powerglide

Interchange Number: 7
Part Number(s): 3909691
Usage: 1967 Chevelle SS 396 Turbo Hydra-Matic 400

Interchange Number: 8
Part Number(s): 3895200
Usage: 1967 Camaro; 1968–70 Nova; both Powerglide only

Interchange Number: 9
Part Number(s): 3912607
Usage: 1967 Camaro; 1968 Nova; both Turbo Hydra-Matic
Notes: Can use with both Turbo Hydra-Matic 350 and Turbo Hydra-Matic 400. But will not fit Powerglide.

Interchange Number: 10
Part Number(s): 3954623
Usage: 1968–69 full-size Chevrolet
Notes: Original part number was 3922547 in 1968. Use with all automatic transmissions.

Interchange Number: 11
Part Number(s): 3920267
Usage: 1968–69 Camaro
Notes: Used with all automatics except Sport shifter.

Interchange Number: 12
Part Number(s): 3952863
Usage: 1968–72 Chevelle
Notes: Not for cars with Sport shifter (ratchet type).

Interchange Number: 13
Part Number(s): 3950179
Usage: 1969–70 Nova Turbo Hydra-Matic

Interchange Number: 14
Part Number(s): 3950179
Usage: 1970–72 Camaro
Notes: Used with all automatics.

Interchange Number: 15
Part Number(s): 3958496
Usage: 1969 Camaro; 1969 Chevelle with Sport shifter
Notes: Rare. Ratchet-type shifter. Looks like regular horseshoe-shaped shifter, but has no shift pattern dial.

Shift Knob

Interchange for the shift knob is based on the original unit. The purpose for the interchange is to help you select a reproduction or NOS (new-old-stock) product. Original units

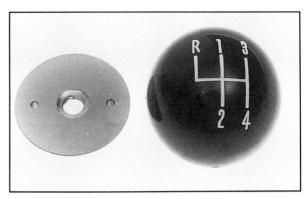

After 1967, this type of knob was used without a console. *Year One*

found in a salvage yard will most likely be too weathered to be used in restoration work.

Some manual transmission knobs had the shift pattern etched in the top of the knob. Floor-shift automatic handles are usually part of the shift lever and are not included in this book. The column-shift automatic knobs were sometimes color keyed (1967–70) to the car's interior. Instead of providing an extensive list of colors here, the interchange indicates what models the particular knob was used in. The part number is for a black knob; all knobs can be painted to match your interior trim. Unless otherwise noted, all column-shift knobs were used with both automatic and three-speed manual on-the-column levers.

Model Identification

ALL EXCEPT FLOOR-MOUNTED MANUAL FOUR-SPEED

Camaro	Interchange Number
1967–70	1

Chevelle	Interchange Number
1964	4
1965	3
1966	2
1967–70	1

Impala	Interchange Number
1959–64	5
1965	3
1966	2
1967–70	1

Chevy II/Nova	Interchange Number
1962–63	6
1964	4
1965	3
1966	2
1967–70	1

Interchange

Interchange Number: 1
Part Number(s): 3973042
Usage: 1967 Pontiac Firebird;
1967–70 Camaro, Chevelle, full-size Chevrolet, Nova; all with column-shift levers

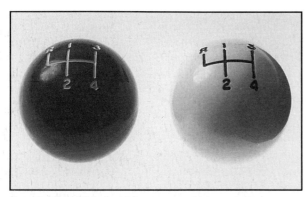

Standard ball knob without console from before 1967. *Year One*

Interchange Number: 2
Part Number(s): 3876965
Usage: 1966 Chevelle; 1966 Chevy II; 1966 full-size Chevrolet, except Caprice

Interchange Number: 3
Part Number(s): 3790368
Usage: 1965 Chevy II; 1965 Chevelle; 1965 full-size Chevrolet

Interchange Number: 4
Part Number(s): 3793123
Usage: 1964 Chevy II; 1964 Chevelle

Interchange Number: 5
Part Number(s): 3782696
Usage: 1959–64 full-size Chevrolet automatic

Interchange Number: 6
Part Number(s): 3790368
Usage: 1962–63 Chevy II with column shift

Model Identification

SHIFT KNOB FOR FLOOR-MOUNTED MANUAL FOUR-SPEED

Interchange

Interchange Number: 1
Part Number(s): 3770344
Color: White
Usage: 1959–63 full-size Chevrolet; 1962–63 Chevy II
Notes: Has inlaid black shift pattern as standard. For options, see interchange number 2

Interchange Number: 2
Part Number(s): 3789168
Color: Black
Usage: 1959–63 full-size Chevrolet; 1963 Chevy II
Notes: Used until 5-20-62.

Interchange Number: 3
Part Number(s): 3857524
Color: White
Usage: 1964–67 full-size Chevrolet except Impala; 1964–67 Chevy II without console; 1965–67 Chevelle without console
Notes: A few 1964 Chevy II models did use the 1963 knob. The change came around mid-November 1963.

Interchange Number: 4
Part Number(s): 3845895
Color: Chrome
Usage: 1964 Impala; 1965–67 full-size Chevrolet with console; optional on 1965–67 Nova SS; 1966–67 Chevelle SS 396; 1968–69 Impala with console; 1968–70 Chevelle or Nova with console

Interchange Number: 5
Part Number(s): 3895201
Usage: Early 1967 Camaro
Notes: One-piece knob changed to a two-piece knob around mid-March 1967.

Interchange Number: 6
Part Number(s): upper, 3920216; lower, 3920218
Usage: 1967 Camaro; 1968–69 full-size Chevrolet; 1968–70 Chevelle; 1968–70 Nova
Notes: All of these models are without a console. Upper lower black with white shift pattern.

Interchange Number: 7
Part Number(s): upper, 3955762; lower, 3955763
Usage: 1968–70 Camaro without console
Notes: Cars with a console used a solid chrome ball below. Lower half was used on three-speed.

Interchange Number: 8
Part Number(s): 3955766
Color: Chrome (ball)
Usage: 1968–70 Camaro with console

Shift Patterns and Dials

Shift patterns are used with manual transmissions, while shift dials are used with automatics. Patterns are used only on cars with a console. On those without a console, the pattern appears on the knob.

Dials are used for all shift lever locations. Again, interchange is based on the original part number. On-the-column types are usually unique to the car line; however, those that were used with consoles are more interchangeable.

Model Identification

Interchange

Interchange Number: 1
Part Number(s): 3786013
Usage: 1959–61 full-size Chevrolet
Notes: Used with a two-part hood retainer.

Interchange Number: 2
Part Number(s): 3817648
Usage: 1962–63 full-size Chevrolet; 1962–65 Chevy II
Notes: Used a one-piece retainer.

Interchange Number: 3
Part Number(s): 3840855
Usage: 1964–65 full-size Chevrolet

Interchange Number: 4
Part Number(s): 3863337
Usage: 1964–65 Chevelle
Notes: Lens retainer from 1964–65 full-size Chevrolet will fit.

Interchange Number: 5
Part Number(s): Powerglide, 3863328; Turbo Hydra-Matic, 3863329
Usage: 1966 full-size Chevrolet
Notes: Powerglide and Turbo Hydra-Matic 400 dials are different and will not interchange.

Interchange Number: 6
Part Number(s): Powerglide, 3899535; Turbo Hydra-Matic, 3899537
Usage: 1967 full-size Chevrolet
Notes: Powerglide and Turbo Hydra-Matic 400 dials are different and will not interchange.

Interchange Number: 7
Part Number(s): 3880633
Usage: 1966 Chevy II, except Nova SS

Interchange Number: 8
Usage: 1966–67 Chevelle
Notes: Part of instrument cluster.
Powerglide and Turbo Hydra-Matic 400 dials are different and will not interchange.

Interchange Number: 9
Part Number(s): 3895209
Usage: 1967 Chevy II, except Nova SS

Interchange Number: 10
Part Number(s): 3895209
Usage: 1967–68 Camaro Powerglide, except Z-28

Interchange Number: 11
Part Number(s): 3909588
Usage: 1967–68 Camaro Turbo Hydra-Matic, except Z-28

Interchange Number: 12
Part Number(s): Powerglide, 6480708
Usage: 1968 full-size Chevrolet

Shift dial for the 1966–67 Chevelle.

Interchange Number: 13
Part Number(s): Turbo Hydra-Matic, 6480709
Usage: 1968 full-size Chevrolet

Interchange Number: 14
Part Number(s): Powerglide, 6482736
Usage: 1969–70 full-size Chevrolet
Notes: Lens assembly with markings.

Interchange Number: 15
Part Number(s): Turbo Hydra-Matic, 6482737
Usage: 1969–70 full-size Chevrolet
Notes: Lens assembly with markings.

Interchange Number: 16
Part Number(s): Powerglide, 6480927; Turbo Hydra-Matic, 6480928
Usage: 1968 Chevelle
Notes: Indicator assembly behind instrument carrier. Powerglide and Turbo Hydra-Matic 400 dials are different and will not interchange.

Interchange Number: 17
Part Number(s): Powerglide, 6483424; Turbo Hydra-Matic, 6483425
Usage: 1969 Chevelle
Notes: Indicator assembly behind carrier. Powerglide and Turbo Hydra-Matic 400 dials are different and will not interchange.

Interchange Number: 18
Part Number(s): Powerglide, 6496316; Turbo Hydra-Matic, 6496317
Usage: 1969–72 Nova
Notes: Indicator assembly behind carrier. Powerglide and Turbo Hydra-Matic units are different and will not interchange.

Interchange Number: 19
Part Number(s): 6483163
Usage: 1969 Camaro Powerglide
Notes: Indicator assembly

Interchange Number: 20
Part Number(s): 6483161
Usage: 1969 Camaro Turbo Hydra-Matic 350 or 400
Notes: Indicator assembly

Interchange Number: 21
Part Number(s): Turbo Hydra-Matic, 6496774
Usage: 1970–72 Chevelle SS; 1970–72 Monte Carlo; 1970–72 Chevelle with gauges
Notes: Indicator assembly behind instrument carrier. Turbo Hydra-Matic only.

Interchange Number: 22
Part Number(s): Powerglide, 6492182; Turbo Hydra-Matic, 6492183
Usage: 1970–72 Chevelle, all except SS
Notes: Indicator assembly behind instrument carrier. Powerglide and Turbo Hydra-Matic 400 dials are different and will not interchange.

Interchange Number: 23
Part Number(s): 3893874
Usage: 1967 Camaro and 1968–70 Nova with Powerglide and console

Interchange Number: 24
Part Number(s): 3919160
Usage: 1968–69 Camaro Powerglide

Interchange Number: 25
Part Number(s): 3880904
Usage: 1966–67 Chevelle Powerglide with console

Interchange Number: 26
Part Number(s): 3990804
Usage: 1968–72 Chevelle Powerglide with console

Interchange Number: 27
Usage: 1964–65 Chevelle with console

Interchange Number: 28
Part Number(s): RH, 3864184; LH, 3864183
Usage: 1965–67 Impala Powerglide with bucket seats (console)

Interchange Number: 29
Part Number(s): 3934231
Usage: 1968–69 Impala Powerglide with console

Interchange Number: 30
Part Number(s): 3864316
Usage: 1965–67 Chevy II with console

Interchange Number: 31
Part Number(s): 3986833
Usage: 1967 Camaro; 1967 Pontiac Firebird; 1968–72 Nova; all Turbo Hydra-Matic with console

Interchange Number: 32
Part Number(s): 3919161
Usage: 1968–69 Camaro Turbo Hydra-Matic with console

Interchange Number: 33
Part Number(s): 3921428
Usage: 1968–72 Chevelle Turbo Hydra-Matic with console

Interchange Number: 34
Part Number(s): RH, 3868998; LH, 3864183
Usage: 1965–67 Impala Turbo Hydra-Matic with console
Notes: Some 1966–67 models used a one-piece design listed as part number 3903970.

Interchange Number: 35
Part Number(s): 3934232
Usage: 1968–69 Impala Turbo Hydra-Matic with console

Interchange Number: 36
Part Number(s): 3919122
Usage: 1968–69 Camaro four-speed manual with console

Interchange Number: 37
Part Number(s): 3919914
Usage: 1968–72 Chevelle four-speed manual with console

Interchange Number: 38
Part Number(s): 3975881
Usage: 1970–72 Camaro four-speed manual with console

Interchange Number: 39
    Part Number(s): 3880912
    Usage: 1966–67 Chevelle four-speed manual with console

Interchange Number: 40
    Part Number(s): 3883709
    Usage: 1966–67 Impala four-speed manual with console
    Notes: Molded into trim plate.

Shift Boots

Interchange is based on part number. Interchange depends primarily on whether the car is equipped with a console or not. Part numbers are for NOS or reproduction parts. Used boots should not be used.

Model Identification

Interchange

Interchange Number: 1
    Part Number(s): 3783383
    Usage: 1959–63 full-size Chevrolet, except Impala SS without console

Interchange Number: 2
    Part Number(s): 3843464
    Usage: 1964 full-size Chevrolet without console, or lower seal with console

Interchange Number: 3
    Part Number(s): 3792165
    Usage: 1962–63 Chevy II four-speed

Interchange Number: 4
    Part Number(s): 3849850
    Usage: 1964–67 Chevy II four-speed without console, or lower seal with console
    Notes: For upper seal, see interchange number

Interchange Number: 5
    Part Number(s): 3842926
    Usage: 1966 Chevelle heavy-duty three- or four-speed without console

Interchange Number: 6
    Part Number(s): 3907663
    Usage: 1966–67 Chevelle heavy-duty three- or four-speed with console
    Notes: This is the upper boot. See interchange number 7 for lower boot.

Interchange Number: 7
    Part Number(s): 3903917
    Usage: 1966–67 Chevelle heavy-duty three- or four-speed with console
    Notes: This is the lower boot. See interchange number 6 for upper boot.

Interchange Number: 8
    Part Number(s): 3893853
    Usage: 1967 Pontiac Firebird; 1967–69 Camaro; both three- or four-speed without console

Interchange Number: 9
    Part Number(s): 3974526
    Usage: 1967 Pontiac Firebird; 1967–69 Camaro; 1968–72 Nova; 1971–72 Pontiac Ventura II; all three- or four-speed with console
    Notes: Lower boot. See interchange number 11 for upper boot.

Interchange Number: 10
    Part Number(s): 3903961
    Usage: 1967 Chevelle heavy-duty three- or four-speed with console

Interchange Number: 11
    Part Number(s): 3921896
    Usage: 1967–69 Camaro; 1968–72 Nova; 1971–72 Pontiac Ventura II; all three- or four-speed with console
    Notes: Upper boot. See interchange number 9 for lower boot.

Interchange Number: 12
    Part Number(s): 3974568
    Usage: 1968–72 Nova; 1971–72 Pontiac Ventura II; all three- or four-speed without console

Interchange Number: 13
    Part Number(s): 3975405

Usage: 1968–72 Chevelle three- or four-speed without console

Interchange Number: 14
Part Number(s): 3931688
Usage: 1968–72 Chevelle heavy-duty three- or four-speed with console
Notes: Lower boot. For upper seal, see interchange number 16.

Interchange Number: 15
Part Number(s): 3973966
Usage: 1970–75 Camaro; 1970–75 Pontiac Firebird; both three- speed or four-speed

Interchange Number: 16
Part Number(s): 3922820
Usage: 1968–72 Chevelle four-speed with console
Notes: Upper seal. Three- speed and four-speed.

Interchange Number: 17
Part Number(s): 3849982
Usage: 1964 Impala four-speed with console
Notes: Upper seal. For lower seal, see interchange number 2.

Interchange Number: 18
Part Number(s): 3877251
Usage: 1965–67 Impala four-speed with console
Notes: Lower seal. For upper seal, see interchange number 19.

Interchange Number: 19
Part Number(s): 3877253
Usage: 1965–67 Impala four-speed with console
Notes: Upper seal. For lower seal, see interchange number 18.

Interchange Number: 20
Part Number(s): 3860183
Usage: 1965–67 Impala four-speed without console

Interchange Number: 21
Part Number(s): 3922871
Usage: 1968–69 Impala four-speed without console

Interchange Number: 22
Part Number(s): 3920391
Usage: 1968–69 Impala four-speed with console
Notes: Lower seal. For upper seal, see interchange number 23.

Interchange Number: 23
Part Number(s): 3920377
Usage: 1968–69 Impala four-speed with console
Notes: Upper seal. For lower seal, see interchange number 22. Also, cover part number 3920397 was used over upper seal. Cover will also interchange for these years.

Interchange Number: 24
Part Number(s): 3863574
Usage: 1964–67 Chevy II four-speed with console
Notes: Upper seal. For lower seal, see interchange number 4.

Driveshaft

Driveshaft interchange is by part number, which includes the slip yoke. Driveshafts can also be identified by overall length. Chevrolet driveshafts are measured from tip to tip. When available, the length is given.

Factors that are involved in a driveshaft swap include the type of transmission and, in some models, the rear axle ratio and engine size.

Model Identification

Interchange

Interchange Number: 1
Part Number(s): 3963870
Overall Length: 24 5/8 inches
Usage: 1959–63 full-size Chevrolet three-speed OD or

Warner four-speed; 1963–64 full-size Chevrolet three-speed OD or Muncie four-speed

Interchange Number: 2
Part Number(s): 3878340
Overall Length: 62-5/32 inches
Usage: 1965–68 full-size Chevrolet, all except automatic

Interchange Number: 3
Part Number(s): 3792720
Overall Length: 31 25/32 inches
Usage: 1962–65 Chevy II; 1966 Chevy II; 1967 Chevy II four-cylinder
Notes: When interchanging from four-speed or from 1964–67 to 1962–62 models, or vice versa, remove yoke.

Interchange Number: 4
Part Number(s): 3938535
Usage: 1966–67 Chevy II V-8; 1967 Chevy II six-cylinder

Interchange Number: 5
Part Number(s): 3958072
Usage: 1968 Nova, all (including 396ci) manual

Interchange Number: 6
Part Number(s): 3950198
Usage: 1969–71 Nova manual, or Powerglide except 1970 four-speed; 1971 Pontiac Ventura manual or two-speed automatic

Interchange Number: 7
Part Number(s): 3898244
Usage: 1964–67 Chevelle; 1968 Chevelle four-door; 1968 El Camino

Interchange Number: 8
Part Number(s): 3924126
Usage: 1968 Chevelle coupe or two-door hardtop

Interchange Number: 9
Part Number(s): 3955598
Usage: 1969–72 Chevelle two-door, except El Camino, all engines except 396 or 454ci

Interchange Number: 10
Part Number(s): 3970519
Usage: 1969–70 El Camino or Chevelle four-door or station wagon with 396ci and Turbo Hydra-Matic 400

Interchange Number: 11
Part Number(s): 3970518
Usage: 1969–72 El Camino or Chevelle four-door or station wagon with 396ci four-speed

Interchange Number: 12
Part Number(s): 7802607
Usage: 1968 Chevelle four-door or station wagon with Turbo Hydra-Matic 400; 1970–72 El Camino 454ci with Turbo Hydra-Matic 400

Interchange Number: 13
Part Number(s): 3955597
Usage: 1968–72 El
Camino with except 396 or 454ci; 1968–72 Chevelle four-door

Interchange Number: 14
Part Number(s): 7801646
Usage: 1968 Chevelle two-door or convertible with Turbo Hydra-Matic 400; 1971–72 Chevelle SS 454 with Turbo Hydra-Matic 400; not for El Camino

Interchange Number: 15
Part Number(s): 3949163
Usage: 1969–72 Chevelle two-door, all except El Camino 396 or 402ci with Turbo Hydra-Matic 400

Interchange Number: 16
Part Number(s): 3910061
Usage: 1967–68 Camaro manual, except 396ci; 1967–68 Z-28

Interchange Number: 17
Part Number(s): 7801406
Usage: 1967–68 Camaro 396ci automatic
Notes: A change occurred around April 1968. Can be identified by a trunnion bearing retaining strap which contracts a step on the bearing housing on the outward end.

Interchange Number: 18
Part Number(s): 3914190
Usage: 1967–68 Camaro 396ci manual

Interchange Number: 19
Part Number(s): 3917578
Usage: 1968 Camaro Powerglide

Interchange Number: 20
Part Number(s): 3950194
Usage: 1968–69 Camaro Turbo Hydra-Matic 350; 1969 Camaro manual or Powerglide
Notes: Exception was 1969 350ci 4bbl.

Interchange Number: 21
Part Number(s): 3970521
Usage: 1969 Camaro Muncie four-speed manual; 1969 Z-28

Interchange Number: 22
Part Number(s): 3981931
Usage: 1969 Camaro Turbo Hydra-Matic 350 and 350ci 4bbl V-8

Interchange Number: 23
Part Number(s): 3950196
Usage: 1969 Camaro Turbo Hydra-Matic 400

Interchange Number: 24
Part Number(s): 3981929
Usage: 1970 Camaro three-speed manual or Powerglide

Interchange Number: 25
Part Number(s): 3981930
Usage: 1970 Camaro Turbo Hydra-Matic 400; 1970–72 Camaro 402 (396ci); 1970–72 Pontiac Firebird 400ci with Turbo Hydra-Matic 400; 1970–73 Camaro Z-28 manual or automatic; 1971 Firebird four-speed; 1973 Firebird 400 or 455ci

Interchange Number: 26
Part Number(s): 3981932
Usage: 1970 Camaro four-speed 350 or 396ci; 1970

Camaro Turbo Hydra-Matic 350; 1970 Pontiac Firebird 400ci four-speed

Interchange Number: 27
Part Number(s): 3963869
Overall Length: 26 13/16 inches
Usage: 1959–64 Impala Powerglide

Interchange Number: 28
Part Number(s): 3871141
Overall Length: 61 7/16 inches
Usage: 1965 Impala Turbo Hydra-Matic

Interchange Number: 29
Part Number(s): 5697871
Overall Length: 60 15/16 inches
Usage: 1966 Impala Turbo Hydra-Matic

Interchange Number: 30
Part Number(s): 7801540
Overall Length: 67 51/64 inches
Usage: 1967–70 Impala Turbo Hydra-Matic Notes:
Caprice models used a different part number, but
the shafts will interchange.

Interchange Number: 31
Part Number(s): 3939255
Overall Length: 67 3/32 inches
Usage: 1967–68 Impala Powerglide

Interchange Number: 32
Part Number(s): 3955596
Usage: 1969–70 Impala Powerglide or Turbo Hydra-
Matic 350

Interchange Number: 33
Part Number(s): 3950261
Usage: 1969–70 Impala Turbo Hydra-Matic 400, except
1970 454ci

Interchange Number: 34
Part Number(s): 3950261
Usage: 1970 Impala 454ci with Turbo Hydra-Matic 400

Interchange Number: 35
Part Number(s): 3961477
Usage: 1969 Impala four-speed

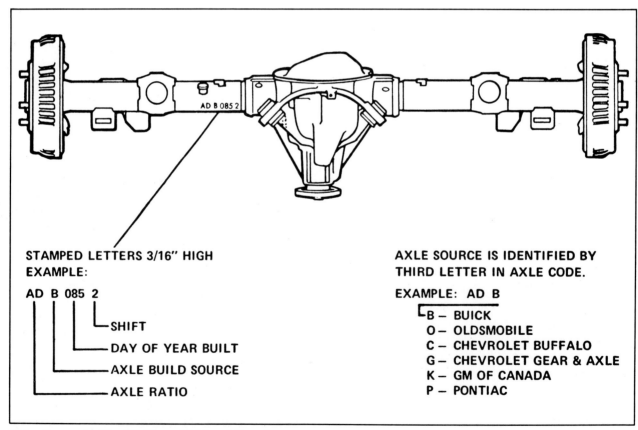

**STAMPED LETTERS 3/16″ HIGH
EXAMPLE:**

AD B 085 2
— SHIFT
— DAY OF YEAR BUILT
— AXLE BUILD SOURCE
— AXLE RATIO

**AXLE SOURCE IS IDENTIFIED BY
THIRD LETTER IN AXLE CODE.**

EXAMPLE: AD B
B — BUICK
O — OLDSMOBILE
C — CHEVROLET BUFFALO
G — CHEVROLET GEAR & AXLE
K — GM OF CANADA
P — PONTIAC

GM axles can be identified by a Divisional Manufacturer's code stamped on the axle tube adjacent to the carrier (see illustration). *Chevrolet*

Interchange Number: 36
    Part Number(s): 3950142
    Usage: 1969–72 Nova Turbo Hydra-Matic

Rear Axle Identification

Axle assembly can be identified quickly and easily by the code that is stamped on the axle housing. This code is located on one of the axle tubes (usually on the driver's side) in numerals that are approximately three inches from the carrier.

The codes represent the manufacturer plant date, build date, and axle gear ratio.

You should be aware that ring gears are easily changed, and that the ratio may not be the same as that of the factory unit. Thus, the code can be used for locating the proper axle housing.

Axle housings are also categorized by their basic design. They will often be referred to as a ten-bolt and a twelve-bolt assembly. This refers to the number of bolts that secure the carrier cover. A ten-bolt axle is a fairly good assembly, but for extreme high-performance applications the twelve-bolt is better.

Ten- and twelve-bolt axles were used with all models. Interchange is based on the fit of the axle and its basic design. Thus, interchange is very good for the specialty cars (Camaro, Nova, and Chevelle); however, Impala interchange is limited to Impalas only.

Codes are given in the charts to help you identify the axle, but the interchange is for the basic axle housing assembly without gears.

Rear Axle Housing

Model Identification

Camaro	Interchange Number
1967–69 ten-bolt	13
1967–69 twelve-bolt	14
1969 twelve-bolt four-disc brakes	15
1970 ten-bolt	16
1970 twelve-bolt	17

Chevelle	Interchange Number
1964	6
1965–66 ten-bolt	7
1965–66 twelve-bolt	8
1967 ten-bolt	9
1967 twelve-bolt	10
1968–70 ten-bolt	12
1968–70 twelve-bolt	11

Impala	Interchange Number
1959–64	1
1965 ten-bolt with three-arm suspension	2
1965–70 ten-bolt with four-arm suspension	3
1965–68 twelve-bolt	4
1969–70 twelve-bolt	5

Chevy II/Nova	Interchange Number
1962–63	19
1964–67 ten-bolt	20
1964–67 twelve-bolt	21
1968–70 ten-bolt	13
1968–70 twelve-bolt	14

Interchange

Interchange Number: 1
    Part Number(s): 3777029
    Usage: 1959–64 full-size Chevrolet, includes 1959–60 El Camino

Interchange Number: 2
    Part Number(s): 3917862
    Usage: 1965 full-size Chevrolet with ten-bolt axle and three-arm suspension

Interchange Number: 3
    Part Number(s): 3866166
    Usage: 1965–70 full-size Chevrolet with ten-bolt axle and four-arm suspension

Interchange Number: 4
    Part Number(s): 3917879
    Usage: 1965–68 full-size Chevrolet with twelve-bolt axle and four-arm suspension

Interchange Number: 5
    Part Number(s): 3981667
    Usage: 1969–70 full-size Chevrolet with twelve-bolt axle

Interchange Number: 6
    Part Number(s): 3846574
    Usage: 1964 Chevelle

Interchange Number: 7
    Part Number(s): 3917878
    Usage: 1965–66 Chevelle with ten-bolt axle

Interchange Number: 8
    Part Number(s): 3917877
    Usage: 1965–66 Chevelle with twelve-bolt axle

Interchange Number: 9
    Part Number(s): 3917876
    Usage: 1967 Chevelle with ten-bolt axle

Interchange Number: 10
    Part Number(s): 3917875
    Usage: 1967 Chevelle with twelve-bolt axle

Interchange Number: 11
    Part Number(s): 3981669
    Usage: 1968, 1970 Buick Skylark; 1968–72 Chevelle; 1970–72 Monte Carlo; 1970–72 Pontiac LeMans; 1970–72 Pontiac Grand Prix; 1971–72 GMC Sprint; all with twelve-bolt axle

Interchange Number: 12
    Part Number(s): 3981668
    Usage: 1968–72 Chevelle; 1970–72 Monte Carlo; both with ten-bolt axle with round cover
    Notes: Some Monte Carlos came with the Pontiac-built ten-bolt axle with a *notched* cover. This unit will not fit a Chevelle.

Interchange Number: 13
    Part Number(s): 3981670
    Usage: 1967–69 Camaro; 1968–71 Nova; 1971 Pontiac Ventura II; all with ten-bolt axle

Interchange Number: 14
    Part Number(s): 3981672
    Usage: 1968–69 Camaro; 1968–71 Nova; 1971 Pontiac Ventura II; all with twelve-bolt axle

Notes: Bare housing, no shafts or gears, will fit those with rear disc brakes. Four-wheel disc brake axle shafts and brake parts must be swapped to the bare axle housing.

Interchange Number: 15
Part Number(s): 3961340
Usage: 1968–69 Camaro with four-wheel disc brakes
Notes: See interchange number 14 without four-wheel disc brakes for bare housing interchange. Although not offered from the factory, this axle will fit the 1968–71 Nova.

Interchange Number: 16
Part Number(s): 3981871
Usage: 1970 Camaro; 1970 Pontiac Firebird; both with ten-bolt axle
Notes: 1971 and up axles will not interchange.

Interchange Number: 17
Part Number(s): 3981872
Usage: 1970 Camaro; 1970 Pontiac Firebird; both with twelve-bolt axle

Interchange Number: 18
Part Number(s): 3921189
Usage: 1967 Camaro with twelve-bolt axle

Interchange Number: 19
Part Number(s): 3792757
Usage: 1962–63 Chevy II

Interchange Number: 20
Part Number(s): 3917874
Usage: 1964–67 Chevy II with ten-bolt axle

Interchange Number: 21
Part Number(s): 3917874
Usage: 1964–67 Chevy II with twelve-bolt axle

Differential Case

The differential case should not be confused with the carrier assembly. This is the internal component that turns the ring gears. Chevrolet used two different cases: those *with* inside gears, used with Positraction axles, and those *without* inside gears, used with the standard axle assembly. Interchange is based on the type of axle (ten-bolt or twelve-bolt), the axle ratio, and whether or not the car is equipped with Positraction.

Model Identification

Interchange

Interchange Number: 1
Part Number(s): 3758046
Usage: 1959–64 full-size Chevrolet with 3.08 gear ratio and Positraction

Interchange Number: 2
Part Number(s): 3863433
Usage: 1964–65 Chevelle; 1964–65 Chevy II; 1964–65 full-size Chevrolet; all with 3.08, 3.36, 3.55 or 3.70 rear axle ratios, ten-bolt axle, and Positraction

Interchange Number: 3
Part Number(s): 3993502
Usage: 1965–67 Chevy II; 1965–70 full-size Chevrolet; 1967–70 Camaro; 1965–72 Chevelle; 1968–71 Nova; 1971 Pontiac Ventura II; all with ten-bolt axle, 3.08 or 3.36 rear axle ratios, and Positraction

Interchange Number: 4
Part Number(s): 3993517
Usage: 1965–69 full-size Chevrolet; 1970–72 Chevelle; both with 4.10, 4.56, or 4.88 rear axle ratios and Positraction

Interchange Number: 5
Part Number(s): 3993516
Usage: 1966–67 Chevy II; 1966–70 full-size Chevrolet; 1966–72 Chevelle; 1967–70 Camaro; 1968–70 Nova; all with 3.07, 3.31, 3.55, or 3.73 rear axle ratios, twelve-bolt axle, and Positraction

Interchange Number: 6
Part Number(s): 3993504
Usage: 1967–69 Camaro; 1967–72 Chevelle; 1968–69 Nova; 1968–69 full-size Chevrolet; all with 2.56 or 2.73 rear axle ratios, ten-bolt axle, and Positraction

Interchange Number: 7
Part Number(s): 3936444
Usage: 1966–70 Chevelle; 1967 Chevy II; 1967–70 Camaro; 1968–70 Nova; 1968–70 full-size Chevrolet with 2.29, 2.56, or 2.73 rear axle, twelve-bolt axle, and Positraction

Interchange Number: 8
Part Number(s): 3947279
Usage: 1968–69 Camaro with four-wheel disc brakes, 2.56 or 2.73 rear axle ratios, and Positraction

Notes: Will fit 1968–71 Nova to allow installation of four-wheel disc brakes.

Interchange Number: 9
Part Number(s): 3947280
Usage: 1968–69 Camaro with four-wheel disc brakes, 3.07, 3.31, 3.55, or 3.73 rear axle ratios, and Positraction
Notes: Will fit 1968–71 Nova to allow installation of four-wheel disc brakes.

Interchange Number: 10
Part Number(s): 3790626
Usage: 1962–66 Chevy II without Positraction

Interchange Number: 11
Part Number(s): 3869789
Usage: 1965–67 Chevy II; 1965–70 full-size Chevrolet; 1965–72 Chevelle; 1967–69 Camaro; 1968–70 Nova; all with 2.73, 2.29, and 2.56 rear axle ratios, automatic, and twelve-bolt axle, but without Positraction

Interchange Number: 12
Part Number(s): 3958109
Usage: 1964–67 Chevy II; 1964–69 full-size Chevrolet; 1964–72 Chevelle; 1967–70 Camaro; 1968–71 Nova; all with 3.08, 3.36, 3.55, or 3.70 rear axle ratios and ten-bolt axle, but without Positraction

Interchange Number: 13
Part Number(s): 3852989
Usage: 1965–67 Chevy II; 1965–70 full-size Chevrolet; 1965–72 Chevelle; 1967–69 Camaro; 1968–70 Nova; all with 3.07, 3.31, 3.55, and 3.73 rear axle ratios and twelve-bolt axle, but without Positraction

Interchange Number: 14
Part Number(s): 3758047
Usage: 1959–63 Impala without Positraction

Rear Axle Shaft

Model Identification

Interchange

Interchange Number: 1
Part Number(s): RH, 3798184; LH, 3798183 (17)
Overall Length: RH, 30 1/2 inches; LH, 29 1/2 inches (flange type)
Usage: 1959–64 full-size Chevrolet
Notes: If using a 1959 axle on newer model, use rear hub bolt part number 3980406 and use the 1959 wheel lug nuts.

Interchange Number: 2
Part Number(s): RH, 3790604; LH, 3790603 (17 splines)
Overall Length: RH, 29 inches; LH, 28 1/4 inches (flange type)
Usage: 1962–63 Chevy II

Interchange Number: 3
Part Number(s): 3847922 (fits either side) (28 splines)
Overall Length: 28 23/64 inches (fits either side)
Usage: 1964 Chevy II

Interchange Number: 4
Part Number(s): 3832417 (fits either side) (28 splines)
Overall Length: 29 inches (fits either side)
Usage: 1964 Chevelle

Interchange Number: 5
Part Number(s): 3969348 (fits either side) (28 splines)
Overall Length: 29 33/64 inches (fits either side)
Usage: 1965–67 Chevelle; 1967–69 Camaro; 1968–71 Nova; 1971–73 Pontiac Ventura II; 1973 Olds Omega; all with ten-bolt axle

Interchange Number: 6
Part Number(s): 3863726 (fits either side) (28 splines)
Overall Length: 28 20/64 inches (fits either side)
Usage: 1965–67 Chevy II with ten-bolt axle

Interchange Number: 7
Part Number(s): 3868992 (fits either side) (30 splines)
Overall Length: 28 27/64 inches (fits either side)
Usage: 1965–67 Chevy II with twelve-bolt axle

Interchange Number: 8
Part Number(s): 3969349 (fits either side) (30 splines)
Overall Length: 30 1/2 inches (fits either side)
Usage: 1965–67 Chevelle; 1967–69 Camaro; 1968–71 Nova; 1971–73 Pontiac Ventura II; 1973 Olds Omega; all with twelve-bolt axle, except 1968–69 Camaro with four-wheel disc brakes

Interchange Number: 9
Part Number(s): 3985720 (fits either side) (30 splines)
Overall Length: 30 17/64 inches (fits either side)
Usage: 1965–70 full-size Chevrolet with twelve-bolt axle

Interchange Number: 10
> Part Number(s): 3914059 (fits either side) (28 splines)
> Overall Length: 31 19/64 inches (fits either side)
> Usage: 1965 full-size Chevrolet with ten-bolt axle

Interchange Number: 11
> Part Number(s): 3985719 (fits either side) (28 splines)
> Overall Length: 31 15/32 inches (fits either side)
> Usage: 1966–68 full-size Chevrolet with ten-bolt axle

Interchange Number: 12
> Part Number(s): 3969284 (fits either side) (28 splines)
> Overall Length: 30 5/32 inches (fits either side)
> Usage: 1968–72 Chevelle; 1970–72 Monte Carlo;
> 1970–73 Camaro; 1970–73 Pontiac Firebird;
> 1971–72 GMC Sprint; all with ten-bolt axle
> Notes: Must have round cover. Notched cover axles are
> different.

Interchange Number: 13
> Part Number(s): 3969285 (fits either side) (30 splines)

Overall Length: 30 5/32 inches (fits either side)
Usage: 1968–72 Chevelle; 1970–72 Monte Carlo;
1970–73 Camaro; 1970–73 Pontiac Firebird;
1971–72 GMC Sprint; all with twelve-bolt axle

Interchange Number: 14
> Part Number(s): 3947206 (fits either side) (30 splines)
> Overall Length: 29 11/16 inches (fits either side)
> Usage: 1968–69 Camaro with four-wheel disc brakes
> Notes: Will fit 1968–71 Nova when modifying to four-
> wheel disc brakes.

Rear Axle Cover

This is a simple interchange. The only requirement is the type of axle used. Thus, all ten-bolt axles with a round cover—whether made by Buffalo, Oldsmobile, Chevrolet Gear and Axle, or St. Catharines in Canada—used the same cover part number 410917. All twelve-bolt axles used part number 3976857. Also, other makes such as Buick, Pontiac, and Oldsmobile used these covers with the twelve-bolt axle up to 1972, and the ten-bolt axle until 1976.

Chapter 6

Frame, Suspension, and Steering

Frame

Several different manufacturers were used to assemble frames for various GM makes and models. Thus, the same frame can be found on Oldsmobile or Pontiacs that will fit your Chevrolet. The actual interchange, though, depends on the particular model and model year, and in some cases the bodystyle.

A frame's identification number is stamped on the outer left-hand side-member, just ahead of the bumper bracket attaching slot. The part number appears along with an abbreviated version of the manufacturer's name. For example, if Pontiac were the manufacturer, the ID would read: Pon. (for Pontiac), S- A.O. Smith, or P.P.S.-Parish Pressed Steel, followed by the part number. The bottom line indicates the build date and shift. Sometimes more than one part number may be listed in the interchange charts. That is because the frame was changed midyear. However, either will fit unless otherwise noted.

Model Identification

Interchange

Interchange Number: 1
> Part Number(s): 3899005 or 3977526
> Usage: 1967–68 Camaro; 1968 Nova; subframe.
> Notes: Will not fit 1969 and later Camaro. Pontiac Firebird will not fit.

Interchange Number: 2
> Part Number(s): 3965600 or 3954642
> Usage: 1969 Camaro; 1969–72 Nova; 1972 Pontiac Ventura; subframe
> Notes: Change occurred 11-11-68; either fit. Will fit 1967–68 Camaro with modification to control arm bumper and sway bar. Pontiac Firebird will not fit.

Interchange Number: 3
> Part Number(s): 3964800 or 3989418
> Usage: 1970–71 Camaro; 1970–71 Pontiac Firebird; subframe

Interchange Number: 4
> Part Number(s): 3837537 or 9773003
> Usage: 1964–65 Chevelle, except convertible, pickup, or station wagon

Interchange Number: 5
> Part Number(s): 3837597
> Usage: 1964–65 Chevelle convertible

Interchange Number: 6
> Part Number(s): 3854299

Usage: 1964–65 El Camino

Notes: Chevelle station wagon fit, but used part number 3837595.

Interchange Number: 7
Part Number(s): 3837527
Usage: 1966–67 Chevelle, except convertible, station wagon, or pickup

Interchange Number: 8
Part Number(s): 3876907
Usage: 1966 El Camino or Chevelle station wagon

Interchange Number: 9
Part Number(s): 3893335
Usage: 1966 El Camino or Chevelle station wagon

Interchange Number: 10
Part Number(s): 3893333
Usage: 1966–67 Chevelle convertible

Interchange Number: 11
Part Number(s): 3893329
Usage: 1967 El Camino or Chevelle station wagon

Interchange Number: 12
Part Number(s): 6263666
Usage: 1968–72 Chevelle hardtop, coupe, or convertible except Monte Carlo; 1968–72 Buick Skylark hardtop, coupe, or convertible except 400 or 455ci; 1968–72 Olds Cutlass coupe, hardtop, or convertible; 1968–72 Pontiac Tempest/LeMans coupe, hardtop, or convertible except with 455ci

Notes: Sedan has a longer frame and will not interchange.

Interchange Number: 13
Part Number(s): 6263665
Usage: 1968–72 El Camino or Chevelle station wagon

Interchange Number: 14
Part Number(s): 3775113
Usage: 1959–60 full-size Chevrolet, except convertible

Interchange Number: 15
Part Number(s): 3780165
Usage: 1959–60 Chevrolet full-size convertible

Interchange Number: 16
Part Number(s): 3857157
Usage: 1961–64 full-size Chevrolet, except convertible

Interchange Number: 17
Part Number(s): 3857165
Usage: 1961–64 full-size Chevrolet convertible

Interchange Number: 18
Part Number(s): 3864763
Usage: 1965 full-size Chevrolet, all but convertible

Interchange Number: 19
Part Number(s): 3864767
Usage: 1965 full-size Chevrolet convertible

Interchange Number: 20
Part Number(s): 38816645
Usage: 1966 full-size Chevrolet convertible

Interchange Number: 21
Part Number(s): 3881649
Usage: 1966 full-size Chevrolet, all but convertible

Interchange Number: 22
Part Number(s): 3916429
Usage: 1967–68 full-size Chevrolet convertible

Interchange Number: 23
Part Number(s): 3916431
Usage: 1967–68 full-size Chevrolet, all but convertible

Interchange Number: 24
Part Number(s): 3939115
Usage: 1969 full-size Chevrolet, all but convertible

Interchange Number: 25
Part Number(s): 3972707
Usage: 1969–70 full-size Chevrolet convertible

Interchange Number: 26
Part Number(s): 3972708
Usage: 1970 full-size Chevrolet, all but convertible

Interchange Number: 26
Part Number(s): 3972708
Usage: 1970 full-size Chevrolet, all but convertible

Front Control Arms

Model Identification

Interchange

Interchange Number: 1

Part Number(s): RH, 3962844; LH, 3963843

Usage: 1967–69 Camaro; 1967–69 Pontiac Firebird; 1968–74 Nova; 1971–74 Pontiac Ventura; 1973–74 Olds Omega

Interchange Number: 2

Part Number(s): RH, 3945518; LH, 3945517

Usage: 1969 Camaro with four-wheel disc brakes

Interchange Number: 3

Part Number(s): RH, 335894; LH, 331277

Usage: 1970–72 Camaro; 1970–72 Pontiac Firebird; 1971–72 full-size Chevrolet

Interchange Number: 4

Part Number(s): RH, 3832350; LH, 3832349

Usage: 1959–64 full-size Chevrolet; 1961–65 Corvair

Interchange Number: 5

Part Number(s): RH, 3865822; LH, 3966931

Usage: 1965–70 full-size Chevrolet, except 427 or 454ci, or taxi or police

Interchange Number: 6

Part Number(s): RH, 3912096; LH, 3966935

Usage: 1965–70 full-size Chevrolet 427 or 454ci, all but taxi or police

Interchange Number: 7

Part Number(s): RH, 3877062; LH, 3974217

Usage: 1964–72 Chevelle; 1970–72 Monte Carlo; 1971–72 GMC Sprint

Notes: 1964–72 Pontiac LeMans, 1964–72 Olds Cutlass, and 1964–72 Buick Skylark will fit, but part number is different.

Interchange Number: 8

Part Number(s): 3849392 (fits either side)

Usage: 1962–67 Chevy II

Notes: No other interchange.

Interchange Number: 9

Part Number(s): RH, 6258452; LH, 6258451

Usage: 1967–69 Camaro; 1967–69 Pontiac Firebird; 1968–74 Nova; 1971–74 Pontiac Ventura; 1973–74 Olds Omega

Interchange Number: 10

Part Number(s): RH, 3955758; LH, 3955757

Usage: 1969 Camaro with four-wheel disc brakes

Interchange Number: 11

Part Number(s): RH, 3964834 RH; LH, 338243

Usage: 1970–72 Camaro; 1970–72 Pontiac Firebird

Interchange Number: 12

Part Number(s): RH, 3990510; LH, 3990509

Usage: 1967–70 Chevelle; 1970–72 Chevelle station wagon; 1970–72 Chevelle SS 396 or 454ci

Notes: 1969–72 Pontiac LeMans will fit; 1969–72 Olds Cutlass may fit.

Interchange Number: 13

Part Number(s): RH, 385230; LH, 3852319

Usage: 1964–66 Chevelle, except 1965 Z-16

Notes: 1965 Z-16 used part numbers 3874690 (RH) and 3874689 (LH).

Interchange Number: 14

Part Number(s): RH, 3846268; LH, 3846267

Usage: 1958–64 full-size Chevrolet without air-assisted suspension

Interchange Number: 15

Part Number(s): RH, 3764450; LH, 3764449

Usage: 1958–59 full-size Chevrolet with air-assisted suspension

Interchange Number: 16

Part Number(s): RH, 3881578; LH, 3881577

Usage: 1965–70 full-size Chevrolet, except Impala SS, or those with heavy-duty suspension (includes taxi or police)

Interchange Number: 17

Part Number(s): RH, 3918840; LH, 3918839

Usage: 1965–70 full-size Impala SS, or those with heavy-duty suspension (included taxi or police sedans)

Interchange Number: 18

Part Number(s): RH, 3882056; LH, 3832055

Usage: 1962–63 Chevy II

Interchange Number: 19

Part Number(s): RH, 3849786; LH, 3849785

Usage: 1965–67 Chevy II

Front Springs

All Chevrolet models covered in this manual used coil springs. The interchange charts is simply a guide to alert you to what models and makes used the same coil springs.

However, there are different tensions available that were used with certain suspension options and/or other options. Thus, springs must be replaced in pairs from a car that has options similar to your own car. *Never* replace only one spring, even if you only *need* one spring. This could cause an imbalance in the car's suspension. Also, never swap one spring from one car and the second from another, even if they have the same options, because springs settle over the years and no two sets of springs settle the same.

Beginning in 1969, springs were selected by a computer and more springs were used per car. So when selecting springs from 1969 to 1972 cars, try to match the same options including engine and bodystyle. Use the accompanying charts to further help you select your springs.

Model Identification

Interchange

Interchange Number: 1

Part Number(s): Varies according to tensions

Usage: 1964–67 Chevelle; 1964–67 Buick Skylark; 1964–67 Olds Cutlass; 1964–67 Pontiac Tempest; 1967–69 Camaro; 1967–69 Pontiac Firebird; 1968–74 Nova; 1971–74 Pontiac Ventura II

Notes: Pontiac, Buick, and Oldsmobile used different part numbers, but will fit. Should be used only when no Chevrolet parts are available, however.

Interchange Number: 2

Part Number(s): Varies with tension

Usage: 1959–70 Impala

Notes: 1969–70 springs are computer selected. See charts.

Interchange Number: 3

Part Number(s): Varies with tension

Usage: 1970–72 Camaro; 1970–72 Pontiac Firebird

Notes: Computer-selected rates. See charts.

Interchange Number: 4

Part Number(s): Varies with tension

Usage: 1968–72 Chevelle; 1968–72 Pontiac LeMans; 1968–72 Olds Cutlass; 1968–72 Buick Skylark; 1968–72 Pontiac Grand Prix; 1970–72 Monte Carlo

Notes: Computer-selected rates. See charts. The 1968–70 full-size Buick, Pontiac, or Oldsmobile will fit.

Interchange Number: 5

Part Number(s): Varies with tension

Usage: 1962–67 Chevy II

Rear Springs

All models but Camaro and Chevy II/Nova used coil rear springs. Like the front springs, several different rates were used in the rear according to model usage and options. Camaros and Novas used leaf rear springs. Leaf springs were also available in different rates by model and option.

When swapping rear springs, regardless of the style, always replace them in pairs from a car that is equipped similar to your own. The interchange lists what models the springs will fit and what they were used on. Springs from

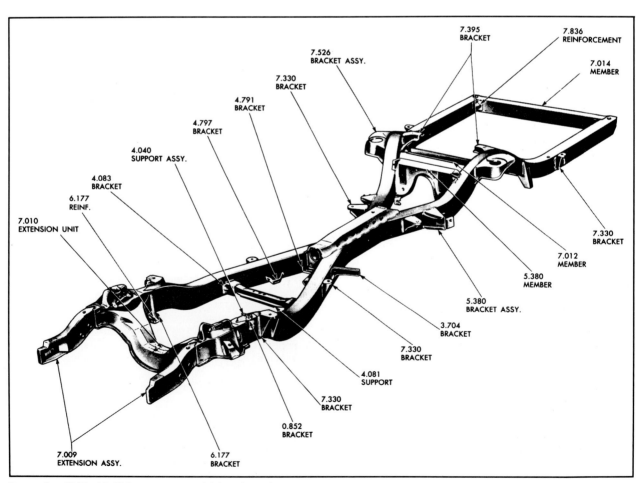

Frame for 1958–64 GM passenger vehicle. *Chevrolet*

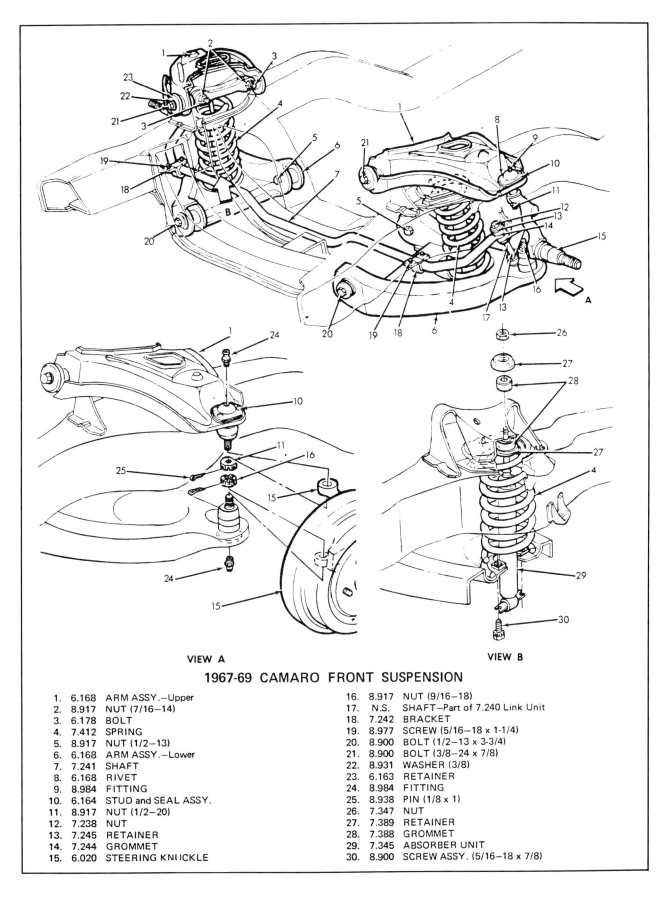

VIEW A

VIEW B

1967-69 CAMARO FRONT SUSPENSION

1.	6.168	ARM ASSY.—Upper
2.	8.917	NUT (7/16—14)
3.	6.178	BOLT
4.	7.412	SPRING
5.	8.917	NUT (1/2—13)
6.	6.168	ARM ASSY.—Lower
7.	7.241	SHAFT
8.	6.168	RIVET
9.	8.984	FITTING
10.	6.164	STUD and SEAL ASSY.
11.	8.917	NUT (1/2—20)
12.	7.238	NUT
13.	7.245	RETAINER
14.	7.244	GROMMET
15.	6.020	STEERING KNUCKLE

16.	8.917	NUT (9/16—18)
17.	N.S.	SHAFT—Part of 7.240 Link Unit
18.	7.242	BRACKET
19.	8.977	SCREW (5/16—18 x 1-1/4)
20.	8.900	BOLT (1/2—13 x 3-3/4)
21.	8.900	BOLT (3/8—24 x 7/8)
22.	8.931	WASHER (3/8)
23.	6.163	RETAINER
24.	8.984	FITTING
25.	8.938	PIN (1/8 x 1)
26.	7.347	NUT
27.	7.389	RETAINER
28.	7.388	GROMMET
29.	7.345	ABSORBER UNIT
30.	8.900	SCREW ASSY. (5/16—18 x 7/8)

1969 and later were computer selected. The charts will also help you to further identify the correct springs for your application.

Model Identification

Camaro ....Interchange Number
1967–69 (leaf)..1
1970...6

Chevelle ....Interchange Number
1964–67..2
1968–70..3

Impala...Interchange Number
1959–64..4
1965–70..5

Chevy II/Nova ....Interchange Number
1962–67..7
1968–70..1

Interchange

Interchange Number: 1
   Part Number(s): Varies with application
   Usage: 1967–69 Camaro; 1967–69 Pontiac Firebird; 1968–70 Nova; all with leaf springs
   Dimensions: 25x31x1-5/8 inches

Interchange Number: 2
   Part Number(s): Varies with application
   Usage: 1964–67 Chevelle, coil springs
   Notes: No other A-body interchange.

Interchange Number: 3
   Part Number(s): Varies with application
   Usage: 1968–72 Chevelle; 1970–72 Monte Carlo
   Notes: 1968–72 Pontiac LeMans, Buick Skylark, Olds Cutlass, and Pontiac Grand Prix will fit, but used a different part number. Be sure to swap to similar models; for example, from a 442 or GTO to an SS 396.

Interchange Number: 4
   Part Number(s): Varies with application
   Usage: 1958–64 full-size Chevrolet
   Notes: No other GM interchange.

Interchange Number: 5
   Part Number(s): Varies with application
   Usage: 1965–70 full-size Chevrolet
   Notes: No other GM interchange. Station wagon rear springs will fit heavy-duty applications like the SS models.

Interchange Number: 6
   Part Number(s): Varies with tension
   Usage: 1970–71 Camaro; 1970–71 Pontiac Firebird

Interchange Number: 7
   Part Number(s): Varies with tension
   Usage: 1962–67 Chevy II, single-leaf

Sway Bar (Front)
   When interchanging sway bars, the rule is always to replace it with a bar of the same diameter or a larger diameter.

Installing a larger diameter bar will improve your car's handling, although the ride won't be as smooth. Using a smaller diameter bar than originally installed can create a dangerous handling condition.

Model Identification

Camaro ....Interchange Number
1967–68..1
1969...2
1970, all but Z-28..4
1970 Z-28..5

Chevelle ....Interchange Number
1964–67, all but SS 396 6
1965–67 SS 396...7
1968–72, all except SS or with F-41 suspension 8
1968–72 SS or 1969–72 with F-41.....................9

Impala...Interchange Number
1959–64..11
1965–70..10

Chevy II/Nova ....Interchange Number
1962–67..12
1968, all except Nova SS 396 1
1968 Nova SS 396..3
1969–70, all but SS or with F-41 suspension 2
1969–70 Nova SS or with F-41 suspension.......................3

Interchange

Interchange Number: 1
   Part Number(s): 3908373
   Usage: 1967–68 Camaro V-8; 1968 Nova V-8, except special high-performance 327 or 396ci; 1968 Nova six-cylinder with heavy-duty suspension

Interchange Number: 2
   Part Number(s): 3955778
   Usage: 1969 Camaro; 1969–74 Nova without special high-performance suspension; 1971–74 Pontiac Ventura II; 1972–74 Olds Omega
   Notes: Interchange number 3 will fit.

Interchange Number: 3
   Part Number(s): 3955782
   Diameter: 0.8125 inch
   Usage: 1969–72 Nova with performance suspension; 1968–70 Nova SS 396 with standard suspension; 1971–74 Pontiac Ventura II with performance suspension; 1974 GTO
   Notes: Will fit 1969 Camaro. Is slightly larger in diameter and provides for better handling.

Interchange Number: 4
   Part Number(s): 3984557
   Diameter: 1.00 inch
   Usage: 1970 Camaro with heavy-duty suspension except Z-28; 1971–72 Camaro except Z-28; 1971–72 Pontiac Firebird except Trans-Am, Formula 400; 1973–74 Camaro with heavy-duty suspension

Interchange Number: 5
   Part Number(s): 3986480
   Diameter: 1.25 inch

Usage: 1970–71 Camaro Z-28; 1970–73 Pontiac Trans-Am or Formula 400

Interchange Number: 6
Part Number(s): 397703
Diameter: 0.8125 inch
Usage: 1964–67 Chevelle except SS 396; 1964–67 Olds Cutlass six-cylinder

Interchange Number: 7
Part Number(s): 397705
Diameter: 0.9375 inch
Usage: 1965–67 Chevelle SS 396; 1964–66 Olds Cutlass station wagon or convertible; 1966–67 Olds 442

Interchange Number: 8
Part Number(s): 401194
Diameter: 1.00 inch
Usage: 1968–69 Pontiac Tempest/LeMans; 1968–70 Olds Cutlass with Rallye suspension; 1968–71 Chevelle, except 1969–71 without performance suspension or with 396 or 454ci; 1968–72 Buick Skylark except GSX, or with Stage IV package; 1969–72 Olds 442 convertible; 1970–71 Monte Carlo except SS 454; 1970–72 Tempest/LeMans, except station wagon and GTO
Notes: Interchange number 9 will fit and provide better handling.

Interchange Number: 9
Part Number(s): 402544
Diameter: 0.1.250 inch
Usage: 1969–71 Chevelle with performance suspension; 1970–71 Chevelle SS; 1970–71 Monte Carlo SS 454; 1970–72 GTO

Interchange Number: 10
Part Number(s): 3868640
Usage: 1965–70 full-size Chevrolet

Interchange Number: 11
Part Number(s): 3760435
Diameter: 0.9375 inch
Usage: 1959–64 full-size Chevrolet

Interchange Number: 12
Part Number(s): 3790740
Usage: 1962–67 Chevy II

Sway Bar (Rear)

Model Identification

Interchange

Interchange Number: 1
Part Number(s): 394926
Diameter: 0.875 inch
Usage: 1964–68 Olds 442 or Cutlass police car; 1965 Z-16 Chevelle SS 396; 1966–67 Buick Gran Sport; 1966–69 Impala SS with special performance suspension; 1968–72 Gran Sport, all outputs with heavy-duty suspension; 1969 Chevelle with F-41 suspension; 1969–72 Cutlass with Rallye or 442 option package; 1970–71 Monte Carlo SS 454; 1970–72 Chevelle SS or with F-41 suspension; 1970–72 Pontiac GTO
Notes: Requires special control arms to mount.

Interchange Number: 2
Part Number(s): 481471
Diameter: 0.562 inch
Usage: 1970–74 Camaro (except Z-28) with F-41 suspension
Notes: Firebird is not a direct interchange, as the Pontiac unit is larger in diameter (0.5.94 inch). But it will fit and provide for better handling.

Interchange Number: 3
Part Number(s): 3983085
Diameter: 0.688 inch
Usage: 1970–75 Camaro Z-28
Notes: Firebird/Trans-Am/Formula 400 is not a direct interchange. The Pontiac unit is larger (0.812 inch) in diameter, but it will fit Camaro and provide for better handling.

Interchange Number: 4
Part Number(s): 3980997
Usage: 1969–72 Nova with F-41 suspension, commonly found on SS models
Notes: Will fit 1968 Nova if 1969–70 hardware is used.

Rear Control Arms

Only Chevelle and Impala are listed in this section, as they are the only two models covered that feature this type of suspension.

The setup consists of a pair of upper and lower arms. Special lower arms were used with the rear sway bar on the Chevelle. Standard lower arms, however, can be modified by drilling mounting holes to adapt their use for a rear sway bar. All 1970–72 Chevelle SS models (this included the low-powered SS 350) were equipped with a rear sway bar, as standard equipment.

Model Identification

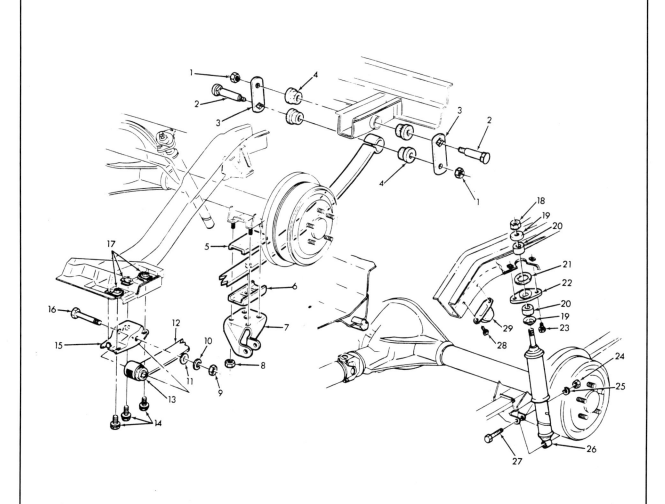

1967-69 CAMARO REAR SUSPENSION

1. 8.917   NUT (7/16–20)
2. N.S.S.   PIN–Part of 7.523 SHACKLE UNIT
3. N.S.S.   SHACKLE–Part of 7.523
           SHACKLE UNIT
4. 7.524   BUSHING
5. 7.545   CUSHION–Upper
6. 7.545   CUSHION–Lower
7. 7.518   PLATE–L.H. and R.H.
8. 7.516   NUT
9. 8.915   NUT (1/2–20)
10. 8.915   L/WASHER (9/16–18)
11. 6.515   WASHER
12. 7.503   SPRING
13. 7.504   BUSHING
14. 8.900   SCREW ASSY. (3/8–16 x 1-1/8)

15. 7.412   BRACKET–L.H. and R.H.
16. 8.900   BOLT (1/2–20)
17. 7.530   NUT ASSY.
18. 7.347   NUT
19. 7.245   RETAINER
20. 7.380   GROMMET
21. N.S.   SEALER
22. 7.395   BRACKET ASSY.
23. 8.900   SCREW ASSY. (5/16–18 x 7/8)
24. 8.915   NUT (7/16–14)
25. 8.931   L/WASHER (7/16)
26. 7.345   SHOCK ABS.
27. 8.900   BOLT (7/16–14)
28. 8.977   SCREW (5/16–18 x 3/4)
29. 7.535   BUMPER ASSY.

1965 Z-16 SS 396
    Upper 1
    Lower 6
1968–69
    Upper 2
    Lower
    Without F-41 8
    Lower with F-41 7
1970
    Upper 2
    Lower without F-41 except SS 8
    Lower with F-41 all SS 7

Impala.....................................*Interchange Number*
1960–64
    Upper 3
    Lower right 9
    Lower left 10
1965–66
    Upper 5
    Lower 11
1967–70
    Upper 7
1967–68
    Lower 11
1969–70
    Lower..12

Interchange

Interchange Number: 1
    Part Number(s): 3869853
    Sides: Fits either side
    Usage: 1964–67 Chevelle

Interchange Number: 2
    Part Number(s): 9790978
    Sides: Fits either side
    Usage: 1968–72 Chevelle

Interchange Number: 3
    Part Number(s): 3758075
    Sides: Fits either side
    Usage: 1960–64 Impala

Interchange Number: 4
    Part Number(s): 3900543
    Sides: Fits either side
    Usage: 1967–70 Impala

Interchange Number: 5
    Part Number(s): 3856386
    Sides: Fits either side
    Usage: 1965–66 Impala

Interchange Number: 6
    Part Number(s): 9791102
    Sides: Fits either side
    Usage: 1965 Chevelle Z-16 SS 396
    Notes: Interchange number 7 or 8 will fit.

Interchange Number: 7
    Part Number(s): 3937877
    Sides: Fits either side
    Usage: 1969 Chevelle with F-41; 1970–71 Monte Carlo

SS 454; 1970–72 Chevelle with SS package, or with F-41 suspension; 1971–72 Pontiac GTO
    Notes: Difference is pre-drilled holes to mount sway bar. Interchange number 8 can be modified to fit.

Interchange Number: 8
    Part Number(s): 9791773
    Sides: Fits either side
    Usage: 1964–72 Chevelle, except 1969–72 with F-41 suspension, or 1970–72 with SS package; 1964–72 Pontiac Tempest, except 1969–72 GTO
    Notes: Has no pre-drilled holes for mounting sway bar. Can fit number 7 if holes are drilled.

Interchange Number: 9
    Part Number(s): 3774121
    Sides: Left-hand
    Usage: 1960–64 Impala, all but station wagon

Interchange Number: 10
    Part Number(s): 3774122
    Sides: Right-hand
    Usage: 1960–64 Impala
    Notes: Also used on left-hand side in station wagon.

Interchange Number: 11
    Part Number(s): 3953592
    Sides: Fits either side
    Usage: 1965–68 Impala

Interchange Number: 12
    Part Number(s): 3953964
    Sides: Fits either side
    Usage: 1969–70 Impala

Steering Gearbox
Interchange for the steering gearbox is categorized by the type of steering used (manual or power-assisted). It is also based on part number and fit. The ratio is given when it is known.

Model Identification

Camaro ....*Interchange Number*
1967–69 without power steering except Z-28...................1
1967–69 Z-28 3
1967 with power steering 10
1968 with power steering 11
1969 with power steering 12
1970 without power steering except Z-28........................8
1970 Z-28 without power steering 7
1970 with power steering except Z-28 or SS 396 13
1970 Z-28 or SS 396 with power steering 14

Chevelle ....*Interchange Number*
1964–69 without power steering except 1965 SS 396......2
1964 with power steering 15
1965–66 with power steering 16
1967–68 with power steering 10
1969 with power steering 17
1970 without power steering 7
1970 with power steering 18

Impala.....................................*Interchange Number*
1959–64 without power steering 9

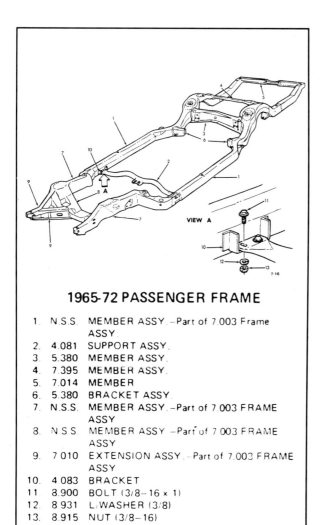

1965-72 PASSENGER FRAME

1. N.S.S. MEMBER ASSY.—Part of 7.003 Frame ASSY.
2. 4.081 SUPPORT ASSY.
3. 5.380 MEMBER ASSY.
4. 7.395 MEMBER ASSY.
5. 7.014 MEMBER
6. 5.380 BRACKET ASSY.
7. N.S.S. MEMBER ASSY.—Part of 7.003 FRAME ASSY
8. N.S.S. MEMBER ASSY.—Part of 7.003 FRAME ASSY
9. 7.010 EXTENSION ASSY.—Part of 7.003 FRAME ASSY
10. 4.083 BRACKET
11. 8.900 BOLT (3/8—16 x 1)
12. 8.931 L/WASHER (3/8)
13. 8.915 NUT (3/8—16)

Frame for 1965–72 GM passenger vehicle. *Chevrolet*

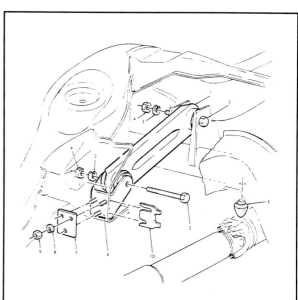

1965-72 PASSENGER UPPER CONTROL ARM & PINION NOSE BUMPER

1. 5.382 ARM ASSY.—upper R.H. (exc. Sta. Wag.) Sta. Wag., (L.H.-R.H.)
2. 5.383 BOLT—upr. & lwr. (5/8—18 x 4-1/4)
3. 8.931 L/WASHER (5/8)
4. 8.915 NUT (5/8—18)
5. 6.176 BUMPER—pinion nose
6. 5.380 BRACKET ASSY.
7. 5.380 REINFORCEMENT
8. 8.931 L/WASHER (7/16)
9. 8.921 NUT

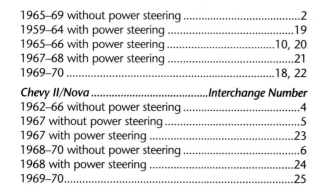

Interchange

Interchange Number: 1
Part Number(s): 7801340
Usage: 1967–68 Pontiac Firebird with a/c, but without power steering; 1967–69 Camaro (except Z-28) without optional steering; 1968–69 Buick Wildcat without power steering

Interchange Number: 2
Part Number(s): 5679270
Usage: 1964–69 Chevelle (except 1965 Z-16) without power steering; 1964–69 Pontiac Tempest (except quick ratio); 1964–69 Olds Cutlass without power steering (except police); 1964–69 full-size Oldsmobile without power steering (except police); 1965–69 Impala without power steering
Notes: Will fit interchange number 6.

Interchange Number: 3
Part Number(s): 7806396
Usage: 1965 Chevelle Z-16 SS 396; 1967–69 Camaro Z-28; 1967–69 Pontiac Firebird with quick-ratio steering; 1967–69 Olds Cutlass police car or with heavy-duty steering option; 1967–69 Pontiac Tempest with heavy-duty or police car; 1967–69 Chevelle police car; all without power steering

Interchange Number: 4
Part Number(s): 5675999
Usage: 1962–66 Chevy II without power steering

Interchange Number: 5
Part Number(s): 5699256
Usage: 1967 Chevy II without power steering

Interchange Number: 6
Part Number(s): 7808549
Usage: 1968–70 Nova; 1970 Oldsmobile with manual steering
Notes: Ratio is 24:1.

Interchange Number: 7
Part Number(s): 7812897
Usage: 1970 Camaro Z-28; 1970 Camaro six-cylinder; 1970 Chevelle; 1970 Pontiac Firebird six-cylinder; 1970 Pontiac Trans-Am or Formula 400; all without power steering

Interchange Number: 8
Part Number(s): 7809504
Usage: 1970 Camaro, except Z-28 or six-cylinder; 1970 Pontiac Firebird, except Trans AM or Formula 400; both without power steering

Interchange Number: 9
Part Number(s): 5679324
Usage: 1959–64 full-size Chevrolet without power steering

Interchange Number: 10
Part Number(s): 5699263 and 7801584
Usage: 1964–66 Olds Cutlass; 1965 Impala; 1967 Camaro; 1967 Pontiac Firebird; 1967–68 Chevelle; 1967–68 Buick Skylark; 1967–68 Pontiac Tempest; all with power steering
Notes: Oldsmobile, Buick, and Pontiac models used different part numbers, but will fit.

Interchange Number: 11
Part Number(s): 3930709
Usage: 1968 Camaro with power steering

Interchange Number: 12
Part Number(s): 7805655
Usage: 1969 Camaro with power steering

Interchange Number: 13
Part Number(s): 7808724
Usage: 1970 Camaro with power steering, except Z-28 or SS 396 or 350 4bbl
Notes: Interchange number 14 will fit and will provide for better handling.

Interchange Number: 14
Part Number(s): 3986004
Usage: 1970 Camaro Z-28; 1970 Camaro 350 4bbl or 396ci; both with power steering

Interchange Number: 15
Part Number(s): 5692398
Usage: 1964 Chevelle with power steering
Notes: Ratio is 17.5:1. Interchange number 16 will fit.

Interchange Number: 16
Part Number(s): 5696113
Usage: 1965–66 Chevelle with power steering
Notes: Ratio is 17.5:1. Will fit 1964 Chevelle. Replacement unit.

Interchange Number: 17
Part Number(s): 7806671
Usage: 1969 Chevelle with power steering; 1969 Pontiac LeMans except GTO; 1969 Buick Skylark; 1969 Pontiac Grand Prix; 1969 Olds Cutlass except 442
Notes: Part number is different for Pontiac, Buick, and Oldsmobile, but will fit.

Interchange Number: 18
Part Number(s): 7811176
Usage: 1970 Chevelle, except El Camino or station wagon; 1970 Monte Carlo; 1970 Impala, except station wagon; all with variable-ratio power steering.
Notes: Interchange number 22 will fit, but ratio will be noticeably different.

Interchange Number: 19
Part Number(s): 5679320
Usage: 1959–64 Impala with power steering

Interchange Number: 20
Part Number(s): 5696112
Usage: 1965–66 Impala with power steering

Interchange Number: 21
Part Number(s): 5699262 and 7806397
Usage: 1967–68 Impala with power steering

Interchange Number: 22
Part Number(s): 7801584
Usage: 1969–70 Impala with power steering, except variable-ratio type
Notes: Interchange number 18 will fit, but ratio will be noticeably different.

Interchange Number: 23
Part Number(s): 5699259
Usage: 1967 Chevy II

Interchange Number: 24
Part Number(s): 7803581
Usage: 1968 Nova V-8 with power steering

Interchange Number: 25
Part Number(s): 7807411
Usage: 1969–70 Nova V-8 with power steering.
Notes: Some are variable-ratio. There will be a noticeable difference when interchanging between variable and non-variable power steering units.

Power Steering Pump

Model Identification

Camaro	Interchange Number
1967–68 V-8	1
1969 V-8 except 302 or 396ci	2
1969 SS 396	3
1970	4

Chevelle	Interchange Number
1964	5
1965, all but 396ci or 327ci/360hp	6
1965 327ci/360hp	7
1965 396ci	8
1966–67 SS 396	9

Interchange

Interchange Number: 1
Part Number(s): 7800515
Usage: 1967–68 Camaro V-8

Interchange Number: 2
Part Number(s): 7805656
Usage: 1969 Camaro (except Z-28) small-block V-8

Interchange Number: 3
Part Number(s): 7806370
Usage: 1969 Camaro 396ci; 1969 Chevelle SS 396 with variable-ratio

Interchange Number: 4
Part Number(s): 7808283
Usage: 1970 Chevelle V-8, except El Camino or station wagon; 1970–72 Monte Carlo; 1970–73 Nova; 1970–74 Camaro V-8; 1971–73 Impala; 1971–72 Chevelle; 1971–73 Pontiac Ventura II

Interchange Number: 5
Part Number(s): 5693781
Usage: 1964 Chevelle, all engine sizes

Interchange Number: 6
Part Number(s): 5693560
Usage: 1965 Chevelle, except 396ci or 327ci 350hp

Interchange Number: 7
Part Number(s): 5696221
Usage: 1965 Chevelle L-79 327ci 360hp

Interchange Number: 8
Part Number(s): 5696016
Usage: 1965 Chevelle SS 396
Notes: Uses a separate reservoir.

Interchange Number: 9
Part Number(s): 5698077
Usage: 1966–67 Chevelle SS 396

Interchange Number: 10
Part Number(s): 7803404
Usage: 1968 Chevelle SS 396

Interchange Number: 11
Part Number(s): 7806371
Usage: 1969 Chevelle V-8, except SS 396 or 427ci

Interchange Number: 12
Part Number(s): 7806372
Usage: 1969 Chevelle SS 396 or COPO 427ci; 1969 Nova SS 396

Interchange Number: 13
Usage: 1959–60 Impala; 1959–60 Buick Special

Interchange Number: 14
Part Number(s): 5692846
Usage: 1961–62 Impala; late 1961 (beginning 10-28-59) Buick Special or Olds F-85

Interchange Number: 15
Part Number(s): 3851310
Usage: 1963–64 Impala

Interchange Number: 16
Part Number(s): 5698072
Usage: 1965–66, Impala except 396 or 409ci

Interchange Number: 17
Part Number(s): 5694537
Usage: 1965 409ci Impala
Notes: No other interchange.

Interchange Number: 18
Part Number(s): 5698075
Usage: 1965 Impala 396ci; 1966–68 Impala 396 or 427ci

Interchange Number: 19
Part Number(s): 7804687
Usage: 1969 Impala, except 396 or 427ci

Interchange Number: 20
Part Number(s): 7804690
Usage: 1969 Impala 396 or 427ci

Interchange Number: 21
Part Number(s): 7808276
Usage: 1970 Impala, all but 454ci or station wagon

Interchange Number: 22
Part Number(s): 7808278
Usage: 1970 Impala 454ci, all but station wagon

Interchange Number: 23
Part Number(s): 5693129
Usage: 1965–66 Chevy II V-8 with power steering

Interchange Number: 24
Part Number(s): 5698079
Usage: 1967–68 Nova V-8 with power steering

Interchange Number: 25
Part Number(s): 7808282
Usage: 1970 El Camino; 1970 Chevelle station wagon

Steering Wheel

Steering wheel interchange is based on the overall design and style number. Both design and color vary from year to year and from model to model, as well as by usage. Thus, color is not part of the interchange. You can either hunt for a wheel that will match your trim, or better yet, you can paint it to match. If you decide to paint one, look for a light-colored wheel since they are the easiest to cover thoroughly. To determine the "correct" color for your steering wheel, consult a restoration guide. (Note that the interchange here is for the bare unit without horn cap or horn shroud.)

Chevrolet used three basic styles of steering wheels. The standard wheel was used in the lower trim models; the Deluxe wheel was optional for the lower trim models and included in higher trim models; and the Sport wheel. The style of wheel is listed under "Type" in the Interchange chart.

Model Identification

Steering gears are identified by the part number that is stamped on the top or bottom cover.

A 1965 Impala steering wheel.

Deluxe steering wheel in the 1967 Camaro.

A 1962–65 Chevy II two-spoke steering wheel.

Interchange

Interchange Number: 1
    Type: All
    Usage: 1959–60 full-size Chevrolet

Interchange Number: 2
    Type: Standard
    Usage: 1962–63 full-size Chevrolet, except Impala or SS

Interchange Number: 3
    Type: Deluxe
    Usage: Optional on 1962–63 Impala; standard on 1962–63 Impala SS

A 1967 Chevelle steering wheel.

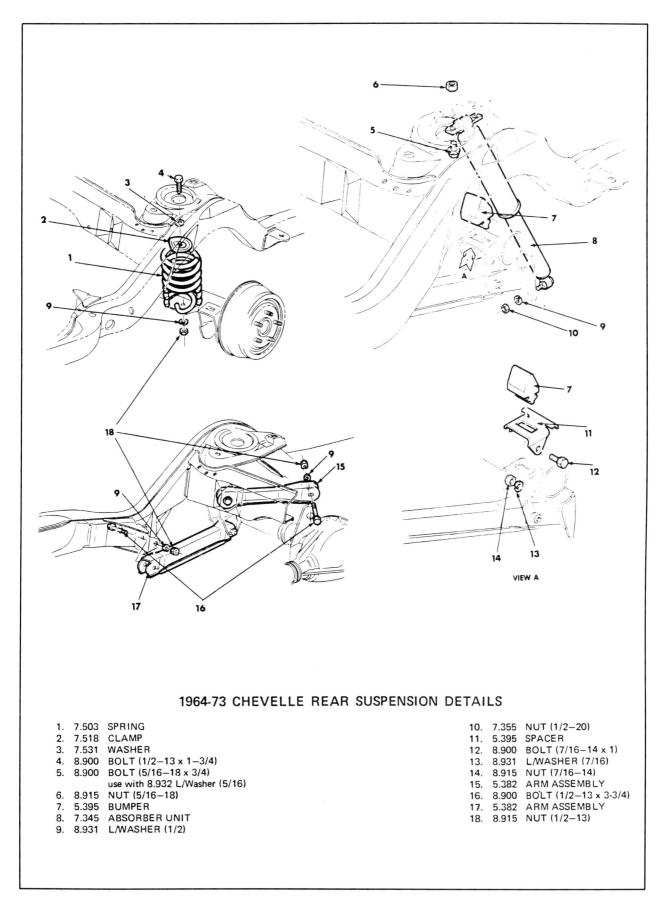

1964-73 CHEVELLE REAR SUSPENSION DETAILS

1. 7.503   SPRING
2. 7.518   CLAMP
3. 7.531   WASHER
4. 8.900   BOLT (1/2–13 x 1–3/4)
5. 8.900   BOLT (5/16–18 x 3/4)
      use with 8.932 L/Washer (5/16)
6. 8.915   NUT (5/16–18)
7. 5.395   BUMPER
8. 7.345   ABSORBER UNIT
9. 8.931   L/WASHER (1/2)

10. 7.355   NUT (1/2–20)
11. 5.395   SPACER
12. 8.900   BOLT (7/16–14 x 1)
13. 8.931   L/WASHER (7/16)
14. 8.915   NUT (7/16–14)
15. 5.382   ARM ASSEMBLY
16. 8.900   BOLT (1/2–13 x 3-3/4)
17. 5.382   ARM ASSEMBLY
18. 8.915   NUT (1/2–13)

The 1964–66 simulated wood rim steering wheel was common in Chevelle and Chevy II models.

Interchange Number: 4
Type: Standard
Usage: 1964 full-size Chevrolet, except Impala or Impala SS

Interchange Number: 5
Type: Deluxe
Usage: Optional on 1964 Impala; standard on 1964 Impala SS

Interchange Number: 6
Type: Standard
Usage: 1965–66 full-size Chevrolet, except Impala, Impala SS, and Caprice
Notes: Interchange number 7 was optional.

A 1964 Chevelle steering wheel.

The Deluxe steering wheel was used in all models for 1969. The horn ID logo, and in some cases the horn shroud, may differ between models.

Interchange Number: 7
Type: Deluxe
Usage: 1965–66 Impala, Impala SS, or Caprice

Interchange Number: 8
Type: Standard
Usage: 1967 full-size Chevrolet, except Impala, Impala SS, or Caprice
Notes: Interchange number 9 was optional.

Interchange Number: 9
Type: Deluxe
Usage: 1967 Caprice, Impala, or Impala SS

Interchange Number: 10
Type: Standard
Usage: 1968 full-size Chevrolet except Impala, Caprice, or Impala SS

Interchange Number: 11
Type: Standard or Deluxe
Usage: 1962–64 Chevy II; 1964–65 Chevelle; 1966 Chevelle, Deluxe steering wheel only on 1966

Interchange Number: 12
Type: Standard
Usage: 1967 Chevy II; 1967–68 Chevelle

Interchange Number: 13
Type: All
Usage: 1967 Camaro
Notes: No other interchange.

Interchange Number: 14
Type: Deluxe
Usage: 1968 Camaro, Nova, or Chevelle

Interchange Number: 15
Type: Standard or Deluxe
Usage: 1969 Camaro, Chevelle, full-size Chevrolet, or Nova

Notes: Shroud differs between standard and Deluxe wheels.

Interchange Number: 16
Type: All
Usage: 1970 Camaro, Chevelle, full-size Chevrolet, or Nova

Interchange Number: 17
Type: Wood rim
Usage: 1964–66 Impala; 1964–66 Chevelle; 1964–66 Olds Cutlass

Interchange Number: 18
Type: Wood rim
Usage: 1967–68 Camaro; 1967–68 Chevelle; 1967–68 Impala; 1967–68 Nova; 1967–68 Olds Cutlass

Interchange Number: 19
Type: Wood rim (Rosewood)
Usage: 1969 Camaro, Chevelle, full-size Chevrolet, or Nova

Interchange Number: 20
Type: Sport wheel vinyl grip
Usage: 1970 Camaro, Chevelle, or Nova

Interchange Number: 21
Type: Standard
Usage: 1966 Chevelle

Interchange Number: 22
Type: Deluxe
Usage: 1967 Chevelle or Chevy II

Steering Column

Steering columns usually interchange by the model and type of transmission and shifter. However, different years and

This steering wheel was used on the 1969–70 Camaro and all other 1970 models. The logo and/or horn shroud may differ between models.

The 1969–70 simulate wood rim steering wheel was offered in a variety of models.

different GM makes and models *will* interchange. This is usually limited to the "family group of cars"—for example, all A-bodies such as the Chevelle, Cutlass, Tempest, and Skylark, or all F-bodies such as the Camaro or Firebird—but not always. Color is no concern here, as the steering column can and should be painted. Certain options like tilt wheel require a special steering column.

Model Identification

Camaro ....*Interchange Number*
1967–68 Camaro
    Three-speed manual on column 2, 7
    Three-speed manual on column with tilt...............2, 7
    Powerglide on column 1
    Powerglide on column with tilt...............................5
    Three- or four-speed automatic on floor.....................3
    Three- or four-speed automatic on floor with tilt 3
    Turbo Hydra-Matic 400 on column 4
    Turbo Hydra-Matic 350 on column (1968) 8
    Turbo Hydra-Matic on column with tilt 5
    Torque drive (six-cylinder) 9
1969 Camaro
    Three-speed on column 12
    Three- or four-speed automatic on floor..................10
    Three- or four-speed automatic on floor with tilt 88
    Automatic on column 11
    Automatic on column with tilt.................................89
1970 Camaro
    Without tilt
    Three- or four-speed automatic on floor..................13
    Three- or four-speed automatic on floor with tilt 15
    Automatic on column 14
    Automatic on column with tilt.................................16

Chevelle ....*Interchange Number*
1964 Chevelle
    Three-speed manual on column 18

Interchange

Interchange Number: 1
    Part Number(s): 7803775
    Transmission Type: Powerglide
    Shifter Location: Column
    Usage: 1967–68 Camaro; 1967–68 Pontiac Firebird

Interchange Number: 2
    Part Number(s): 7803602
    Transmission Type: Manual

Shifter Location: Column
Usage: 1967 Camaro; 1967 Pontiac Firebird

Interchange Number: 3
Part Number(s): 7803777
Transmission Type: All
Shifter Location: Floor
Usage: 1967–68 Camaro; 1967–68 Pontiac Firebird

Interchange Number: 4
Part Number(s): 7803780
Transmission Type: Turbo Hydra-Matic 400
Shifter Location: Column
Usage: 1967–68 Camaro; 1967–68 Pontiac Firebird.

Interchange Number: 5
Part Number(s): 7803778
Transmission Type: Automatic
Shifter Location: Column
Usage: 1967–68 Camaro; 1967–69 Pontiac Firebird;
both with tilt wheel

Interchange Number: 6
Part Number(s): 7803779
Transmission Type: All
Shifter Location: Floor
Usage: 1967–68 Camaro; 1967–68 Pontiac Firebird;
both with tilt wheel

Interchange Number: 7
Part Number(s): 7803567
Transmission Type: Manual three-speed
Shifter Location: Column
Usage: 1968 Camaro; 1968 Pontiac Firebird

Interchange Number: 8
Part Number(s): 7803781
Transmission Type: Turbo Hydra-Matic 350
Shifter Location: Floor
Usage: 1968 Camaro; 1968 Pontiac Firebird

Interchange Number: 9
Part Number(s): 7806050
Transmission Type: Torque drive
Shifter Location: floor
Usage: 1968 Camaro

Interchange Number: 10
Part Number(s): 7804300
Transmission Type: All
Shifter Location: Floor
Usage: 1969 Camaro; 1969 Pontiac Firebird; 1969–72
Nova; 1971–72 Pontiac Ventura II

Interchange Number: 11
Part Number(s): 7812231
Transmission Type: Automatic
Shifter Location: Column
Usage: 1969 Camaro; 1969 Pontiac Firebird; 1969–72
Nova; 1971–72 Pontiac Ventura II

Interchange Number: 12
Part Number(s): 7812235
Transmission Type: Manual three-speed
Shifter Location: Column
Usage: 1969 Camaro; 1969 Pontiac Firebird; 1969–72
Nova; 1971–72 Pontiac Ventura II

Interchange Number: 13
Part Number(s): 7812204
Transmission Type: All
Shifter Location: Floor
Usage: 1970–74 Camaro; 1970–74 Pontiac Firebird;
both with tilt wheel

Interchange Number: 14
Part Number(s): 7808582
Transmission Type: Automatic
Shifter Location: Column
Usage: 1970 Camaro; 1970 Pontiac Firebird; both with-
out tilt wheel

Interchange Number: 15
Part Number(s): 7812229
Transmission Type: All
Shifter Location: Floor
Usage: 1970–74 Camaro; 1970–74 Pontiac Firebird;
both with tilt wheel

Interchange Number: 16
Part Number(s): 7812203
Transmission Type: Automatic
Shifter Location: Column
Usage: 1970–74 Camaro; 1970–74 Pontiac Firebird;
both with tilt wheel

Interchange Number: 17
Part Number(s): 7812224
Transmission Type: Automatic
Shifter Location: Column
Usage: 1970–74 Camaro; 1970–74 Pontiac Firebird

Interchange Number: 18
Part Number(s): 3854381
Transmission Type: Manual three-speed
Shifter Location: Column
Usage: 1964 Chevelle

Interchange Number: 19
Part Number(s): 3854244
Transmission Type: All
Shifter Location: Floor
Usage: 1964 Chevelle

Interchange Number: 20
Part Number(s): 3864545
Transmission Type: All
Shifter Location: Floor
Usage: 1965 Chevelle

Interchange Number: 21
Part Number(s): 5693760
Transmission Type: All
Shifter Location: Floor
Usage: 1964–65 Chevelle with tilt wheel

Interchange Number: 22
Part Number(s): 5691416
Transmission Type: Manual three-speed
Shifter Location: Column
Usage: 1966 Chevelle, except SS 396

Interchange Number: 23
Part Number(s): 5692597
Transmission Type: All

Shifter Location: Floor
Usage: 1966 Chevelle SS 396

Interchange Number: 24
Part Number(s): 5692598
Transmission Type: Automatic
Shifter Location: Column
Usage: 1966 Chevelle

Interchange Number: 25
Part Number(s): 5697070
Transmission Type: Automatic
Shifter Location: Column
Usage: 1966–67 Chevelle with tilt wheel

Interchange Number: 26
Part Number(s): 5697065
Transmission Type: All
Shifter Location: Floor
Usage: 1966–67 Chevelle with tilt wheel

Interchange Number: 27
Part Number(s): 7802716
Transmission Type: Automatic
Shifter Location: Column
Usage: 1967 Chevelle, all except SS 396

Interchange Number: 28
Part Number(s): 7802717
Transmission Type: Manual three-speed
Shifter Location: Column
Usage: 1967 Chevelle, except SS 396

Interchange Number: 29
Part Number(s): 7802718
Transmission Type: All
Shifter Location: Floor
Usage: 1967 Chevelle, except SS 396

Interchange Number: 30
Part Number(s): 7802722
Transmission Type: All
Shifter Location: Floor
Usage: 1967 SS 396 only

Interchange Number: 31
Part Number(s): 7802416
Transmission Type: Turbo Hydra-Matic 400
Shifter Location: Column
Usage: 1968 Chevelle SS 396

Interchange Number: 32
Part Number(s): 7802909
Transmission Type: Turbo Hydra-Matic 400
Shifter Location: Column
Usage: 1968 SS 396 with tilt wheel

Interchange Number: 33
Part Number(s): 7803695
Transmission Type: Powerglide
Shifter Location: Column
Usage: 1968 SS 396 with tilt wheel

Interchange Number: 34
Part Number(s): 7803696
Transmission Type: All

Shifter Location: Floor
Usage: 1968 SS 396

Interchange Number: 35
Part Number(s): 7803752
Transmission Type: All
Shifter Location: Floor
Usage: 1968 SS 396 with tilt wheel

Interchange Number: 36
Part Number(s): 7802059
Transmission Type: All
Shifter Location: Floor
Usage: 1968 Chevelle, all but SS 396

Interchange Number: 36
Part Number(s): 7801973
Transmission Type: All
Shifter Location: Floor
Usage: 1968 Chevelle with tilt wheel, all but SS 396

Interchange Number: 37
Part Number(s): 7801972
Transmission Type: Powerglide
Shifter Location: Column
Usage: 1968 Chevelle with tilt wheel, except SS 396

Interchange Number: 38
Part Number(s): 7802068
Transmission Type: Powerglide
Shifter Location: Column
Usage: 1968 Chevelle, all but SS 396

Interchange Number: 39
Part Number(s): 7812236
Transmission Type: All
Shifter Location: Floor
Usage: 1969–72 Chevelle, except SS 396 or SS 454;
    1970 Monte Carlo, except SS 396 or 454

Interchange Number: 40
Part Number(s): 7808147
Transmission Type: All
Shifter Location: Floor
Usage: 1969 Chevelle with tilt wheel, except SS 396

Interchange Number: 41
Part Number(s): 7808150
Transmission Type: Manual
Shifter Location: Floor
Usage: 1969 SS 396 with tilt wheel

Interchange Number: 42
Part Number(s): 7804954
Transmission Type: Automatic
Shifter Location: Column
Usage: 1969 Chevelle SS 396

Interchange Number: 43
Part Number(s): 7804956
Transmission Type: Powerglide
Shifter Location: Floor
Usage: 1969 Chevelle SS 396

Interchange Number: 44
Part Number(s): 7808149
Transmission Type: Turbo Hydra-Matic 400

Shifter Location: Floor
Usage: 1969 Chevelle SS 396 or 427

Interchange Number: 45
Part Number(s): 7812207
Transmission Type: Automatic
Shifter Location: Column
Usage: 1969–72 Chevelle with tilt wheel, except SS

Interchange Number: 46
Part Number(s): 7812208
Transmission Type: Automatic
Shifter Location: Floor
Usage: 1970–72 Chevelle; 1970 Monte Carlo; both with tilt wheel

Interchange Number: 47
Part Number(s): 7812230
Transmission Type: Automatic
Shifter Location: Column
Usage: 1969–71 Chevelle with tilt wheel, except SS 396 or SS 454

Interchange Number: 48
Part Number(s): 7812237
Transmission Type: Manual
Shifter Location: Floor
Usage: 1969–72 Chevelle SS 396 or SS 454 with tilt wheel

Interchange Number: 49
Part Number(s): 7812234
Transmission Type: Manual three-speed
Shifter Location: Column
Usage: 1969–72 Chevelle with tilt wheel, except SS 396 or SS 454

Interchange Number: 50
Part Number(s): 5673152
Transmission Type: Manual three-speed
Shifter Location: Column
Usage: 1959–64 full-size Chevrolet

Interchange Number: 51
Part Number(s): 3888737
Transmission Type: Manual three-speed
Shifter Location: Column
Usage: 1965–66 full-size Chevrolet

Interchange Number: 52
Part Number(s): 3779645
Transmission Type: Powerglide
Shifter Location: Column
Usage: 1959–62 full-size Chevrolet

Interchange Number: 53
Part Number(s): 3840281
Transmission Type: Automatic
Shifter Location: Column
Usage: 1963–64 full-size Chevrolet

Interchange Number: 54
Part Number(s): 3868463
Transmission Type: Automatic
Shifter Location: Column
Usage: 1965–66 full-size Chevrolet

Interchange Number: 55
Transmission Type: All
Shifter Location: Floor
Usage: 1959–62 full-size Chevrolet

Interchange Number: 56
Transmission Type: All
Shifter Location: Floor
Usage: 1963–64 full-size Chevrolet

Interchange Number: 57
Transmission Type: All
Shifter Location: Floor
Usage: 1965–66 full-size Chevrolet

Interchange Number: 58
Part Number(s): 7803526
Transmission Type: All
Shifter Location: Floor
Usage: 1967–68 full-size Chevrolet

Interchange Number: 59
Part Number(s): 7803774
Transmission Type: Automatic
Shifter Location: Column
Usage: 1967–68 full-size Chevrolet with tilt wheel

Interchange Number: 60
Part Number(s): 7803773
Transmission Type: Automatic
Shifter Location: Column
Usage: 1967–68 full-size Chevrolet

Interchange Number: 61
Part Number(s): 7803567
Transmission Type: Manual three-speed
Shifter Location: Column
Usage: 1967–68 full-size Chevrolet

Interchange Number: 62
Part Number(s): 7804295
Transmission Type: Automatic
Shifter Location: Column
Usage: 1969 full-size Chevrolet

Interchange Number: 63
Part Number(s): 7804296
Transmission Type: Manual three-speed
Shifter Location: Column
Usage: 1969 full-size Chevrolet

Interchange Number: 64
Part Number(s): 7804297
Transmission Type: All
Shifter Location: Floor
Usage: 1969 full-size Chevrolet

Interchange Number: 65
Part Number(s): 7810030
Transmission Type: Automatic
Shifter Location: Column
Usage: 1969 full-size Chevrolet with tilt wheel

Interchange Number: 66
Part Number(s): 7808152
Transmission Type: All
Shifter Location: Floor
Usage: 1969 full-size Chevrolet with tilt wheel

Interchange Number: 67
Part Number(s): 7810030
Transmission Type: Automatic
Shifter Location: Column
Usage: 1970 full-size Chevrolet with tilt wheel

Interchange Number: 68
Part Number(s): 7804295
Transmission Type: Automatic
Shifter Location: Column
Usage: 1970 full-size Chevrolet

Interchange Number: 69
Part Number(s): 7804296
Transmission Type: Manual three-speed
Shifter Location: Column
Usage: 1970 full-size Chevrolet with tilt wheel.

Interchange Number: 70
Part Number(s): 7807862
Transmission Type: Manual three-speed
Shifter Location: Column
Usage: 1970 full-size Chevrolet

Interchange Number: 71
Part Number(s): 3792717
Transmission Type: Manual three-speed
Shifter Location: Column
Usage: 1962–63 Chevy II (to build date 6-7-62)

Interchange Number: 72
Part Number(s): 3793789
Transmission Type: Manual three-speed
Shifter Location: Column
Usage: 1963 (after 6-8-62) to 1964 Chevy II

Interchange Number: 73
Part Number(s): 3864755
Transmission Type: Manual three-speed
Shifter Location: Column
Usage: 1965 Chevy II

Interchange Number: 74
Part Number(s): 3886537
Transmission Type: Manual three-speed
Shifter Location: Column
Usage: 1966 Chevy II

Interchange Number: 75
Part Number(s): 3790855
Transmission Type: Automatic
Shifter Location: Column
Usage: 1962 Chevy II

Interchange Number: 76
Part Number(s): 3793793
Transmission Type: Automatic
Shifter Location: Column
Usage: 1963–64 Chevy II, except SS

Interchange Number: 77
Part Number(s): 3864759
Transmission Type: Automatic
Shifter Location: Column
Usage: 1965 Chevy II, except SS

Interchange Number: 78
Part Number(s): 3879773
Transmission Type: Automatic
Shifter Location: Column
Usage: 1966 Chevy II

Interchange Number: 79
Part Number(s): 3792717
Transmission Type: All
Shifter Location: Floor
Usage: 1962–63 Chevy II (to 6-8-62)

Interchange Number: 80
Part Number(s): 3793789
Transmission Type: All
Shifter Location: Floor
Usage: 1963 (after 6-7-62) to 1964 Chevy II

Interchange Number: 81
Part Number(s): 3864755
Transmission Type: All
Shifter Location: Floor
Usage: 1965 Chevy II

Interchange Number: 82
Part Number(s): 3886537
Transmission Type: All
Shifter Location: Floor
Usage: 1966 Chevy II

Interchange Number: 83
Part Number(s): 7803532
Transmission Type: Powerglide
Shifter Location: Column
Usage: 1967 Chevy II

Interchange Number: 84
Part Number(s): 7803533
Transmission Type: Manual three-speed
Shifter Location: Column
Usage: 1967 Chevy II

Interchange Number: 85
Part Number(s): 7803534
Transmission Type: All
Shifter Location: Floor
Usage: 1967 Chevy II

Interchange Number: 86
Part Number(s): 7803782
Transmission Type: All
Shifter Location: Floor
Usage: 1968 Nova

Interchange Number: 87
Part Number(s): 7803783
Transmission Type: Manual three-speed
Shifter Location: Column
Usage: 1968 Nova

Interchange Number: 88
Transmission Type: All
Shifter Location: Floor
Usage: 1969 Camaro; 1969 Pontiac Firebird; 1969–72 Nova; all with tilt column

Interchange Number: 89
Transmission Type: Automatic

Shifter Location: Column
Usage: 1969 Camaro; 1969 Pontiac Firebird; 1969–72 Nova; all with tilt column

Interchange Number: 90
Part Number(s): 5679130
Transmission Type: All
Shifter Location: Floor
Usage: 1962–64 Impala without tachometer,
Note: Will fit 1959–62 Impalas.

Interchange Number: 91
Part Number(s): 679395
Transmission Type: All
Shifter Location: Floor
Usage: 1963–64 Impala with tachometer,
Note: Will fit 1959–62 Impalas.

Interchange Number: 92
Part Number(s): 5694250
Transmission Type: Powerglide
Shifter Location: Column
Usage: 1963–64 Impala with tachometer,
Note: Will fit 1965–66 Impalas.

Interchange Number: 93
Part Number(s): 5695705
Transmission Type: Turbo Hydra-matic 400
Shifter Location: Column
Usage: 1965–66 Impalas.

Interchange Number: 94
Part Number(s): 5694295
Transmission Type: All
Shifter Location: Floor
Usage: 1963–64 Impala with tachometer,
Note: Will fit 1965–66 Impalas.

Steering Knuckle

Interchange of the steering knuckle is based on part number. Interchange factors include model year, model type, and brakes type. A steering knuckle from a car with drum brakes will not fit a car with disc brakes.

Model Identification

Interchange

Interchange Number: 1
Part Number(s): 3966159
Brake Type: Drum
Usage: 1967–69 Camaro; 1967–72 Chevelle; 1968–74 Nova; 1971–72 GMC Sprint; 1971–74 Pontiac Ventura II; 1973–74 Olds Omega; 1973–74 Buick Apollo
Notes: All interchange vehicles must have drum brakes.

Interchange Number: 2
Part Number(s): 3966151
Brake Type: Disc
Usage: 1967–69 Camaro, except 1969 Z-28 or with special steering; 1967–72 Chevelle; 1967–72 Buick Skylark; 1967–72 Olds Cutlass; 1968–74 Nova; 1970–72 Monte Carlo; 1971–72 GMC Sprint; 1971–74 Pontiac Ventura II; 1973–74 Buick Apollo; 1973–74 Olds Omega
Notes: Part number is different on Oldsmobile and Buick but will fit.

Interchange Number: 3
Part Number(s): RH, 3954868; LH, 3954867
Brake Type: Four-wheel disc
Usage: 1969 Camaro

Interchange Number: 4
Part Number(s): RH, 3954870; LH, 3954869
Brake Type: Four-wheel disc
Usage: 1969 Camaro Z-28

Interchange Number: 5
Part Number(s): RH, 329350; LH, 329349
Brake Type: Disc

Usage: 1970–76 Camaro; 1973–76 Chevelle; 1973–76 Monte Carlo; 1973–76 Olds Cutlass; 1973–76 Buick Skylark/Regal; 1973–76 Pontiac Grand Prix; 1973–76 Pontiac LeMans; 1973–76 GMC Sprint; 1975–76 Nova; 1975–76 Pontiac Ventura II; 1975–76 Buick Apollo

Interchange Number: 6
Part Number(s): 38815124
Brake Type: Drum
Usage: 1964–66 Chevelle, except Z-16
Notes: Service part has 5/8 inch diameter anchor hole. This was the standard part for late 1965–66. The 1964 to mid-1965 part used a 1/2 inch diameter hole. Change occurred in May 1965. Don't use the earlier style on later style models. But you can use the 5/8 diameter hole on 1964–66 models, except for the 1965 Z-16.

Interchange Number: 7
Part Number(s): RH, 3872944; LH, 3872943
Brake Type: Drum, heavy-duty 11 inch diameter
Usage: 1965 Z-16 Chevelle SS 396

Interchange Number: 8
Brake Type: Drum
Usage: 1959–62 full-size Chevrolet
Notes: Stamped 3754168.

Interchange Number: 9
Part Number(s): 3828580
Brake Type: Drum
Usage: 1963–64 full-size Chevrolet
Notes: Used as a replacement part for 1959–62 models.

Interchange Number: 10
Part Number(s): 3855004
Brake Type: Drum
Usage: 1965–67 full-size Chevrolet

Interchange Number: 11
Part Number(s): 3924383
Brake Type: Drum
Usage: 1967–68 full-size Chevrolet

Interchange Number: 12
Part Number(s): 3924384
Brake Type: Disc
Usage: 1967–68 full-size Chevrolet

Interchange Number: 13
Part Number(s): 3953416
Brake Type: 1968 disc without power-assist; 1969–70 disc
Usage: 1968–70 full-size Chevrolet

Interchange Number: 14
Part Number(s): 3953415
Brake Type: Drum
Usage: 1969–70 full-size Chevrolet

Interchange Number: 15
Part Number(s): 3790426
Brake Type: Drum
Usage: 1962–63 Chevy II

Interchange Number: 16
Part Number(s): 3847927
Brake Type: Drum
Usage: 1964 to early 1965 Chevy II
Notes: Has a 1/2 inch diameter anchor hole. Change occurred May 1965. Interchange number 17 will also fit.

Interchange Number: 17
Part Number(s): RH, 3885908; LH, 3885907
Brake Type: Drum
Usage: 1965 (after May) to 1966 Chevy II
Notes: Due to the change in design, early and late styles are not 100 percent interchangeable. To use the later style on earlier models, you must use the brake shoe anchor bolt and lock from the later style. Will fit 1964–65 models, but hardware must be included.

Interchange Number: 18
Part Number(s): 3902968
Brake Type: Drum
Usage: 1967 Chevy II

Interchange Number: 19
Part Number(s): 3901211
Brake Type: Disc
Usage: 1967 Chevy II
Notes: Can be adapted to 1962–66 Chevy II.

Chapter 7

Brakes

Master Cylinder

Interchange for the master cylinder is based on part number. Type of braking system is an important factor in interchange. Two types were used, drum and disc, and they are *not* interchangeable. Thus, a drum brake master cylinder can not be used on a car with drum brakes, and vice versa. Before disc brakes were offered in 1966, metallic drum brakes were available. In most cases, these also used a special master cylinder.

Beginning in 1967, all master cylinders were restyled to a dual-circuit system. This system is easily recognized by its two separate reservoirs. Single-reservoir master cylinders should *never* be used on a 1967 or newer model.

Master cylinder manufacture must also be considered. Chevrolet used the Moraine brand from Delco, and the Bendix brand. For best braking operation, the proper manufacture should be used.

Model Identification

A dual-reservoir master cylinder.

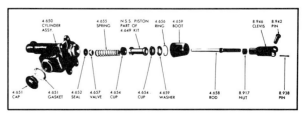

Exploded view of a 1957–61 master brake cylinder.

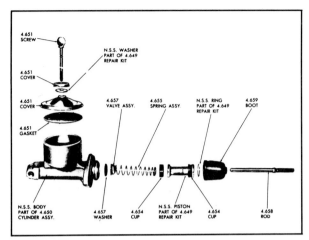

Exploded view of a 1962–63 master brake cylinder.

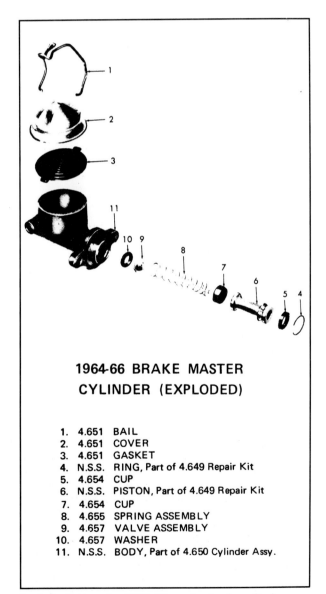

1964-66 BRAKE MASTER CYLINDER (EXPLODED)

1. 4.651 BAIL
2. 4.651 COVER
3. 4.651 GASKET
4. N.S.S. RING, Part of 4.649 Repair Kit
5. 4.654 CUP
6. N.S.S. PISTON, Part of 4.649 Repair Kit
7. 4.654 CUP
8. 4.655 SPRING ASSEMBLY
9. 4.657 VALVE ASSEMBLY
10. 4.657 WASHER
11. N.S.S. BODY, Part of 4.650 Cylinder Assy.

Exploded view of a 1964–66 master brake cylinder.

Interchange

Interchange Number: 1
  Part Number(s): 5456789
  Manufacturer: Moraine

"Delco Moraine" is stamped into the booster chamber.

Usage: 1959–66 full-size Chevrolet with or without power brakes; 1962–66 Chevy II; 1963–66 Chevy pickup or C-10 van; 1963–66 GMC C-10 pickup; 1964–66 Chevelle

Notes: All are without metallic linings and are Moraine systems.

Interchange Number: 2
Part Number(s): 3853776
Manufacturer: Bendix (618105)
Usage: 1964–66 full-size Chevrolet; 1964–66
Chevelle; 1964–66 Chevy II; 1964–66 Chevrolet C-10 to C-30 pickup
Notes: All have Bendix power brake systems.

Interchange Number: 3
Part Number(s): 5458523
Manufacturer: Bendix (stamped BS)
Usage: 1967–70 Chevelle; 1967–70 Camaro; 1967–70 Chevy II; 1967–69 Corvair
Notes: Dual-circuit type. All are without metallic linings. Interchange number 5 will fit.

Interchange Number: 4
Part Number(s): 5463267
Manufacturer: Moraine (stamped AT)
Usage: 1967–70 full-size Chevrolet with power brakes
Notes: Dual-circuit cylinder.

Interchange Number: 5
Part Number(s): 3912145
Manufacturer: Bendix
Usage: 1967–70 full-size Chevrolet without power brakes or metallic linings
Notes: Dual-circuit cylinder.

Interchange Number: 6
Part Number(s): 5464345
Manufacturer: Moraine
Usage: 1962–66 full-size Chevrolet; 1962–66 Chevy II; 1964–66 Chevelle; 1966 full-size Pontiac; all with power drum brakes
Notes: Single-circuit style.

Interchange Number: 7
Part Number(s): 5463284
Manufacturer: Moraine (stamped AU)
Usage: 1967 Chevelle; 1967 Camaro; both with metallic brakes
Notes: Will fit 1968 models with metallic drum brakes.

Interchange Number: 8
Part Number(s): 5458524
Manufacturer: Moraine (stamped AR)
Usage: 1967 Impala with metallic brakes

Interchange Number: 9
Part Number(s): 5469489
Manufacturer: Moraine (stamped SA)
Usage: 1967 Chevelle; 1967–70 full-size Chevrolet with power brakes; 1967–68 Camaro
Notes: Interchange number 11 will fit.

Interchange Number: 10
Part Number(s): 5468813
Manufacturer: Moraine (stamped AD)

Usage: 1967 Chevy II; 1967 Camaro; 1968–69 full-size Chevrolet without power brakes

Interchange Number: 11
Part Number(s): 5463492
Manufacturer: Moraine
Usage: 1967 Pontiac Firebird; 1968 Nova
Notes: Interchange number 9 will fit.

Interchange Number: 12
Part Number(s): 5468811
Manufacturer: Moraine
Usage: 1968 Chevelle
Notes: Has 1 1/8 inch diameter piston. No other interchange.

Interchange Number: 13
Part Number(s): 5463751
Manufacturer: Moraine (stamped US)
Usage: 1969 Camaro; 1969 Nova; both with power brakes

Interchange Number: 14
Part Number(s): 5461184
Manufacturer: Moraine
Usage: 1968–72 Corvette; 1969 Chevelle; both with power brakes

Interchange Number: 15
Part Number(s): 5470665
Manufacturer: Moraine
Usage: 1970 Chevelle; 1970 Monte Carlo; both with power brakes

Interchange Number: 16
Part Number(s): 5470664
Manufacturer: Moraine
Usage: 1970–74 Camaro with power brakes

Interchange Number: 17
Part Number(s): 3979629
Manufacturer: Bendix
Usage: 1970 full-size Chevrolet with power brakes

Interchange Number: 18
Part Number(s): 5470721
Manufacturer: Moraine
Usage: 1970–74 Nova; 1971–74 Pontiac Ventura II; 1973–74 Buick Apollo; 1973–74 Olds Omega; all with power brakes

Booster Chamber

Vacuum chambers, often called booster chambers, were keyed to the type of brake system used on a car. Disc brakes and drum brakes used a different chamber and are not interchangeable. However, unlike the master cylinder, the same vacuum chamber was used on both metallic drum and nonmetallic brakes.

There are two boost chamber manufacturers, Moraine and Bendix. The two brands cannot be interchanged and must be used with the identical brand of master cylinder. Chambers are clearly marked either Moraine Delco or Bendix. Some chambers may also be coded with a letter or number that is used for identification.

1964-69 MORAINE POWER BRAKE PISTON—EXPLODED

1. 4.935 RING
2. 4.924 ROD
3. 4.922 RING
4. 4.934 RETAINER
5. 4.934 PLATE
6. 4.934 LEVER
7. 4.918 SPRING
8. 4.918 BUMPER
9. 4.918 RETAINER
10. 4.918 RING
11. 4.922 PISTON
12. 4.922 SUPPORT
13. 4.922 DIAPHRAGM
14. 4.918 RING
15. N.S.S. VALVE, Part of 4.658 Valve Assy.
16. N.S.S. ROD, Part of 4.658 Valve Assy.
17. N.S.S. VALVE ASSY., Part of 4.658 Valve Assy.
18. N.S.S. SEAT, Part of 4.658 Valve Assy.
19. 4.955 SPRING
20. 4.935 RETAINER
21. 4.935 RETAINER
22. 8.934 SPRING
23. 4.913 FILTER
24. 4.913 SILENCER

Exploded view of 1964–69 Moraine power brake piston.

Model Identification

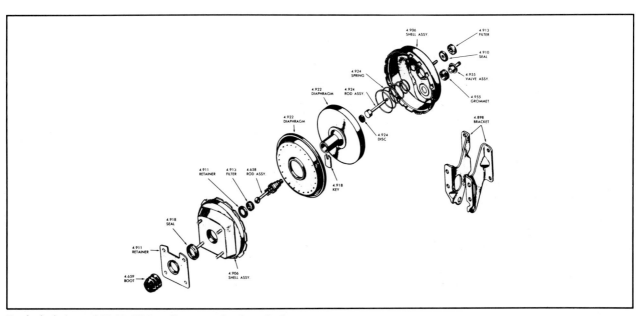

Exploded view of 1962–71 Bendix power brake cylinder.

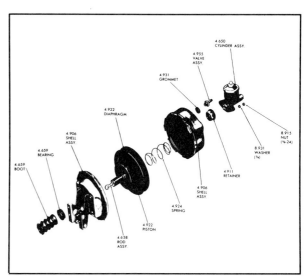

Exploded view of 1962–63 Moraine power brake housing.

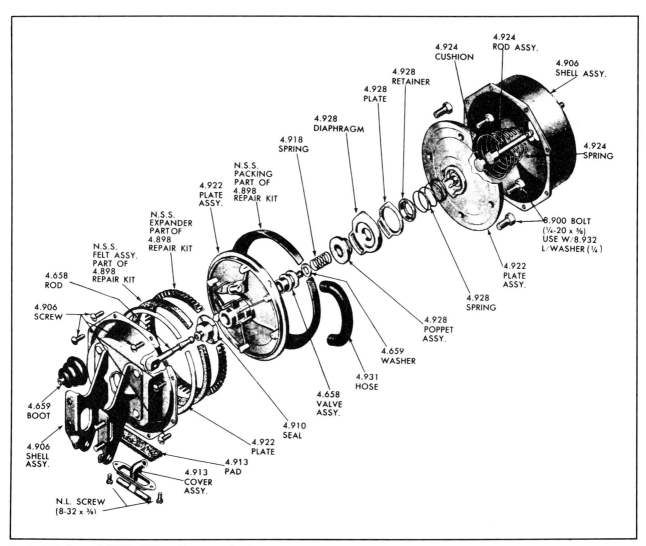

Exploded view of 1959–61 Bendix power brake.

Interchange

Interchange Number: 1

    Part Number(s): 5459121
    Manufacturer: Moraine

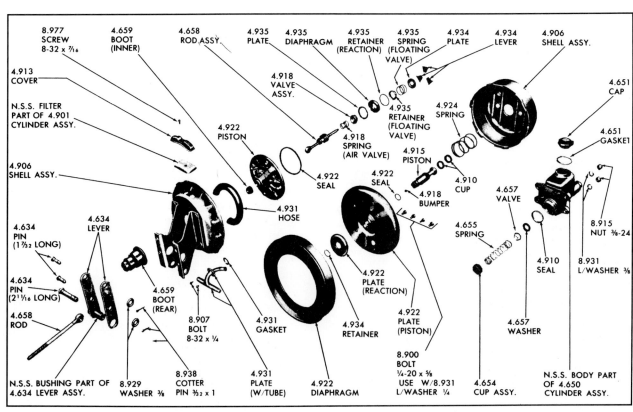

Exploded view of 1959–61 Moraine power brake piston.

Usage: 1959 full-size Chevrolet

Interchange Number: 2
Part Number(s): 3764358
Manufacturer: Bendix (stamped C)
Usage: 1959–60 full-size Chevrolet

Interchange Number: 3
Part Number(s): 3764358
Manufacturer: Bendix (stamped C-1)
Usage: 1961 full-size Chevrolet

Interchange Number: 4
Part Number(s): 5459910
Manufacturer: Moraine (stamped 5459520)
Usage: 1960–61 full-size Chevrolet

Interchange Number: 5
Part Number(s): 5460880
Manufacturer: Moraine
Usage: 1962 full-size Chevrolet

Interchange Number: 6
Part Number(s): 5460880
Manufacturer: Moraine (stamped 5464700)
Usage: 1963 full-size Chevrolet

Interchange Number: 7
Part Number(s): 3831860
Manufacturer: Bendix (stamped C-2)
Usage: 1962 full-size Chevrolet

Interchange Number: 8
Part Number(s): 3831860
Manufacturer: Bendix (stamped C-3)
Usage: 1963 full-size Chevrolet

Interchange Number: 9
Part Number(s): 5464301
Manufacturer: Moraine (stamped 5464280)
Usage: 1964 full-size Chevrolet

Interchange Number: 10
Part Number(s): 3849950
Manufacturer: Bendix (stamped C-5)
Usage: 1964 full-size Chevrolet

Interchange Number: 11
Part Number(s): 2501128
Manufacturer: Bendix (stamped H)
Usage: 1962–63 Chevy II

Interchange Number: 12
Part Number(s): 5464811
Manufacturer: Moraine (stamped 5464810)
Usage: 1964 Chevy II

Interchange Number: 13
Part Number(s): 3869465
Manufacturer: Bendix (stamped H-1)
Usage: 1964 Chevy II

Interchange Number: 14
Part Number(s): 3849010
Manufacturer: Bendix (stamped H-2)
Usage: 1965 (up to 8-7-64) Chevy II

Interchange Number: 15
Part Number(s): 3868647

Manufacturer: Bendix (stamped H-3)
Usage: 1965 (after 8-7-64) to 1966 Chevy II

Interchange Number: 16
Part Number(s): 5464800
Manufacturer: Moraine (stamped 5464779 or 5467250)
Usage: 1965 (up to 8-7-64) Chevy II

Interchange Number: 17
Part Number(s): 5467251
Manufacturer: Moraine (stamped 5467250)
Usage: 1965 (after 8-7-64) to 1966 Chevy II

Interchange Number: 18
Part Number(s): 3848934
Manufacturer: Bendix (stamped C-4)
Usage: 1964–66 Chevelle

Interchange Number: 19
Part Number(s): 5464361
Manufacturer: Moraine (stamped 5464900)
Usage: 1964 Chevelle

Interchange Number: 20
Part Number(s): 5465341
Manufacturer: Moraine (stamped 5464900 or 5464901)
Usage: 1965–66 Chevelle
Notes: Will fit 1964 Chevelle.

Interchange Number: 21
Part Number(s): 5465511
Manufacturer: Moraine (stamped 5464900)
Usage: 1965–66 full-size Chevrolet

Interchange Number: 22
Part Number(s): 3857829
Manufacturer: Bendix (stamped C-4)
Usage: 1965–66 full-size Chevrolet
Notes: Interchange number 18 will fit.

Interchange Number: 23
Part Number(s): 3979596
Manufacturer: Bendix
Usage: 1967–71 Chevelle; 1971–72 GMC Sprint
Notes: This is replacement part number. Original varies but all the same unit.

Interchange Number: 24
Part Number(s): 5460620
Manufacturer: Moraine (stamped 2505715)
Usage: 1967–70 full-size Chevrolet 396, 427, or 454ci without disc brakes
Notes: Rare!

Interchange Number: 25
Part Number(s): 5462049
Manufacturer: Moraine
Usage: 1967–68 Camaro; 1968 Nova

Interchange Number: 26
Part Number(s): 5462030
Manufacturer: Moraine
Usage: 1967 Chevelle

Interchange Number: 27
Part Number(s): 3918715

Parking brake pad for 1959–63 models.

Parking brake pad for 1967–70 models.

Manufacturer: Bendix
Usage: 1967–68 Camaro; 1968 Nova

Interchange Number: 28
Part Number(s): 5468804
Manufacturer: Moraine
Usage: 1968 Chevelle with finned brake drums

Interchange Number: 29
Part Number(s): 5469396
Manufacturer: Moraine (stamped 2505689)
Usage: 1969–70 Chevelle

Interchange Number: 30
Part Number(s): 5469397
Manufacturer: Moraine
Usage: 1969 Camaro; 1969–70 Nova

Interchange Number: 31
Part Number(s): 3974365
Manufacturer: Bendix
Usage: 1969–70 Camaro; 1969–74 Nova; 1971–74
    Pontiac Ventura II; 1973–74 Buick Apollo; 1973–74
    Olds Omega

Interchange Number: 32
Part Number(s): 5470735
Manufacturer: Moraine
Usage: 1970 Camaro; 1970 Pontiac Firebird, except
    Trans-Am

Interchange Number: 33
Part Number(s): 5463968
Manufacturer: Moraine
Usage: 1967–70 full-size Chevrolet

Interchange Number: 34
Part Number(s): 5458828
Manufacturer: Moraine
Usage: 1967–68 Camaro;1968 Nova with disc brakes

Interchange Number: 35
Part Number(s): 5468819
Manufacturer: Moraine (tagged CL)
Usage: 1968 Chevelle with disc brakes
Notes: No other interchange.

Interchange Number: 36
Part Number(s): 5469405
Manufacturer: Moraine
Usage: 1969 Camaro; 1969–70 Nova with disc brakes

Parking brake pad for 1964–66 models.

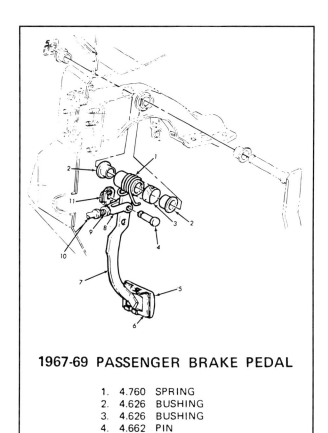

1967-69 PASSENGER BRAKE PEDAL

1. 4.760 SPRING
2. 4.626 BUSHING
3. 4.626 BUSHING
4. 4.662 PIN
5. 4.630 PLATE
6. 4.630 COVER
7. 4.625 PEDAL ASSY.
8. 8.946 CLEVIS (3/8)
9. 8.916 NUT (3/8–24)
10. 4.658 ROD
11. 4.662 RETAINER

Brake pedal assembly for 1967–69 passenger vehicles.

Interchange Number: 37
Part Number(s): 5469400
Manufacturer: Moraine
Usage: 1969–70 Chevelle with disc brakes

Interchange Number: 38
Part Number(s): 3979624
Manufacturer: Moraine
Usage: 1967–70 full-size Chevrolet with disc brakes

Interchange Number: 39
Part Number(s): 5460428
Manufacturer: Moraine
Usage: 1967 Chevelle with disc brakes

Interchange Number: 40
Part Number(s): 5458777
Manufacturer: Moraine
Usage: 1967 Chevy II with drum brakes

Interchange Number: 41
Part Number(s): 5458826
Manufacturer: Moraine
Usage: 1967 Chevy II with disc brakes

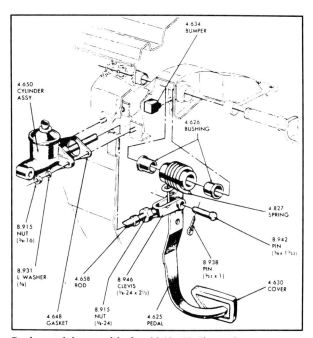

Brake pedal assembly for 1962–67 Chevrolet.

Brake Drum

Brake drums are largely interchangeable. However, front and rear drum brakes are different and will not interchange. Models with metallic brakes used special drums and therefore cannot use nonmetallic brake drums.

Model Identification

Camaro 1967–70 ....*Interchange Number*
Front (without fins) 4
Rear (without fins)...9
Front (with fins) 6
Rear (with fins)..11
Metallic linings
    Front (without fins)....................................5
    Rear (without fins) 10

Chevelle 1964–70 ....*Interchange Number*
Front (without fins) 4
Rear (without fins)...9
Front (with fins) 6
Rear (with fins)..11
Metallic linings
    Front (without fins)....................................5
    Rear (without fins) 10

Impala 1959–70...................................*Interchange Number*
Front (without fins) 1
Rear (without fins)...7
Metallic linings
    Front 2
    Rear 8

Chevy II/Nova ....*Interchange Number*
1962–63
    Front 3
    Rear 12

1968 Chevelle SS 396 Sport Coupe. *Chevrolet*

Interchange

Interchange Number: 1

Part Number(s): 3872326 (fits either side)
Usage: 1959–70 full-size Chevrolet without metallic brakes

Interchange Number: 2

Part Number(s): 3872384 (fits either side)
Usage: 1959–67 full-size Chevrolet with metallic brakes

Interchange Number: 3

Part Number(s): 3830169 (fits either side)
Usage: 1962–63 Chevy II without metallic brakes

Interchange Number: 4

Part Number(s): 3845258
Usage: 1964–68 Chevelle, except 1965 SS 396 Z-16; 1964–68 Chevy II/Nova; 1967–68 Camaro; all without metallic brakes

Interchange Number: 5

Part Number(s): 3845282
Usage: 1964–68 Chevelle, except 1965 SS 396 Z-16; 1964–68 Chevy II/Nova; 1967–68 Camaro; all with metallic brakes

Interchange Number: 6

Part Number(s): 3996670
Usage: 1968 Pontiac Firebird; 1968–70 Camaro; 1968–72 Chevelle, except 1969–72 SS; 1968–74 Nova; 1971–74 Pontiac Ventura II; 1973–74 Buick Apollo; 1973–74 Olds Omega Notes: Drums have fins.

Interchange Number: 7

Part Number(s): 385944
Usage: 1959–70 full-size Chevrolet without metallic brakes; 1961–65 Corvair (front or rear drums); 1971

Chevrolet C-10 pickup with standard 11x2 inch drums

Interchange Number: 8
Part Number(s): 3869537
Usage: 1959–65 Corvette; 1959–67 full-size Chevrolet; all with metallic brakes

Interchange Number: 9
Part Number(s): 3987445
Usage: 1964–68 Chevelle, except 1965 SS 396 Z-16; 1964–68 Chevy II/Nova; 1967–68 Camaro; 1969–74 Nova with front disc brakes; 1970–72 Chevelle with round axle cover; all without fins or metallic brakes

Interchange Number: 10
Part Number(s): 3998266
Usage: 1964–67 Chevelle, all but 1965 SS 396 Z-16; 1967 Camaro; 1964–67 Chevy II/Nova; all with metallic brakes Notes: A few 1968 models were built with metallic brakes using these drums.

Interchange Number: 11
Part Number(s): 3996135
Usage: 1969–72 Chevelle; 1969–74 Nova with front drums; 1969–74 Camaro with drums in 1969–70; 1970–72 Pontiac Firebird; 1971–74 Pontiac Ventura with front drum brakes

Interchange Number: 12
Part Number(s): 385107
Usage: 1962–63 Chevy II without metallic brakes

Disc Brake Rotor

Model Identification

Interchange

Interchange Number: 1
Part Number(s): 3933936
Usage: 1967–68 full-size Chevrolet
Notes: Four-piston design only in 1968.

Interchange Number: 2
Part Number(s): 3986083
Usage: 1968–70 full-size Chevrolet
Notes: Single-piston design only in 1968.

Interchange Number: 3
Part Number(s): 3901098
Usage: 1967–68 Pontiac Firebird; 1967–68 Pontiac Tempest; 1967–69 Camaro; 1967–69 Olds Cutlass; 1967–71 Buick Skylark; 1967–72 Chevelle; 1967–72 Nova; 1970–72 Monte Carlo; 1971–72 GMC Sprint; 1971–74 Pontiac Ventura II; 1973–74 Buick Apollo
Notes: Not for four-wheel disc brake system.

Interchange Number: 4
Part Number(s): 3996663 (fits front or rear, rotor only)
Usage: 1968–69 Camaro with four-wheel disc brake system

Interchange Number: 5
Part Number(s): 334348
Usage: 1970–75 Camaro; 1970–75 Pontiac Firebird; 1973–75 Olds Cutlass; 1973–76 Pontiac LeMans; 1973–76 Buick Century/Regal; 1973–76 Pontiac Grand Prix; 1973–76 Monte Carlo; 1975 Pontiac Ventura II; 1975 Buick Apollo

Brake Pedal

Transmission type is relevant to the type of brake pedal used. Manual transmissions used a smaller brake pedal step plate than cars with automatics, so they are not interchangeable.

Model Identification

Interchange

Interchange Number: 1
Part Number(s): 3776831
Used: 1959–61 full-size Chevrolet manual

Interchange Number: 2
Part Number(s): 3798255
Usage: 1962–64 full-size Chevrolet manual

Interchange Number: 3
Part Number(s): 3926959
Usage: 1965–70 full-size Chevrolet manual

Interchange Number: 4
Part Number(s): 3793879
Usage: 1962–66 Chevy II manual

Interchange Number: 5
Part Number(s): 3843931
Usage: 1964–66 Chevelle manual

Interchange Number: 6
Part Number(s): 3937889
Usage: 1967–72 Chevelle; 1967–70 Olds Cutlass; 1970–72 Monte Carlo; all manual

Interchange Number: 7
Part Number(s): 3923541
Usage: 1967–68 Camaro; 1967–68 Pontiac Firebird; 1968 Nova; all manual

Interchange Number: 8
Part Number(s): 3908345
Usage: 1967 Chevy II manual

Interchange Number: 9
Part Number(s): 3953287
Usage: 1969 Camaro; 1969 Pontiac Firebird; 1969–74 Nova; 1971–74 Pontiac Ventura II; 1973–74 Olds Omega; 1973–74 Buick Apollo; all manual

Interchange Number: 10
Part Number(s): 3965697
Usage: 1970–74 Camaro; 1970–74 Pontiac Firebird; both manual

Interchange Number: 11
Part Number(s): 3798259
Usage: 1962–64 full-size Chevrolet automatic

Interchange Number: 12
Part Number(s): 3937893

Usage: 1965–68 full-size Chevrolet; 1967–72 Chevelle; 1967–72 Olds Cutlass; 1967–72 Pontiac Le-Mans; 1967–72 Skylark; all automatic

Interchange Number: 13
Part Number(s): 3923545
Usage: 1967–68 Camaro; 1967–68 Pontiac Firebird; 1968 Nova; all automatic

Interchange Number: 14
Part Number(s): 3908767
Usage: 1969–70 full-size Chevrolet automatic

Interchange Number: 15
Part Number(s): 3953291
Usage: 1969 Camaro; 1969–74 Nova; 1971–74 Pontiac Ventura II; 1973–74 Buick Apollo; all automatic

Interchange Number: 16
Part Number(s): 3972201
Usage: 1970–74 Camaro; 1970–74 Pontiac Firebird; both automatic

Interchange Number: 17
Part Number(s): 3972201
Usage: 1970–74 Camaro; 1970–74 Pontiac Firebird; both automatic

Interchange Number: 18
Part Number(s): 3843935
Usage: 1964–66 Chevelle; 1964–66 Pontiac LeMans; 1964–66 Olds Cutlass; 1964–66 Buick Skylark; all automatic

Interchange Number: 19
Part Number(s): 3776832
Usage: 1959–61 full-size Chevrolet automatic

Brake Pedal Pad
Even though the brake pedal was changed many times, the brake pedal pad, or cover, was not. As a result, there is ample interchange available. This section is not so much for salvage yard hunting, but for NOS or reproduction parts.

Another point of interest is that those pads used with manual transmissions are the exact same covers used on the clutch. Models with disc brakes used a special pad that featured trim identifying it for use with disc brakes.

Model Identification

Interchange

Interchange Number: 1
Part Number(s): 3744748
Type: Manual
Usage: 1959–70 full-size Chevrolet with drum brakes, except 1967–68 SS or Caprice

Interchange Number: 2
Part Number(s): 3884850
Type: Manual
Usage: 1964–68 Impala SS; 1966–70 Caprice; 1967–70 Impala with disc brakes

Interchange Number: 2
Part Number(s): 3884850
Type: Manual
Usage: 1966–70 Caprice; 1967–68 Impala SS; 1967–70 Impala with disc brakes

Interchange Number: 3
Part Number(s): 3745991
Type: Automatic
Usage: 1964–70 full-size Chevrolet with drum brakes, except Caprice (used a trim plate)

Interchange Number: 4
Part Number(s): 3745991
Type: Automatic
Usage: 1959–64 full-size Chevrolet

Interchange Number: 5
Part Number(s): 3858198
Type: Manual
Usage: 1962–67 Chevy II; 1964–71 Chevelle; 1964–72 Olds Cutlass; 1964–72 Buick Skylark; 1971 Buick LeSabre; 1975–76 Astre; 1975–76 Monza/Vega; all with drum brakes

Interchange Number: 6
Part Number(s): 3858199
Type: Automatic
Usage: 1962–67 Chevy II; 1964–72 Chevelle; 1964–72 Olds Cutlass; 1964–72 Buick Skylark; 1971 Buick LeSabre; 1975–76 Astre; 1975–76 Monza/Vega; all with drum brakes

Interchange Number: 7
Part Number(s): 3934000
Type: Manual
Usage: 1967 Chevy II; 1967–72 Chevelle; 1967–72 Olds Cutlass; 1967–72 Buick Skylark; 1971 Buick LeSabre; 1975–76 Astre; 1975–76 Monza/Vega; all with disc brakes
Notes: Pad has bright circle with the words "disc brakes" on it.

Interchange Number: 8
Part Number(s): 3934002
Type: Automatic
Usage: 1967 Chevy II; 1967–72 Chevelle; 1967–72 Olds Cutlass; 1967–72 Buick Skylark; 1971 Buick LeSabre; 1975–76 Astre; 1975–76 Monza/Vega; all with disc brakes

Interchange Number: 9
Part Number(s): 3888680
Type: Manual
Usage: 1964–72 Pontiac Tempest; 1965–70 full-size Pontiac; 1966–70 Pontiac Grand Prix; 1967–74 Camaro; 1967–74 Pontiac Firebird; 1968–74 Nova; 1974–75 Buick Apollo; all with drum brakes

Interchange Number: 10
Part Number(s): 3921648
Type: Manual
Usage: 1964–72 Pontiac Tempest; 1965–70 full-size Pontiac; 1966–70 Pontiac Grand Prix; 1968–70 Camaro; 1968–70 Nova; 1968–70 Pontiac Firebird; 1974–75 Buick Apollo; all with disc brakes

Interchange Number: 11
Part Number(s): 3888682
Type: Automatic
Usage: 1967–74 Camaro; 1967–75 Pontiac Firebird; 1968–74 Nova; 1971–75 Pontiac Ventura II; 1973–75 Buick Apollo; 1973–75 Olds Omega; all with drum brakes

Interchange Number: 12
Part Number(s): 3930091
Type: Automatic
Usage: 1968–74 Camaro; 1968–74 Nova; both with disc brakes

Interchange Number: 13
Part Number(s): 3881784
Type: Automatic
Usage: 1967–70 Impala with disc brakes

Interchange Number: 14
Part Number(s): 3888680
Type: Manual
Usage: 1974–75 Buick Apollo; 1968–74; ; 1971–75 Pontiac Ventura II; all with drum brakes

Calipers

For calipers, interchange is based on right- and left-hand sides and on number of pistons. Early models used a four-piston design, while the later ones used a single-piston design. Single-piston calipers must be used with the single-piston rotors; four-piston calipers must be used with corresponding rotors.

Model Identification

Camaro	Interchange Number
1967–68	5
1969 without four-wheel disc brakes	7
1969 with four-wheel disc brakes	6
1970	8

Chevelle	Interchange Number
1967–68	3
1969–70	4

Impala	Interchange Number
1967–68	1
1968–70	2

Chevy II/Nova	Interchange Number
1967–68	5
1969–70	7

Interchange

Interchange Number: 1
Part Number(s): *inner*: RH, 5468555, LH, 5468554; *outer*: 5456479 (fits either side)
Usage: 1967–68 full-size Chevrolet, four-piston type

Interchange Number: 2
Part Number(s): RH, 5472814; LH, 5472815
Usage: 1968–70 full-size Chevrolet, single-piston type

Interchange Number: 3
Part Number(s): *inner*: RH, 5468364, LH, 5468365; *outer*: 5456076 (fits either side)
Usage: 1967 Buick Skylark; 1967–68 Chevelle; 1967–68 Olds Cutlass; 1967–68 Pontiac Tempest; all four-piston type

Interchange Number: 4
Part Number(s): RH, 5472162; LH, 5472161
Usage: 1969–72 Chevelle; 1969–72 Pontiac LeMans; 1969–72 Grand Prix; 1970–72 Monte Carlo; 1970–72 Olds Cutlass; 1971–72 Buick Skylark; 1971–72 GMC Sprint; all single-piston type

Interchange Number: 5
Part Number(s): *inner*: RH, 5468377, LH, 5468376; *outer*: 5455534 (fits either side)
Usage: 1967–68 Camaro; 1967–68 Chevy II/Nova; both with four-piston type

Interchange Number: 6
Part Number(s): *Front, inner:* RH, 5469486, LH, 5469487; *outer*: 2621206 (fits either side) *Rear, inner*: 5461992 (fits either side) *outer*: 5462017 (fits either side)
Usage: 1969 Camaro with four-wheel disc brakes; right-hand side of 1968–72 Corvette with heavy-duty brake option

Notes: Parts actually appeared on late 1967 Corvettes on the right-hand side. The left-hand side of a Corvette will not Interchange.

Interchange Number: 7
Part Number(s): RH, 5472434; LH, 5472433
Usage: 1969 Camaro without four-wheel disc brakes; 1969–74 Nova; 1971–75 Pontiac Ventura II; 1973 Olds Omega; 1973–74 Buick Apollo

Interchange Number: 8
Part Number(s): RH, 5472533; LH, 5472532
Usage: 1970–71 Camaro; 1970–71 Pontiac Firebird

Parking Brake

Model Identification

Camaro	Interchange Number
1967–68	11
1969	15
1970	14

Chevelle	Interchange Number
1964 67	10
1968–69	12
1970	13

Impala	Interchange Number
1959–60	1
1961–62	2
1963–64	3
1965–66	4
1967	5
1968	6
1969–70	7

Chevy II/Nova	Interchange Number
1962–65	8
1966–67	9
1968	11
1969	15

Interchange

Interchange Number: 1
Part Number(s): 3769569
Usage: 1959–60 full-size Chevrolet

Interchange Number: 2
Part Number(s): 3805264
Usage: 1961–62 full-size Chevrolet

Interchange Number: 3
Part Number(s): 3823197
Usage: 1963–64 full-size Chevrolet

Interchange Number: 4
Part Number(s): 3903063
Usage: 1965–66 full-size Chevrolet

Interchange Number: 5
Part Number(s): 3898221
Usage: 1967 full-size Chevrolet

Interchange Number: 6
    Part Number(s): 3925075
    Usage: 1968 full-size Chevrolet

Interchange Number: 7
    Part Number(s): 3939223
    Usage: 1969–70 full-size Chevrolet

Interchange Number: 8
    Part Number(s): 3790897
    Usage: 1962–65 Chevy II

Interchange Number: 9
    Part Number(s): 3877515
    Usage: 1966–67 Chevy II

Interchange Number: 10
    Part Number(s): 3908775
    Usage: 1964–67 Chevelle

Interchange Number: 11
    Part Number(s): 3928357
    Usage: 1967–68 Camaro; 1968 Nova

Interchange Number: 12
    Part Number(s): 3946779
    Usage: 1968–69 Chevelle

Interchange Number: 13
    Part Number(s): 3960783
    Usage: 1970–72 Chevelle

Interchange Number: 14
    Part Number(s): 330291
    Usage: 1970–72 Camaro

Interchange Number: 15
    Part Number(s): 330293
    Usage: 1969 Camaro; 1969–72 Nova; 1971–72 Pontiac
    Ventura II

Chapter 8

Wheels

Two determining factors in wheel interchange are diameter and width. A third important consideration is offset, the distance the wheel is set back from the brake drum or rotor. Offset can be measured by noting the distance from the centerline of the rim to the inner side of the wheel.

Incorrect offset can interfere with brake operation or cause tire clearance problems. (When offsets are known, they are given in the charts.) There is generally a "one-plus" rule in swapping wheels. This means you can usually, but not always, go up one wheel size without a problem. For example, if your car is equipped with 14x5 inch wheels, you can usually install 14x6 inch wheels. Try to avoid large offset changes, though. If you have a wheel with, say, a 1/4 inch offset, you should not go to a wheel with a 3.00 inch offset.

Another suggestion for wheel swapping: If the wheels in question were an option on your model, they will usually fit your car.

The Model Identification interchange chart is divided into two categories: plain steel wheels, and styled wheels. The styled types include Rallye and Super Sport wheels. Styled wheels came without trim ring or center caps.

Model Identification

Interchange

Interchange Number: 1
    Part Number(s): 3989423
    Size: 14x5 inches (19/32 inch offset)
    Usage: 1959–69 full-size Chevrolet; 1967 Camaro; 1968–72 Nova; 1971–72 Chevelle, except station wagon; 1971–72 GMC Sprint; 1971–72 Pontiac Le-Mans; 1971–72 Pontiac Ventura II
    Notes: Stamped D-D.

Interchange Number: 2
    Part Number(s): 3960347
    Size: 14x6 inches (1/16 inch offset)
    Usage: 1959–69 full-size Chevrolet, except with disc brakes
    Notes: Has nine hubcap attaching clips.

Interchange Number: 3
    Part Number(s): 2354750
    Size: 15x5 1/2 inches (9/16 inch offset)
    Usage: 1957–64 full-size Chevrolet
    Notes: Wheel is riveted. Has three wheel cover attaching clips and six lug nut holes. Use with tube tires only.

This type of wheel is commonly referred to as an SS, or Super Sport, wheel.

Interchange Number: 4
    Part Number(s): 9792737
    Size: 14x5 inches
    Usage: 1967 Chevelle with Rallye Spare Wheel; 1968–69 Camaro; 1968–69 Pontiac Firebird; both with spare saver tire
    Notes: Stamped HI.

Interchange Number: 5
    Part Number(s): 3834956
    Size: 15x5 inches (9/16 inch offset)
    Usage: 1959–67 full-size Chevrolet
    Notes: Wheel riveted. Has no wheel cover clips.

Interchange Number: 6
    Part Number(s): 3838080
    Size: 15x5 1/2 inches (7/16 inch offset)
    Usage: 1962–66 full-size Chevrolet police car
    Notes: Wheel riveted. Has no wheel cover clips.

Interchange Number: 7
    Part Number(s): 3793396

Rallye wheels were used on a variety of models. This is the 1968–70 style center cap.

The 1967 Rallye wheel center cap.

Size: 14x5 inches (1/4 inch offset)
Usage: 1962–63 Chevy II with 6.50x14 inch tires

Interchange Number: 8
Part Number(s): 3872276
Size: 14x5 inches
Usage: 1964–67 Chevy II; 1964–68 Chevelle;
1964–68 Buick Skylark, except GS 350 or GS 400;
1964–68 Pontiac LeMans, except GTO; 1964–68
Olds Cutlass, except 442; 1968–69 Nova, except SS
or with disc brakes

Interchange Number: 9
Part Number(s): 3928297
Size: 14x6 inches (11/32 inch offset)
Usage: 1965 Chevelle Z-16; 1966–69 Chevelle, except
SS 396

Interchange Number: 10
Part Number(s): 3871919
Size: 14x6 inches (1 inch offset)
Usage: 1964–66 Pontiac GTO; 1964–66
Oldsmobile J-88; 1965–70 Chevrolet or GMC C-10 van;
1966–68 Chevelle SS 396 or 1968–69 Chevelle with
F70x14 tires; 1966 Buick Gran Sport; 1966–68 Buick
Skylark with heavy-duty suspension; 1966–68 Olds
Cutlass with heavy duty suspension; 1967 Pontiac
LeMans; all with drum brakes

Interchange Number: 11
Part Number(s): 3970535
Size: 14x6 inches
Usage: 1967–69 Camaro

Interchange Number: 12
Part Number(s): 3914894
Size: 15x6 inches
Usage: 1967–68 Camaro Z-28 with disc brakes

Interchange Number: 13
Part Number(s): 3901696
Size: 15x5 inches (1/4 inch offset)
Usage: 1967 full-size Chevrolet

Interchange Number: 14
Part Number(s): 3928294
Size: 14x5 inches
Usage: 1968 Chevelle, except SS 396; 1968 Nova, ex-
cept SS; both with drum brakes

Interchange Number: 15
Part Number(s): 3938983
Size: 14x6 inches
Usage: 1968–69 Camaro, except with space saver tire;
1968–70 Nova, except Nova SS or with space saver
spare tire; both with disc brakes

Interchange Number: 16
Part Number(s): 334397 or 362052
Size: 14x7 inches (13/32 inch offset)
Usage: 1969 Camaro SS 350 or SS 396; 1969 Pontiac
Firebird; 1969–70 Nova SS; 1969–70 Pontiac Grand
Prix; 1973–74
Camaro; 1973–74 Pontiac Firebird; 1973–74 Nova;
1973–74 Pontiac LeMans

Notes: Some stamped IF. Standard wheels with F70
tires.

Interchange Number: 17
Part Number(s): 3964071
Size: 15x5 inches (2 29/32 inch offset)
Usage: 1968–70 full-size Chevrolet
Notes: Wheel is welded; has no wheel cover clips. Bare-
painted wheel, used with 8.25x15 inch tires.

Interchange Number: 18
Part Number(s): 9791450
Size: 14x6 inches
Usage: 1968 Olds Cutlass with disc brakes; 1968 Buick
Skylark with disc brakes; 1968 Pontiac LeMans with
disc brakes; 1968–72 Pontiac LeMans; 1969–72
Buick Skylark; 1970–72 Chevelle, except SS;
1970–72 Olds Cutlass; 1970–72 Pontiac Grand Prix
Notes: This is the standard painted wheel.

Interchange Number: 19
Part Number(s): 3984792
Size: 15x6 inches (1/16 inch offset)
Usage: 1968–70 full-size Chevrolet with disc brakes and
8.15x15 inch tires that are externally balanced

Interchange Number: 20
Part Number(s): 333274
Size: 14x6 inches (1/2 inch offset)
Usage: 1970–72 Camaro; 1970–72 Pontiac Firebird;
1971–72 Pontiac Ventura II; all with E78 or F78 tires
except cars with 4bbl
Notes: Stamped XJ.

Interchange Number: 21
Part Number(s): 3975667
Size: 14x7 inches (11/32 inch offset)
Usage: 1970–72 Camaro; 1970–72 Pontiac Firebird;
1971–72 Nova; 1971–72 Pontiac Grand Prix
Notes: Used with 4bbl equipped cars and F78 tires.
Stamped CL.

Interchange Number: 22
Part Number(s): 3918077
Size: 14x5 inches (1/2 inch offset)
Type: Rallye
Usage: 1967 Chevy II; 1967–68 Camaro; 1967–68
Chevelle; 1968 Nova; all with disc brakes Notes: Not
for SS-equipped Chevelle or Camaro. Stamped XA.

Interchange Number: 23
Part Number(s): 3918078
Size: 14x6 inches
Type: Rallye
Usage: 1967 Chevelle SS 396; 1968–69 Chevelle with
F70 tires; 1970 Chevelle, except El Camino

Interchange Number: 24
Part Number(s): 3998532
Size: 15x7 inches (9/32 inch offset)
Type: Five-spoke steel
Usage: 1970–72 Camaro Z-28; 1971–72 Chevelle SS;
1971–72 GMC Sprint

Interchange Number: 25
Part Number(s): 3975671

Size: 14x7 inches (13/32 inch offset)
Type: Super Sport (Magnum 500 style)
Usage: 1969 Camaro SS 350 or 396; 1969–70 Chevelle SS 396; 1969–70 Nova SS
Notes: Stamped AO.

Interchange Number: 26
Part Number(s): 3970530
Size: 14x7 inches
Type: Rallye wheel
Usage: 1969 Camaro; 1970 Nova
Notes: Stamped YJ.

Interchange Number: 27
Part Number(s): 334330
Size: 14x7 inches (11/32 inch offset)
Type: Rallye wheel
Usage: 1970–72 Camaro; 1971–72 Nova
Notes: Stamped AV.

Interchange Number: 28
Part Number(s): 3997899
Size: 15x7 inches (19/32 inch offset)
Type: Rallye wheel
Usage: 1968–69 Camaro with four-wheel disc brakes; 1969 Camaro Z-28; 1970–74 Monte Carlo; 1973–74 Chevelle
Notes: Stamped Z.

Interchange Number: 29
Part Number(s): 3938984
Size: 14x6 inches
Type: Rallye wheel
Usage: 1968–69 Camaro; 1968–70 El Camino

Interchange Number: 30
Part Number(s): 3968773
Size: 15x6 inches
Type: Rallye wheel
Usage: 1967–70 Impala; 1968–69 Camaro, except Z-28 or with four-wheel disc brakes

Wheel Covers

Wheel covers should not be confused with hubcaps. Hubcaps cover only the inner portion of the wheel and the lug nuts, while wheel covers hide the entire face of the wheel.

Wheel covers are identified by their design and size (diameter). Sometimes a cover can be slightly modified, such as changing the inner emblem, and it will still fit on another model. A description is given in the charts to help you identify the cover. If it can be adapted to another model, the modification is described under "Notes." The diameter given is for the wheel, not the cover itself.

Model Identification

Camaro ....Interchange Number
1967 except SS, mag, or wire 21
1967–69 SS 15
1967–69 mag 17
1967–68 wire 18
1968–69 six-spoke 23
1969–70 wire 24

1969–70 mag 35
1969–70 except SS, mag, or wire 38
1970 Deluxe cover...39
1970 ribbed 30

Chevelle ....Interchange Number
1964–66 wire cover 9
1966 except mag or wire 10
1967 except mag or wire 16
1968 except mag or wire 22
1967–68 mag 17
1967–68 wire 18
1968–69 six-spoke 23
1969–70 wire 24
1969 except mag or wire 25
1970 multi-ribbed 15 inch 29
1970 multi-ribbed 14 inch 30
1969–70 mag 35

Impala ....Interchange Number
1959 finned cover...1
1960 eight-spline...2
1961 deep-dish except Impala SS 3
1961 Impala SS..4
1962 twelve-spline except Impala SS 5
1962 Impala SS..6
1964–66 wire 9
1965–66 Impala SS...7
1965 except SS, wire, or mag 8
1966 except SS, wire, or mag 11
1967–69 mag 17
1967 except wire or mag 19
1967 Caprice 20
1968–69 six-spoke 23
1969–70 wire basket 24
1968 except six-spoke, wire, or mag 26
1968–69 15 inch 27
1968–70 wire 15 inch 28
1969–70 multi-ribbed 15 inch 29
1969–70 multi-ribbed 14 inch 30
1969 Deluxe cover 31
1968 mag 36
1969–70 mag 37

Chevy II/Nova ....Interchange Number
1962 twelve-spline..5
1964–66 wire 9
1965 except wire or Nova SS 12
1965 Nova SS...15
1966 except wire or Nova SS 12
1966 Nova SS...13
1967–69 mag 17
1967 except mag, wire, or Nova SS.......................................32
1967 Nova SS..7
1967–68 wire 18
1968 Nova except mag or wire 33
1968–69 six-spoke 23
1968–69 Deluxe cover..34
1969–70 wire 24
1969–70 mag 35
1970 ribbed 30

Interchange

Interchange Number: 1
Part Number(s): 3760050
Diameter: 14 inches
Description: Cross flags in center, bordered by eight splines dividing fin pattern.
Usage: 1959 full-size Chevrolet

Interchange Number: 2
Part Number(s): 3769530
Diameter: 14 inches
Description: Cross flags in center, bordered by solid chrome band. Outer diameter of cover features eight splines separating eight slots.
Usage: 1960 full-size Chevrolet

Interchange Number: 3
Part Number(s): 3783336
Diameter: 14 inches
Description: Plastic-covered model emblem reads "Chevrolet" sitting in deep-dish cover. Outer edge of cover has thirty divider bars.
Usage: 1961 full-size Chevrolet, except SS; 1961 Corvair
Notes: Interchange number 4 can be adapted to fit.

Interchange Number: 4
Part Number(s): 3787678
Diameter: 14 inches
Description: Features center tri-spoke center cap that is marked with bow-tie emblems. Outer edge has many small square slots.
Usage: 1961 Impala SS
Notes: Interchange number 3 can be adapted to fit. To Interchange between 3 and 4, change center caps accordingly.

Interchange Number: 5
Diameter: 14 inches
Description: Plastic cover center ID that features bow-tie emblem. Bordered by twelve bent "legs" that protrude from center cap.
Usage: 1962 full-size Chevrolet; 1962 Chevy II; 1962 Corvair
Notes: Interchange number 6 can be adapted to fit. See notes under Interchange number 6.

Interchange Number: 6
Part Number(s):
Diameter: 14 inches
Description: Tri-spoke center cap. Broader by twelve bent "legs" that protrude from the center cap.
Usage: 1962 Impala SS
Notes: Replace center ID cap with tri-spoke cap to Interchange between numbers 5 and 6.

Interchange Number: 7
Part Number(s): 3964523
Diameter: 14 inches
Description: Highlighted by a tri-bar "spinner" style center cap with the SS logo in the center.
Background of the spinner in a multi-fin pattern. On the outer edge of this pattern are twelve slots.
Usage: 1965–66 Impala SS; 1967 Nova SS.
Notes: 1965 Caprice cover will Interchange, but the Caprice center insert must be switched to the SS unit.

Interchange Number: 8
Part Number(s): 3860204
Diameter: 14 inches
Description: Plastic cover bow-tie emblem dominates the center dome. Circling the dome is a fine-finned pattern. Dividing the finned pattern are five small bars that connect to the outer rim of the cover.
Usage: 1965 full-size Chevrolet, except SS or Caprice; 1965 Corvair

Interchange Number: 9
Part Number(s): 3834904
Diameter: 14 inches
Description: Wire spoke wheel cover, with tri-spinner center cap.
Usage: 1964–66 full-size Chevrolet, Chevelle, Chevy II, or Corvair

Interchange Number: 10
Part Number(s): 3875041
Diameter: 14 inches
Description: Outer edge of cover is highlighted with two rows of elliptical-shaped slots. In the center is a bow-tie emblem that is surrounded by a starburst design. Between the slots and the center dome is a ribbed section.
Usage: 1966 Chevelle

Interchange Number: 11
Part Number(s): 3875029
Diameter: 14 inches
Description: Center section with bow-tie emblem deep inset. Highlighted on the outer edge by eight bars. In between these bars are small louvers.
Usage: 1966 full-size Chevrolet, except Impala SS or Caprice

Interchange Number: 12
Part Number(s): 3866210
Diameter: 14 inches
Description: Raised center ID dome with bow-tie emblem placed in inset starburst pattern. Outer edge of cover features thirty-two small square slots.
Usage: 1965 Chevy II, except Nova SS

Interchange Number: 13
Part Number(s): 3890162
Diameter: 14 inches
Description: Dominated by a tri-spinner looking center cap with the SS logo. Cap is placed over multi-louvers. The louvers are trimmed with chrome and painted flat black. Do not confuse it with 1965 Chevelle SS unit which does not have the trim louvers.
Usage: 1966 Nova SS

Interchange Number: 14
Part Number(s): 3876956
Diameter: 14 inches
Description: Louvered design dominates most of the cover. Center Chevy II ID logo.
Usage: 1966 Chevy II, except Nova SS

Interchange Number: 15

Part Number(s): 3871174

Diameter: 14 inches

Description: Dominated by a larger tri-bar "spinner" type cap. Bars run from ribbed cap that reads "SS" to other edge of cover. In between each set of bars are three elliptical slots.

Usage: 1965 Nova SS; 1968–69 Camaro SS

Interchange Number 16

Part Number(s): 3890691

Diameter: 14 inches

Description: Raised center dome holds model ID insert. Five spokes run from the dome to the outer edge of cover. In between the spokes is a ribbed section.

Usage: 1967 Chevelle (cover is same for all)

Notes: To Interchange, the inserts must be changed since they differ by model. The standard Chevelle used a bow-tie, the Concours a medallion, and the Super Sport read "SS."

Interchange Number: 17

Part Number(s): 3903086

Diameter: 14 inches

Description: Mag-style cover. Looks like five-spoke mag wheel. Has light grey spokes with bright-plated simulated lug nuts. Bow-tie symbol in the center hub.

Usage: 1967 Chevy II; 1967–69 Chevelle; 1967–69 Camaro; 1967–69 full-size Chevrolet; 1968–69 Nova;

Interchange Number: 18

Part Number(s): 3908761

Diameter: 14 inches

Description: Wire spoke wheel covers. Round center hub imprinted with bow-tie symbol and the words "Chevrolet Motor Division."

Usage: 1967 Chevy II; 1967–68 Chevelle; 1967–68 Camaro; 1968 Nova

Interchange Number: 19

Part Number(s): 3893358

Diameter: 14 inches

Description: Center model ID dome surrounded by twelve rectangular-shaped slots.

Usage: 1967 full-size Chevrolet, except Caprice

Notes: Cover is the same between SS and standard Chevrolet, but inserts must be changed to Interchange covers. Super Sport used the SS logo and the others used the bow-tie symbol.

Interchange Number: 20

Part Number(s): 3893350

Diameter: 14 inches

Description: High raised center dome with Caprice Medallion. The dome is supported by bent-down legs.

Usage: 1967 Caprice

Interchange Number: 21

Part Number(s): 3888699

Diameter: 14 inches

Description: Large center dome with bow-tie symbol. Three wide arms protrude from the dome to the inner outer edge of the cover. Between the arms are two elliptical slots.

Usage: 1967 Camaro

Interchange Number: 22

Part Number(s): 3918054

Diameter: 14 inches

Description: Very large center dome with model ID insert. Dome supports outer ring of cover by five small bars.

Usage: 1968 Chevelle

Notes: Insert differs between models. Super Sport reads "SS 396." Concours used a medallion, and the rest used a bow-tie symbol. Change insert to Interchange.

Interchange Number: 23

Part Number(s): 3918080

Diameter: 14 inches

Description: Six-spoke design. In between each set of spokes are two elliptical slots. The spokes run stem from a larger center dome that is imprinted with the words "Chevrolet Motor Division."

Usage: 1968–69 Chevelle, Camaro, Nova, or full-size Chevrolet

Interchange Number: 24

Part Number(s): 3957061

Diameter: 14 inches

Description: Simulated wire wheel basket. Large diameter wires protrude from center cap that is imprinted with the words "Chevrolet Motor Division."

The cap also features three small knobs.

Usage: 1969–70 Chevelle, Camaro, Nova, or full-size Chevrolet

Interchange Number: 25

Part Number(s): 3937879

Diameter: 14 inches

Description: Outer edge of cover is highlighted by thirty-two small slots. Main portion of cover is inset and smooth where it is attached to a center cap with eight small arms. Cap is imprinted with the words "Chevrolet Motor Division."

Usage: 1969 Chevelle, except SS 396

Interchange Number: 26

Part Number(s): 3916408

Diameter: 15 inches

Description: Very large center dome that is raised And supported by many small bent legs that attach it to outer ring of cover. In the middle of the Dome are the words "Chevrolet Motor Division" on smaller dome that is part of the larger dome.

Usage: 1968 full-size Chevrolet

Interchange Number: 27

Part Number(s): 3930774

Diameter: 15 inches

Description: Raised center cap with bow-tie in the middle of an inset portion of the cover. At the outer edge of the cover are several small slots.

Usage: 1968–69 full-size Chevrolet

Interchange Number: 28

Part Number(s): 3957059

Diameter: 15 inches

Description: Simulated wire wheel basket. Large diame-

ter wires protrude from center cap that is imprinted with the words "Chevrolet Motor Division." The cap also features three small knobs.
Usage: 1969–70 full-size Chevrolet

Interchange Number: 29
Part Number(s): 3963405
Diameter: 15 inches
Description: Multi-ribbed cover. Center cap with cross flags.
Usage: 1969–72 full-size Chevrolet; 1969–72 Corvette; 1970–72 Chevelle; 1971–72 Monte Carlo; 1971–72 Nova; 1971–72 Camaro

Interchange Number: 30
Part Number(s): 3972260
Diameter: 14 inches
Description: Multi-ribbed cover. Center cap with cross flags.
Usage: 1969–72 full-size Chevrolet (after 2-2-69); 1970–72 Nova; 1970–72 Camaro; 1970–72 Chevelle

Interchange Number: 31
Part Number(s): 3939273
Diameter: 14 inches
Description: Large ribbed dome dominates most of cover. In center of dome it is imprinted with a Bow-tie symbol and the words "Chevrolet Motor Division." Ribbed dome is connected to outer ring of cover with nine small bars.
Usage: 1969 full-size Chevrolet

Interchange Number: 32
Part Number(s): 3895218
Diameter: 14 inches
Description: Large center dome is made of several ring-shaped designs. Between the dome and the outer ring of the cover are ten elongated slots. Center of dome is bow-tie symbol.
Usage: 1967 Chevy II, except Nova SS

Interchange Number: 33
Part Number(s): 3923556
Diameter: 14 inches
Description: Center cap holds model name. Cap is placed in deep inset dome. Between dome and outer ring are thirty-two small oval-shaped slots.
Usage: 1968 Nova
Notes: All Novas used this wheel cover. Super Sport models used insert with SS logo, while other Novas used insert with the bow-tie symbol. Change insert accordingly to interchange.

Interchange Number: 34
Part Number(s): 3962724
Diameter: 14 inches
Description: Very large center dome that is raised and supported by many small bent legs that attach it to outer ring of cover. In the middle of the dome are the words "Chevrolet Motor Division" on smaller dome that is part of larger dome.
Usage: 1969–70 Nova

Interchange Number: 35
Part Number(s): 3963434
Diameter: 14 inches
Description: Five-spoke mag wheel style. Black spokes with trim around the outline, bright-plated simulated lug nuts. Center cap has bow-tie symbol.
Usage: 1969–72 Chevelle, Camaro, or Nova; 1970–72 Monte Carlo

Interchange Number: 36
Part Number(s): 3883390
Diameter: 14 inches
Description: Simulated five spokes. In between the spokes lay twin elliptical slots trimmed with chrome. Spokes connect to center dome that reads "Chevrolet Motor Division" and are supported by many small bent legs that attach it to outer ring of the cover. In the middle of the dome appear the same words on a smaller dome that is part of the larger one.
Usage: 1968 full-size Chevrolet

Interchange Number: 37
Part Number(s): 3968716
Diameter: 15 inches
Description: Five-spoke mag wheel style. Black Spokes with trim around the outline, bright-plated simulated lug nuts. Center cap has bow-tie symbol.
Usage: 1969–72 full-size Chevrolet

Interchange Number: 38
Part Number(s): 3925886
Diameter: 14 inches
Description: Large center raised dome dominates the cover. Dome is supported by five wide, bent-down legs that connect to the outer ring of the cover. In the middle of the dome is the bow-tie symbol.
Usage: 1969–70 Camaro, except SS

Interchange Number: 39
Part Number(s): 3980992
Diameter: 14 inches
Description: Outer edge of cover is ribbed; inward portion contains simulated five spokes that connect to center portion with bow-tie symbol.
Usage: 1970 Camaro with Deluxe wheel cover

Hubcaps for Styled Wheels
The hubcaps listed in the charts are not the standard dog-dish-style caps. These are not attractive on a show car, nor are they popular with restorers, so they are not included. Instead, the interchange information is for styled wheel hubcaps.

Model Identification

Interchange

Interchange Number: 1
Part Number(s): Cap, 3901715 cap; ornament,
   3901715
Type: Rallye
Description: Chrome-plated ornament; cap reads "disc
   brakes."
Usage: 1967 Chevelle; 1967 full-size Chevrolet
Notes: Used with 14 or 15 inch wheels.

Interchange Number: 2
Part Number(s): 3925801
Type: Rallye
Description: Die-cast brightly plated. Ribbed sides. Im-
   printed with "Chevrolet Motor Division."
Usage: 1968–72 Chevelle; 1968–72 Camaro; 1968–70
   Nova; 1970–72 Monte Carlo

Interchange Number: 3
Part Number(s): 3956770
Diameter: 14 inches
Type: Super Sport
Usage: 1968–70 Nova SS; 1968–70 Camaro SS 350 or
   SS 396; 1969–70 Chevelle SS 396
Notes: First design. Change in 1970. Attaches with re-
   tainer.

Interchange Number: 4
Part Number(s): 3983323
Description: Cap holds SS long insert.
Type: Super Sport
Usage: Late 1970 Chevelle SS 396 or Nova SS; Camaro
   SS 350 or SS 396
Notes: Second design. Attaches with three screws.

Interchange Number: 5
Part Number(s): 3989478
Description: Small cap has bow-tie symbol.
Type: Steel spoke (Z-28 type)
Usage: 1971–72 Chevelle or Nova; 1971–73 Camaro

Wheel Trim Rings

Model Identification

Interchange

Interchange Number: 1
Part Number(s): 3901704
Type: Rallye (15 inch)
Width: 1 3/4 inches
Usage: 1967 full-size Chevrolet; 1967–69 Camaro Z-28;
   1969 full-size Chevrolet; 1970 Monte Carlo

Interchange Number: 2
Part Number(s): 3901708
Type: Rallye (15x7 inch)
Width: 2 3/8x16 5/8 inch overall diameter
Usage: 1967–69 full-size Chevrolet;1967–69 Camaro;
   1970–72 Monte Carlo.

Interchange Number: 3
Part Number(s): 3923522
Type: Rallye (14x6 inch)
Width: 15 5/8 inch overall diameter; 1.86 inch offset
Usage: 1967–72, all models
Notes: Attaches with four clips.

Interchange Number: 4
Part Number(s): 3934892
Type: Rallye (14x7 inch)
Width: 15 5/8 inch overall diameter; 2.24 inch offset
Usage: 1968–72, all models

Interchange Number: 5
Part Number(s): 9796919
Type: Super Sport (14 inch)
Usage: 1968–70 Chevelle, Camaro, or Nova, all with SS
   wheels; 1969–72 Pontiac Firebird; 1969–72 Pontiac
   Grand Prix; 1972 Pontiac GTO; all Pontiacs with Ral-
   lye II wheels; 1970–72 Olds Cutlass with SS wheels;
   1972 Buick Skylark with Rallye wheels

Interchange Number: 6
Part Number(s): 3984524
Type: Steel spoke (15x7 inch)
Usage: 1971–72 Chevelle; 1971–73 Camaro or Nova;
   all with SS package or Z-28 Camaro

Chapter 9

Electrical System

Starter

Chevrolet's starter motor is a GM-built unit that can be found on many different GM models, so there is ample interchange. Starters can be identified by a number stamped on the side of the housing. While a starter may "physically fit," it may not have enough power to properly turn over a high-performance engine. The rule when interchanging is that the output should be the same as or greater than the original unit. A starter that is able to start a car in the summertime may not prove as capable in the middle of a cold Midwest winter.

Some motors will be stamped with an ID number on the housing. This number can be used for identification. (When the number is known, it is stated in the chart.)

Model Identification

Starters are stamped with their part number.

Interchange

Interchange Number: 1
Part Number(s): 1108361
ID Number(s): 1107320, 1108361
Usage: 1965–68 Chevelle 327ci; 1967 Camaro 327ci;1968 full-size Chevrolet 327ci without heavy-duty clutch or Turbo Hydra-Matic; 1968–69 Nova 327 or 350ci, except premium fuel; 1969 Chevelle or Camaro 350ci (except with regular fuel) with Powerglide or first-design Turbo Hydra-Matic 350; 1969 full-size Chevrolet 350ci automatic, except Turbo Hydra-Matic 400

Interchange Number: 2
ID Number(s): 1107242
Usage: 1962–64 full-size Chevrolet 327ci automatic
Notes: Interchange number 1 will fit, but this Interchange will not fit post-1965 models.

Interchange Number: 3
Part Number(s): 1108366
ID Number(s): 1108365,1108366,1108367

Usage: 1962–64 Chevelle; 1962–64 Chevy II; 1965–67 Chevelle or Chevy II, all but 327 or 396ci; 1965–69 full-size Chevrolet six-cylinder 283ci V-8 or 307ci V-8, all without AIR, or heavy-duty clutch, or Turbo Hydra-Matic 400; 1967–69 Camaro, except 350 or 396ci; 1968 Nova, all except 350 or 396ci; 1968–71 Buick Skylark six-cylinder; 1970–73 Camaro, Chevelle, Nova, Impala, C-10 Chevy pickup, C-10 GMC pickup, C-10 Chevy van, all six-cylinder or 307ci; 1970–73 Pontiac Firebird six-cylinder; 1971–74 Pontiac Ventura II six-cylinder or 307ci; 1973–74 Olds Omega six-cylinder or 307ci; 1973–74 Buick Apollo six-cylinder

Notes: Interchange number 4 will fit and provide for more starting power.

Interchange Number: 4
Part Number(s): 1108400
ID Number(s): 1107365, 1108338, 1108382, 1108400, 1108418
Usage: 1959–61 full-size Chevrolet 348 or 283ci; 1962–65 full-size Chevrolet 409ci; 1965–68 full-size Chevrolet 396 or 427ci; 1965–68 Chevelle 396ci; 1967–68 Camaro 396ci; 1967–69 full-size Chevrolet Turbo Hydra-Matic 400; 1968 Nova 396ci; 1969 Camaro or Chevelle 350ci 4bbl; 1969 full-size Chevrolet 350 4bbl; 1969 Camaro, Chevelle, Nova, Impala, or C-10 Chevy pickup, all 396 or 427ci; 1970–71 C-10 Blazer 350ci automatic; 1970–72 Impala manual; 1970–72 Camaro, Chevelle, or Nova V-8, except 307ci; 1970–74 Monte Carlo
Notes: This unit will fit smaller engines like the regular 350 2bbl and 283, and provide for more cranking power and faster starts. Great for a modified 350ci. Should not be used with special high-performance 396 (375hp) or 427ci (425hp).

Interchange Number: 5
Part Number(s): 1108350
ID Number(s): 1108350
Usage: All with heavy-duty battery in 1969—standard on 396ci 375hp and 427ci 425hp; 1969–70 C-10 van or pickup with heavy-duty battery

Interchange Number: 6
Part Number(s): 11880420
ID Number(s): 1108420
Usage: 1969 Nova, Chevelle, or full-size Chevrolet; all with second-design Turbo Hydra-Matic 350
Notes: Used with 12-3/4 inch ring gear.

Distributor Housing

The unit described here is a bare distributor housing without cap, breaker plate, points, condenser, or vacuum control. Engine size and output, and in some cases emission controls, will have an effect on distributor interchange.

Distributors are grouped together under their replacement part number. Identification numbers, stamped on a band on the distributor housing itself, can be used to identify the assembly, but should not be relied on since more than one ID number can be used in the same interchange.

Model Identification

CAMARO/CHEVELLE/IMPALA/NOVA/CHEVY II

Engine ....Interchange Number
283ci
1959–65 1
1966–67 without AIR..2
1966–67 with AIR 3
327ci
1962...5
1963–64...6
1965–67 without AIR except special high-performance 7
1965–67 with special high-performance.........................13
1968–69 2bbl manual 8
1968–69 2bbl automatic 9
1968 250hp...2
1968 275hp manual 10
1968 275hp automatic 11
1968 325hp...12
348ci
1959–61 20
350ci
1968–70 4bbl with manual except 1970 Z-28 16
1968–70 4bbl with automatic except 1970 Z-28 17
1969–70 2bbl with manual.................................18
1969–70 2bbl with automatic 19
1970 Z-28..32
396ci
1965 except 425hp or with transistor ignition.................25
1965 425hp without transistor ignition 24
1965–66 375hp without transistor ignition 24
1965–68 375hp with transistor ignition 26
1966–69 325hp without transistor ignition 27
1966–68 325hp with transistor ignition 33
1966–68 350hp except transistor ignition 27
1966–68 350hp with transistor ignition 33
1967–70 375hp except transistor ignition 28
1967–68 350hp except transistor ignition 28
1969 350hp automatic 28
1969–70 350hp manual......................................29
409ci
1962–65 without transistor ignition except with high-performance or multi-carbs 20
1963–65 with transistor ignition except with high-performance or multi-carbs 22
1963–65 without transistor ignition with high-performance or multi-carbs 21
1963–65 with transistor ignition with high-performance or multi-carbs...23
427ci
1966 425hp without transistor ignition 24
1966–68 425hp with transistor ignition........................26
1966–69 390hp without transistor ignition 27
1966–68 390hp with transistor ignition.........................33
1967–69 425hp except transistor ignition 28
1969 335hp 27
454ci
1970 except 450hp 30
1970 450hp 31

123

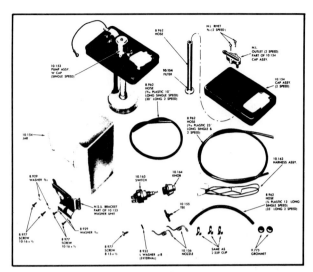

Washer jar for 1964–69 models.

Interchange

Interchange Number: 1
Part Number(s): 1111015
ID Number(s): 1110946, 1110947, 1111015
Usage: 1959–65 283ci V-8

Interchange Number: 2
Part Number(s): 1111500
ID Number(s): 1111150
Usage: 1966–67 283ci without AIR; 1968 Impala 327ci 250hp

Interchange Number: 3
Part Number(s): 1111256
ID Number(s): 1111256
Usage: 1966–67 283ci V-8 with AIR

Interchange Number: 4
Part Number(s): 1111480
ID Number(s): 1111480, 1111467
Usage: 1967–69 Z-28 302ci

Interchange Number: 5
Part Number(s): 1110987
ID Number(s): 1110987
Usage: 1962 full-size Chevrolet 327ci

Interchange Number: 6
Part Number(s): 1111016
ID Number(s): 1111016
Usage: 1963–64 327ci

Interchange Number: 7
Part Number(s): 1111249
ID Number(s): 1111107, 1111249, 1111152, 1111193
Usage: 1965–67 327ci without AIR except 350 or 360hp versions

Interchange Number: 8
Part Number(s): 1111482
ID Number(s): 1111482, 1111440
Usage: 1968–69 Camaro 327ci 2bbl manual

Interchange Number: 9
Part Number(s): 1111443
ID Number(s): 1111443
Usage: 1968 Camaro 327ci 2bbl automatic

Interchange Number: 10
Part Number(s): 1111298
ID Number(s): 1111298
Usage: 1968 327ci 275hp 4bbl manual

Interchange Number: 11
Part Number(s): 1111297
ID Number(s): 1111297
Usage: 1968 327 275hp 4bbl automatic

Interchange Number: 12
Part Number(s): 1111478
ID Number(s): 1111478
Usage: 1968 327ci 325hp

Interchange Number: 13
Part Number(s): 1111195
ID Number(s): 1111195, 1111154, 1111108, 1111071
Usage: 1965–66 Chevelle 327ci 350hp; 1967 Chevelle or Chevy II 327ci 325hp

Interchange Number: 14
Part Number(s): 1111995
ID Number(s): 1111995, 1111439, 1111257
Usage: 1968–70 307ci manual; 1969 327ci

Interchange Number: 15
Part Number(s): 1112005
ID Number(s): 1112005, 1111483
Usage: 1968–70 307ci automatic; 1971–72 350ci 2bbl

Interchange Number: 16
Part Number(s): 1111996
ID Number(s): 1111996, 1111488, 1111264
Usage: 1968–70 350ci 4bbl manual, except 1970 Z-28

Interchange Number: 17
Part Number(s): 1111997
ID Number(s): 1111997, 1111489, 1111265
Usage: 1968–70 350ci 4bbl automatic, except 1970 Z-28 or 225hp version in 1969 Impala

Interchange Number: 18
Part Number(s): 1112001
ID Number(s): 1112001, 1111486
Usage: 1969–70 350ci 2bbl manual

Interchange Number: 19
Part Number(s): 1112002
ID Number(s): 1111487, 1112002
Usage: 1969–70 350ci 2bbl automatic

Interchange Number: 20
Part Number(s): 1111023
ID Number(s): 1111023, 1111006, 1110948, 1110919
Usage: 1959–61 348ci; 1962–65 409ci without twin 4bbl or high-performance package, or with transistor ignition

Interchange Number: 21
Part Number(s): 1111085
ID Number(s): 1111085

Usage: 1963–65 409ci with twin 4bbl or high-performance package, but without transistor ignition

Interchange Number: 22
Part Number(s): 1111059
ID Number(s): 1111059
Usage: 1963–65 409ci with transistor ignition, except with two 4bbl or high-performance package

Interchange Number: 23
Part Number(s): 1111086
ID Number(s): 1111086
Usage: 1963–65 409ci with twin 4bbl or high-performance package and with transistor ignition

Interchange Number: 24
Part Number(s): 1111100
ID Number(s): 1111100,
Usage: 1965 396ci 425hp; 1965–66 396ci 375hp; 1966 427ci 425hp; all without transistor ignition

Interchange Number: 25
Part Number(s): 1111098
ID Number(s): 1111098
Usage: 1965 Impala 396ci, except 425hp or with transistor ignition

Interchange Number: 26
Part Number(s): 1111074
ID Number(s): 1111074
Usage: 1965–66 396ci 375hp; 1965 396ci 425hp; 1966 427ci 425hp; all with transistor ignition

Interchange Number: 27
Part Number(s): 1111497
ID Number(s): 1111497,1111169,1111109,1111073
Usage: 1965–69 396ci, except 375hp or with transistor ignition; 1967–69 427ci, except 425hp

Interchange Number: 28
Part Number(s): 1111499
ID Number(s): 1111499,1111278,1111170,1111138, 1111112
Usage: 1967–70 396ci 375hp; 1967–68 396ci 350hp; 1969 396ci 350hp automatic; 1967–69 427ci 425hp; 1966 427ci 390hp without transistor ignition

Interchange Number: 29
Part Number(s): 1111999
ID Number(s): 1111999, 1111498, 1111445
Usage: 1969 396ci 350hp manual; 1970 396ci (402) 350hp manual

Interchange Number: 30
Part Number(s): 1111963
ID Number(s): 1111963
Usage: 1970 454ci, except 450hp

Interchange Number: 31
Part Number(s): 1111437
ID Number(s): 1111437
Usage: 1970 454ci 450hp

Interchange Number: 32
Part Number(s): 1112019
ID Number(s): 1112019

Usage: 1970 Camaro Z-28 350ci 360hp
Notes: No other interchange.

Interchange Number: 33
Part Number(s): 1111137
ID Number(s): 1111137
Usage: 1966–68 396ci 325hp or 350hp with transistor ignition

Ignition Coil

Only three ignition coils were used, making for an easy interchange. The type depends on whether the ignition system is regular or transistorized. *Never* use a regular coil on a transistorized ignition system, or vice versa. A coil can be identified by the number stamped on it.

Model Identification

CAMARO/CHEVELLE/IMPALA/NOVA/CHEVY II

Year	Interchange Number
1959–64	1
1965–70 without transistor ignition	2
1964–67 with transistor ignition	3

Interchange

Interchange Number: 1
Part Number(s): 1115202
ID Number(s): 202-12V
Usage: 1955–64, all except with transistor ignition (includes Chevrolet, Oldsmobile [up to 1963], Buick [up to 1974], and Pontiac [up to 1961])
Notes: Also used on 1964–72 Chevrolet six-cylinder; 1964–68 Pontiac six-cylinder; and on 1971–74 Pontiac 250ci six-cylinder.

Interchange Number: 2
Part Number(s): 1115238
ID Number(s): 238-BR
Usage: 1963–72 Pontiac V-8 with standard ignition; 1964–72 V-8 Chevrolet, except with transistor ignition; 1964–72 Oldsmobile V-8, except with UHV ignition (Ultra High Voltage); 1974 Buick V-8, except with pointless ignition

Interchange Number: 3
Part Number(s): 1115207
ID Number(s): 176-12V
Usage: 1964–66 Pontiac transistor ignition; 1964–67 V-8 Chevrolet with transistor ignition

Alternator and Generator

Chevrolet used a generator until the 1962 model year. The alternator's ability to provide more power when needed and on a steadier basis made the generator obsolete. Many people still refer to the alternator as a generator, even in service manuals, but the two are not interchangeable, so don't confuse them. Both are easily recognized by their shape and design.

The generator can be found in a long, round housing that uses an armature to create a DC electric current to recharge the battery as the energy is used. The alternator is usually contained in a round, aluminum two-piece housing that creates an AC current which is rectified to run the car's electrical system.

Both the alternator and the generator are identified by a number stamped on the housing. There are different levels (outputs) of alternators and generators. If you've added more accessories to your car than what came as original equipment, then a higher output unit could be a wise interchange. Part number, ID number, and output are given in the charts. Interchange is based on the part number.

Generator

Model Identification

CAMARO/CHEVELLE/IMPALA/NOVA

Year and Type	Interchange Number
1959–64 30 amp	1
1959–62 35 amp	2
1959 35 amp with power steering	6, 7
1959–62 40 amp	4
1959 40 amp with power steering	5
1959–62 50 amp	3

Interchange

Interchange Number: 1
Part Number(s): 1102110
Output: 30 amp
ID Number(s): 110210, 1102096, 1120292, 1102087, 1102086, 1102082, 1106069, 1102067, 1102061, 11020251, 1102053, 61-U, 97-U
Usage: 1957–60 Oldsmobile without power steering or a/c; 1958–64 Chevrolet, all engines, all models without power steering or a/c; 1959–62 Pontiac without power steering or a/c
Notes: Has rubber mounts.

Interchange Number: 2
Part Number(s): 1102195
Output: 35 amp
ID Number(s): 1102268, 1102173, 38U
Usage: 1959–61 348ci with high-lift cam; 1960–62 with power steering 1962 409ci
Notes: Solid mount. Dual ball bearing end frames. Last two ID numbers are for rebuilt units.

Interchange Number: 3
Part Number(s): 1106681
Output: 50 amp, low-cut type
ID Number(s): 1106681
Usage: 1959–62 full-size Chevrolet or pickup with a/c

Interchange Number: 4
Part Number(s): 1105123
Output: 40 amp
ID Number(s): 1105123
Usage: 1959–62 Chevrolet, except with power steering in 1959
Notes: Optional unit from base 30 amp unit.

Interchange Number: 5
Part Number(s): 1105124
Output: 40 amp
ID Number(s): 1105124
Usage: 1959 full-size Chevrolet with gear drive power steering

Interchange Number: 6
Part Number(s): 1102084
Output: 35 amp
ID Number(s): 1102084
Usage: 1959 full-size Chevrolet with gear drive power steering; standard unit with power steering

Interchange Number: 7
Part Number(s): 1105118
Output: 35 amp, low-cut type
ID Number(s): 1105118
Usage: 1959 full-size with gear drive power steering; requires special regulator

Alternator

Interchanging factors for alternators include the output range and the original factory-installed options on the car. Dealer-installed options such as air conditioning may have required a different alternator that would have come from the factory. As is the norm, interchange is based on the original part number. When and if a change was made during the model year, the date of the change is given, if known, in the charts. In most cases, the part number is the same as the identification number. From 1962 to 1964 the alternator was optional, and from 1965 on it was standard.

Model Identification

CAMARO/CHEVELLE/IMPALA/NOVA/CHEVY II

Year and Type	Interchange Number
1962, 42-amp	1, 2
1962, 52-amp	3, 4
1962, 62-amp	5, 6
1963, 32-amp	7
1963, 42-amp	8
1963, 52-amp	9
1964, 32-amp	10
1964, 37-amp	11
1964, 42-amp	12
1964, 55-amp	13
1964, 60-amp	14
1965–67, 37-amp	15
1965–67, 42-amp	16
1965, 55-amp	17
1965, 60-amp	18
1966, 62-amp	20
1967, 61-amp	19
1967, 62-amp	21
1968, 37-amp	22, 23, 24
1968, 42-amp	25
1968, 61-amp	26, 27
1969–70, 37-amp	28, 29, 30
1969–70, 42-amp	31
1969–70, 61-amp	32

Interchange

Interchange Number: 1
Part Number(s): 1100613
Output: 42-amp
ID Number(s): 1100613
Usage: 1962 full-size Chevrolet or Chevy II
Notes: Until 2-23-62. Standard with a/c until same date.

Interchange Number: 2
Part Number(s): 1100620
Output: 42-amp
ID Number(s): 1100620
Usage: 1962 full-size Chevrolet or Chevy II
Notes: After 2-23-62. Standard with a/c after same date. Will interchange number with 1.

Interchange Number: 3
Part Number(s): 1100600
Output: 52-amp
ID Number(s): 1100600
Usage: 1962 full-size Chevrolet or Chevy II
Notes: Until 2-23-62. Interchange number 4 will fit.

Interchange Number: 4
Part Number(s): 1100615
Output: 52-amp
ID Number(s): 1100615
Usage: 1962 full-size Chevrolet or Chevy II
Notes: After 2-23-62. Interchange number 3 will fit.

Interchange Number: 5
Part Number(s): 1100601
Output: 62-amp
ID Number(s): 1100601
Usage: 1962 full-size Chevrolet or Chevy II
Notes: Until 2-23-62.

Interchange Number: 6
Part Number(s): 1100618
Output: 62-amp
ID Number(s): 1100618
Usage: 1962 full-size Chevrolet or Chevy II
Notes: After 2-23-62.

Interchange Number: 7
Part Number(s): 1100630
Output: 32-amp
ID Number(s): 1100630
Usage: 1963 full-size Chevrolet or Chevy II

Interchange Number: 8
Part Number(s): 1100629
Output: 42-amp
ID Number(s): 1100629
Usage: 1963 full-size Chevrolet or Chevy II; 1963 C-10 Chevrolet pickup
Notes: Standard unit with a/c.

Interchange Number: 9
Part Number(s): 1100633
Output: 52-amp
ID Number(s): 1100633
Usage: 1963 full-size Chevrolet or Chevy II

Interchange Number: 10
Part Number(s): 1100670
Output: 32-amp
ID Number(s): 1100670
Usage: 1964 full-size Chevrolet, Chevy II, or Chevelle

Interchange Number: 11
Part Number(s): 1100668
Output: 37-amp
ID Number(s): 1100668
Usage: 1964 full-size Chevrolet, Chevy II, or Chevelle; 1964 Pontiac Tempest

Interchange Number: 12
Part Number(s): 1100669
Output: 42-amp
ID Number(s): 1100669
Usage: 1964 full-size Chevrolet, Chevy II, or Chevelle, all with a/c

Interchange Number: 13
Part Number(s): 1100665
Output: 55-amp
ID Number(s): 1100665
Usage: 1964 full-size Chevrolet, Chevy II, or Chevelle; 1964 Pontiac Tempest

Interchange Number: 14
Part Number(s): 1100684
Output: 60-amp
ID Number(s): 1100684
Usage: 1964 full-size Chevrolet; 1964 Pontiac with transistor ignition and a/c

Interchange Number: 15
Part Number(s): 1100693
Output: 37-amp
ID Number(s): 1100693
Usage: 1965–67 full-size Chevrolet, Chevy II, or Chevelle; 1967 Camaro

Interchange Number: 16
Part Number(s): 1100696
Output: 42-amp
ID Number(s): 1100696
Usage: 1965–67 full-size Chevrolet, Chevy II, or Chevelle; 1967 Camaro
Notes: Use with a/c.

Interchange Number: 17
Part Number(s): 1100694
Output: 55-amp
ID Number(s): 1100694
Usage: 1965 full-size Chevrolet, Chevy II, or Chevelle

Interchange Number: 18
Part Number(s): 1100697
Output: 60-amp
ID Number(s): 1100697
Usage: 1965–67 full-size Chevrolet; 1965–67 Pontiac
Notes: Uses with 396 and 427ci standard in 1966.

Interchange Number: 19
Part Number(s): 1100750
Output: 61-amp

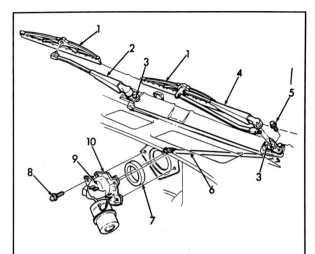

1970-72 CHEVELLE WINDSHIELD WIPER MOTOR, TRANS. ROD & BLADE ASSY.

1.	10.146	BLADE ASSY	3913614
2.	10.147	ROD ASSY. R.H.	3913612
3.	8.908	SCREW ASSY.' (10 - 24 x 1/2)	
4.	10.147	ROD ASSY. L. H.	3913613
5.	8.900	SCREW ASSY. (1/4 - 20 x 5/16)	
6.	10.159	TRAN. & MOTOR DRIVE	
		LINK ASSY. R.H.	4918758
	10.159	TRANS. & CONN. LINK ASSY.	
		L.H. (EXC. CONN. LINK ASSY.)	
		L.H. (Spec. (w/w)	4918624
	10.159	TRANS. & CONN. LINK ASSY.	
		L.H. (Exc. Spec. w/w)	4918620
7.	10.152	GASKET	542675
8.	8.908	SCREW ASSY. (10 - 24 x 3/4)	
9.	10.150	MOTOR ASSY.	4939586
10.	10.153	PUMP ASSY..	4918180

ID Number(s): 1100750
Usage: 1967 full-size Chevrolet; 1967 Camaro

Interchange Number: 20
Part Number(s): 1117754
Output: 62-amp
ID Number(s): 1117754
Usage: 1966 full-size Chevrolet, Chevy II, or Chevelle

Interchange Number: 21
Part Number(s): 1117767
Output: 62-amp
ID Number(s): 1117767
Usage: 1967 full-size Chevrolet and Chevelle; 1968 full-size Chevrolet, Chevelle, Camaro, or Nova

Interchange Number: 22
Part Number(s): 1100693
Output: 37-amp
ID Number(s): 1100693
Usage: 1968 full-size Chevrolet, Chevelle, Camaro, or Nova

Interchange Number: 23
Part Number(s): 1100813
Output: 37-amp
ID Number(s): 1100813
Usage: 1968 full-size Chevrolet, Chevelle, Camaro, or Nova; all with dual-groove pulley.
Notes: Will fit interchange number 22. Will fit interchange number 24 if pulleys are swapped.

Interchange Number: 24
Part Number(s): 1100794
Output: 37-amp
ID Number(s): 1100794
Usage: 1968 full-size Chevrolet, Chevelle, Camaro, or Nova; all with single-groove pulley.
Notes: Will fit interchanges 22 or 23 if pulleys are switched.

Interchange Number: 25
Part Number(s): 1100696
Output: 42-amp
ID Number(s): 1100696, 1100795
Usage: 1968 full-size Chevrolet, Chevelle, Camaro, or Nova

Interchange Number: 26
Part Number(s): 1100796
Output: 61-amp
ID Number(s): 1100796
Usage: 1968 full-size Chevrolet, Chevelle, Camaro, or Nova; all with single-groove pulley
Notes: Will fit interchange number 27 if pulleys are switched.

Interchange Number: 27
Part Number(s): 1100817
Output: 61-amp
ID Number(s): 1100817
Usage: 1968 full-size Chevrolet, Chevelle, Camaro, or Nova; all with dual-groove pulley
Notes: Used when K76 and C60 are ordered together. Will fit interchange number 26.

Interchange Number: 28
Part Number(s): 1100837
Output: 37-amp
ID Number(s): 1100837
Usage: 1969 Impala SS 427; 1969 Nova 396ci 375hp; 1969 Camaro Z-28; 1969–70 Chevelle SS 396ci 375hp; 1970–71 Chevelle SS 454 with 450 or 425hp (LS-6 option); all with single-groove pulley
Notes: Will fit interchange number 29. Will fit interchange number 30 if pulleys are swapped.

Interchange Number: 29
Part Number(s): 1100834
Output: 37-amp
ID Number(s): 1100834
Usage: 1969–70 full-size Chevrolet, Chevelle, Camaro, or Nova (all except 1969 302ci, 1969–70 396ci 375hp, and 1970 350ci in Camaro); all with single-groove pulley
Notes: Will fit interchange number 28. Will fit interchange number 30 if pulleys are swapped.

Interchange Number: 30
 Part Number(s): 1100836
 Output: 37-amp
 ID Number(s): 1100836
 Usage: 1969–70 full-size Chevrolet, Chevelle, Camaro, or Nova; all with dual-groove pulley
 Notes: Will fit interchange number 28 or 29.

Interchange Number: 31
 Part Number(s): 1100842
 Output: 42-amp
 ID Number(s): 1100842
 Usage: 1969–70 Chevelle or Nova; 1969 full-size Chevrolet

Interchange Number: 32
 Part Number(s): 1100843
 Output: 61-amp
 ID Number(s): 1100843
 Usage: 1969–70 full-size Chevrolet, Chevelle, Camaro, or Nova; all with V-8
 Notes: Those with six-cylinder and 61-amp unit will not interchange.

Regulator

The type of regulator chosen as an interchange depends upon the type of charging accessory (alternator or generator) and the output of the alternator or generator. Regulators are identified by a number stamped on them. Also, note that the regulator is a GM part and can be found on a variety of GM makes and models. For further identification, see the listings for "Generator" or "Alternator."

Model Identification

CAMARO/CHEVELLE/IMPALA/NOVA/CHEVY II

Year and Model	Interchange Number
1959–62 30-amp generator	1
1959–62 35-amp generator	2
1959–62 50-amp generator	3
1959–62 40-amp generator	4

Air conditioning compressor.

1959–62 60-amp alternator	5
1962–70 alternator, except 62 or 63-amp	6
1963–70 62-amp alternator	7
1963–70 63-amp alternator	8

Interchange

Interchange Number: 1
 Type of Charging System: Generator
 Part Number(s): 1119261
 ID Number(s): 1119663, 1119003, 1119261
 Usage: 1956–62 GM models with 30-amp generator

Interchange Number: 2
 Type of Charging System: Generator
 Part Number(s): 1118956
 ID Number(s): 1119604, 1119618, 118956
 Usage: 1956–62 GM models with 35-amp generator

Interchange Number: 3
 Type of Charging System: Generator

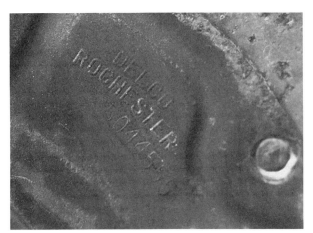

Heater motor is identified by a part number stamped on the outer case. Code includes assembly plant as well. This motor was made at the Rochester plant.

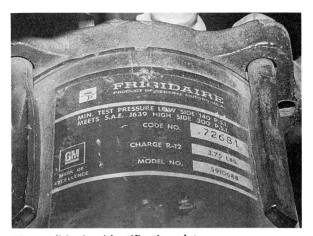

Air conditioning identification plate.

Part Number(s): 1119619
ID Number(s): 1119619
Usage: 1958 Pontiac with 45-amp generator; 1959–61 Chevrolet with 50-amp generator

Interchange Number: 4
Type of Charging System: Generator
Part Number(s): 1119610
ID Number(s): 1119610
Usage: 1957 Pontiac with 40-amp generator; 1959–61 Chevrolet with 40-amp generator

Interchange Number: 5
Type of Charging System: Alternator
Part Number(s): 9000554
ID Number(s): 9000554
Usage: 1959–61 Chevrolet with 60-amp alternator; 1961–62 Oldsmobile with 60-amp alternator
Notes: Regulator is transistorized type.

Interchange Number: 6
Type of Charging System: Alternator
Part Number(s): 1119515
ID Number(s): 1119515, 1119512, 1119506
Usage: 1962–72 GM models with alternator, except with 62 or 63-amp alternators

Interchange Number: 7
Type of Charging System: Alternator
Part Number(s): 1116378
ID Number(s): 1116378, 1116368
Usage: 1963–70 GM models with 62-amp alternator

Interchange Number: 8
Type of Charging System: Alternator
Part Number(s): 1119519
ID Number(s): 1119519
Usage: 1965–68 Corvair with 45-amp alternator; 1966 Impala SS 396 or SS 427; 1967 full-size Chevrolet Turbo Hydra-Matic 400 with a/c; 1970–71 Chevelle, Monte Carlo, Buick Skylark and Buick LeSabre, all with 63-amp alternator; 1970–72 Oldsmobile with 63-amp alternator

Battery Tray

Model Identification

Interchange

Interchange Number: 1
Part Number(s): 3794016
Usage: 1959–63 full-size Chevrolet; 1962–67 Chevy II

Interchange Number: 2
Part Number(s): 3848270
Usage: 1964–65 full-size Chevrolet or Chevelle

Interchange Number: 3
Part Number(s): 3893882
Usage: 1966 full-size Chevrolet; 1966 Chevelle; 1967–69 Camaro; 1967–69 Pontiac Firebird

Interchange Number: 4
Part Number(s): 3895138
Usage: 1967 full-size Chevrolet or Chevelle

Interchange Number: 5
Part Number(s): 3915471
Usage: 1968 full-size Chevrolet, 1968–72 Chevelle

Interchange Number: 6
Part Number(s): 3916658
Usage: 1968–72 Nova; 1971–72 Pontiac Ventura II

Interchange Number: 7
Part Number(s): 3938000
Usage: 1969 full-size Chevrolet

Interchange Number: 8
Part Number(s): 3957233
Usage: 1970 full-size Chevrolet

Interchange Number: 9
Part Number(s): 3967157
Usage: 1970–72 Camaro

Windshield Wiper Motor

Several different types of windshield wiper motors were used by Chevrolet. Interchange variables include the number of blade speeds and the type. Concealed and non-concealed wipers are not interchangeable. Concealed wipers became available on 1968 models. They were standard on the higher trim models like the Malibu, and optional on the lower trim models. Concealed wipers differed from the non-concealed type in that the resting position of the blades was underneath the rear edge of the hood. The motor itself was responsible for the positioning of the wipers, not the hood.

Wiper motors are stamped with an identification number. Using these and the accompanying photographs, you can identify a particular wiper motor.

Model Identification

Interchange

Interchange Number: 1
Motor Type: Single-speed
Part Number(s): 4907734 (replacement)
ID Number(s): 5045283 (1961 unit)
Usage: 1959–61 full-size Chevrolet; 1959–61 Oldsmobile;1959–61 Buick;1959–61Pontiac
Notes: Not *all* original units will interchange. Most later units will fit earlier models but not vice versa. Part number is for 1961 unit.

Interchange Number: 2
Motor Type: Single-speed
Part Number(s): 4909555
Usage: 1962 full-size Chevrolet

Interchange Number: 3
Motor Type: Two-speed
Part Number(s): 4909107
ID Number(s): 4760468
Usage: 1959–62 full-size Chevrolet; 1961–62 Olds Delta 88

Interchange Number: 4
Motor Type: Single-speed
Part Number(s): 4910214
Usage: 1962 Chevy II; 1962 Corvair

Interchange Number: 5
Motor Type: Two-speed
Part Number(s): 4910144
Usage: 1962 Chevy II; 1962 Corvair

Interchange Number: 6
Motor Type: Two-speed
Part Number(s): 4911476
ID Number(s): 4911476, 5045430, 5045508, 5045462, 9899321

Usage: 1963–67 Chevy II; 1965–67 Chevelle; 1967 Camaro

Interchange Number: 7
Motor Type: Two-speed
Part Number(s): 4914164
ID Number(s): 4914164, 5044594
Usage: 1964 Chevelle (round type)

Interchange Number: 8
Motor Type: Single-speed
Part Number(s): 4911945
ID Number(s): 4911945, 5045325
Usage: 1963–65 Chevy II; 1963–65 Corvair; 1964–65 Chevelle; 1964–65 Olds Cutlass; 1964–65 Buick Skylark; 1964–65 Pontiac Tempest

Interchange Number: 9
Motor Type: Single-speed
Part Number(s): 4911528
ID Number(s): 4911528, 9994599
Usage: 1963–65 full-size Chevrolet

Interchange Number: 10
Motor Type: Two-speed
Part Number(s): 4917639
ID Number(s): 5044626, 5044670, 4917639
Usage: 1967 full-size Chevrolet
Notes: No other interchange.

Interchange Number: 11
Motor Type: 4918342
Part Number(s): Two-speed concealed wipers
ID Number(s): 9822412
Usage: 1968–72 full-size Chevrolet; 1968–72 full-size Buick; 1968–72 full-size Oldsmobile; 1968–72 full-size Pontiac; 1968–72 Cadillac
Notes: This unit was used in early 1973 production models, including midsize GM models. Approximate date of change is 1-1-73.

Interchange Number: 12
Motor Type: Two-speed concealed wipers
Part Number(s): 4939586

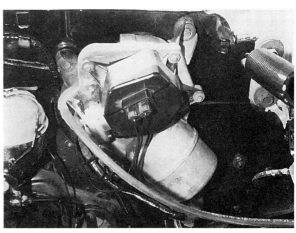

A 1969–70 two-speed wiper motor with concealed blades.

Usage: 1968–72 Chevelle; 1968–72 Pontiac LeMans; 1968–72 Olds Cutlass without shaft lever control; 1968–72 Buick Skylark without shaft lever control; 1970–72 Camaro; 1970–72 Monte Carlo; 1970–72 Pontiac Firebird; 1970–72 GMC Sprint

Interchange Number: 13

Motor Type: Two-speed non-concealed wipers
Part Number(s): 4918442
Usage: 1968–72 Chevelle; 1968–72 Pontiac LeMans; 1968–72 Olds Cutlass without shaft lever control; 1968–72 Buick Skylark without shaft lever control; 1968–74 Camaro; 1968–74 Nova; 1970–72 Monte Carlo; 1970–74 Pontiac Firebird; 1971–74 Vega; 1971–74 Pontiac Ventura II; 1973–74 Olds Omega; 1973–74 Buick Apollo

Interchange Number: 14

Motor Type: Two-speed with headlamp washer
Part Number(s): 4919624
ID Number(s): 4919642, 5045605
Usage: 1969 Camaro, Chevelle, or Nova
Notes: Unit has additional nipple for headlamp washer outlet.

Interchange Number: 15

Motor Type: Two-speed with headlamp washers
Part Number(s): 4919325
Usage: 1969 full-size Chevrolet with headlamp washers

Windshield Wiper Arms

Windshield wiper arms may seem like a general fit item, but this is not the case. Different models used different sized arms. Even in early Camaros, bodystyle can affect usage because the convertible and coupe used two different sets of arms that are not interchangeable.

Interchange can get confusing for models with the concealed wiper system arm. Chevelles used a special arm on the driver's side but not the passenger's, while Camaros used special arms on both sides.

Also, most models used two different brands of wiper blades, Trico and Anco. Usually the Anco blade comes a little longer than the Trico, sometimes requiring a different set of arms. If special arms are needed, they are listed in the charts. If not, only Trico is listed even though Anco blades *may* have been used. This procedure did not require special arms.

Model Identification

Interchange

Interchange Number: 1

Part Number(s): RH, 3756358; LH, 3756357
Type/Manufacturer: Trico
Usage: 1959–64 full-size Chevrolet with single-speed wipers

Interchange Number: 2

Part Number(s): RH, 3758740; LH, 3758739
Type/Manufacturer: Anco
Usage: 1959–64 full-size Chevrolet with single-speed wipers (optional arms)

Interchange Number: 3

Part Number(s): RH, 3824128; LH, 3824129
Type/Manufacturer: Trico
Usage: 1961–64 full-size Chevrolet with two-speed wipers

Interchange Number: 4

Part Number(s): 3886675 (fits either side)
Type/Manufacturer: Trico
Usage: 1962–67 Chevy II

Interchange Number: 5

Part Number(s): 3888671 (fits either side)
Type/Manufacturer: Anco
Usage: 1962–67 Chevy II
Notes: Early until build date of 11-30-66 (optional arm). Interchange number 6 will fit.

Interchange Number: 6

Part Number(s): 3919099 (fits either side)
Type/Manufacturer: Anco
Usage: 1967 Chevy II

Notes: Late beginning at build date 12-1-66. Will fit 1962 to early 1967 models. Interchange number 5 will not interchange.

Interchange Number: 7
Part Number(s): 3887573 (fits either side)
Type/Manufacturer: Trico
Usage: 1964–66 Chevelle
Notes: No optional arm on the Chevelle. The 1964–65 models used a different part number, but arm is the same and will fit.

Interchange Number: 8
Part Number(s): 3916689 (fits either side)
Type/Manufacturer: Trico
Usage: 1967–69 Camaro coupe

Interchange Number: 9
Part Number(s): 3916690 (fits either side)
Type/Manufacturer: Anco
Usage: 1967–69 Camaro coupe (optional arm)

Interchange Number: 10
Part Number(s): 3916687 (fits either side)
Type/Manufacturer: Trico
Usage: 1967–69 Camaro convertible

Interchange Number: 11
Part Number(s): 3916688 (fits either side)
Type/Manufacturer: Anco
Usage: 1967–69 Camaro convertible

Interchange Number: 12
Part Number(s): 393832 (fits either side)
Type/Manufacturer: Trico
Usage: 1964–67 Buick Skylark; 1964–67 Pontiac LeMans; 1964–67 Olds Cutlass; 1967 Chevelle

Interchange Number: 13
Part Number(s): 3914789 (fits either side)
Type/Manufacturer: Trico
Usage: 1968–72 Nova coupe
Notes: Four-door models will *not* interchange to a coupe.

Interchange Number: 14
Part Number(s): RH, 3913612; LH, 3913611
Type/Manufacturer: Trico
Usage: 1968–72 Chevelle with 1968–71 Pontiac LeMans; 1968–72 Olds Cutlass; 1968–72 Buick Skylark; all without concealed wipers
Notes: Not for 1969–72 SS or Malibu; not found on higher trim models.

Interchange Number: 15
Part Number(s): RH, 3913612; LH, 3913613
Type/Manufacturer: Trico
Usage: 1968–72 Chevelle; 1968–72 Pontiac LeMans; 1968–72 Olds Cutlass;1968–72 Buick Skylark; all with concealed wipers
Notes: Standard affair on 1969–72 Malibu or SS Models.

Interchange Number: 16
Part Number(s): RH, 3919947; LH, 3919948
Type/Manufacturer: Trico
Usage: 1968–70 full-size Chevrolet

Interchange Number: 17
Part Number(s): RH, 3927634; LH, 3926741
Type/Manufacturer: Anco
Usage: 1968–70 full-size Chevrolet

Interchange Number: 18
Part Number(s): RH, 3859776; LH, 3859775
Type/Manufacturer: Trico
Usage: 1965 full-size Chevrolet with single-speed wipers

Interchange Number: 19
Part Number(s): RH, 3862390; LH, 3862389
Type/Manufacturer: Trico
Usage: 1965 full-size Chevrolet with two-speed wipers

Interchange Number: 20
Part Number(s): RH, 3887570; LH, 3887569
Type/Manufacturer: Trico
Usage: 1966–67 full-size Chevrolet
Notes: Has a dull finish.

Interchange Number: 21
Part Number(s): 9806040 (fits either side)
Type/Manufacturer: Trico
Usage: 1970–75 Camaro without concealed wipers
Notes: Not for RS or higher trim models; 1970–75 Pontiac Firebird without concealed wipers; not for Trans-Am or higher trim models.

Interchange Number: 22
Part Number(s): RH, 9806042; LH, 9806043
Type/Manufacturer: Trico
Usage: 1970–75 Camaro; 1970–75 Pontiac Firebird; both with concealed wipers. Standard on higher trim Models like RS or Trans-Am.

Windshield Washer Jar

Interchange parts include the white jar and lid. Some early models (before 1968) came with a flat black washer jug and cap as optional equipment. Also, some (those before 1966) did not come standard with a washer jar. This option could be ordered separately or as part of the ZO1 Comfort and Convenience option group.

Model Identification

Camaro ....Interchange Number
1967–69..4
1970...5

Chevelle ....Interchange Number
1964–69..4
1970...5

Impala...Interchange Number
1959...1
1960–61..2
1962–63..3
1964–69..4
1970...5

Chevy II/Nova ....Interchange Number
1962–63..3
1964–70..4

133

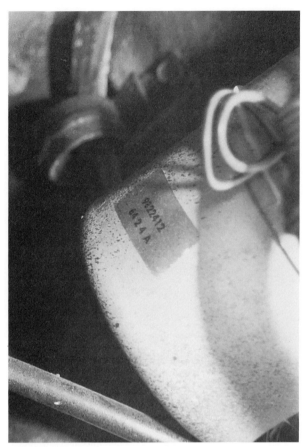

1959–62 washer jar and components.

Interchange

Interchange Number: 1
Part Number(s): 3760336
Usage: 1959 full-size Chevrolet; 1959 full-size Oldsmobile; 1959 full-size Pontiac
Notes: Deep rectangular shape with full-size top cover that held the pump assembly.

Interchange Number: 2
Part Number(s): 6256921
Usage: 1960–61 full-size Chevrolet

Interchange Number: 3
Part Number(s): 3798370
Usage: 1962–63 (up to 11-30-62) full-size Chevrolet or Chevy II. Used with bracket 3792790.
Notes: Jar in interchange number 4 will fit, if above 1962–63 bracket is used.

Interchange Number: 4
Part Number(s): 3840083
Usage: 1963–67 (after 11-30-62) Chevy II; 1963–69 (after 11-30-62) full-size Chevrolet; 1964–67 Olds Cutlass; 1964–67 Pontiac LeMans; 1964–67 Buick Sky-

lark; 1964–69 Chevelle; 1967 Pontiac Firebird; 1967–69 Camaro; 1968–70 Nova
Notes: All used bracket part number 548935. Location varies and makes the bracket appear different, but it is the same bracket. Exceptions: 1965–67 Chevy II with two-speed wipers, which used bracket part number 3863488; 1965–66 full-size Chevrolet with two-speed wipers, which used part number 3833218; and the 1969 full-size Chevrolet without retractable headlamp covers, which used part number 3951208.

Interchange Number: 5
Part Number(s): 3961557
Usage: 1970 full-size Chevrolet, Chevelle, or Camaro; 1970–74 Pontiac Firebird; 1971–74 Nova; 1971–74 Pontiac Ventura II
Notes: Bracket was not required; jar supported itself.

Windshield Wiper Linkage Assembly

These are the bars that transfer the power from the motor to the wiper arms. Some bars were coded, while others were not. They are largely interchangeable due to the fact that they are of GM design.

Model Identification

Camaro	Interchange Number
1967	8
1968–69	9
1970 without concealed wipers	10
1970 with concealed wipers	11

Chevelle	Interchange Number
1964–65 single-speed	14
1964–67 two-speed	13
1968–70	12

Impala	Interchange Number
1959–60	1
1961–62	2
1963–64	3
1965–67	4
1968–70	5

Chevy II/Nova	Interchange Number
1962–67	6
1968–70	7

Interchange

Interchange Number: 1
Part Number(s): RH, 4759125; LH, 4759126
Usage: 1959–60 full-size Chevrolet; 1959–60 full-size Oldsmobile; both sport coupes or convertibles only
Notes: Sedans will not interchange.

Interchange Number: 2
Part Number(s): 4910279 (one-piece design)
Usage: 1961–62 full-size Chevrolet

Interchange Number: 3
Part Number(s): RH, 4913095; LH, 4913096
Usage: 1963–64 full-size Chevrolet

Interchange Number: 4
> Part Number(s): RH, 4915370; LH, 4915369
> Usage: 1965–67 full-size Chevrolet

Interchange Number: 5
> Part Number(s): RH, 4918610; LH, 4918612
> Usage: 1968–70 full-size Chevrolet

Interchange Number: 6
> Part Number(s): RH, 4916746; LH, 4916756
> Usage: 1962–67 Chevy II

Interchange Number: 7
> Part Number(s): RH, 4918670; LH, 4918672
> Usage: 1968–75 Nova; 1971–75 Pontiac Ventura II; 1973–75 Olds Omega; 1973–75 Buick Apollo

Interchange Number: 8
> Part Number(s): RH, 4917574; LH, 4917576
> Usage: 1967 Camaro; 1967 Pontiac Firebird
> Notes: Right-hand unit used until 1969 and will fit interchange number 9. Left-hand unit unique to this year only and will not fit 1968–69 Camaro.

Interchange Number: 9
> Part Number(s): RH, 4917574; LH, 4918754
> Usage: 1968–69 Camaro; 1968–69 Pontiac Firebird
> Notes: 1967 right-hand unit in interchange number 8 will fit.

Interchange Number: 10
> Part Number(s): RH, 4939192; LH, 4939196
> Usage: 1970–75 Camaro; 1970–75 Pontiac Firebird; both without concealed wiper arms

Interchange Number: 11
> Part Number(s): RH, 4939184; LH, 4939188
> Usage: 1970–75 Camaro; 1970–75 Pontiac Firebird; both with concealed wiper arms

Interchange Number: 12
> Part Number(s): 4918624 (see notes); RH, 4918758; LH, 4918620
> Usage: 1968–72 Chevelle; 1968–72 Olds Cutlass; 1968–72 Buick Skylark; 1968–72 Pontiac LeMans; 1969–72 Pontiac Grand Prix
> Notes: Part number 4918624 was used with concealed wipers. Left-hand assembly differs from those with concealed wipers. Right-hand assembly is the same with or without option.

Interchange Number: 13
> Part Number(s): RH, 4913654; LH, 4913665
> Usage: 1964–67 Chevelle; 1964–67 Pontiac LeMans; 1964–67 Olds Cutlass; 1964–67 Buick Skylark
> Notes: Two-speed wipers.

Interchange Number: 14
> Part Number(s): 4913871
> Usage: 1964–65 Chevelle; 1964–65 Pontiac LeMans; 1964–65 Olds Cutlass; 1964–65 Buick Skylark
> Notes: Single-speed wipers.

Windshield Wiper Switch

The wiper switch interchange is the bare switch without its decorative knob. Interchange is based on part number. Type and number of wiper blade speeds will affect interchangeability.

Model Identification

Interchange

Interchange Number: 1
> Part Number(s): 1993441
> Usage: 1959–64 full-size Chevrolet; 1960 Olds Delta 88; 1961–63 Olds Cutlass (F-85); 1961–66 Buick Skylark; 1962–64 Chevy II; 1964 full-size Pontiac; 1964–65 Pontiac LeMans; all with single-speed wiper without washer

Interchange Number: 2
> Part Number(s): 1993541
> Usage: 1959–61 full-size Oldsmobile; 1959–63 full-size Chevrolet; 1961 Olds F-85; 1961 Buick Skylark; 1961 full-size Pontiac; 1962–64 Chevy II; all with single-speed wipers with washer

Interchange Number: 3
> Part Number(s): 1993543
> Usage: 1959–61 full-size Oldsmobile; 1959–63 full-size Chevrolet; both with two-speed wipers

Interchange Number: 4
> Part Number(s): 1993642
> Usage: 1964 full-size Chevrolet with single-speed wipers and washers

Interchange Number: 5
> Part Number(s): 1993643
> Usage: 1964 full-size Chevrolet with two-speed wipers and washers

Interchange Number: 6
> Part Number(s): 1993527
> Usage: 1961–63 Olds F-85 1962 Chevy II with two-speed wipers without washers;

Interchange Number: 7
> Part Number(s): 1993584
> Usage: 1963–64 Chevy II with two-speed wipers and washers

Interchange Number: 8
> Part Number(s): 1993634
> Usage: 1964 Chevelle; 1964 Olds Cutlass; 1964 Pontiac Tempest; 1964 Buick Skylark; all with single-speed wipers.

Interchange Number: 9
> Part Number(s): 1993633
> Usage: 1964 Chevelle; 1964 Olds Cutlass; 1964 Buick Skylark; 1964 Pontiac LeMans; all with two-speed wipers
> Notes: First design. Interchange 11 will fit.

Interchange Number: 10
> Part Number(s): 1993678
> Usage: 1965–66 full-size Chevrolet, with comfort and convenience equipment in 1965 full-size

Interchange Number: 11
> Part Number(s): 1993665
> Usage: 1964–65 Chevelle; 1964–65 Olds Cutlass; 1964–65 Buick Skylark; 1964–65 Pontiac LeMans; all with two-speed wipers

Interchange Number: 12
> Part Number(s): 1993677
> Usage: 1965 Chevelle, full-size Chevrolet, or Chevy II, all without CC equipment

Interchange Number: 13
> Part Number(s): 1993680
> Usage: 1965 Chevelle, Chevy II, or full-size Chevrolet, all with single-speed wipers and washers

Interchange Number: 14
> Part Number(s): 1993679
> Usage: 1965–66 Chevy II with CC equipment and two-speed wipers; 1966 Chevelle

Interchange Number: 15
> Part Number(s): 1993394
> Usage: 1967 full-size Chevrolet

Interchange Number: 16
> Part Number(s): 1993395
> Usage: 1967 Chevy II; 1967–68 Camaro; 1967–68 Chevelle; 1968 Nova

Interchange Number: 17
> Part Number(s): 1993442
> Usage: 1968 Chevelle; 1968–70 full-size Chevrolet, both with concealed wipers

Interchange Number: 18
> Part Number(s): 1993464
> Usage: 1969 Camaro; 1969–71 Nova; 1969–71 Chevelle (except Malibu or SS or with concealed wipers); 1971 Pontiac Ventura II

Interchange Number: 19
> Part Number(s): 1993465
> Usage: 1969–71 Chevelle Malibu, SS, or those with concealed wipers; 1970–71 Monte Carlo

Interchange Number: 20
> Part Number(s): 1994097
> Usage: 1970–71 Camaro with concealed wiper blades

Interchange Number: 21
> Part Number(s): 1994098
> Usage: 1970–71 Camaro, except RS or those with concealed wiper blades

Heater Motor Assembly

The biggest determining factor in interchanging the heater motor assembly is whether or not it was installed with factory air conditioning. The dealer-installed air conditioning used the same unit as those models that came from the factory without air conditioning. Motors with factory air conditioning are not interchangeable with cars without factory air or with dealer-installed air.

If the air conditioning unit looks like it has been added on, then it's a dealer-installed unit. Those integrated into the dash—often called Four Seasons—are factory-installed units.

Motors are identified by a number stamped onto the case. This number usually matches the part number, and is followed by the build date represented by the month and last two digits of the year. For example, "11 68" would represent November 1968.

Model Identification

Camaro .... *Interchange Number*
1967–70
> Without factory-installed a/c 4
> With factory-installed a/c..9

Chevelle ....*Interchange Number*
1964–70
> Without factory-installed a/c 4
> With factory-installed a/c..9

Impala..*Interchange Number*
1959–62
> Without factory a/c non-reciprocating heater.............1
> Without factory a/c reciprocating heater 2
1959–60
> With factory-installed a/c...6
1961–62
> With factory-installed a/c...7

Interchange

Interchange Number: 1
    Part/ID Number(s): 5044338
    Usage: 1959–62 full-size Chevrolet

Interchange Number: 2
    Part/ID Number(s): 5044331
    Usage: 1959–61 full-size Chevrolet with reciprocating type heater

Interchange Number: 3
    Part/ID Number(s): 5044531
    Usage: 1963 full-size Chevrolet

Interchange Number: 4
    Part Number(s): 4960505
    ID Number(s): 5044555, 5044695, 5044531
    Usage: 1964–74 Chevelle; 1964–74 full-size Chevrolet; 1964–74 Pontiac LeMans; 1964–74 Olds Cutlass; 1964–74 Buick Skylark; 1967–74 Camaro; 1967–74 Pontiac Firebird; 1968–74 Nova; 1969–74 Pontiac Grand Prix; 1969–74 full-size Oldsmobile; 1969–74 full-size Buick, except 1969–70 Riviera; 1970–74 Monte Carlo; 1970 74 full size Pontiac; 1971–74 Pontiac Ventura II; 1971–74 GMC Sprint; 1973–74 Buick Apollo; 1973–74 Olds Omega

Interchange Number: 5
    Part Number(s): 4914921
    ID Number(s): 5044578 (1964–67), 5044486 (1962–63)
    Usage: 1962–67 Chevy II
    Notes: All years will interchange even though they are different numbers.

Interchange Number: 6
    Part Number(s): 5044340
    ID Number(s):
    Usage: 1959–60 full-size Chevrolet with factory-installed a/c

Interchange Number: 7
    Part Number(s): 3149416
    ID Number(s): 5044487, 3149416
    Usage: 1961–62 full-size Chevrolet with factory-installed a/c

Interchange Number: 8
    Part Number(s): 5044522
    ID Number(s): 5044522

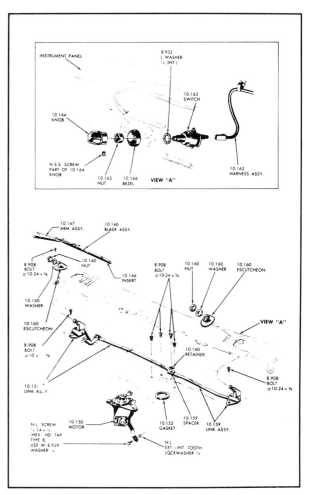

Typical washer arm and jar.

    Usage: 1963 full-size Chevrolet with factory-installed a/c
    Notes: Interchange number 9 will fit.

Interchange Number: 9
    Part Number(s): 4960538
    ID Number(s): 5044559, 4960538, 89977733
    Usage: 1963–74 full-size Chevrolet; 1964–70 Olds Cutlass; 1964–72 Chevelle; 1964–72 Buick Skylark; 1964–72 Pontiac LeMans; 1967–74 Camaro; 1967 74 Pontiac Firebird; 1968–74 Nova; 1968–74 full-size Buick; 1969–72 Pontiac Grand Prix; 1969–74 full-size Oldsmobile; 1970–72 Monte Carlo; 1970–74 full-size Pontiac; 1971–72 GMC Sprint; 1971–74 Pontiac Ventura II; 1973–74 Buick Apollo; 1973–74 Olds Omega; all with factory-installed a/c

Heater Core Assembly

    Interchange of the heater core is determined by whether or not factory air conditioning was installed. Dealer-installed air used the same core as those units without factory air conditioning. Engine size may also affect interchange.

Model Identification

Interchange

Interchange Number: 1
    Part Number(s): 3022069
    Usage: 1963–68 full-size Chevrolet; 1964–67 Chevelle;
      1964–67 Pontiac LeMans; 1964–67 Olds Cutlass;
      1964–67 Buick Skylark; all without a/c

Interchange Number: 2
    Part Number(s): 3011414
    Usage: 1969–70 full-size Chevrolet without a/c

Interchange Number: 3
    Part Number(s): 3014083
    Usage: 1968–72 Chevelle; 1968–72 Pontiac LeMans;
      1968–72 Buick Skylark; 1968–72 Olds Cutlass;
      1969–72 Pontiac Grand Prix; 1970–72 Monte Carlo;
      1971–72 GMC Sprint; all without a/c

Interchange Number: 4
    Part Number(s): 3022071
    Usage: 1967 Camaro, except SS 396; 1967 Pontiac Fire-
      bird without 400ci or HO V-8; both without a/c
    Notes: This unit was phased out of production and the
      396ci unit (interchange number three) took its
      place.

Interchange Number: 5
    Part Number(s): 3022072
    Usage: 1967–68 Camaro 396ci without a/c

Interchange Number: 6
    Part Number(s): 3022074
    Usage: 1968 Camaro, except SS 396; 1968 Nova, ex-
      cept Nova SS 396; all without a/c

Interchange Number: 7
    Part Number(s): 3016842
    Usage: 1969–74 Nova, except 396ci; 1969–75 Camaro;
      1969–75 Pontiac Firebird; 1971–75 Pontiac Ventura
      II; 1973–75 Buick Apollo; 1973–75 Olds Omega; all
      without a/c

Interchange Number: 8
    Part Number(s): 3005383
    Usage: 1962–67 Chevy II without a/c

Interchange Number: 9
    Part Number(s): 3000133
    Usage: 1963–64 full-size Chevrolet with a/c

Interchange Number: 10
    Part Number(s): 3021826
    Usage: 1965–68 full-size Chevrolet; 1968 Chevelle;
      1965–68 full-size Pontiac; all with A/c

Interchange Number: 11
    Part Number(s): 3014782
    Usage: 1969–70 full-size Chevrolet; 1969–72 Chevelle;
      1969–72 Pontiac LeMans; 1969–72 Buick Skylark;
      1969–72 Pontiac Grand Prix; 1969–72 Olds Cutlass;
      1970–72 Monte Carlo; 1971–72 GMC Sprint; all
      with a/c

Interchange Number: 12
    Part Number(s): 3004817
    Usage: 1964–67 Chevelle; 1964–67 Pontiac LeMans;
      1964–67 Olds Cutlass; 1964–67 Buick Skylark; all
      with a/c

Interchange Number: 13
    Part Number(s): 3022068
    Usage: 1967–68 Camaro; 1967–68 Pontiac Firebird;
      both with a/c

Interchange Number: 14
   Part Number(s): 3018489
   Usage: 1968–74 Nova; 1969 Pontiac Firebird; 1969–71 Camaro; 1971–74 Pontiac Ventura II; 1973–74 Buick Apollo; all with a/c

Interchange Number: 15
   Part Number(s): 3018864
   Usage: 1968–70; ; 1968–70 Nova SS 396; 1969 Camaro SS 396; 1969 Pontiac Firebird 400 with Ram Air; all without a/c

Interchange Number: 16
   Part Number(s): 3151212
   Usage: 1959–61 full-size Chevrolet without a/c, but with recirculating heater in 1961

Interchange Number: 17
   Part Number(s): 3144756
   Usage: 1959–62 full-size Chevrolet with a/c

Interchange Number: 18
   Part Number(s): 3153941
   Usage: 1962 full-size Chevrolet without a/c

Air Conditioning Compressor

The interchange for an air conditioning compressor is based on the original part number for the entire compressor. Interchange is quite large if you go by fit alone. In fact, compressors from other GM makes and models will interchange. For example, a compressor from a 1966–74 Cutlass will fit the 1966 and up Chevelle. Although it may fit properly, the number may be incorrect for that particular model year.

If you want to go the route of using the correct part number, try to focus your interchange on the same model year and engine type. For example, if you are looking for a compressor for your 1969 Camaro, you might try a unit from a 1969 full-size car (remember, other GM makes will fit). Part numbers were generally the same for all models for that particular compressor.

Factory-installed air conditioning and dealer-installed or "hang on" units used two different compressors, thus they are not interchangeable. The Four Seasons integrated units are much more common than the hang-on type. So if your car is equipped with the a dealer-installed unit, your search is going to be somewhat limited.

Model Identification

Camaro ....*Interchange Number*
1967–70
   Without factory-installed a/c 4
   With factory-installed a/c...............................1

Chevelle ....*Interchange Number*
1964–70
   Without factory-installed a/c 4
   With factory-installed a/c...............................1

Impala.......................................*Interchange Number*
1959–60
   Without factory a/c 2
1961
   With factory-installed a/c...............................3
1962–70
   With factory-installed a/c...............................1

1964–70 washer jar.

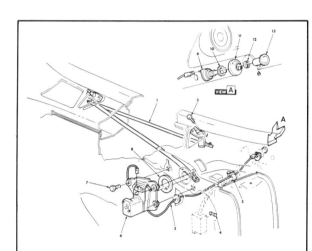

1965-67 PASSENGER WINDSHIELD WIPER LINKAGE

1.	10.159	LINK ASSY.	4915369-70
2.	N.L.	SCREW	
3.	2.559	RETAINER	3816G59
4.	8.965	FUSE (20 Amp.)	
5.	N.S.	WIRE ASSY. (#16 ga. wire)	
6.	*	MOTOR ASSY	
7.	8.908	SCREW (#10–24 x 1)	
8.	10.152	GASKET	542675
9.	10.163	SWITCH ASSY.	1993677
10.	8.932	L. WASHER (1/2)	
11.	10.166	BEZEL (Biscayne, Bel Air)	3859223
	10.166	BEZEL (Impala)	3859224
12.	10.163	NUT	3820531
13.	10.164	KNOB	3859221

*Removed From Service

Interchange

Interchange Number: 1

Part/ID Number(s): 5910486, 6598423, 5910435, 5910495, 5910431

Usage: 1962–71 full-size Chevrolet; 1962–71 full-size Pontiac; 1962–71 Buick Skylark; 1962–71 full-size Buick; 1962–71 Olds Cutlass; 1964–71 Chevelle; 1964–71 Pontiac LeMans; 1964–71 full-size Oldsmobile; 1967–71 Camaro; 1967–71 Pontiac Firebird; 1968–71 Nova; 1969–71 Pontiac Grand Prix; 1971 GMC Sprint; all with factory-installed a/c

Notes: Compressors from 1972–75 models will fit, but have a heat switch while the earlier compressor has no heat switch. Bypass heat switch when installing.

Interchange Number: 2

Part/ID Number(s): 5910347

Usage: 1959–60 full-size Chevrolet; 1959–60 full-size Oldsmobile; 1959–60 full-size Buick; 1959–60 full-size Pontiac; all with factory-installed a/c

Notes: Interchange number 3 will fit.

Interchange Number: 3

Part/ID Number(s): 5910425, 6550153

Usage: 1961 full-size Chevrolet; 1961 full-size Oldsmobile; 1961 Buick; 1961 full-size Pontiac; 1961 Buick Skylark; 1961 Olds F-85; all with factory-installed a/c

Interchange Number: 4

Part/ID Number(s): 5910432

Usage: 1962–65 full-size Impala with hang-on a/c; 1962–65 full-size Pontiac with hang-on a/c; 1962–67 Chevy II; 1962–67 Buick Skylark with hang-on a/c; 1964–67 Olds Cutlass with hang-on a/c; 1964–70 hang-on a/c; 1964–70 Pontiac LeMans with hang-on a/c; 1967–70 Camaro with hang-on a/c; 1968–70 Nova hang-on a/c

Notes: Will not fit factory-integrated a/c systems. Used with dealer-installed a/c. Factory-installed in 1962–67 Chevy II.

Air Conditioning Condenser

Model Identification

Interchange

Interchange Number: 1

Part Number(s): 8529972

Usage: 1959–60 full-size Chevrolet

Interchange Number: 2

Part Number(s): 8530135

Usage: 1961 full-size Chevrolet

Interchange Number: 3

Part Number(s): 3819444

Usage: 1962–63 full-size Chevrolet

Interchange Number: 4

Part Number(s): 3899793

Usage: 1967 Camaro; 1967 Chevelle; 1967 full-size Chevrolet; 1968 Nova; 1967–68 Pontiac Firebird; all with factory a/c

Notes: Also used on 1968 Chevelle, Camaro, and full-size Chevrolet with dealer-installed a/c.

Interchange Number: 5
Part Number(s): 3925731
Usage: 1968 Camaro with factory a/c

Interchange Number: 6
Part Number(s): 3937170
Usage: 1969 Camaro with factory a/c

Interchange Number: 7
Part Number(s): 3940259
Usage: 1969–70 Camaro, Chevelle, Nova, or full-size Chevrolet; 1970 Monte Carlo; all with dealer-installed a/c

Interchange Number: 8
Part Number(s): 3967920
Usage: 1970 Camaro with factory a/c
Notes: Was used for the first month of the 1971 production run.

Interchange Number: 9
Part Number(s): 3859770
Usage: 1964–66 Chevelle

Interchange Number: 10
Part Number(s): 3919596
Usage: 1968 Chevelle with factory-installed a/c

Interchange Number: 11
Part Number(s): 3937140
Usage: 1969 Chevelle with factory-installed a/c

Interchange Number: 12
Part Number(s): 3967948
Usage: 1970–72 Chevelle; 1970–72 Monte Carlo; 1970–72 GMC Sprint; all with factory-installed a/c

Interchange Number: 13
Part Number(s): 3840310
Usage: 1964 full-size Chevrolet

Interchange Number: 14
Part Number(s): 3856228
Usage: 1965–66 full-size Chevrolet

Interchange Number: 15
Part Number(s): 3919577
Usage: 1968 full-size Chevrolet with factory-installed a/c

Interchange Number: 16
Part Number(s): 3997404
Usage: 1969 full-size Chevrolet with factory-installed a/c

Interchange Number: 17
Part Number(s): 3967935
Usage: 1970 full-size Chevrolet with factory-installed a/c

Interchange Number: 18
Part Number(s): 3857132
Usage: 1962–66 Chevy II

Interchange Number: 19
Part Number(s): 3895999
Usage: 1967 Chevy II

Interchange Number: 20
Part Number(s): 3937190
Usage: 1969 Nova with factory-installed a/c

Interchange Number: 21
Part Number(s): 3973752
Usage: 1970–72 Nova; 1971–72 Pontiac Ventura V-8

Horns

The car horn has fewer interchange possibilities than you'd expect—if you interchange the horn along with its mounting bracket, that is. Each model and model year had various mounting locations, so the only interchange is usually the same model and same model year. An exception is the 1968–72 Nova, which used the same exact horn assembly for all five years.

Interchange likelihood becomes much greater, however, if you remove the horn from the bracket. Full-size Chevrolets from 1955 to 1964 and Chevy II models from 1962 to 1964 used the same two horns. The high-note horn was listed as part number 9000239 and stamped the same. The low-note horn was listed as part number 9000011 and stamped 9000014.

Beginning in 1965, the high-note horn was listed as part number 1892164, and the low-note horn was part number 1892162. These continued into the1975 model year for the high-note, and up to 1971 for the low-note. The horns were used in all GM makes and models and will interchange.

Horn Relay

Only four relays were used on earlier horns. Their usage depended on the model year and, in some cases, the model. From 1959 to 1962 all GM models (including Pontiac, Oldsmobile, Buick, and Chevrolet) used part number 1116920. Beginning in 1963 and continuing into 1964, Chevrolet used part number 1115824. Then it was used on the 1965 Chevelle and Chevy II. The 1965 full-size Chevrolet and all other GM models from 1966–71 used part number 1115889.

Signal Lever

The biggest concern with the signal lever is the column type. The levers used with the tilt steering column differed from those units used without the option. Also, the levers with speed control used a special stalk that doubled as the speed control switch. Another factor to watch for includes model usage, for some types.

Model Identification

Camaro .... Interchange Number
1967–68
    Without cruise control 3
    With cruise control 4
1969–70
    Without cruise control 5
    With cruise control 4

Chevelle ....Interchange Number
1964–67
    Without tilt steering....................................2
    With tilt steering 6
    With cruise control (1967) 4

1968

Interchange

Interchange Number: 1
Part Number(s): 3782964 and 3854303
Usage: 1959–66 Chevrolet; 1963–65 Chevy II; both
without tilt column

Interchange Number: 2
Part Number(s): 3840903
Usage: 1964–67 Chevelle; 1966 Chevy II; both without
tilt column

Interchange Number: 3
Part Number(s): 3909580
Usage: 1967 Chevy II; 1967 Pontiac Firebird; 1967–68
full-size Chevrolet; 1967–68 Camaro; 1968 Chevelle; 1968 Nova; all without cruise control

Interchange Number: 4
Part Number(s): 6465256
Usage: 1967–72 full-size Chevrolet, Chevelle, Nova, or
Camaro; 1967–72 Pontiac LeMans; 1967–72 Buick
Skylark; 1968–74 full-size Pontiac; 1970–74 Monte
Carlo; all with cruise control
Notes: Look for this option in full-size cars or personal
luxury models like the Monte Carlo. It was more
commonly used on those models.

Interchange Number: 5
Part Number(s): 3961517
Usage: 1969–70 full-size Chevrolet, Camaro Chevelle,
or Nova; 1970 Monte Carlo; all without cruise control

Interchange Number: 6
Part Number(s): 3783459
Usage: 1959–66 full-size Chevrolet; 1962–65 Chevy II;
1964–66 Chevelle; all with tilt column

Headlamp Switch

The headlamp switch interchange involves the bare unit
without the knob. Interchange is possible largely because the
switch is a GM-made part. An important thing to watch for,
though, is cars with retractable headlamp covers. They require a special switch and will not work or interchange properly with a car lacking this feature.

Model Identification

Interchange

Interchange Number: 1
Part Number(s): 1995096
Usage: 1957–63 full-size Chevrolet; 1962–63 Chevy II

Interchange Number: 2
Part Number(s): 1995179
Usage: 1964–67 full-size Chevrolet, except 1966
Caprice with bucket seats; 1964–67 Chevy II; 1964–67
Pontiac LeMans; 1964–67 Olds Cutlass; 1964–67
Buick Skylark; 1964–67 full-size Buick; 1964–69
Chevelle; 1967 Pontiac Firebird; 1967 full-size
Oldsmobile, except front-wheel drive; 1967–68 Ca-
maro, except with retractable headlamp covers;
1968–74 Nova; 1968–74 full-size Pontiac; 1971–74
Pontiac Ventura II; 1972 Chevelle

Interchange Number: 3
Part Number(s): 1995142
Usage: 1966 Caprice with bucket seats
Notes: No other interchange.

Interchange Number: 4
Part Number(s): 1995165
Usage: 1968 full-size Chevrolet, except with option T-83
retractable headlamps.
Notes: No other interchange.

Interchange Number: 5
Part Number(s): 1995166
Usage: 1968 full-size Chevrolet with retractable head-
lamp covers

Interchange Number: 6
Part Number(s): 1995176
Usage: 1967–68 Camaro RS with retractable headlamp covers; 1969 Camaro RS without console gauges

Interchange Number: 7
Part Number(s): 1995183
Usage: 1969 Camaro with console gauges except RS equipped; 1969–72 full-size Chevrolet, except with headlamp covers; 1970–71 Chevelle; 1970–72 Camaro

Interchange Number: 8
Part Number(s): 19951174
Usage: 1969 full-size Chevrolet with retractable headlamp covers
Notes: No other interchange.

Interchange Number: 9
Part Number(s): 1995175
Usage: 1969 Camaro with exposed headlamps but without console gauges
Notes: No other interchange.

Interchange Number: 10
Part Number(s): 1995177
Usage: 1969 Camaro RS with console gauges
Notes: No other interchange.

Interchange Number: 11
Part Number(s): 3973678
Usage: 1970–71 full-size Chevrolet with headlamp delay

Convertible Top Motor

Most Chevrolet models came with a power-operated convertible top. The procedure was powered by a hydraulic motor. Like many other components, this is a GM part and therefore has numerous possibilities for interchange. Generally speaking, only a few motor types were used. Factors that will affect interchangeability are model and model year. All interchange includes the hydraulic pump.

Model Identification

Camaro	Interchange Number
1967–69	5

Chevelle	Interchange Number
1964–70	5

Impala	Interchange Number
1959–60	1
1961	2
1962–64	3
1965–70	6

Chevy II	Interchange Number
1962–63	4

Interchange

Interchange Number: 1
Part Number(s): 4813039
Usage: 1959–60 full-size Chevrolet, Buick, Pontiac, or Oldsmobile

Notes: This is a late 1959 unit. Earlier 1959 units will not fit later-built models. The later style unit is identified by the number "5044368" stamped on top the end plate.

Interchange Number: 2
Part Number(s): 4815145
Usage: 1961 full-size Chevrolet, Pontiac, Buick, or Oldsmobile; 1962 Cadillac

Interchange Number: 3
Part Number(s): 4461121
Usage: 1962–64 full-size Chevrolet, Buick, Pontiac, or Oldsmobile

Interchange Number: 4
Part Number(s): 4879190
Usage: 1962–63 Chevy II; 1962–63 Buick Skylark; 1962–63 Pontiac Tempest

Interchange Number: 5
Part Number(s): 7710923
Usage: 1964–72 Chevelle; 1964–72 Pontiac LeMans; 1964–72 Buick Skylark; 1964–72 Olds Cutlass; 1966–67 Chevy II; 1967–69 Camaro; 1967–69 Pontiac Firebird
Notes: Replacement part number will fit earlier models, but original motors from earlier designs will not fit later models. Break down 1964, 1965, 1966–67 and this part number which was used from 1968 to 1972.

Interchange Number: 6
Part Number(s): 7598791
Usage: 1965–70 full-size Chevrolet, Pontiac, Buick, or Oldsmobile
Notes: 1965 original motor will not fit 1966–70 models, but the 1966–70 motor will fit 1965 models.

Convertible Top Switch

This is the power switch that was placed on the instrument panel that operated the top. It is the bare switch without the bezel. Tip: Look at station wagons with a power rear window; the switch is the same.

Model Identification

Camaro	Interchange Number
1967	6
1968	5
1969	7

Chevelle	Interchange Number
1964–66	5
1967	6
1968	5
1969	7
1970	8

Impala	Interchange Number
1959–60	1
1961–62	2
1963	3
1964	4
1965–66	5

Interchange

Interchange Number: 1
> Part Number(s): 4761829
> Usage: 1959–60 full-size Chevrolet convertible; 1959–60 full-size station wagon with power rear window

Interchange Number: 2
> Part Number(s): 3814719
> Usage: 1961–62 full-size with power top

Interchange Number: 3
> Part Number(s): 4634122
> Usage: 1963 full-size convertible; 1963 full-size wagon with power rear window

Interchange Number: 4
> Part Number(s): 4423037
> Usage: 1964 full-size convertible; 1964 full-size wagon with power rear window

Interchange Number: 5
> Part Number(s): 3840095
> Usage: 1964–66 Chevelle, Pontiac Tempest, Olds Cut-

lass, or Buick Skylark convertible or station wagon with power rear window; 1965–66 full-size convertible; 1965–66 full-size wagon with power rear window; 1968 Camaro or Pontiac Firebird; 1968 Malibu or SS 396; 1968 Chevelle Concours wagon

Interchange Number: 6
> Part Number(s): 3906118
> Usage: 1967 Chevelle or Camaro; 1967–68 full-size Chevrolet convertible or station wagon with power rear window

Interchange Number: 7
> Part Number(s): 3959230
> Usage: 1969 Camaro or Chevelle; 1969 Pontiac Le-Mans; 1969 Buick Skylark; 1969 Olds Cutlass; 1969 mid-size GM station wagon with power rear window; 1969–70 full-size Chevrolet convertible or station wagon with power rear window

Interchange Number: 8
> Part Number(s): 3973644
> Usage: 1970–72 Chevelle convertible; 1970–72 Chevelle station wagon with power rear window

Interchange Number: 9
> Part Number(s): 3814719
> Usage: 1962–63 Chevy II Nova convertible; 1962–66 Chevy II station wagon with electric rear window;

Chapter 10

Body Panels

Hood

Hood interchange means the bare hood *only* without trim, emblems, or hinges. It's based on the original replacement part number and on original model usage. For example, some performance models such as the Chevelle SS 396 came with a special hood. Even though the interchange will say SS 396 *only*, the hood *can* be adapted to fit a regular Chevelle. Another example is the 1969 cowl induction Z-28 hood, which will fit other Camaro models, but may not be historically correct.

Model Identification

All 1966–67 Chevy II deck lids are interchangeable.
Chevrolet

The 1967–69 Camaro SS 350 or 396 hood. Interchange is without simulated vents.

Interchange

Interchange Number 1
Part Number(s): 3938617
Special Usage Description: Standard flat hood
Usage: 1967–69 Camaro, except SS 350 or SS 396
Notes: 1967–68 hood will fit 1969 models, but when swapping a 1969 hood to an earlier model the insulation hole at the rear edge will have to be reworked.

Interchange Number: 2
Part Number(s): 3838619
Special Usage Description: Super Sport hood. Special indention on each side to hold simulated Louvers.
Usage: 1967–69 Camaro SS 350 or SS 396
Notes: Will fit non-SS models. Interchange without simulated hood louvers.

Interchange Number: 3
Part Number(s): 3949708
Special Usage Description: Cowl induction scooped hood
Usage: 1969 Camaro
Notes: Originally designed for 1969 models but will fit 1967–68 Camaros.

Interchange Number: 4
Part Number(s): 3962967
Special Usage Description: Standard flat hood
Usage: 1970–74 Camaro

Interchange Number: 5
Part Number(s): 3854140
Special Usage Description: Standard flat hood
Usage: 1964 Chevelle

Interchange Number: 6
Part Number(s): 3856895
Special Usage Description: Standard flat hood
Usage: 1965 Chevelle

Interchange Number: 7
Part Number(s): 3896557
Special Usage Description: Standard flat hood
Usage: 1966 Chevelle, except SS 396

Interchange Number: 8
Part Number(s): 3896559
Special Usage Description: Super Sport hood with special indentations to hold louvers.
Usage: 1966 Chevelle SS 396
Notes: Interchange with or without louvers.

Interchange Number: 9
Part Number(s): 3885987
Special Usage Description: Standard flat hood
Usage: 1967 Chevelle, except SS 396

Interchange Number: 10
Part Number(s): 3897504
Special Usage Description: Super Sport hood with special indention on each side to hold simulated air vent.
Usage: 1967 Chevelle SS 396
Notes: Interchange with or without vents.

Interchange Number: 11
Part Number(s): 3940657
Special Usage Description: Standard flat hood
Usage: 1968 Chevelle, except SS 396

Interchange Number: 12
Part Number(s): 3940660
Special Usage Description: Super Sport hood; twin-dome design with cutouts at rear edge of hood to support louvers
Usage: 1968 Chevelle SS 396

A popular option was the 1969 cowl induction hood. It will fit the 1967–68 Camaro.

Notes: *Use caution:* Two different hoods were used. Both will fit, but each used unique hinges and hood springs. You will need those parts to interchange.

Interchange Number: 13
Part Number(s): 3940631
Special Usage Description: Standard flat hood
Usage: 1969 Chevelle, except SS 396

Interchange Number: 14
Part Number(s): 3940632
Special Usage Description: Super Sport hood; twin-dome design with cutouts at rear edge
Usage: 1969 Chevelle SS 396
Notes: Although similar, 1968 and 1969 hood will not interchange.

Interchange Number: 15
Part Number(s): 3977767
Special Usage Description: Standard flat hood
Usage: 1970–72 Chevelle, except SS 350, SS 396, or SS 454

Interchange Number: 16
Part Number(s): 3987022
Special Usage Description: Super Sport hood with center dome but without induction cutout
Usage: 1970–72 Chevelle SS
Notes: 1970 Chevelle used a different part number, but 1971–72 hood will fit. Not for those with cowl induction.

Interchange Number: 17
Part Number(s): 3987028
Special Usage Description: Super Sport hood with ZL-2 cowl induction. Features cutout on center dome.
Usage: 1970–72 Chevelle SS, except 1971–72 SS 350

Interchange Number: 18
Part Number(s): 3752792
Special Usage Description: Standard flat hood
Usage: 1959 full-size Chevrolet

Interchange Number: 19
Part Number(s): 3764273
Special Usage Description: Standard flat hood
Usage: 1960 full-size Chevrolet

Interchange Number: 20
Part Number(s): 3772989
Special Usage Description: Standard flat hood
Usage: 1961 full-size Chevrolet

Interchange Number: 21
Part Number(s): 3786160
Special Usage Description: Standard flat hood
Usage: 1962 full-size Chevrolet

Interchange Number: 22
Part Number(s): 3817605
Special Usage Description: Standard flat hood
Usage: 1963 full-size Chevrolet

Interchange Number: 23
Special Usage Description: Standard flat hood
Usage: 1964 full-size Chevrolet
Notes: Four different hoods were used. (1) Impala model used a special hood that allowed it to mount special crown moldings. Will not correctly interchange to other models or vice versa without modification. (2) Impala model with power brakes had an indentation that allowed clearance for the power booster. (3) All other models without power brakes. (4) All other models with power brakes.

The 1970–72 Chevelle hoods are interchangeable. SS type is shown. *Chevrolet*

Interchange Number: 24
> Part Number(s): 3876590
> Special Usage Description: Standard flat hood
> Usage: 1965–66 full-size Chevrolet

Interchange Number: 25
> Part Number(s): 3885974
> Special Usage Description: Standard flat hood
> Usage: 1967 full-size Chevrolet, except SS 427

Interchange Number: 26
> Part Number(s): 3901921
> Special Usage Description: SS 427 hood; center dome with center cutout
> Usage: 1967 Impala SS 427

Interchange Number: 27
> Part Number(s): 3907647
> Special Usage Description: Standard flat hood
> Usage: 1968 full-size Chevrolet, except SS 427

Interchange Number: 28
> Part Number(s): 3917444
> Special Usage Description: SS 427 hood; large center dome with cutout at the rear edge of hood
> Usage: 1968 Impala SS 427

Interchange Number: 29
> Special Usage Description: Standard flat hood
> Usage: 1969 full-size Chevrolet
> Notes: While all will fit, note that Impala, SS, and Caprice models used a hood with pre-drilled holes for the model name across the front center. All other models used the Chevrolet script at the LH edge.

Interchange Number: 30
> Part Number(s): 3945690
> Special Usage Description: Standard flat hood
> Usage: 1970 full-size Chevrolet

Interchange Number: 31
> Part Number(s): 3872697
> Special Usage Description: Standard flat hood
> Usage: 1962–65 Chevy II

Interchange Number: 32
> Part Number(s): 3872998
> Special Usage Description: Standard flat hood
> Usage: 1966–67 Chevy II

Interchange Number: 33
> Part Number(s): 3974588
> Special Usage Description: Standard flat hood
> Usage: 1968–72 Nova, except SS

Interchange Number: 34
> Part Number(s): 3974591
> Special Usage Description: Super Sport hood; twin indentations hold simulated louvers
> Usage: 1968–72 Nova SS
> Notes: Interchange with or without louvers.

Hood Hinges

Interchange is based on part number, and is widely available. Can be interchanged with a variety of GM makes and models. Hood springs are not included, except for on the 1968 Chevelle SS 396.

Model Identification

Interchange

Interchange Number: 1
> Part Number(s): RH, 3910668; LH, 3910667
> Usage: 1965–67 Chevelle; 1965–67 full-size Chevrolet; 1966–67 Chevy II; 1967–69 Pontiac Firebird; 1967–69 Camaro

Interchange Number: 2
> Part Number(s): RH, 3910680; LH, 3910679
> Usage: Early-built (before 11-30-67) 1968 Chevelle
> Notes: Interchange 3 will fit if rear bolt slot is elongated. 1968–72 hinges from Pontiac LeMans will fit, but may have to be modified.

Interchange Number: 3
> Part Number(s): RH, 39266830; LH, 39126829
> Usage: Late-built (beginning 12-1-67) 1968 Chevelle; 1968 full-size Chevrolet; 1968–74 Nova; 1971–74 Pontiac Ventura II; 1973–74 Olds Omega; 1973–74 Buick Apollo
> Notes: 1968–72 Pontiac LeMans hinges will fit, but may have to be modified.

Interchange Number: 4
> Part Number(s): RH, 3949202; LH, 3949201
> Usage: 1969 Chevelle or full-size Chevrolet

Interchange Number: 5
> Part Number(s): RH, 3793528; LH, 3793527
> Usage: 1962 Chevy II

Interchange Number: 6
> Part Number(s): RH, 3864682; LH, 3864681
> Usage: 1963–64 full-size Chevrolet; 1963–65 Chevy II; 1964 Chevelle

Door handles are widely interchangeable.

Hood Hinge Springs

Hood hinge springs are universal fit. That means the spring on the right-hand side will fit the left-hand side. Springs can also be found on a variety of GM makes and models, even on those that do not use the same hood hinges.

Model Identification

Interchange

Interchange Number: 1
Part Number(s): 3848272
Free length: 8-25/64 inches
Usage: 1963–64 Chevy II; 1963–66 full-size Chevrolet; 1964–65 Chevelle; 1964–67 Pontiac LeMans; 1964–67 Olds Cutlass; 1966–67 Chevelle SS 396;

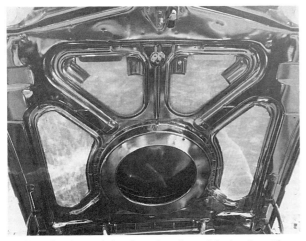

Underside view of the functional cowl induction Chevelle hood.

The 1969 Camaro used special molding on the quarter panels.

This 1966 Chevelle SS 396 used a special hood.

1967–68 Pontiac Firebird; 1967–69 Camaro SS 350 or SS 396; 1969–70 full-size Pontiac; 1969 Pontiac Firebird (except 400ci); 1970 full-size Chevrolet; 1970 Pontiac Firebird; 1971 Chevelle SS; 1971–72 Monte Carlo or El Camino; 1971–72 Pontiac Le-Mans; 1972 Chevelle SS or Heavy Chevy

Notes: Do *not* use in 1963 Chevrolet with Z-11 option; severe hood damage will occur.

Interchange Number: 2
Part Number(s): 3791291
Usage: 1962 Chevy II

Interchange Number: 3
Part Number(s): 3907626
Usage: 1967 full-size Chevrolet; 1969 full-size Chevrolet; 1970 Monte Carlo; 1970–72 Camaro

Interchange Number: 4
Part Number(s): 3864680
Free length: 8 13/32 inches
Usage: 1965 Chevy II; 1966–67 Chevelle, except SS 396; 1968 Chevelle second design; 1968 full-size Chevrolet; 1969–72 Chevelle, except 1971–72 SS or Heavy Chevy

Interchange Number: 5
Part Number(s): 3926800
Free length: 8-3/4 inches
Usage: 1968 Chevelle first design; 1968–70 Pontiac Le-Mans; 1968–75 Nova; 1971–72 LeMans (with chrome bumper); 1971–75 Pontiac Ventura II; 1973 LeMans

Interchange Number: 6
Part Number(s): 409025
Usage: 1966–67 Chevy II; 1967–69 Camaro, except SS 396 or SS 350; 1971–72 full-size Oldsmobile, except Toronado; 1973–75 Buick Apollo

Interchange Number: 7
Part Number(s): 3781357
Free length: 8-1/16 inches
Usage: 1961 full-size Chevrolet

Interchange Number: 8
Part Number(s): 3758875
Usage: 1959–60 full-size Chevrolet

Interchange Number: 9
Part Number(s): 3819353
Usage: 1962 full-size Chevrolet

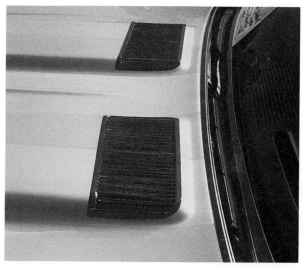

Hood vents are the same in the 1968 and 1969 Chevelle SS 396, but the hoods are not.

Front Fenders

Due to design changes such as side-marker lamps, there is very little interchanging in the front fenders. There are also special models like the 1967–69 Camaro RS that used special fenders. In this case, a regular non-RS Camaro fender will not interchange.

Interchange is for the bare unit only without name-plates, wheel well trim, or side moldings. However, these factors do come into play as side trim and nameplates require holes to be matched or drilled. To mount the fender, existing holes may have to be filled and new ones drilled, depending on your intended usage. Remember, it is always easier to drill new holes than it is to cover up existing ones. So look for a fender that matches your particular application or without any other trim, if possible.

Model Identification

Interchange

Interchange Number: 1
    Part Number(s): RH, 3904686; LH, 3904685
    Usage: 1967 Camaro, except RS

Interchange Number: 2
    Part Number(s): RH, 3904688; LH, 3904687
    Usage: 1967 Camaro RS
    Notes: Non-RS fender will not accommodate the hide-
      away headlamps.

Interchange Number: 3
    Part Number(s): RH, 3941966; LH, 3941965
    Usage: 1968 Camaro without RS
    Notes: Fender has provisions for side lamps.

Interchange Number: 4
    Part Number(s): RH, 3941968; LH, 3941967
    Usage: 1968 Camaro RS
    Notes: Non-RS fender will not accommodate hideaway
      headlamps. Fenders have provisions for side lamps.

Interchange Number: 5
    Part Number(s): RH, 3953856; LH, 3953855
    Usage: 1969 Camaro without RS

Interchange Number: 6
    Part Number(s): RH, 39453858; LH, 3953857
    Usage: 1969 Camaro with RS
    Notes: Non-RS fender will not accommodate hideaway
      headlamps.

Interchange Number: 7
    Part Number(s): RH, 3981842; LH, 3981841
    Usage: 1970–75 Camaro, all option packages

Interchange Number: 8
    Part Number(s): RH, 3858944; LH, 38589943
    Usage: 1964 Chevelle

Interchange Number: 9
    Part Number(s): RH, 38737899; LH, 38737898
    Usage: 1965 Chevelle

Interchange Number: 10
    Part Number(s): RH, 3886308; LH, 3886307
    Usage: 1966 Chevelle

Interchange Number: 11
    Part Number(s): RH, 3904677; LH, 3904676
    Usage: 1967 Chevelle

Interchange Number: 12
    Part Number(s): RH, 3924118; LH, 3924117
    Usage: 1968 Chevelle

Interchange Number: 13
    Part Number(s): RH, 3953854; LH, 3953853
    Usage: 1969 Chevelle

Interchange Number: 14
    Part Number(s): RH, 3970612; LH, 3970611
    Usage: 1970 Chevelle station wagon or El Camino
    Notes: Sedan, coupe, or convertible fenders will not fit.

Interchange Number: 15
    Part Number(s): RH, 3970610; LH,3970609
    Usage: 1970 Chevelle sedan, coupe, or convertible
    Notes: Fenders from El Camino or station wagon will
      not fit.

Interchange Number: 16
    Part Number(s): RH, 3764710; LH, 3764709
    Usage: 1959 full-size Chevrolet

Interchange Number: 17
    Part Number(s): RH, 3764272; LH, 3764271
    Usage: 1960 full-size Chevrolet

Interchange Number: 18
    Part Number(s): RH, 3783148; LH, 3783147
    Usage: 1961 full-size Chevrolet

Interchange Number: 19
    Part Number(s): RH, 3786162; LH, 3786161
    Usage: 1962 full-size Chevrolet

Interchange Number: 20
    Part Number(s): RH, 3828592; LH, 3828591
    Usage: 1963 full-size Chevrolet, except Z-11

Interchange Number: 21
    Part Number(s): RH, 3828594; LH, 3828593
    Usage: 1963 full-size Chevrolet Z-11
    Notes: Fenders are lightweight aluminum. Extremely
      rare.

Interchange Number: 22
    Part Number(s): RH, 3858942; LH, 3858941
    Usage: 1964 full-size Chevrolet

Interchange Number: 23
    Part Number(s): RH, 3865816; LH, 3865815
    Usage: 1965 full-size Chevrolet

Interchange Number: 24
    Part Number(s): RH, 3886310; LH, 3886309
    Usage: 1966 full-size Chevrolet

Interchange Number: 25
    Part Number(s): RH, 3904678; LH, 3904677
    Usage: 1967 full-size Chevrolet

Interchange Number: 26
Part Number(s): RH, 3924116; LH, 3924115
Usage: 1968 full-size Chevrolet

Interchange Number: 27
Part Number(s): RH, 3953694; LH, 3953693
Usage: 1969 full-size Chevrolet

Interchange Number: 28
Part Number(s): RH, 3970608; LH, 3970607
Usage: 1970 full-size Chevrolet

Interchange Number: 29
Part Number(s): RH, 3859177; LH, 3859178
Usage: 1962–65 Chevy II

Interchange Number: 30
Part Number(s): RH, 3888237; LH, 3888236
Usage: 1966 Chevy II

Interchange Number: 31
Part Number(s): RH, 3892222; LH, 3892221
Usage: 1967 Chevy II

Interchange Number: 32
Part Number(s): RH, 3953852; LH, 3953851
Usage: 1968–69 Nova

Interchange Number: 33
Part Number(s): RH, 6258338; LH, 6258337
Usage: 1970–72 Nova

Front Doors

On most models, doors were changed only when a significant design change occurred, so the interchange is larger than it may at first appear. Factors to consider are that they are unique to each side of the car and to different bodystyles. Interchange is the complete door, minus the interior door panel and any exterior trim moldings. In this chapter, two-door sedan means a pillar coupe.

Some doors may have to be stripped of their glass and other hardware to interchange. This is especially true when swapping a hardtop door to a convertible.

Model Identification

Interchange

Interchange Number: 1
Part Number(s): RH, 7645892; LH, 7645893
Usage: 1967 Camaro; 1967 Pontiac Firebird

Interchange Number: 2
Part Number(s): RH, 7742292; LH, 7742293
Usage: 1968 Camaro; 1968 Pontiac Firebird

Interchange Number: 3
Part Number(s): RH, 8723785; LH, 8723786
Usage: 1969 Camaro; 1969 Pontiac Firebird
Notes: Right-hand door only on Firebird. Left-hand door slightly different on Firebird due to way mirror mounts. Still will fit 1969 Camaro if Pontiac mirror is used.

Interchange Number: 4
Part Number(s): RH, 9681671; LH, 9681672
Usage: 1970–73 Camaro
Notes: Firebird doors will not interchange.

Interchange Number: 5
Part Number(s): RH, 4492500; LH, 4492501
Usage: 1964–65 Chevelle two-door sedan
Notes: Will not fit El Camino.

Interchange Number: 6
Part Number(s): RH, 4492506; LH, 4492507
Usage: 1964–65 Chevelle two-door hardtop or convertible
Notes: When swapping from hardtop to convertible, glass and all hardware must be removed and replaced with convertible components.

Interchange Number: 7
Part Number(s): RH, 4492504; LH, 4492505
Usage: 1964–65 El Camino
Notes: Unique door. Station wagon door will not interchange.

Interchange Number: 8
Part Number(s): RH, 7661576; LH, 7661577
Usage: 1966–67 Chevelle two-door sedan
Notes: Will not fit El Camino.

Interchange Number: 9
Part Number(s): RH, 7661578; LH, 7661579
Usage: 1966–67 El Camino
Notes: Unique door assembly. Station wagon will not fit.

Interchange Number: 10
Part Number(s): RH, 7661580; LH, 76615181
Usage: 1966–67 Chevelle two-door hardtop or convertible

Interchange Number: 11
Part Number(s): RH, 7742314; LH, 7742315
Usage: 1968 Chevelle two-door hardtop or convertible

Interchange Number: 12
Part Number(s): RH, 8716906; LH, 8716907
Usage: 1968–69 Chevelle two-door sedan
Notes: Will not fit El Camino.

Interchange Number: 13
Part Number(s): RH, 9888121; LH, 9888122
Usage: 1968–72 El Camino; 1971–72 GMC Sprint
Notes: Unique door; station wagon will not fit.

Interchange Number: 14
Part Number(s): RH, 8716910; LH, 8716911
Usage: 1969 Chevelle two-door hardtop or convertible

Interchange Number: 15
Part Number(s): RH, 9861034; LH, 9888153
Usage: 1970–71 Chevelle coupe or convertible
Notes: Driver's side door will interchange from 1970–72, but right-hand door in 1972 will not fit earlier models.

Interchange Number: 16
Part Number(s): RH, 4770669; LH, 4770670
Usage: 1959 full-size Chevrolet, Pontiac, or Oldsmobile; all two-door sedan

Interchange Number: 17
Part Number(s): RH, 4770675; LH, 4770676
Usage: 1959 full-size Chevrolet or Oldsmobile; both two-door hardtop or convertible

Interchange Number: 18
Part Number(s): RH, 4776927; LH, 4776928
Usage: 1959 El Camino
Notes: Unique door assembly.
Station wagon will not fit.

Interchange Number: 19
Part Number(s): RH, 4787756; LH, 4787757
Usage: 1960 full-size Chevrolet two-door sedan

Interchange Number: 20
Part Number(s): RH, 4787742; LH, 4787743
Usage: 1960 full-size Chevrolet two-door hardtop or convertible

Interchange Number: 21
Part Number(s): RH, 47877548; LH, 4787749
Usage: 1960 El Camino
Notes: Unique door assembly. Station wagon will not fit.

Interchange Number: 22
Part Number(s): RH, 4813620; LH, 4813621
Usage: 1961–62 full-size Chevrolet two-door sedan
Notes: In 1961 models new locks were phased in. These were continued into 1962. To interchange a 1962 door to an early 1961 model, the locks must be switched.

Interchange Number: 23
Part Number(s): RH, 4815062; LH, 4815063
Usage: 1961–62 full-size Chevrolet two-door hardtop or convertible
Notes: See notes under interchange number 22 this section.

Interchange Number: 24
Part Number(s): RH, 4415778; LH, 4415779
Usage: 1963–64 full-size Chevrolet two-door sedan

Interchange Number: 25
Part Number(s): RH, 4415780; LH, 4415781
Usage: 1963–64 full-size Chevrolet two-door hardtop or convertible

Interchange Number: 26
Part Number(s): RH, 44195141; LH, 44195142
Usage: 1965–66 full-size Chevrolet two-door sedan

Interchange Number: 27
Part Number(s): RH, 4495147; LH, 4495147
Usage: 1965 full-size Chevrolet two-door hardtop or convertible

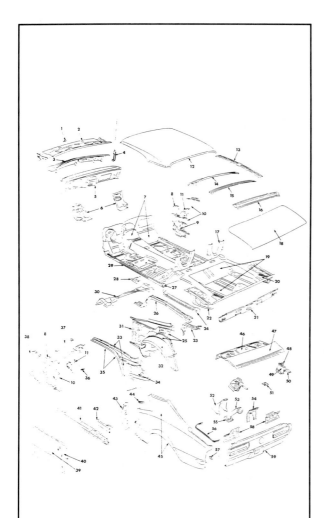

1967-69 CAMARO (SPT. CPE.) BODY SHEET METAL

1. 10.027 SUPPORT—Windshield Glass
2. 12.803 PANEL ASSY.—Shroud Upper
3. 12.804 PANEL ASSY.—Shroud Vent Duct Center
4. 10.230 BRACE—Instrument Panel to Center Duct
5. 10.230 PANEL ASSY.—Instrument
6. 12.650 BRACE ASSY.—Dash to Motor Mount Rail (Component of Item 7)
7. 12.804 PANEL ASSY.—Dash (Includes Item 6)
8. 12.804 PANEL—Shroud Vent Duct Side
9. 12.659 REINFORCEMENT—Front Body Hinge Pillar to Rocker
10. 12.840 PANEL ASSY.—Front Body Hinge Pillar
11. 12.659 REINFORCEMENT ASSY.—Front Body Hinge Pillar to Duct (Includes Item 36)
12. 12.810 PANEL—Roof
13. 12.952 BOW—Roof Longitudinal
14. 12.807 FRAME ASSY.—Windshield Inner Upper
15. 12.952 BOW—Roof
16. 12.964 PANEL—Back Window Inner
17. N.L. BRACE—Rear Seat Back Diagonal
18. 12.181 LID ASSY.—Rear Compartment
19. 12.981 PAN—Rear Compartment
20. 12.986 RAIL—Rear End Cross
21. 12.981 FILLER—Compartment Pan to Quarter Panel
22. 12.971 EXTENSION—Shelf Panel (Component of Item 25)
23. 12.981 REINFORCEMENT ASSY.—Compartment Pan at Gas Tank
24. 12.944 PANEL ASSY.—Wheelhouse (Includes Item 23-31-32-33-34)
25. 12.986 RAIL ASSY.—Rear Compartment Side
26. 12.934 FILLER—Rocker Inner Panel Rear
27. 12.980 REINFORCEMENT—Floor Pan at Rear Spring Front
28. 12.934 PANEL—Rocker Inner
29. 12.981 BAR ASSY.—Compartment Pan Cross Front
30. 12.941 PANEL—Rear Quarter Inner Low (Component of Item 25)

31. 12.944 PANEL—Wheelhouse Outer (Component of Item 25)
32. 12.956 RAIL ASSY.—Side Roof (Includes Item 35—Component of Item 25)
33. 12.941 PANEL—Rear Quarter Inner Upper (Component of Item 25)
34. 12.075 MOLDING—Roof Drip (Component of Item 33)
35. 10.230 SUPPORT—Instrument Panel End (Component of Item 11)
36. 12.075 MOLDING—Windshield Pillar Drip
37. 12.804 PANEL—Shroud Lower
38. 12.895 PANEL ASSY.—Front Door Outer (Component of Item 40)
39. 10.351 DOOR ASSY.—Front (Includes Item 39)
40. 12.934 PANEL ASSY.—Door Opening Rocker Outer
41. 12.934 REINFORCEMENT—Rocker Outer Panel
42. 12.942 REINFORCEMENT—Body Lock Pillar
43. 12.941 FILLER—Quarter Window Lower Rear Corner 20.
44. 12.971 PANEL ASSY.—Rear Seat Back Shelf
45. 12.971 PANEL ASSY.—Rear Compartment Front
46. 12.186 PIN—Compartment Lid Hinge
47. 12.184 SUPPORT—Compartment Lid Hinge
48. 12.187 STRAP—Compartment Lid Hinge
49. 12.981 SUPPORT ASSY.—Spare Tire Clamp Anchor Plate
50. 12.945 COVER—Gas Tank Filler Neck Tube Protector
51. 12.945 HOSE—Gas Tank Filler Neck Tube Protector
52. 12.237 PLATE—Compartment Lid Lock Striker Anchor
53. 12.945 RETAINER—Gas Tank Filler Neck Tube Protector
54. 12.996 GUTTER—Compartment Lid Side
55. 7.836 SUPPORT—Rear Bumper
56. N.L. REINFORCEMENT—Rear End Panel (Component of Item 59)
57. 12.966 PANEL—Rear End

1967-69 CAMARO (CONVERTIBLE) BODY SHEET METAL

1. 10.027 SPORT—Windshield Glass
2. 12.803 PANEL ASSY., Shroud Upper
3. 12.804 PANEL ASSY., Shroud Vent Duct Center
4. 10.230 BRACE, Instrument Panel to Center Duct
5. 12.804 REINFORCEMENT, Shroud Vent Center Duct Panel Side at Windshield
6. 10.230 PANEL ASSY., Instrument
7. 12.650 BRACE ASSY., Dash to Motor Mount Rail (Component of Item 8)
8. 12.804 PANEL ASSY., Dash (Includes Item 7)
9. 12.807 FRAME ASSY., Windshield Inner Upper
10. 14.050 RAIL ASSY., Front Roof
11. 12.659 REINFORCEMENT ASSY., Front Body, Hinge Pillar to Duct (Includes Item 35)
12. 12.804 PANEL, Shroud Vent Duct Side
13. 12.840 PANEL ASSY., Front Body Hinge Pillar
14. 12.659 REINFORCEMENT, Front Body Hinge Pillar to Rocker
15. 12.944 REINFORCEMENT, Wheelhouse Inner Panel (Component of Item 24)
16. 12.181 LID ASSY., Rear Compartment
17. 12.981 PAN, Rear Compartment
18. 7.836 SUPPORT ASSY., Rear Bumper Inner
19. 12.986 RAIL, Rear End Cross
20. 12.981 FILLER, Compartment Pan to Quarter Panel
21. 12.981 REINFORCEMENT ASSY., Compartment Pan at Gas Tank
22. 12.986 RAIL ASSY., Rear Compartment Side
23. 12.948 BRACE, Folding Top Mounting Support to Wheelhouse (Component of Item 24)
24. 12.944 PANEL ASSY., Wheelhouse (Includes Items 15-23-25-27-28)
25. 12.944 PANEL, Wheelhouse Outer (Component of Item 24)
26. 12.948 SUPPORT, Folding Top Mounting
27. 12.941 PANEL, Rear Quarter Inner Rear (Component of Item 24)
28. 12.941 PANEL, Rear Quarter Inner Front (Component of Item 24)
29. 12.684 BRACE, Body Lock Pillar to Folding Top Mounting Support
30. 12.981 BAR ASSY., Compartment Pan Cross Front

31. 12.934 FILLER, Rocker Inner Panel Rear
32. 12.980 REINFORCEMENT, Floor Pan at Rear Spring Front
33. 12.934 PANEL, Rocker Inner
34. 12.684 BRACE, Body Lock Pillar to Floor Pan
35. 10.230 SUPPORT, Instrument Panel End (Component of Item 11)
36. 12.804 PANEL, Shroud Lower
37. 12.895 PANEL ASSY., Front Door Outer (Component of Item 38)
38. 10.351 DOOR ASSY., Front (Includes Item 37)
39. 12.934 PANEL ASSY., Door Opening Rocker Outer
40. 12.934 REINFORCEMENT, Rocker Outer Panel Rear
41. 12.942 REINFORCEMENT, Body Lock Pillar
42. 12.940 REINFORCEMENT, Rear Quarter Outer Panel at Belt
43. 12.940 PANEL, Rear Quarter Side Outer
44. 12.971 PANEL ASSY., Rear Compartment Front
45. 12.186 PIN, Compartment Lid Hinge
46. 12.184 SUPPORT, Compartment Lid Hinge
47. 12.187 STRAP, Comprtment Lid Hinge
48. 12.981 SUPPORT ASSY., Spare Tire Clamp Anchor Plate
49. 12.945 COVER, Gas Tank Filler Neck Tube Protector
50. 12.945 HOSE, Gas Tank Filler Neck Tube Protector
51. 12.945 RETAINER, Gas Tank Filler Neck Tube Protector
52. 12.996 GUTTER, Compartment Lid Side
53. 7.836 SUPPORT, Rear Bumper
54. 12.237 PLATE, Compartment Lid Lock Striker Anchor
55. N.L. REINFORCEMENT, Rear End Panel (Component of Item 56)
56. 12.966 PANEL, Rear End
57. 12.989 BRACE ASSY., Folding Top Upper
58. 12.989 BRACE ASSY., Folding Top Lower
59. 12.684 BRACE, Body Lock Pillar to Quarter Panel

58. N.L. REINFORCEMENT—Rear End Panel (Component of Item 59)
59. 12.966 PANEL—Rear End

ITEM 58 FOR 1967-1968 ONLY

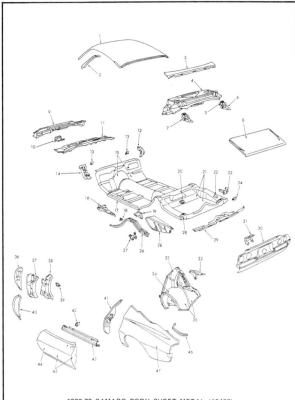

1970-73 CAMARO BODY SHEET METAL (12487)

1. 12.810 PANEL ASM.–Roof (Incl. Item 2)
2. 12.840 PANEL ASM.–Front Body Hinge Pillar Upper
   (Comp. of Item 1)
3. 12.971 PANEL ASM.–Compartment Front
4. 12.971 PANEL ASM.–Rear Seat to Back Window
   (Incl. Items 5,6,7)
5. 12.186 PIN–Rear Compartment Lid Hinge (Comp.
   of Item 4)
6. 12.187 STRAP–REAR Compartment Lid Hinge (Comp.
   of Item 4)
7. 12.184 SUPPORT–Rear Compartment Lid Hinge (Comp.
   of Item 4)
8. 12.181 LID ASM.–Compartment
9. 12.804 PANEL ASM.–Shroud Vent Center Duct
10. 6.760 PLATE ASM.–Steering Column Support Anchor
    Lower
11. 12.804 PANEL ASM.–Shroud Upper and Instrument
12. 12.804 DEFLECTOR–Shroud Air Conditioning Blower
    Water-Right Side
13. 8.141 SUPPORT ASM.–Front Fender on Dash
14. 12.650 BRACE ASM.–Dash to Motor Mount Rail
    (Comp. of Item 15)
15. 12.804 PANEL ASM.–Dash (Incl. Item 14)
16. 12.986 REINDORCEMENT ASM.–Floor Pan at Rear Spring
    Front (Comp. of Item 26)
17. 12.934 PANEL ASM.–Rocker Inner
18. 4.785 SUPPORT–Parking Brake Cable on Rail
    (Comp. of Item 26)
19. 12.986 HOUSING ASM.–Rear Shock Absorber (Comp.
    of Item 26)
20. 12.981 SUPPORT–Spare Tire Clamp Anchor Plate
21. 12.981 PAN ASM.–Rear Compartment (Incl. Items
    26,28,29)
22. 12.966 EXTENSION–Rear End Panel Outer Reinforcement
23. 12.966 REINFORCEMENT ASM.–Rear End Panel Outer
24. 12.986 EXTENSION–Rear End Cross Rail to Quarter
    Panel Filler
25. 12.981 FILLER–Rear Compartment Pan to Quarter Panel
26. 12.986 RAIL ASM.–Rear Compartment Pan Side
    (Comp. of Item 21)
27. 12.986 SUPPORT–Stabilizer Bar on Compartment Side
    Rail
28. 7.836 SUPPORT–Rear Bumper Outer Mounting
    (Comp. of Item 21)
29. 12.986 RAIL–Rear End Cross (Comp. of Item 21)
30. 12.966 PANEL ASM.–Rear End
31. 12.237 PLATE–Rear Compartment Lid Lock Anchor-Body
    Side
32. 12.971 EXTENSION–Rear Seat to Back Window Panel
    (Comp. of Item 35)
33. 12.941 BRACE–Quarter Inner Upper to Wheelhouse
    (Comp. of Item 35)
34. 12.944 PANEL–Wheelhouse Outer (Comp. of Item 35)
35. 12.944 PANEL ASM.–Wheelhouse (Incl. Items
    32,33,34)
36. 12.804 PANEL–Shroud Vent Side Duct Front
37. 12.840 PANEL ASM.–Front Body Hinge Pillar Lower
38. 12.804 PANEL ASM.–Shroud Vent Duct Side
39. 10.230 SUPPORT ASM.–Instrument Panel End
40. 12.804 PANEL–Shroud Lower
41. 12.934 REINFORCEMENT–Body Lock Pillar
42. 12.942 PLATE–Rocker Outer Panel Baffle-Right Side
43. 12.934 PANEL–Rocker Outer
44. 12.895 PANEL ASM.–Front Door Outer (Comp. of Item 45)
45. 10.351 DOOR ASM.–Front (Incl. Item 44)
46. 12.996 GUTTER–Rear Compartment Lid Side
47. 12.940 PANEL–Rear Quarter Outer

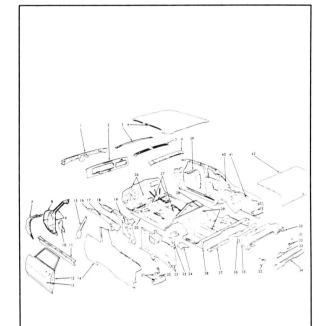

1964-65 CHEVELLE SHEET METAL—TWO DOOR

1. 12.804 PANEL ASSEMBLY, Upper Dash and Duct
2. 10.230 PANEL ASSEMBLY, Instrument
3. 12.807 FRAME, Windshield Inner Upper
4. 12.810 PANEL, Roof
5. 12.952 BOW ASSEMBLY, Roof
6. 12.964 PANEL, Back Window Inner
7. 12.804 PANEL, Shroud Side
8. 12.804 PANEL ASSEMBLY, Shroud Side Duct
9. 12.840 PANEL ASSY., Front Body Hinge Pillar
10. 12.659 REINF., Frt. Body Pillar to Duct
11. 12.934 PANEL, Door Opening Rocker Outer
12. 10.351 DOOR ASSEMBLY
13. 12.895 PANEL ASSEMBLY, Front Door Outer
14. 12.940 PANEL, Quarter Outer
15. 12.942 PANEL ASSY., Body Lock Pillar
16. 12.075 MOULDING, Roof Drip Front
17. 12.956 RAIL ASSEMBLY, Side Roof Outer
18. 12.957 RAIL, Side Roof Inner Front
19. 12.957 RAIL ASSEMBLY, Side Roof Inner Rear
20. 12.934 PANEL, Rocker Inner
21. 12.943 PLATES, Tail Lamp Mounting
22. 12.940 PANEL, Rear Quarter Outer Extension
23. 12.944 PANEL ASSEMBLY, Wheelhouse
24. 12.944 BRACE, Wheelhouse Inner Panel
25. 12.971 EXTENSION, Shelf Panel
26. 12.804 PANEL ASSEMBLY, Dash Lower
27. 12.980 PAN ASSEMBLY, Floor
28. N.S.S. BRACE, Rear Seat Back
29. 12.981 PAN ASSEMBLY, Rear
30. 12.187 STRAP, Rear Compartment Lid Inner
31. 12.184 SUPPORT, Rear Compartment Lid Hinge
32. 12.237 PLATE, Rr. Compt. Striker Anchor
33. 12.996 BRACE, Rear Compartment Gutter
34. 12.966 PANEL, Rear End
35. 12.971 PANEL, Rear Compartment Front
36. 12.971 PANEL, Rear Seat Back Shelf
37. 12.986 BAR, Rear Cross
38. 12.981 FILLER, Compartment Pan
39. 12.804 PANEL, Shroud Side
40. 12.964 FILLER, Back Window Lower
41. 12.966 PANEL, Rear End
42. 12.181 LID ASSEMBLY, Rear Compartment

Notes: When swapping between convertible and hard-top, glass and all hardware must be removed.

Interchange Number: 28
Part Number(s): RH, 7587232; LH, 7587233
Usage: 1966 full-size Chevrolet two-door hardtop or convertible
Notes: To interchange the Impala and Caprice, the door must be stripped of glass and the wing window frame, and the correct ones used. Same holds true for hardtop and convertible.

Interchange Number: 29
Part Number(s): RH, 7660376; LH, 7660377
Usage: 1967 full-size Chevrolet two-door sedan

Interchange Number: 30
Part Number(s): RH, 7660378; LH, 7660379
Usage: 1967 full-size Chevrolet two-door hardtop or convertible
Notes: When interchanging between hardtop and convertible, door glass and wing window frame must be removed. Also, when swapping between Caprice and other models, door glass must be removed.

Interchange Number: 31
Part Number(s): RH, 7748876; LH, 7748877
Usage: 1968 full-size Chevrolet two-door sedan

Interchange Number: 32
Part Number(s): RH, 7748882; LH, 7748883
Usage: 1968 full-size Chevrolet two-door hardtop and convertible
Notes: (1) When interchanging between hardtops and convertibles, remove door glass and vent window frame. (2) When swapping between hardtops And fastbacks, door glass must be removed. (3) Caprice models used different door and will not interchange.

Interchange Number: 33
Part Number(s): RH, 8728776; LH, 8728777
Usage: 1969 full-size Chevrolet two-door sedan

Interchange Number: 34
Part Number(s): RH, 8728782; LH, 8728783
Usage: 1969–70 full-size Chevrolet two-door hardtop or convertible
Notes: Interchange without glass only.

Interchange Number: 35
Part Number(s):RH, 4450626; LH, 4450627
Usage: 1962–65 Chevy II two-door sedan
Notes: Locks differ between 1962 models and later models and must be changed appropriately.

Interchange Number: 36
Part Number(s): RH, 4487210; LH, 4487211
Usage: 1962–65 Chevy II two-door hardtop or 1962–64 convertible

Interchange Number: 37
Part Number(s): RH, 4545144; LH, 4545145
Usage: 1966 Chevy II two-door sedan

Interchange Number: 38
Part Number(s): RH, 4545146; LH, 4545147
Usage: 1966 Chevy II two-door hardtop

Interchange Number: 39
Part Number(s): RH, 7643068; LH, 7643069
Usage: 1967 Chevy II two-door sedan

Interchange Number: 40
Part Number(s): RH, 7689127; LH, 7689128
Usage: 1967 Chevy II two-door hardtop

Interchange Number: 41
Part Number(s): RH, 9873610; LH, 9877671
Usage: 1968–72 Nova sport coupe; 1971–72 Pontiac Ventura II sport coupe

Front Door Hinges

Hinges are greatly interchangeable, and model or bodystyle does not affect the interchange as much as you might think.

Hinges are differentiated by the position in which they are used: upper and lower. When replacing a hinge, both upper and lower units should be replaced at the same time. Also, you should be aware that on some models there is distinct difference between the right and left sides of the car. Thus, door hinges from the passenger's side may not fit the driver's side door.

Model Identification

Camaro	Identification Number
1967	
Upper	1
Lower	15
1968	
Upper	2
Lower	16
1969	
Upper	3
Lower	17
1970	
Upper	4
Lower	18

Chevelle	Identification Number
1964–65	
Upper	5
Lower	19
1966–67	
Upper	1
Lower	15
1968–70	
Upper	6
Lower	20

Impala	Identification Number
1959–60	
Upper	7
Lower	21
1961–64	
Upper	8
Lower	22
1965–66	
Upper	9
Lower	23
1967–68	
Upper	10

Interchange

Interchange Number: 1
 Part Number(s): 7642529 (fits either side)
 Usage: 1966 Olds Cutlass; 1966–67 Chevelle; 1966–67
 Buick Skylark; 1966–67 Pontiac LeMans; 1967 Ca-
 maro; 1967 Pontiac Firebird

Interchange Number: 2
 Part Number(s): RH, 8736244; LH, 8736245
 Usage: 1968 Camaro; 1968 Pontiac Firebird

Interchange Number: 3
 Part Number(s): RH, 9817406; LH, 9817407
 Usage: 1969 Camaro; 1969 Pontiac Firebird; 1969–74
 Nova; 1971–74 Pontiac Ventura; 1973–74 Buick
 Apollo; 1973–74 Olds Omega

Interchange Number: 4
 Part Number(s): RH, 9868457; LH, 9868458
 Usage: 1970–74 Pontiac Firebird; 1970–75 Camaro;
 1971–74 full-size Buick; 1971–74 full-size Pontiac;
 1971–74 full-size Oldsmobile; 1971–75 full-size
 Chevrolet

Interchange Number: 5
 Part Number(s): 4409743 (fits either side)
 Usage: 1964–65 Chevelle; 1964–65 Buick Skylark;
 1964–65 Olds Cutlass; 1964–65 Pontiac LeMans

Interchange Number: 6
 Part Number(s): 7722170 (fits either side)
 Usage: 1968–72 Chevelle; 1968–72 Pontiac LeMans;
 1968–72 Olds Cutlass; 1968–72 Buick Skylark;
 1969–72 Pontiac Grand Prix; 1970–72 Monte Carlo;
 1971–72 GMC Sprint

Interchange Number: 7
 Part Number(s): *Spring-type:* RH, 4301364, LH,
 4301365; *strap-type:* RH, 4301370, LH, 4301371
 Usage: 1959–60 full-size Chevrolet, Pontiac, Oldsmobile, or Buick

Interchange Number: 8
 Part Number(s): *Spring-type:* 4309528 (fits either side);
 strap-type: 4307840 (fits either side)
 Usage: 1961–64 full-size Chevrolet, Pontiac, Oldsmobile, or Buick

Interchange Number: 9
 Part Number(s): *Spring-type:* 5719425 (fits either side);
 strap-type: 5719426 (fits either side)
 Usage: 1965–66 full-size Chevrolet, Pontiac, Oldsmobile, or Buick

Interchange Number: 10
 Part Number(s): *Spring-type:* 9710342 (fits either side);
 strap-type: 9714726 (fits either side)
 Usage: 1967–68 full-size Chevrolet, Pontiac, Oldsmobile, or Buick

Interchange Number: 11
 Part Number(s): RH, 8720943; LH, 8720944
 Usage: 1969–70 full-size Chevrolet, Pontiac, Oldsmo-
 bile, or Buick

Interchange Number: 12
 Part Number(s): 7580738 (fits either side)
 Usage: 1962–66 Chevy II

Interchange Number: 13
 Part Number(s): 7642529 (fits either side)
 Usage: 1967 Chevy II

Interchange Number: 14
 Part Number(s): RH, 7722192; LH, 7722193
 Usage: 1968 Nova

Interchange Number: 15
 Part Number(s): RH, 7663424; LH, 7663425
 Usage: 1966 Olds Cutlass; 1966–67 Chevelle; 1966–67
 Buick Skylark; 1966–67 Pontiac LeMans; 1967 Ca-
 maro; 1967 Pontiac Firebird

Interchange Number: 16
 Part Number(s): RH, 8736248; LH, 8736249
 Usage: 1968 Camaro; 1968 Pontiac Firebird

Interchange Number: 17
 Part Number(s): RH, 9817408; LH, 9817409
 Usage: 1969 Camaro; 1969 Pontiac Firebird; 1969–74
 Nova; 1971–74 Pontiac Ventura; 1973–74 Buick
 Apollo; 1973–74 Olds Omega

Interchange Number: 18
 Part Number(s): 9816926 (fits either side)
 Usage: 1969–74 full-size Chevrolet, Pontiac, Oldsmo-
 bile, or Buick; 1970–74 Pontiac Firebird; 1970–75
 Camaro

Interchange Number: 19
 Part Number(s): RH, 4506971; LH, 4506972
 Usage: 1964–65 Chevelle; 1964–65 Buick Skylark;
 1964–65 Olds Cutlass; 1964–65 Pontiac LeMans

Interchange Number: 20
 Part Number(s): RH, 7722087; LH, 7722088
 Usage: 1968–72 Chevelle; 1968–72 Pontiac LeMans;
 1968–72 Olds Cutlass; 1968–72 Buick Skylark;
 1969–72 Pontiac Grand Prix; 1970–72 Monte Carlo;
 1971–72 GMC Sprint

Interchange Number: 21
 Part Number(s): *Spring-type:* 4301376 (fits either side);
 strap-type: 4301369 (fits either side)
 Usage: 1959–60 full-size Chevrolet, Pontiac, Oldsmobile, or Buick

Part Number(s): *Spring-type:* RH, 4309530, LH, 4309531; *strap-type:* RH, 5711928, LH, 5711929

Usage: 1961–64 full-size Chevrolet, Pontiac, Oldsmobile, or Buick

Interchange Number: 23

Part Number(s): *Spring-type:* RH, 5719594, LH, 5719595; *strap-type:* RH, 5719598, LH, 5719599

Usage: 1965–66 full-size Chevrolet, Pontiac, Oldsmobile, or Buick

Interchange Number: 24

Part Number(s): *Spring-type:* RH, 9709314, LH, 9709315; *strap-type:* RH, 9709318, LH, 9709319

Usage: 1967 full-size Chevrolet, Pontiac, Oldsmobile, or Buick

Interchange Number: 25

Part Number(s): *Spring-type:* RH, 9713086, LH, 9713087; *strap-type:* RH, 9713090, LH, 9713091

Usage: 1968 full-size Chevrolet, Pontiac, Oldsmobile, or Buick

Interchange Number: 26

Part Number(s): RH, 4841356; LH, 4841357

Usage: 1962–67 Chevy II

Interchange Number: 27

Part Number(s): RH, 7722194; LH, 7722195

Usage: 1968 Nova

Outside Door Handle

Exterior door handles are widely interchangeable and can be found on other GM models besides Chevrolet. While this section deals with front door handles *only*, in some cases, and on some models, the same handle can be found on the rear door. Normally, handles are also reversible, meaning one side will fit the other. There are exceptions, however, such as the 1968 and later Nova which has special handles that are unique to each side. If there are special circumstances, they are listed in the charts under "Restrictions."

Model Identification

Camaro	Interchange Number
1967–69	1
1970	2

Chevelle	Interchange Number
1964–67	1
1968–69	3
1970	
except El Camino	4
El Camino	3

Impala	Interchange Number
1959–68	5
1969–70	4

Chevy II/ Nova	Interchange Number
1962–64	6
1966–67	7

Interchange

Interchange Number: 1

Part Number(s): RH, 5716870; LH, 5716871

Usage: 1960 full-size Chevrolet (except sport sedan); 1963–64 full-size Buick; 1964–67 Chevelle; 1966–67 Pontiac LeMans; 1966–67 Buick Skylark (rear door only); 1967–69 Pontiac Firebird; 1967–69 Camaro; 1968–75 Nova; 1969–70 Electra (rear door only); 1970–72 Buick Skylark (front and rear doors); 1971–75 Pontiac Ventura II; 1973–75 Olds Omega (front and rear doors)

Restrictions: See usage.

Interchange Number: 2

Part Number(s): RH, 9827570; LH, 9827571

Usage: 1970–75 Camaro; 1970–75 Pontiac Firebird; 1971–75 full-size Chevrolet; 1971–75 Vega; 1971–75 Monza; 1975 Buick Skyhawk; 1975 Pontiac Astre

Restrictions: Astre SJ is not interchangeable.

Interchange Number: 3

Part Number(s): RH, 9712350; LH, 9712351

Usage: 1968–72 Chevelle; 1968–72 Pontiac LeMans; 1969–70 full-size Chevrolet four-door; 1970–72 Chevelle station wagon or El Camino

Interchange Number: 4

Part Number(s): RH, 9717592; LH, 9717593

Usage: 1969–70 full-size Chevrolet; 1969–70 full-size Pontiac; 1969–70 full-size Buick (front only in 1969); 1970–72 Chevelle

Restrictions: All 1970–72 Chevelle bodystyles except station wagon or El Camino. Coupe or convertible only on full-size models.

Interchange Number: 5

Part Number(s): RH, 9702886; LH, 9702887

Usage: 1959–67 full-size Pontiac; 1959–68 full-size Chevrolet; 1960 full-size Buick; 1962–64 Chevy II; 1963–64 Riviera

Restrictions: Front door only on full-size models.

Interchange Number: 6

Usage: 1962–64 Chevy II (front or rear doors)

Interchange Number: 7

Part Number(s): RH, 5719142; LH, 5719143

Usage: 1966–67 Chevy II; 1969–70 full-size Chevrolet four-door

Roof Assembly

Model Identification

Camaro	Interchange Number
1967–69	1
1970	2

Chevelle	Interchange Number
1964–65	
Two-door sedan	3
Two-door hardtop	4
El Camino	5

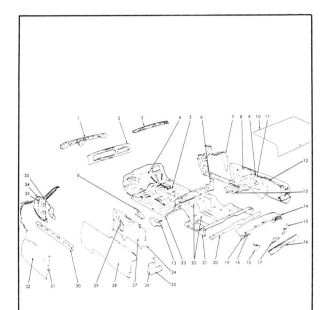

1964-65 CHEVELLE SHEET
METAL—CONVERTIBLE

1. 12.804 PANEL ASSY., Upper Dash and Duct
2. 10.230 PANEL ASSEMBLY, Instrument
3. 12.807 FRAME ASSY., Windshield Upper
4. 12.804 PANEL ASSY., Lower Dash
5. N.L. PAN ASSY., (Only Serviced Current Model)
6. 12.684 BRACE, Lock Pillar to Pan
7. 12.804 PANEL, Shroud Side
8. 12.940 REINFORCEMENT, Panel at Belt
9. 12.989 PANEL, Top Compartment Rear
10. 12.181 LID ASSY., Rear Compartment
11. 12.768 FILLER, Top Compt. Side to Rear
12. 12.996 GUTTER, Rear Compartment Lid
13. 12.768 BRACE, Top Compartment to Wheelhouse
14. 12.971 PANEL, Rear Compartment Front
15. 12.996 BRACE, Compartment Gutter to Pan
16. 12.966 PANEL, Rear End
17. 12.237 PLATE, Lid Lock Striker Anchor
18. 12.187 STRAP, Lid Hinge
19. 12.184 BOX, Lid Hinge
20. 12.986 BAR, Rear Cross
21. 12.981 FILLER, Compartment Pan to Panel
22. 12.981 PAN ASSY., Rear Compartment
23. 12.934 PANEL, Rocker Inner
24. 12.944 PANEL ASSEMBLY, Wheelhouse
25. 12.940 PANEL, Rear Outer Extension
26. 12.943 PLATE, Tail Lamp Mounting
27. 12.944 PANEL, Wheelhouse Outer
28. 12.940 PANEL, Rear Quarter Outer
29. 12.941 PANEL ASSY., Rear Quarter Inner Front
30. 12.934 PANEL, Rocker Outer
31. 10.351 DOOR ASSEMBLY
32. 12.895 PANEL ASSEMBLY, Door Outer
33. 12.840 PANEL ASSEMBLY, Hinge Pillar
34. 12.804 PANEL ASSEMBLY, Shroud Side Duct
35. 12.659 REINFORCEMENT, Hinge Pillar to Duct

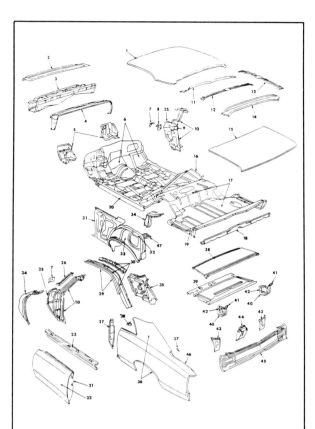

1966 CHEVELLE SHEET METAL—TWO DOOR HARDTOP

1. 12.810 PANEL, Roof
2. 12.800 GRILLE, Shroud Top Vent
3. 12.804 PANEL ASSY., Upr. Dash and Duct
4. 10.230 PANEL ASSY., Instrument
5. 12.650 BRACE ASSY., Dash to Chassis
6. 12.804 PANEL ASSY., Dash Lower (Incl. Item 5)
7. 12.659 REINF., Frt. Body Hge. Plr. to Duct
8. 12.659 REINF., Frt. Body Hge. Plr. at Upr. Hge.
9. 10.230 SUPPORT ASSY., Inst. Panel End
10. 12.840 PANEL ASSY., Frt. Body Hge. Pillar
11. 12.807 FRAME, Windshield Inner Upper
12. 12.952 BOW ASSY., Roof
13. 12.952 BOW, Roof Longitudinal
14. 12.964 PANEL, Back Wind Inner
15. 12.181 LID ASSY., Rear Compartment
16. N.L. BRACE, Rr. Seat Back Diag.
17. 12.981 PAN ASSY., Rear Compartment
         (Incl. Item 18)
18. 12.986 BAR ASSY., Rear Cross
19. 12.981 FILLER, Rr. Compt. Pan. to Qtr. Pnl.
20. 12.934 PANEL, Rocker Inner
21. 10.351 DOOR ASSY., Front (Incl. Item 22)
22. 12.895 PANEL ASSY., Frt. Door Outer
23. 12.934 PANEL, Door Opng. Rocker Outer
24. 12.804 PANEL, Shroud Lower Side
25. 12.804 PANEL, Shroud Vent Duct Side
26. 12.808 FRAME, W/shield Outer Side
27. 12.042 REINF., Body Lock Pillar
28. 12.941 FILLER, Qtr. Wind Lwr. Rr. Corner
29. 12.075 MOULDING, Roof Drip
30. 12.956 RAIL, Side Roof (Incl. Item 29)
31. 12.941 PANEL, Rear Qtr. Inner Lower
32. 12.944 PANEL, Wheelhouse (Incl. Items 31-33-49)
33. 12.944 PANEL, Wheelhouse Outer (Part of Item 32)
34. 12.971 EXTENSION, Shelf Panel
35. 12.941 PANEL, Rear Qtr. Inner Upper
36. 12.940 PANEL, Rear Qtr. Side Outer
37. 12.940 REINF., Compt. Lid Opng. Upr. Corner
38. 12.971 PANEL, Rear Compartment Front
39. 12.971 PANEL, Rear Seat Back Shelf
40. 12.184 SUPPORT, Rear Compt. Lid Hinge
41. 12.187 HINGE, Rr. Compt. Lid
42. 12.186 PIN, Rr. Compt. Lid Hinge
43. 12.996 BRACE, Compt. Gutr. to Compt. Pan.
44. 12.237 PLATE, Rr. Compt. Lid Lk. Strkr. Anchor
45. 12.966 PANEL ASSY., Rear End (Incl. Item 48)
46. 12.996 GUTTER, Rear Compt. Lid Side
47. 12.944 BRACE, Whse. to Compt. Lid Gutter

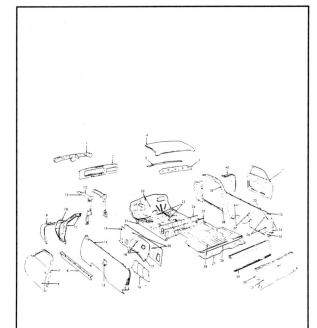

1964-66 EL CAMINO SHEET METAL

1. 12.804 PANEL ASSEMBLY, Upper Dash
2. 10.230 PANEL ASSEMBLY, Instrument
3. 12.807 FRAME, W/Shield Inner Upper
4. 12.810 PANEL, Roof
5. 12.964 PANEL, Back Window Inner
6. 12.895 PANEL ASSEMBLY, Door Outer
7. 10.351 DOOR ASSEMBLY
8. 12.934 PANEL, Door Opening Rocker Quarter
9. 12.804 PANEL, Shroud Side
10. 12.804 PANEL ASSEMBLY, Shroud Side Duct
11. 12.840 PANEL ASSY., Front Body Hinge Pillar
12. 12.075 MOULDING, Roof Drip Front
13. 12.956 RAIL ASSEMBLY, Side Roof Outer
14. 12.940 PANEL, Rear Qtr. Side Outer
15. 12.945 FILLER, Gas Tank Door Opening
16. 12.981 FILLER, Compartment Pan
17. 12.944 PANEL, Wheelhouse Outer
18. 12.944 PANEL ASSEMBLY, Wheelhouse
19. 12.942 PANEL, Body Lock Pillar
20. 12.941 PANEL, Rear Quarter Inner Front
21. 12.934 PANEL, Rocker Outer
22. 12.804 PANEL ASSEMBLY, Dash Lower
23. 12.980 PAN ASSEMBLY, Floor
24. 12.971 PANEL ASSY., Rr. Compt. Div. Lower
25. N.L.   SUPPORT, Rear Compartment Floor
26. 12.986 BAR ASSEMBLY, Rear Cross Front
27. 12.986 BAR, Rear Cross Rear
28. 12.981 PAN ASSEMBLY, Rear Compartment
29. 12.971 PANEL ASSY., Rr. Compt. Div. Upper
30. 12.179 GATE ASSEMBLY, Tail
31. 12.179 PANEL ASSEMBLY, Tail Gate Outer
32. 12.940 FILLER, Quarter Outer Panel
33. 12.968 PANEL ASSY., Back Body Pillar
34. 12.940 PANEL, Rear Quarter Outer Ext.
35. 12.940 FILLER, Rear Quarter Rear Lower
36. 12.941 PANEL, Rear Quarter Inner Rear
37. 12.941 PANEL, Rear Quarter Inner Front
38. 12.942 PANEL, Body Lock Pillar Inner Lower
39. N.S.   PANEL, Part of 12.940 Panel
40. 12.804 PANEL, Shroud Side

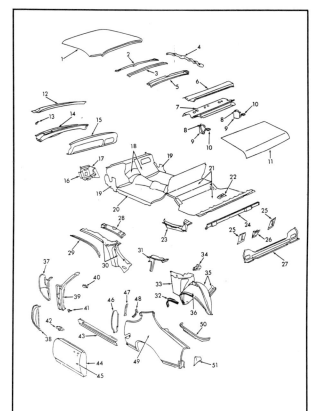

1968-69 CHEVELLE SHEET METAL—TWO DOOR

1. 12.810 PANEL, Roof
2. 12.807 FRAME, Windshield Inner Upper
3. 12.952 BOW, Roof
4. 12.952 BOW, Roof Longitudinal
5. 12.964 PANEL, Back Window Inner
6. 12.971 PANEL, Rear Compartment Front
7. 12.971 PANEL, Rear Seat to Back Window
8. 12.186 PIN, Rear Compartment Lid Hinge
9. 12.184 SUPPORT, Rear Compartment Lid Hinge
10. 12.187 STRAP & LINK, Rear Compartment
        Lid Hinge
11. 12.181 LID ASSY., Rear/Compartment
12. 12.804 PANEL ASSY., Shroud Upper
13. 10.027 SUPPORT, Windshield Glass
14. 12.804 PANEL ASSY., Shroud Vent Duct Center
15. 10.230 PANEL ASSY., Instrument
16. 8.153 SUPPORT ASSY., Front Fender Skirt on
        Brace (Comp. Item 17)
17. 12.650 BRACE ASSY., Dash to Chassis Frame
        (Comp. Item 18—Incl. Item 16)
18. 12.804 PANEL ASSY., Dash (Incl. Item 17)
19. 12.659 REINFORCEMENT, Front Body Hinge
        Pillar to Rocker
20. 12.934 PANEL, Rocker Inner
21. 12.981 PAN ASSY., Rear Compartment
        (Incl. Items 22-23-24)
22. 12.981 SUPPORT, Spare Tire Clamp Anchor
        Plate (Comp. Item 21)
23. 12.981 FILLER, Compartment Pan to Quarter
        Panel (Comp. Item 21)
24. 12.986 BAR ASSY., Rear Cross (Comp. Item 21)
25. 12.996 BRACE, Compartment Gutter to
        Compartment Pan
26. 12.237 PLATE, Compartment Lid Lock
        Striker Anchor
27. 12.966 PANEL ASSY., Rear End
28. N.S.S. RAIL, Side Roof Inner (Comp. Item 30)
29. 12.075 MOLDING, Roof Drip (Comp. Item 30)
30. 12.956 RAIL ASSY., Side Roof (Incl.
        Items 28-29)
31. 12.971 EXTENSION, Rear Seat to Back
        Window Panel
32. 12.944 REINFORCEMENT, Wheelhouse
        Outer Panel (Comp. Item 35)
33. 12.941 PANEL ASSY., Rear Quarter Inner
        Lower (Comp. Item 35)
34. 12.941 EXTENSION, Quarter Inner Panel Rear
35. 12.944 PANEL ASSY., Wheelhouse (Incl.
        Items 32-33-36)
36. 12.944 PANEL, Wheelhouse Outer (Comp. Item 35)
37. 12.804 PANEL, Shroud Vent Duct Side
38. 12.804 PANEL, Shroud Lower
39. 12.840 PANEL ASSY., Front Body Hinge Pillar
40. 10.230 SUPPORT, Instrument Panel End
41. 8.141 SUPPORT ASSY., Front Fender on Dash
42. 10.657 REINFORCEMENT, Front Door
        Outer Panel at Vent
43. 12.934 PANEL, Door Opening Rocker Outer
44. 10.351 DOOR ASSY., Front (Incl. Item 45)
45. 12.895 PANEL ASSY., Front Door Outer
        (Comp. Item 44)
46. 12.942 REINFORCEMENT, Body Lock Pillar
47. 12.942 PANEL ASSY., Body Lock Pillar
        Upper (27 Styles)
48. 12.941 FILLER, Quarter Window Lower
        Rear Corner
49. 12.940 PANEL, Rear Quarter Side Outer
50. 12.996 GUTTER, Rear Compartment Lid Side
51. 12.940 EXTENSION, Quarter Outer at Tail Lamp

Interchange

Interchange Number: 1

Part Number(s): 7585083

Usage: 1967–69 Camaro; 1967–69 Pontiac Firebird

Interchange Number: 2

Part Number(s): 8787543

Usage: 1970 Camaro; 1970 Pontiac Firebird

Notes: No other interchange. Due to rear window design, later models will not interchange.

Interchange Number: 3

Part Number(s): 4533800

Usage: 1964–65 Chevelle two-door sedan

Interchange Number: 4

Part Number(s): 4533802

Usage: 1964–65 Chevelle; 1964–65 Pontiac LeMans; 1964–65 Buick Skylark; 1964–65 Olds Cutlass; all two-door hardtop

Interchange Number: 5

Part Number(s): 7596481

Usage: 1964–67 El Camino

Interchange Number: 6

Part Number(s): 4498668

Usage: 1966–67 Chevelle two-door sedan

Interchange Number: 7

Part Number(s): 4534268

Usage: 1966–67 Chevelle; 1966–67 Pontiac LeMans; 1966–67 Buick Skylark; 1966–67 Olds Cutlass; all two-door hardtops

Interchange Number: 8

Part Number(s): 7790418

Usage: 1968–72 Chevelle two-door sedan, or two-door hardtop; 1968–72 Olds Cutlass except Supreme; 1968–72 Pontiac LeMans; 1968–72 Buick Skylark

Interchange Number: 9

Part Number(s): 7790424

Usage: 1968–72 El Camino

Interchange Number: 10

Part Number(s): 4803030

Usage: 1959–60 full-size Chevrolet, Pontiac, or Oldsmobile; all two- or four-door sedan

Interchange Number: 11

Part Number(s): 4803023

Usage: 1959–60 full-size Chevrolet, Pontiac, or Oldsmobile; all two-door hardtop

Interchange Number: 12

Part Number(s): 4803070

Usage: 1959–60 El Camino

Interchange Number: 13

Part Number(s): 4794709

Usage: 1961 full-size Chevrolet, Pontiac, or Oldsmobile; all two- or four-door sedan

Interchange Number: 14

Part Number(s): 4794822

Usage: 1961–62 full-size Chevrolet; 1961 full-size Pontiac; 1961 full-size Oldsmobile; all two-door hardtops

Notes: 1962 Bel Air only.

Interchange Number: 15

Part Number(s): 4823127

Usage: 1962–64 full-size Chevrolet, Pontiac, or Oldsmobile; 1964 Buick Wildcat; 1964 Buick LeSabre; all two- or four-door sedan

Interchange Number: 16

Part Number(s): 4839263

Usage: 1962–64 full-size Chevrolet, Pontiac, or Oldsmobile; 1963–64 Buick LeSabre; 1963–64 Buick Wildcat; all two-door hardtops

Notes: Will not fit 1962 Bel Air.

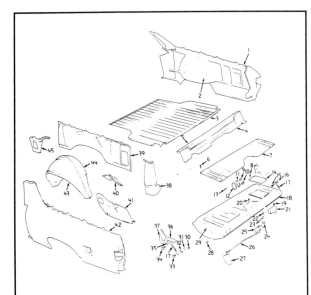

1970-72 EL CAMINO REAR END SHEET METAL

1. 12.940 PANEL, OUTER 8761648
2. 12.941 PANEL, rear inner
   front upper 7671562
3. 12.981 PANEL, Rear Compartment 9806819
4. 12.986 BAR ASSY., Rear Cross . . . 9611258
5. 12.986 BAR ASSY., Rear Cross
   Front 9809167
6. 8.977 SCREW
7. 12.195 PANEL 7671589
8. 8.977 SCREW (8-18 x 3/8)
9. 10.571 PLATE, Lock Striker upr. . 4849938
10. 10.571 PLATE, Lock Striker
    rear 4649282
11. 12.237 SPACER, Lock Striker 4800021
12. 12.237 STRIKER 4754469-70
13. 12.237 SCREW 4892566
14. 12.195 COVER 7712098
15. 12.184 BOLT 7740373
16. 8.929 WASHER (3/8 X1X 3/32)
17. 12.203 CABLE 7732274
18. 12.179 PANEL ASSY., Outer . . . 9862702
19. 8.977 SCREW (8-18 x 3/8)
20. 10.474 SCREW 8788000
21. 12.195 PLATE 8731353
22. 12.242 SCREW 4422699
23. 12.242 HANDLE 4411638
24. 12.242 ESCUTCHEON 4409003
25. 12.242 LOCK ASSY. 7741883
26. 12.242 ROD, R.H. 7725971
    12.242 ROD, L.H. 7726253
27. 12.242 LOCK ASSY. 7733777-78
28. 8.977 SCREW
29. 12.197 GATE ASSY. 9862703
30. 8.970 PLUG, Black Plastic (5/16)
31. 12.237 WASHER 4469196
32. 12.203 SPRING 7736132-33
33. 12.184 BOLT 7740374
34. 12.184 BOLT 7668482
35. 12.184 PIN 9712980
36. 12.184 STRAP, Hinge Gate
    Side 9719758-59
37. 12.184 STRAP, Hinge Body
    Side 9712976-77
38. 12.941 PANEL, Rear Inner 7671536-37
39. 12.941 PANEL, Rear Inner
    Front Upper 7671563
40. 12.981 EXTENSION, Pan to outer
    Panel Filler Front 7723600
41. 12.981 FILLER, Pan to Qtr.
    Panel 9814156-57
42. 12.940 PANEL, Outer 8761649
43. 12.944 PANEL, Wheelhouse Outer 9815030
44. 12.944 PANEL, Wheelhouse . . . 9814166-67
45. 12.941 PANEL, Rear Qtr. Inner
    Front 7787061-62

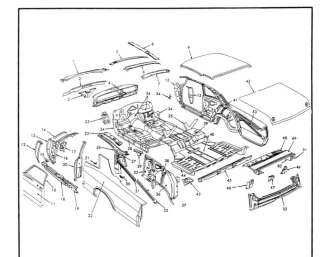

1965-68 PASSENGER SHEET METAL—TWO DOOR SEDAN

1. 12.803 PANEL ASSY., Shroud Upper
2. 12.804 PANEL ASSY., Shroud Vent. Duct Ctr.
3. 9.779 OUTLET ASSY., w/Shield Defroster
4. 10.230 PANEL ASSY., Instrument
5. 12.807 FRAME ASSY., w/Shield Inner Upper
6. 12.952 BOW, Roof
7. 12.964 PANEL ASSY., Back Window Inner
8. 12.952 BOW, Roof Longitudinal
9. 12.810 PANEL, Roof
10. 10.351 DOOR ASSY., (Incl. Item 11)
11. 12.895 PANEL ASSY., Door Outer
12. 12.804 PANEL, Shroud Lower
13. 12.804 PANEL, Shroud Vent Duct Side
14. 12.075 MOLDING, w/Shield Pillar Drip
15. 12.934 SUPPORT, Front Fender
16. 12.840 PANEL ASSY., Frt. Body Hinge Pillar
    (Incl. Item 15)
17. 12.659 BRACE ASSY., Frt. Body Hinge Pillar
    to Duct
18. 12.934 PANEL ASSY., Door Opening Rocker Outer
19. 12.940 REINF., Floor Pan to Quarter Outer Pnl.
20. 12.942 PANEL ASSY., Body Lock Pillar
21. 12.964 PANEL, Back Window Lower Corner
22. 12.940 PANEL, Rear Quarter Side Outer
23. 12.650 BRACE ASSY., Dash to Chassis Frame
24. 12.659 REINF., Frt. Body Hinge Pillar to Rocker
25. 12.957 RAIL ASSY., Side Roof Inner
26. 12.075 MOLDING, Roof Drip
27. 12.956 RAIL ASSY., Side Roof Outer (Incl.
    Item 26)
28. 12.934 PANEL, Rocker Inner
29. 12.971 EXTENSION, Shelf Panel
30. 12.964 FILLER, Back Window Lower Corner
31. 12.944 BRACE, Rear Quarter Diag. Front
32. 12.944 BRACE, Rear Quarter Diag. Rear
33. 12.941 PANEL, Rear Quarter Inner Lower
34. 10.230 PANEL, Instrument Panel End
35. N.L. BRACE, Rear Seat Back Diag.
36. 12.944 PANEL, Wheelhouse Outer
37. 12.944 PANEL ASSY., Wheelhouse
    (Incl. Items 33—36—38)
38. 12.944 PLATE, Wheelhouse to Quarter
    Baffle Upper
39. 12.981 SUPPORT ASSY., Spare Tire Clamp Plt.
40. 12.181 PAN ASSY., Rear Compt. (Incl. Item 45)
41. 12.941 PANEL, Rear Quarter Inner Upper Rear
42. 12.181 LID ASSY., Rear Compartment
43. 12.944 BRACE, Compartment Gutter to
    Wheelhouse
44. 12.981 FILLER, Compartment Pan to Quarter
    Panel
45. 12.986 BAR ASSY., Rear Cross
46. 12.996 BRACE, Compartment Gutter to Compt.
    Pan
47. 12.237 PLATE, Compartment Lid Lock Striker
    Anchor
48. 12.971 PANEL, Rear Seat Back Shelf
49. 12.971 PANEL, Rear Compartment Front
50. 12.184 BOX ASSY., Rear Compartment Lid Hinge
51. 12.187 STRAP & LINK ASSY., Rear Compartment
    Lid Hge.
52. 12.966 PANEL ASSY., Rear End
53. 12.966 GUTTER, Rear Compartment Lid Side
54. 12.803 PANEL ASSY., Dash (Incl. Item 23)

Interchange Number: 17

Part Number(s): 7717833

Usage: 1965–66 full-size Chevrolet or Pontiac; both two-door sedan

Interchange Number: 18

Part Number(s): 7596485

Usage: 1965–66 full-size Chevrolet; 1965–66 full-size Pontiac except Grand Prix; 1965–66 Buick Wildcat; 1965–66 Buick LeSabre; all two-door hardtops

Notes: 1966 Caprice will not fit.

Interchange Number: 19

Part Number(s): 7717833

Usage: 1967–68 full-size Chevrolet or Pontiac; both two-door sedan

Interchange Number: 20

Part Number(s): 7592993

Usage: 1967–68 full-size Chevrolet (except 1968 Impala Custom); 1967–68 full-size Pontiac (except Grand Prix); 1967–68 full-size Oldsmobile (except Delta 98); 1967–68 Buick LeSabre; 1967–68 Buick Wildcat; all two-door hardtop

Interchange Number: 21

Part Number(s): 7701024

Usage: 1968 Impala Custom; 1968 Caprice

Interchange Number: 22

Part Number(s): 7749319

Usage: 1969–70 full-size Chevrolet two-door hardtop, except Caprice or Impala Custom

Interchange Number: 23

Part Number(s): 7753001

Usage: 1969–70 Impala Custom or Caprice; both two-door hardtop

Interchange Number: 24

Part Number(s): 4834205

Usage: 1962–64 Chevy II two-door sedan

Interchange Number: 25

Part Number(s): 4835451

Usage: 1962–65 Chevy II two-door hardtop

Interchange Number: 26

Part Number(s): 4462033

Usage: 1965 Chevy II two-door sedan

Interchange Number: 27

Part Number(s): 45120155

Usage: 1966–67 Chevy II two-door sedan

Interchange Number: 28

Part Number(s): 7715931

Usage: 1966–67 Chevy II two-door hardtop

Interchange Number: 29

Part Number(s): 7722875

Usage: 1968–72 Nova; 1971–72 Pontiac Ventura II

Quarter Panels

Interchange is based on a cutout quarter panel from an original car. A new replacement panel can also be used using the same interchange. Bodystyle greatly influences the interchange, as do minor changes in model year.

If you salvage a used fender, try to pick a unit that is as close as possible to your original unit in trim and emblem usage; otherwise, you may have to fill pre-drilled holes before you can use it. Better yet, find a clean unit that is free of any trim or emblems and then drill the holes that are needed. Part numbers are given in pairs (one for each side) in the interchange charts.

Model Identification

Interchange

Interchange Number: 1
   Part Number(s): RH, 7585084; LH, 7585085
   Usage: 1967 Camaro coupe

Interchange Number: 2
   Part Number(s): RH, 7585086 LH, 7585087
   Usage: 1967 Camaro convertible

Interchange Number: 3
   Part Number(s): RH, 7738673; LH, 7738674
   Usage: 1968 Camaro coupe

Interchange Number: 4
   Part Number(s): RH, 7741301; LH, 7741302
   Usage: 1968 Camaro convertible

Interchange Number: 5
   Part Number(s): RH, 7779476; LH, 7779477
   Usage: 1969 Camaro coupe

Interchange Number: 6
   Part Number(s): RH, 7779480; LH, 7779481
   Usage: 1969 Camaro convertible

Interchange Number: 7
   Part Number(s): RH, 9868287; LH, 9868288
   Usage: 1970–72 Camaro
   Notes: Replacement interchange only. Cutoff inter-
   change 1970 only.

Interchange Number: 8
   Part Number(s): RH, 4409810; LH, 4409811
   Usage: 1964 Chevelle two-door hardtop
   Notes: Two-door sedan quarter will not fit.

Interchange Number: 9
   Part Number(s): RH, 4468406; LH, 4468407
   Usage: 1964 Chevelle two-door sedan
   Notes: Two-door hardtop quarter will not fit.

Interchange Number: 10
   Part Number(s): RH, 4490695; LH, 4490696
   Usage: 1964–65 El Camino

Interchange Number: 11
   Part Number(s): RH, 4533825; LH, 4533826
   Usage: 1965 Chevelle two-door sedan
   Notes: Two-door hardtop quarter will not fit.

Interchange Number: 12
   Part Number(s): RH, 4484741; LH, 4484742
   Usage: 1965 Chevelle two-door hardtop
   Notes: Two-door sedan quarter will not fit.

Interchange Number: 13
   Part Number(s): RH, 4484743; LH, 4484744
   Usage: 1965 Chevelle convertible

Interchange Number: 14
   Part Number(s): RH, 4409812; LH, 4409813
   Usage: 1964 Chevelle convertible

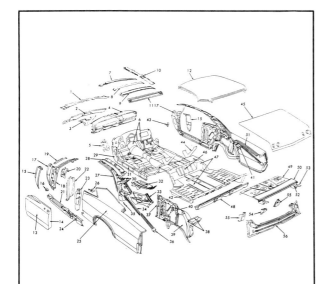

1965-68 PASSENGER SHEET METAL—SPORT COUPE

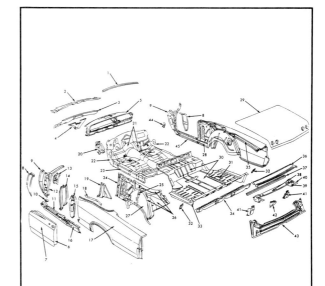

1965-68 PASSENGER SHEET METAL—CONVERTIBLE

1. 12.803 PANEL ASSY., Shroud Upper
2. 12.804 PANEL ASSY., Shroud Vent Duct Ctr.
3. 9.779 OUTLET ASSY., w/Shield Defroster
4. 10.230 PANEL ASSY., Instrument
5. 12.650 BRACE ASSY., Dash to Chassis Frame
6. 12.803 PANEL ASSY., Dash (Incl. Item 5)
7. 12.807 FRAME ASSY., w/Shield Inner Upper
8. 12.952 BOW, Auxiliary Roof
9. 12.952 BOW, Roof
10. 12.952 BOW, Roof Longitudinal
11. 12.964 PANEL ASSY., Back Wind. Inner
12. 12.810 PANEL, Roof
13. 10.351 DOOR ASSY., (Incl. Item 14)
14. 12.895 PANEL ASSY., Door Outer
15. 12.804 PANEL, Shroud Lower
16. 12.934 SUPPORT, Front Fender
17. 12.804 PANEL, Shroud Vent Duct Side
18. 12.840 PANEL ASSY., Frt. Body Hge. Plr.
　(Incl. Item 16)
19. 12.075 MOLDING, w/Shield Pillar Drip
20. 12.659 BRACE ASSY., Frt. Body Hge. Plr. to Duct
21. 12.934 PANEL ASSY., Door Opng. Rckr. Outer
22. N.S.S. Part of 12.940 Panel
23. 12.942 REINF., Body Lock Pillar
24. 12.940 REINF., Floor Pan to Qtr. Pnl.
25. 12.940 PANEL, Rear Quarter Side Outer
26. 12.941 FILLER, Qtr. Wind. Lwr. Rr. Corner
27. 12.075 MOLDING, Roof Drip
28. 12.957 RAIL ASSY., Side Roof Inner
29. 12.659 REINF., Frt. Body Hge. Plr. to Rckr.
30. 12.956 RAIL ASSY., Side Roof Outer (Incl. Item 27)
31. 12.934 PANEL, Rocker Inner
32. 12.971 EXTENSION, Shelf Panel
33. 12.941 PANEL, Quarter Inner Extension
34. 12.944 BRACE, Rr. Qtr. Diagonal Front
35. 12.964 FILLER, Back Wind. Lwr. Corner
36. 12.944 BRACE, Rr. Qtr. Diagonal Rear
37. 12.941 PANEL, Rr. Qtr. Inner Lwr.
38. 12.944 PANEL ASSY., Wheelhouse (Incl. Item 37)
39. 12.944 PANEL, Wheelhouse Outer
40. 12.944 PLATE, Whse. to Qtr. Baffle Upr.
41. 12.996 BRACE, Compt. Gutr. to Whse.
42. 12.981 FILLER, Compt. Pan to Qtr. Pnl.
43. 10.230 SUPPORT, Inst. Panel End
44. N.L. BRACE, Rear Seat Back Diag.
45. 12.181 LID ASSY., Rear Compt.
46. 12.981 SUPPORT ASSY., Spare Tire Clamp Plt.
47. 12.981 PAN ASSY., Rear Compt. (Incl. Item 48)
48. 12.986 BAR ASSY., Rear Cross
49. 12.971 PANEL, Rr. Seat Back Shelf
50. 12.971 PANEL, Rr. Compt. Front
51. 12.996 GUTTER, Rear Compt. Lid Side
52. 12.184 BOX ASSY., Rr. Compt. Lid Hge.
53. 12.187 STRAP & LINK ASSY., Rr. Compt. Lid Hge.
54. 12.237 PLATE, Compt. Lid Lk. Stkr. Anchor
55. 12.996 BRACE, Compt. Gutr. to Compt. Pan
56. 12.966 PANEL ASSY., Rr. End

1. 12.807 FRAME ASSY., w/Shield Inner Upper
2. 12.803 PANEL ASSY., Shroud Upper
3. 12.804 PANEL ASSY., Shroud Vent Duct Ctr.
4. 9.779 OUTLET ASSY., w/Shield Defroster
5. 10.230 PANEL ASSY., Instrument
6. 10.351 DOOR ASSY., (Incl. Item 7)
7. 12.895 PANEL ASSY., Door Outer
8. 12.804 PANEL, Shroud Lower
9. 12.804 PANEL, Shroud Vent Duct Side
10. 12.934 SUPPORT, Front Fender
11. 12.934 PNL. ASSY., Door Opng. Rckr. Otr.
12. 12.840 PNL. ASSY., Frt. Body Hge. Plr. (Incl. Item 10)
13. 12.659 BRACE ASSY., Frt. Body Hge. Plr. to Duct
14. N.S.S. Part of 12.940 Panel
15. 12.942 REINF., Body Lock Pillar
16. 12.940 REINF., Floor Pan to Qtr. Otr. Pnl.
17. 12.940 PANEL, Rear Qtr. Side Outer
18. 12.940 REINF., Rr. Qtr. Pnl. at Belt
19. 12.684 BRACE ASSY., Body Lock Plr. to Pan
20. 12.650 BRACE ASSY., Dash to Chassis Frame
21. 12.803 PANEL ASSY., Dash (Incl. Item 20)
22. 12.659 REINF., Frt. Body Hge. to Rckr.
23. 12.934 PANEL, Rocker Inner
24. 12.941 PANEL ASSY., Rear Qtr. Inner
25. 12.944 PLATE, Whse. to Qtr. Baffle Upr.
26. 12.944 PANEL ASSY., Wheelhouse (Incl. Items 24, 25, 27)
27. 12.944 PANEL, Wheelhouse Outer
28. 12.934 REINF., Rocker Outer Panel Rear
29. 12.181 LID ASSY., Rear Compt.
30. 12.981 PAN ASSY., Rear Compt. (Incl. Item 34)
31. 12.981 SUPT. ASSY., Spare Tire Clamp Plt.
32. 12.981 EXT., Qtr. Otr. to Compt. Pan Filr.
33. 12.981 FILLER, Compt. Pan to Qtr. Pnl.
34. 12.986 BAR ASSY., Rear Cross
35. 12.996 GUTTER, Rear Compt. Lid Side
36. 12.971 PANEL, Rear Compt. Front
37. 12.989 PANEL, Fldg. Top Compt. Rear
38. 12.971 REINF. Rear Compt. Front Panel
39. 12.184 BOX ASSY., Rear Compt. Lid Hinge
40. 12.187 STRAP & LINK ASSY., Rr. Compt. Lid Hge.
41. 12.996 BRACE, Compt. Gutr. to Compt. Pan
42. 12.237 PLATE, Compt. Lid Lock Stkr. Anch.
43. 12.966 PANEL ASSY., Rr. End
44. 10.230 SUPPORT, Inst. Pnl. End
45. 12.934 REINF., Rocker Outer Panel Frt.

Interchange Number: 15
Part Number(s): RH, 7580122; LH, 7580123
Usage: 1966–67 Chevelle two-door sedan
Notes: Do not include taillamp extension in interchange.

Interchange Number: 16
Part Number(s): RH, 7580162; LH, 7580163
Usage: 1966–67 Chevelle two-door hardtop
Notes: Do not include taillamp extension in interchange.

Interchange Number: 17
Part Number(s): RH, 7580164; LH, 7580165
Usage: 1966–67 Chevelle convertible
Notes: Do not include taillamp extension in interchange.

Interchange Number: 18
Part Number(s): RH, 4542622; LH, 4542623
Usage: 1966 El Camino

Interchange Number: 19
Part Number(s): RH, 7598638; LH, 7598639
Usage: 1967 El Camino

Interchange Number: 20
Part Number(s): RH, 7761614; LH, 7761615
Usage: 1968 Chevelle two-door sedan

Interchange Number: 21
Part Number(s): RH, 7761616; LH, 7761617
Usage: 1968 Chevelle two-door hardtop

Interchange Number: 22
Part Number(s): RH, 7793617; LH, 7793618
Usage: 1968 Chevelle convertible

Interchange Number: 23
Part Number(s): RH, 7671477; LH, 7671478
Usage: 1968 El Camino, first design
Notes: Panel has side-marker lamp mounted below taillamp level line.

Interchange Number: 24
Part Number(s): RH, 8738084; LH, 8738085
Usage: Late 1968 El Camino, second design; 1969 El Camino
Notes: Panel has side-marker lamp mounted level with taillamp.

Interchange Number: 25
Part Number(s): RH, 7757064; LH, 7757065
Usage: 1969 Chevelle two-door sedan

Interchange Number: 26
Part Number(s): RH, 8768754; LH, 8768755
Usage: 1969 Chevelle two-door hardtop

Interchange Number: 27
Part Number(s): 8770136 RH, 8770137 LH,
Usage: 1969 Chevelle convertible

Interchange Number: 28
Part Number(s): RH, 9815404; LH, 9815405
Usage: 1970–72 Chevelle two-door hardtop

Interchange Number: 29
Part Number(s): RH, 8735905; LH, 8735906
Usage: 1970–72 Chevelle convertible

Interchange Number: 30
Part Number(s): RH, 8761648; LH, 8761649
Usage: 1970–72 El Camino; 1971-9172 GMC Sprint

Interchange Number: 31
Part Number(s): RH, 4779183; LH, 4779184
Usage: 1959 full-size Chevrolet two-door sedan, hardtop, or convertible

Interchange Number: 32
Part Number(s): RH, 4781495; LH, 4781496
Usage: 1959 El Camino, or lower portion 1959 full-size Chevrolet two-door delivery sedan

Interchange Number: 33
Part Number(s): RH, 4787704; LH, 4787705
Usage: 1960 full-size Chevrolet two-door sedan

Interchange Number: 34
Part Number(s): RH, 4787706; LH, 4787707
Usage: 1960 full-size Chevrolet two-door hardtop

Interchange Number: 35
Part Number(s): RH, 4774804; LH, 4774805
Usage: 1960 full-size Chevrolet convertible

Interchange Number: 36
Part Number(s): RH, 4778094; LH, 4778094
Usage: 1960 El Camino

Interchange Number: 37
Part Number(s): RH, 4827480; LH, 4827481
Usage: 1961 full-size Chevrolet two-door sedan

Interchange Number: 38
Part Number(s): RH, 4827484; LH, 4827485
Usage: 1961 full-size Chevrolet two-door hardtop

Interchange Number: 39
Part Number(s): RH, 4794840; LH, 4794841
Usage: 1961 full-size Chevrolet two-door convertible

Interchange Number: 40
Part Number(s): RH, 4853165; LH, 4853166
Usage: 1962 full-size Chevrolet two-door sedan

Interchange Number: 41
Part Number(s): RH, 4823144; LH, 4823145
Usage: 1962 Bel Air two-door hardtop
Notes: Impala quarter will not interchange.

Interchange Number: 42
Part Number(s): RH, 4823172; LH, 4823173
Usage: 1962 Impala two-door hardtop
Notes: Bel Air quarter will not interchange.

Interchange Number: 43
Part Number(s): RH, 4823168; LH, 4823169
Usage: 1962 full-size Chevrolet two-door convertible

Interchange Number: 44
Part Number(s): RH, 4405620; LH, 4405621
Usage: 1963 full-size Chevrolet two-door sedan

Interchange Number: 45
Part Number(s): RH, 4405614; LH, 4405615
Usage: 1963 full-size Chevrolet two-door hardtop

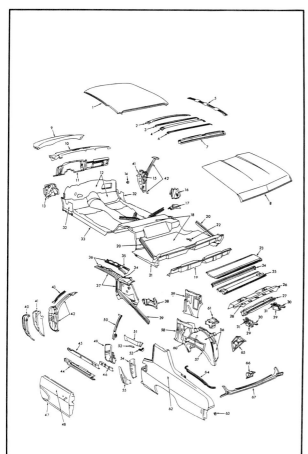

1969-70 PASSENGER SHEET METAL COUPE, CONVERTIBLE
(15411-15611-16437-47-67-16647)

1. 12.810 PANEL, Roof (11-37-47 Styles Only)
2. 12.807 FRAME ASSY. Windshield Inner Upper
3. 12.952 BOW, Auxiliary Roof Front (47 Styles Only)
4. 12.952 BOW, Roof (11-47 Styles Only)
5. 12.952 BOW, Roof Longitudinal (11-37-47 Styles Only)
6. 12.952 BOW, Auxiliary Roof Rear (47 Styles Only)
7. 12.964 PANEL, Back Window Inner (11-37-47 Styles Only)
8. 12.181 LID ASSY. Compartment
9. 12.804 PANEL ASSY., Shroud Vent Duct Center
10. 12.804 PANEL ASSY., Upper Shroud & Instr.
11. 10.230 PANEL ASSY., Instrument Lower
12. 12.804 PANEL ASSY., Dash (Incl. Item 13)
13. 12.650 BRACE, Dash To Chassis Frame (Comp. of Item 12)
14. 10.230 SUPPORT, Instrument Panel End
15. 12.659 BRACE, Front Body Hinge Pillar to Duct
16. 12.684 BRACE ASSY. Body Lock Pillar to Floor Pan (37-47-67 Styles Only)
17. 12.942 REINFORCEMENT, Floor Pan At Lock Pillar (37-47-67 Styles Only)
18. 12.981 PAN ASSY., Compartment (Incl. Item 19)
19. 12.986 BAR ASSY., Rear Cross (Comp. of Item 18)
20. 12.944 BRACE, Quarter Diagonal Rear (11-37-47 Styles Only)
21. 12.981 FILLER, Compartment Pan To Quarter Panel
22. 12.981 SUPPORT ASSY., Spare Tire Clamp Anchor Plate
23. 12.971 PANEL, Compartment Front (11-37-67 Styles Only)
24. 12.989 PANEL, Folding Top Compartment Rear (67 Style Only)
25. 12.971 REINFORCEMENT, Compartment Front Panel (67 Style Only)
26. 12.971 PANEL, Rear Seat To Back Window (11-37-47 Styles Only)
27. 12.971 REINFORCEMENT, Rear Seat To Back Window Panel (47 Styles Only)
28. 12.971 SUPPORT, Compartment Front Panel (47 Styles Only)
29. 12.184 BOX ASSY., Rear Compartment Lid Hinge
30. 12.187 STRAP & LINK ASSY., Rear Compartment Lid Hinge
31. 12.186 PIN, Rear Compartment Lid Hinge
32. 12.659 REINFORCEMENT, Front Body Hinge Pillar To Rocker
33. 12.934 PANEL, Rocker Inner
34. 12.956 RAIL ASSY., Side Roof Outer (Incl. Item 37) (11 Styles Only)
35. 12.957 RAIL ASSY., Side Roof Inner (11 Styles Only)
36. 12.956 RAIL ASSY., Side Roof (Incl. Items 34-35-37) (37-47 Styles Only)
37. 12.075 MOULDING, Drip Roof (Comp. of Items 34-36) (11-37-47 Styles Only)
38. 12.941 PANEL, Quarter Inner Extension (37-47 Styles Only)
39. 12.944 BRACE, Quarter Diagonal Front (11-37-47 Styles Only)
40. 12.804 PANEL, Shroud Lower
41. 12.804 PANEL, Shroud Vent Duct
42. 12.840 PANEL ASSY. Front Body Hinge Pillar
43. 12.075 MOULDING, Drip Windshield Pillar (11-37-47 Styles Only)
44. 12.934 PANEL, Rocker Outer
45. 12.934 REINFORCEMENT, Rocker Outer Panel Front (67 Style Only)
46. 12.934 REINFORCEMENT, Rocker Outer Panel Rear (67 Style Only)
47. 10.351 DOOR ASSY. (Incl. Item 48)
48. 12.895 PANEL, Door Outer (Comp. of Item 47)
49. 12.942 REINFORCEMENT, Body Lock Pillar
50. 12.942 PANEL ASSY. Body Lock Pillar Upper (11 Styles Only)
51. 12.684 BRACE, Body Lock Pillar to Wheelhouse (67 Style Only)
52. 12.940 REINFORCEMENT, Quarter Outer Panel At Belt (37-67 Styles Only)
53. 12.941 FILLER, Quarter Window Lower Rear Corner (11-47 Styles Only)
54. 12.942 REINFORCEMENT, Body Lock Pillar Lower Front (11 Style Only)
55. 12.942 REINFORCEMENT, Body Lock Pillar Lower Rear (11 Style Only)
56. 12.944 PANEL ASSY., Wheelhouse (Incl. Items 57-58-59-60)
57. 12.944 PANEL, Wheelhouse Outer (Comp. of Item 56)
58. 12.941 PANEL ASSY., Quarter Inner Lower (Comp. of Item 56) (11-37-47 Styles Only)
59. 12.941 PANEL ASSY., Quarter Inner (Comp. of Item 56) (67 Style Only)
60. 12.944 REINFORCEMENT, Wheelhouse Outer (Comp. of Item 56) (67 Style Only)
61. 12.971 EXTENSION, Rear Seat To Back Window Panel (11-37-47 Styles Only)
62. 12.940 PANEL, Quarter Outer
63. 12.981 REINFORCEMENT, Compartment Pan To Quarter Panel Filler
64. 12.996 GUTTER, Compartment Lid Side
65. 12.996 BRACE, Compartment Gutter to Wheelhouse (11-37 Styles Only)
66. 12.237 PLATE, Compartment Lid Lock Striker Anchor
67. 12.966 PANEL, Rear End

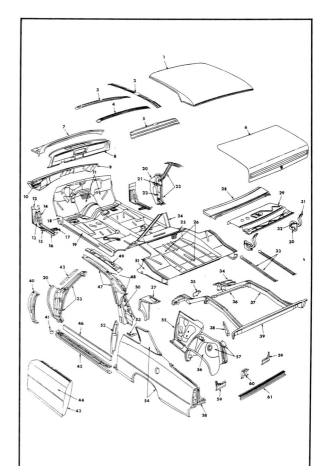

1966-67 CHEVY II SHEET METAL—TWO DOOR HARDTOP

1. 12.810 PANEL, Roof
2. 12.952 BOW, Roof Longitudinal
3. 12.807 FRAME ASSY., Windshield Inner Upper
4. 12.952 BOW, Roof
5. 12.964 PANEL, Back Window Inner
6. 12.181 LID ASSY., Rear Compartment
7. 12.803 PANEL ASSY., Shroud Upper
8. 10.230 PANEL ASSY., Instrument
9. 12.804 PANEL ASSY., Shroud Top Vent. Duct. Ctr.
10. 12.804 PLATE ASSY., Frt. Fend. Anch. on Duct Pnl.
11. 12.804 PLATE ASSY., Dash (Incl. Items 12-13-14-15-16-17)
12. 12.650 BRACE, Dash to Motor Mount Rail Frt.
13. 12.650 BRACE, Dash to Mtr Mount Rail Rr. Ctr.
14. 12.650 BRACE, Dash to Mtr. Mount Rail Rr. Inr.
15. N.L. GUIDE, Parking Brake Cable Frt. On Rail
16. 12.981 RAIL ASSY., Floor Pan. Side
17. 12.980 BAR, Floor Pan. No. 1
18. 12.934 EXTENSION, Rocker Inner Panel Frt.
19. 12.934 PANEL, Rocker Inner
20. 12.804 PANEL, Shroud Top Vent. Duct. Side
21. 12.659 REINF. ASSY., Frt. Body Hge. Plr. to Duct
22. 12.659 REINF., Frt. Body Hge. Plr. To Rocker
23. 12.840 BRACE, Frt. Body Hinge Pillar (Incl. Items 20—22)
24. N.L. BRACE, Rear Seat Back Diag.
25. 12.981 SUPPORT ASSY., Spare Tire Clamp Anch Plt.
26. 12.981 PAN, Rear Compartment
27. 12.971 EXTENSION, Compt Shelf Panel
28. 12.971 PANEL, Rear Compartment Front
29. 12.971 PANEL, Rear Seat Back Shelf
     .184 SUPPORT, Rear Compartment Lid Hinge
31. 12.187 HINGE, Rr. Compt. Lid
32. 12.186 PIN, Rear Compt. Lid Hinge
33. 12.981 REINF., Rr. Compt. Pan. at Gas Tank
34. 7.112 SUPPORT ASSY., Rear Spring Front
35. 4.785 GUIDE, Parking Brake Cable Rr. on Floor
36. N.L. BAR, Rear Seat Pan. Cross (at kick up)
37. 12.986 RAIL ASSY., Rear Compt. Pan. Side
38. 12.986 BRACE, Rear Compt. Side Rail to Rr. Rail
39. 12.986 RAIL, Rear End Cross
40. 12.804 PANEL, Shroud Lower
41. 12.934 FILLER, Rocker Outer Panel
42. 12.075 MOULDING, Windshield Pillar Drip
43. 10.351 DOOR ASSY., Front (Incl. Item 44)
44. 12.895 PANEL, Front Door Outer
45. 12.934 PANEL ASSY., Door Opening Rocker Outer (Incl. Item 41)
46. 12.934 REINF. Rocker Outer Panel
47. 12.075 MOULDING, Roof Drip
48. 12.956 RAIL ASSY., Side Roof Outer
49. 12.957 RAIL, Side Roof Inner Front
50. 12.957 RAIL, Side Roof Inner Rear
51. 12.981 FILLER, Compt. Pan. To Qtr. Pnl.
52. 12.942 REINF., Body Lock Pillar
53. 12.941 FILLER, Qtr. Wind. Lwr. Rr. Cor. Otr.
54. 12.940 PANEL, Rear Qtr. Side Outer Ext.
55. 12.941 PANEL, Rear Quarter Inner
56. 12.944 PANEL, Wheelhouse Outer (Part of Item 57)
57. 12.944 PANEL ASSY., Wheelhouse (Incl. Items 55-56)
58. 12.940 PANEL, Rear Qtr. Side Outer
59. 12.996 BRACE ASSY., Rr. Compt. Gutter to Rr. Rail
60. 12.237 PLATE, Rr. Compt. Lid Lk. Striker Anch.
61. 12.966 PANEL, Rear End

Interchange Number: 46
Part Number(s): 4405875 RH, 4405876 LH,
Usage: 1963 full-size Chevrolet two-door convertible

Interchange Number: 47
Part Number(s): RH, 4411356; LH, 4411357
Usage: 1964 full-size Chevrolet two-door sedan

Interchange Number: 48
Part Number(s): RH, 4437496; LH, 4437497
Usage: 1964 full-size Chevrolet two-door hardtop

Interchange Number: 49
Part Number(s): RH, 4437498; LH, 437499
Usage: 1964 full-size Chevrolet two-door convertible

Interchange Number: 50
Part Number(s): RH, 4490423; LH, 4490424
Usage: 1965 full-size Chevrolet two-door sedan

Interchange Number: 51
Part Number(s): RH, 7595544; LH, 7595545
Usage: 1965 full-size Chevrolet two-door hardtop

Interchange Number: 52
Part Number(s): RH, 4427012; LH, 4427013
Usage: 1965 full-size Chevrolet two-door convertible

Interchange Number: 53
Part Number(s): RH, 4544646; LH, 4544647
Usage: 1966 full-size Chevrolet two-door sedan

Interchange Number: 54
Part Number(s): RH, 4507248; LH, 4507249
Usage: 1966 full-size Chevrolet two-door hardtop, all
except Caprice

Interchange Number: 55
Part Number(s): RH, 4534227; LH, 4534228
Usage: 1966 Caprice coupe
Notes: Other models will not interchange.

Interchange Number: 56
Part Number(s): RH, 4507258; LH, 4507259
Usage: 1966 full-size Chevrolet two-door convertible

Interchange Number: 57
Part Number(s): RH, 7593046; LH, 7593047
Usage: 1967 Caprice coupe
Notes: Other models will not interchange.

Interchange Number: 58
Part Number(s): RH, 7660362; LH, 7660363
Usage: 1967 full-size Chevrolet two-door sedan

Interchange Number: 59
Part Number(s): RH, 7681954; LH, 7681955
Usage: 1967 full-size Chevrolet two-door hardtop, ex-
cept Caprice

Interchange Number: 60
Part Number(s): RH, 7681952; LH, 7681953
Usage: 1967 full-size Chevrolet two-door convertible

Interchange Number: 61
Part Number(s): RH, 7684378; LH, 7684379
Usage: 1968 Caprice coupe
Notes: Other models will not interchange.

Interchange Number: 62
Part Number(s): RH, 7730326; LH, 7730327
Usage: 1968 full-size Chevrolet two-door sedan

Interchange Number: 63
Part Number(s): RH, 7730334; LH, 7730335
Usage: 1968 full-size Chevrolet two-door hardtop, ex-
cept Impala Custom or Caprice

Interchange Number: 64
Part Number(s): RH, 7763290; LH, 7763291
Usage: 1968 Impala Custom

Interchange Number: 65
Part Number(s): RH, 8712910; LH, 8712911
Usage: 1968 full-size Chevrolet two-door convertible

Interchange Number: 66
Part Number(s): RH, 8788937; LH, 8788938
Usage: 1969 full-size Chevrolet two-door sedan

Interchange Number: 67
Part Number(s): RH, 8788940; LH, 8788941
Usage: 1969 full-size Chevrolet two-door hardtop, ex-
cept Impala Custom or Caprice

Interchange Number: 68
Part Number(s): RH, 7749630; LH, 7749631
Usage: 1968 Caprice or 1969 Impala Custom
Notes: Other models will not interchange.

Interchange Number: 69
Part Number(s): RH, 8788946; LH, 8788947
Usage: 1969 full-size Chevrolet two-door convertible

Interchange Number: 70
Part Number(s): RH, 8738232; LH, 8738233
Usage: 1970 full-size Chevrolet two-door hardtop, ex-
cept Impala Custom or Caprice

Interchange Number: 71
Part Number(s): RH, 8738234; LH, 8738235
Usage: 1970 Impala Custom; 1970 Caprice
Notes: Other models will not interchange.

Interchange Number: 72
Part Number(s): RH, 8738238; LH, 8738238
Usage: 1970 full-size Chevrolet two-door convertible

Interchange Number: 73
Part Number(s): RH, 4409682; LH, 4409683
Usage: 1962–64 Chevy II two-door sedan

Interchange Number: 74
Part Number(s): RH, 4409684; LH, 4409685
Usage: 1962–65 Chevy II two-door hardtop
Notes: Replacement part only on 1965 model.

Interchange Number: 75
Part Number(s): RH, 4409688; LH, 4409689
Usage: 1962–64 Chevy II two-door convertible

Interchange Number: 76
Part Number(s): RH, 7600822; LH, 7600823
Usage: 1966–67 Chevy II two-door sedan

Interchange Number: 77
Part Number(s): RH, 7690146; LH, 7690147
Usage: 1966–67 Chevy II two-door hardtop

Interchange Number: 78
　　Part Number(s): RH, 8778516; LH, 8778517
　　Usage: 1968–69 Nova coupe

Interchange Number: 79
　　Part Number(s): RH, 8756530; LH, 8756531
　　Usage: 1970–72 Nova; 1971–72 Pontiac Ventura II
　　Notes: Interchange is for replacement panel only. Cut-off interchange 1970 Nova only.

Interchange Number: 80
　　Part Number(s): RH, 4453980; LH, 4459381
　　Usage: 1965 Chevy II two-door sedan

Deck Lid

When interchanging deck lids, find a replacement unit that is similar in trim and that has the same emblems as your car. Be aware that some models used special trim that may require additional hole drilling. While holes *can* be filled if you find an improper match, I do not recommend it for something that takes the abuse a deck lid does. Try to find a good match, or find a clean deck lid that is free of any additional trim or moldings. Note also that spoilers or rear deck luggage racks can require additional hole drilling into the deck lid, further complicating interchanges. Interchange does not include any trim nameplates or hinges.

Model Identification

Interchange

Interchange Number: 1
　　Part Number(s): 8746031
　　Usage: 1967 Pontiac Firebird; 1967 to early 1968 Camaro
　　Notes: Interchange number 2 will fit.

Interchange Number: 2
　　Part Number(s): 8783521
　　Usage: Late 1968 to 1969 Camaro; 1968–69 Pontiac Firebird

Interchange Number: 3
　　Part Number(s): 9819030
　　Usage: 1970–74 Camaro; 1970–74 Pontiac Firebird

Interchange Number: 4
　　Part Number(s): 4493013
　　Usage: 1964–65 Chevelle, except 1965 Malibu SS
　　Notes: Due to more pre-drilled holes.

Interchange Number: 5
　　Part Number(s): 4490148
　　Usage: 1965 Malibu SS
　　Notes: Will fit number 4, but not vice versa.

Interchange Number: 6
　　Part Number(s): 7620526
　　Usage: 1966–67 Chevelle

Interchange Number: 7
　　Part Number(s): 8761214
　　Usage: 1968–72 Chevelle; 1970–72 Monte Carlo; 1970–72 Buick Skylark

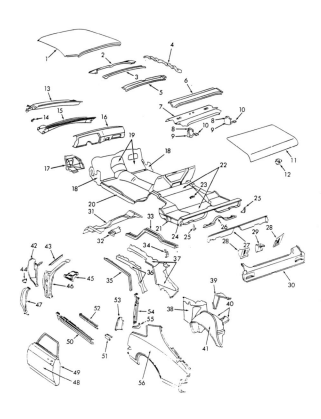

1968-73 CHEVY II—NOVA SHEET METAL—TWO DOOR SEDAN

1. 12.810 PANEL, Roof
2. 12.807 FRAME, Windshield Inner Upper
3. 12.952 BOW, Roof
4. 12.952 BOW, Roof Longitudinal
5. 12.964 PANEL, Back Window Inner
6. 12.971 REINFORCEMENT, Rear Seat to Back
    Window Panel
7. 12.971 PANEL, Rear Seat to Back Window
8. 12.186 PIN, Rear Compartment Lid Hinge
9. 12.184 SUPPORT, Rear Compartment Lid Hinge
10. 12.187 STRAP & LINK ASSY., Rear
    Compartment Lid Hinge
11. 12.181 LID ASSY., Rear Compartment
12. 12.237 STRIKER ASSY., Rear Compartment
    Lid Lock
13. 12.804 PANEL ASSY., Shroud Upper
14. 10.027 SUPPORT, Windshield Glass
15. 12.804 PANEL ASSY., Shroud Vent Duct Center
16. 10.230 PANEL ASSY., Instrument
17. 12.650 BRACE ASSY., Dash to Motor Mount
    Rail (Comp. Item 19)
18. 12.659 REINFORCEMENT, Front Body Hinge
    Pillar to Rocker
19. 12.804 PANEL ASSY., Dash (Incl. Item 17)
20. 12.804 PANEL ASSY., Rocker Inner
21. 12.981 FILLER, Compartment Pan to Quarter
    Panel
22. 12.981 PAN, Rear Compartment
23. 12.981 SUPPORT ASSY., Spare Tire Clamp
    Anchor Plate
24. 12.981 EXTENSION, Compartment Pan to Quarter
    Panel Filler
25. 12.981 FILLER, Compartment Pan to Rear
    Cross Bar
26. 12.986 RAIL, Rear End Cross Front
27. 12.986 RAIL, Rear End Cross Rear
28. 12.996 BRACE, Compartment Gutter to Rear
    Cross Rail
29. 12.237 PLATE, Compartment Lid Lock
    Striker Anchor

30. 12.966 PANEL ASSY., Rear End
31. 12.981 BAR ASSY., Compartment Pan Cross Front
32. 12.980 REINFORCEMENT, Floor Pan at Rear
    Spring Front
33. 12.986 RAIL ASSY., Rear Compartment Pan Side
34. 12.986 BRACE, Compartment Side Rail
    to Rear Rail
35. 12.075 MOLDING, Roof Drip (Comp. Item 36)
36. 12.956 RAIL ASSY., Side Roof Outer (Incl.
    Item 35)
37. 12.957 RAIL, Side Roof Inner
38. 12.941 PANEL, Rear Quarter Inner Lower (Comp.
    Item 40)
39. 12.971 EXTENSION, Rear Seat to Back
    Window Panel
40. 12.944 PANEL ASSY., Wheelhouse (Incl.
    Items 38-41)
41. 12.944 PANEL, Wheelhouse Outer
    (Comp. Item 40)
42. 12.804 PANEL, Shroud Vent Duct Side
43. 12.075 MOLDING, Windshield Pillar Drip
44. 12.804 PLATE, Shroud Side Duct Panel Baffle
45. 12.659 REINFORCEMENT ASSY., Front Body
    Hinge Pillar to Duct
46. 12.840 PANEL ASSY., Front Body Hinge Pillar
47. 12.804 PANEL, Shroud Lower
48. 12.895 PANEL ASSY., Front Door Outer (Comp.
    Item 49)
49. 10.351 DOOR ASSY., Front (Incl. Item 48)
50. 12.934 PANEL, Door Opening Rocker Outer
51. 12.934 REINFORCEMENT, Rocker Outer
    Panel Rear
52. 12.934 REINFORCEMENT, Rocker Outer
    Panel Front
53. 12.942 REINFORCEMENT, Body Lock Pillar
    Outer Panel
54. 12.942 PANEL ASSY., Body Lock Pillar Upper
55. 12.941 FILLER, Quarter Window Lower
    Rear Corner
56. 12.940 PANEL, Rear Quarter Side Outer

Interchange Number: 8
Part Number(s): 4750850
Usage: 1959 full-size Chevrolet convertible or two- or four-door sedan
Notes: A two-door hardtop deck lid will not interchange.

Interchange Number: 9
Part Number(s): 4750853
Usage: 1959 full-size Chevrolet two-door hardtop
Notes: Other bodystyles will not interchange.

Interchange Number: 10
Part Number(s): 4777627
Usage: 1960 full-size Chevrolet, all bodystyles including convertible—except two-door hardtop

Interchange Number: 11
Part Number(s): 4777629
Usage: 1960 full-size Chevrolet two-door hardtop

Interchange Number: 12
Part Number(s): 4838386
Usage: 1961 Bel Air or Biscayne

Interchange Number: 13
Part Number(s): 4838388
Usage: 1961 Impala
Notes: Others will not correctly interchange due to tail-lamp design.

Interchange Number: 14
Part Number(s): 4830067
Usage: 1962 Impala
Notes: Taillamp design different than other models.

Interchange Number: 15
Part Number(s): 4830066
Usage: 1962 Bel Air or Biscayne

Interchange Number: 16
Part Number(S): 4446254
Usage: 1963 Bel Air or Biscayne

Interchange Number: 17
Part Number(s): 4402727
Usage: 1963 Impala
Notes: Taillamp design differs.

Interchange Number: 18
Part Number(s): 4401099
Usage: 1964 Bel Air or Biscayne

Interchange Number: 19
Part Number(s): 4419897
Usage: 1964 Impala
Notes: Taillamp design differs.

Interchange Number: 20
Part Number(s): 4439520
Usage: 1965 Bel Air or Biscayne

Interchange Number: 21
Part Number(s): 4439521
Usage: 1965 Impala four-door sedan or two-door convertible
Notes: Impala two-door hardtop will not interchange, nor will other models due to taillamp design.

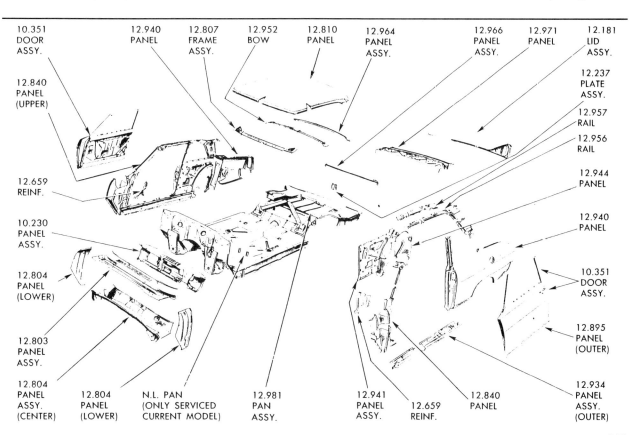

10.351 DOOR ASSY.

12.940 PANEL

12.807 FRAME ASSY.

12.952 BOW

12.810 PANEL

12.964 PANEL ASSY.

12.966 PANEL ASSY.

12.971 PANEL

12.181 LID ASSY.

12.840 PANEL (UPPER)

12.237 PLATE ASSY.

12.957 RAIL

12.956 RAIL

12.659 REINF.

12.944 PANEL

10.230 PANEL ASSY.

12.940 PANEL

12.804 PANEL (LOWER)

10.351 DOOR ASSY.

12.803 PANEL ASSY.

12.895 PANEL (OUTER)

12.804 PANEL ASSY. (CENTER)

12.804 PANEL (LOWER)

N.L. PAN (ONLY SERVICED CURRENT MODEL)

12.981 PAN ASSY.

12.941 PANEL ASSY.

12.659 REINF.

12.840 PANEL

12.934 PANEL ASSY. (OUTER)

Interchange Number: 22
Part Number(s): 4461753
Usage: 1965 Impala two-door hardtop
Notes: Other bodystyles will not fit. Other models will not interchange due to taillamp design.

Interchange Number: 23
Part Number(s): 7619931
Usage: 1966 full-size Chevrolet, all except two-door hardtop Impala
Notes: Will fit 1966 Impala convertible.

Interchange Number: 24
Part Number(s): 7637032
Usage: 1966 Impala two-door hardtop
Notes: Other bodystyles will not fit.

Interchange Number: 25
Part Number(s): 7611954
Usage: 1967 Impala two-door hardtop
Notes: Other bodystyles will not fit.

Interchange Number: 26
Part Number(s): 7665143
Usage: 1967 full-size Chevrolet, all except two-door Impala
Notes: Will fit convertible.

Interchange Number: 27
Part Number(s): 7722128
Usage: 1968 full-size Chevrolet, all but Impala two-door hardtop

Interchange Number: 28
Part Number(s): 7696314
Usage: 1968 Impala two-door hardtop
Notes: Other bodystyles will not fit.

Interchange Number: 29
Part Number(s): 9813061
Usage: 1969–70 full-size Chevrolet, except two-door hardtop

Interchange Number: 30
Part Number(s): 9813059
Usage: 1969–70 full-size Chevrolet two-door hardtop, including Impala Custom and Caprice
Notes: Other bodystyles will not fit.

Interchange Number: 31
Part Number(s): 4896947
Usage: 1962–64 Chevy II

Interchange Number: 32
Part Number(s): 4488606
Usage: 1965 Chevy II

Interchange Number: 33
Part Number(s): 7661139
Usage: 1966–67 Chevy II

Interchange Number: 34
Part Number(s): 9600856
Usage: 1968–72 Nova; 1971–72 Pontiac Ventura II
Notes: 1973 Buick Apollo, 1973 Olds Omega, 1973 Nova, and 1973 Pontiac Ventura II coupe or sedan will fit, but hatchback will not.

Tailgate (El Camino only)

Interchange

Interchange Number: 1
Part Number(s): 4756626
Usage: 1959 El Camino

Interchange Number: 2
Part Number(s): 4810203
Usage: 1960 El Camino

Interchange Number: 3
Part Number(s): 4526810
Usage: 1964–66 El Camino

Interchange Number: 4
Part Number(s): 7660966
Usage: 1967 El Camino

Interchange Number: 5
Part Number(s): 7687327
Usage: 1968 El Camino

Interchange Number: 6
Part Number(s): 9862703
Usage: 1969–72 El Camino

Deck Lid Hinges
Interchange includes the bare hinge *with* mounting bracket but *without* torque rod. In some models, bodystyle will be a factor. Also, some hinges have a universal fit, meaning one hinge will fit either the right- or left-hand side of the car while others will fit only one side or the other.

Model Identification

1968

Interchange

Interchange Number: 1

Part Number(s): RH, 9709424; LH, 9709425
Usage: 1967–69 Camaro; 1967–69 Pontiac Firebird

Interchange Number: 2

Part Number(s): RH, 9723492; LH, 9723493
Usage: 1970–75 Camaro; 1970–75 Pontiac Firebird

Interchange Number: 3

Part Number(s): 5717153 (fits either side)
Usage: 1964–65 Chevelle; 1964–65 Olds Cutlass; 1964–65 Buick Skylark; 1964–65 Pontiac LeMans

Interchange Number: 4

Part Number(s): RH, 9706258; LH, 9706259
Usage: 1966–67 Chevelle; 1966–67 Chevy II; 1966–67 Olds Cutlass; 1966–67 Buick Skylark; 1966–67 Pontiac LeMans

Interchange Number: 5

Part Number(s): 9722033 (fits either side)
Usage: 1968–70 Olds Cutlass four-door only; 1968–72 Chevelle (except convertible)
Notes: 1968–70 Olds Cutlass two-door will not interchange.

Interchange Number: 6

Part Number(s): 9720628 (fits either side)
Usage: 1968–72 Chevelle convertible; 1968–72 Olds Cutlass convertible; 1970–72 Buick Skylark convertible

Interchange Number: 7

Part Number(s): 5717538 (fits either side)
Usage: 1961–64 full-size Chevrolet except Convertible; late 1963–64 Pontiac Starfire; 1964 Olds Jetstar I

Interchange Number: 8

Part Number(s): 5717540
Usage: 1961–64 full-size Chevrolet convertible

Interchange Number: 9

Part Number(s): 9707446 (fits either side)
Usage: 1965 Olds Delta 98; 1965–66 full-size Chevrolet; 1965–66 full-size Oldsmobile; 1965–67 full-size Pontiac; 1965–67 full-size Buick; all two-door hardtop
Notes: Other bodystyles will not fit.

Interchange Number: 10

Part Number(s): 9721855 (fits either side)
Usage: 1965–70 full-size Chevrolet, except 1965–68 convertible or two-door hardtop; 1965–70 full-size Oldsmobile, except convertible or two-door; 1965–70 full-size Pontiac, except two-door or convertible; 1965–70 full-size Buick four-door

Interchange Number: 11

Part Number(s): 9708167 (fits either side)
Usage: 1965–66 full-size Chevrolet convertible; 1965–66 full-size Buick convertible; 1965–67 full-size Pontiac convertible; 1965–68 Olds Delta 98 convertible; 1966–67 full-size Oldsmobile convertible

Interchange Number: 12

Part Number(s): 9710020 (fits either side)
Usage: 1967 full-size Chevrolet, Pontiac, Oldsmobile, or Buick; all two-door hardtop
Notes: Other bodystyles will not interchange.

Interchange Number: 13

Part Number(s): 9715312 (fits either side)
Usage: 1968–70 full-size Impala; 1968–70 full-size Oldsmobile except Delta 98 or Toronado; 1968–70 full-size Buick; 1968–70 full-size Pontiac; all two-door hardtop
Notes: Not for 1969–70 Impala Custom or Caprice.

Interchange Number: 14

Part Number(s): 9610894 (fits either side)
Usage: 1969–72 Impala Custom or Caprice, both Coupe

Interchange Number: 15

Usage: 1962–64 Chevy II

Interchange Number: 16

Usage: 1965 Chevy II

Interchange Number: 17

Part Number(s): 9714082 (fits either side)
Usage: 1968–72 Nova; 1971–72 Pontiac Ventura II

Interchange Number: 18

Usage: 1968–70 Impala convertible; 1968–70 full-size Buick convertible; 1968–70 full-size Pontiac convertible; 1968–70 full-size Oldsmobile convertible, except Delta 98

Chapter 11

Bumpers and Grille

Front Bumper

Due to changes in design, there are few bumpers that are exactly the same over the span of one year. In fact, each model and model year are different and will not interchange—except for the following:

- 1967–68 Camaro used same bumper
- 1970–72 Camaro except RS used same bumper
- 1970–72 Camaro RS used same two-piece bumpers
- 1962–64 Chevy II used same bumper
- 1968–69 Nova used same bumper
- 1970–72 Nova used same bumper

Rear Bumper

Only the bumpers listed in the charts can be found on more than one model or were used for more than one model year. Therefore, those that are *not* listed are unique for that particular model and model year.

Model Identification

Interchange

Interchange Number: 1
    Part Number(s): 3886603
    Usage: 1967–68 Camaro

Interchange Number: 2
    Part Number(s): 3927424
    Usage: 1969 Camaro

Interchange Number: 3
    Part Number(s): 3949772
    Usage: 1970–72 Camaro, all except Z-28 or with bumper guards

Interchange Number: 4
    Part Number(s): 3982006
    Usage: 1970–72 Camaro Z-28 or with bumper guards
    Notes: Features pre-drilled holes to mount bumper guard strips.

Interchange Number: 5
    Part Number(s): 3837999
    Usage: 1964 Chevelle
    Notes: Interchange without back braces. Braces differed between pickup/station wagon and other bodystyles.

Interchange Number: 6
    Part Number(s): 3858438
    Usage: 1965 Chevelle
    Notes: Interchange without back braces. Braces differed between pickup/station wagon and other bodystyles.

The early Rallye Sport Camaro featured hideaway head-lamps. This 1969 model has the Z-28 package.

Interchange Number: 7
Part Number(s): 3869724
Usage: 1966 El Camino or Chevelle station wagon

Interchange Number: 8
Part Number(s): 3869756
Usage: 1966 Chevelle, except station wagon or El Camino

Interchange Number: 9
Part Number(s): 3895146
Usage: 1967 Chevelle, except station wagon or El Camino

Interchange Number: 10
Part Number(s): 3895162
Usage: 1967 El Camino; 1967 Chevelle station wagon

Interchange Number: 11
Part Number(s): 3907622
Usage: 1968 Chevelle except El Camino, station wagon, Malibu, or SS 396

Interchange Number: 12
Part Number(s): 3907669
Usage: 1968 Malibu or SS 396, except El Camino or station wagon

Interchange Number: 13
Part Number(s): 3935692
Usage: 1968 Chevelle station wagon; 1968–72 El Camino
Notes: 1969–72 El Camino may require the bumper to be notched to provide clearance form the tailgate hinges.

Interchange Number: 14
Part Number(s): 3927689
Usage: 1969 Chevelle, all but station wagon or El Camino

Interchange Number: 15
Part Number(s): 3975450
Usage: 1970 Chevelle, all but station wagon or El Camino
Notes: 1970 SS models used a rubber insert.

Interchange Number: 16
Part Number(s): 3848996
Usage: 1962–65 Chevy II

Interchange Number: 17
Part Number(s): 3866564
Usage: 1966–67 Chevy II

Interchange Number: 18
Part Number(s): 3903515
Usage: 1968–72 Nova; 1971–72 Pontiac Ventura II

Grille

Grille design usually changes from year to year and between some models and sub-models. However, you can modify (paint) some grilles to adapt to another model. For example, the 1968 Chevelle SS 396 used a black-accented grille while other models from the same year used a bright-plated one. Grille interchange includes headlamp doors or headlamp bezels, as they were usually a continuation of the grille.

Model Identification

Camaro ....*Interchange Number*
1967
    except RS 0
    RS 1
1968
    except RS 2
    RS
1969
    except RS 3
    RS 4
1970
    except RS 5
    RS 6

Chevelle ....*Interchange Number*
1964..7
1965..8
1966..9
1967
    except SS 10
    SS 396 11
1968..12
1969
    except Malibu 13
    Malibu 14

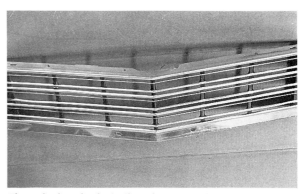

Though they look similar, the 1967 Chevelle grilles are not interchangeable due to the holes in the top. SS 396 models do not have these holes.

Interchange

Interchange Number: 0
    Usage: 1967 Camaro, all except RS
    Main Section: 3905746
    Headlamp Bezels: RH, 3886614; LH, 3886615

Interchange Number: 1
    Usage: 1967–68 Camaro RS
    Main Section: 3929281
    Headlamp Bezels/Doors: RH, 3898150; LH, 3898149
    Notes: Can be adapted to non-1967–68 RS Camaros. Requires special fenders.

Interchange Number: 2
    Usage: 1968 Camaro, all except RS
    Main Section: 3914773
    Headlamp Bezels: RH, 3914770; LH, 3914769

Interchange Number: 3
    Usage: 1969 Camaro, all except RS
    Main Section: 3957062
    Headlamp Bezels: Part of main section.

Interchange Number: 4
    Usage: 1969 Camaro RS
    Main Section: 3938641
    Headlamp Bezels/Doors: *Outer:* RH, 3958004, LH, 3958003; *inner:* RH, 3958006, LH 3958005
    Notes: Can be adapted to non-1969 Camaro RS models. Requires special fenders.

Interchange Number: 5
    Usage: 1970–71 Camaro, except RS
    Main Section: 3967175
    Notes: SS models were painted in black enamel.

Interchange Number: 6
    Usage: 1970–73 Camaro RS
    Main Section: RH, 3962974; LH, 3962973
    Headlamp Bezels: Not used in grille
    Notes: Two-part design. Mounts in frame. Can be adapted to non-1970–72 RS Camaros. Requires special bumper.

Interchange Number: 7
    Usage: 1964 Chevelle
    Main Section: 3854130
    Headlamp Bezels: RH, 3830724; LH, 3830723

Interchange Number: 8
    Usage: 1965 Chevelle
    Main Section: 3875756
    Headlamp Bezels: RH, 3856900; LH, 3856899

Interchange Number: 9
    Usage: 1966 Chevelle
    Main Section: 3873795
    Extensions: RH, 3876424; LH, 3876423
    Notes: Regular Chevelle grille can be painted with black enamel to fit SS 396.

Interchange Number: 10
    Usage: 1967 Chevelle, all except SS 396 or Concours
    Main Section: 3885980
    Extensions: RH, 3893976; LH, 3893975
    Notes: Cannot be adapted to 1967 SS 396 due to pre-drilled emblem mounting holes. Extensions were used on all models including SS 396.

Interchange Number: 11
    Usage: 1967 Chevelle SS 396
    Main Section: 3892182
    Extensions: RH, 3893976; 3893975
    Notes: Extension same on all 1967 Chevelles.

Interchange Number: 12
    Usage: 1968 Chevelle
    Main Section: 3915400
    Notes: Main section same on all models. Paint with black enamel for SS 396. Extensions differ. All but SS 396 used part numbers: RH, 3926808; LH, 3926807. SS 396 used part numbers: RH, 3926804; LH, 3926803. Due to difference in molding usage, they are not interchangeable.

Interchange Number: 13
    Usage: 1969 Chevelle, except Malibu or Concours
    Main Section: 3942789
    Extensions: RH, 3938112; LH, 3938111
    Notes: Extensions were used on all models.

Interchange Number: 14
    Usage: 1969 Malibu or Concours, with SS 396 (except pillar coupe)
    Main Section: 3938180
    Extensions: RH, 3893976; 3893975
    Notes: Grille should be painted black to be used on SS 396. Base Chevelle grille will not interchange.

Interchange Number: 15
    Usage: 1970 Chevelle
    Main Section: 3956117

Notes: Grille should be painted black for SS 396 or SS 454. Interchange with moldings, but without emblems.

Interchange Number: 16
Usage: 1959 full-size Chevrolet
Main Section: 3767700
Extensions/Headlamp Bezels: 3764500 (fits either side)

Interchange Number: 17
Usage: 1960 full-size Chevrolet
Main Section: 3768435

Interchange Number: 18
Usage: 1961 full-size Chevrolet
Main Section: Upper, 3796727; lower, 3777175

Interchange Number: 19
Usage: 1962 full-size Chevrolet
Main Section: 33788244
Extensions/Headlamp Bezels: RH, 3799346; LH, 3799345
Notes: Main section part interchanges with filler panel and upper molding.

Interchange Number: 20
Usage: 1963 full-size Chevrolet
Main Section: 3817606

Interchange Number: 21
Usage: 1964 full-size Chevrolet
Main Section: 3830700
Notes: Interchange with all moldings and bezels and nameplate.

Interchange Number: 22
Usage: 1965 full-size Chevrolet
Main Section: 3850210
Notes: Interchange with all moldings.

Interchange Number: 23
Usage: 1966 full-size Chevrolet
Extensions/Headlamp Bezels: RH, 3869748; LH, 3869747
Notes: Main grille two-part design: upper, 3869745; lower, 3869746.

Interchange Number: 24
Usage: 1967 full-size Chevrolet
Main Section: 3885962
Extensions/Headlamp Bezels: RH, 3885964, LH, 3885963; end plates, RH, 3905728, LH, 3905729
Notes: Caprice will interchange, but does not include end plates. Paint as required for SS models.

Interchange Number: 25
Usage: 1968 full-size Chevrolet, all except with hideaway headlamps
Extensions/Headlamp Bezels: RH, 3917468; LH, 3917467
Notes: Main section two-part design: upper, 3910612; lower, 3910613.

Interchange Number: 26
Usage: 1968 full-size Chevrolet, all with T-83 hideaway headlamps
Lower, RH, 3934262, LH, 3934261; upper, RH,

3926882, LH, 3926881
Notes: Very rare. Door looks like production grille. Production main grille may have been used.

Interchange Number: 27
Usage: 1969 full-size Chevrolet, all except with T-83 hideaway headlamps
Main Section: Upper, 3929895; lower, 3934560
Extensions/Headlamp Bezels: RH, 3964556; LH, 3964555
Notes: Lower main assembly will fit cars with T-83 option.

Interchange Number: 28
Usage: 1969 full-size Chevrolet, all with T-83 hideaway headlamps
Main Section: Upper, 3929897; lower, 3934560
Extensions/Doors: RH, 3934564; LH, 3934563
Notes: Lower main assembly can be found in cars with or without the T-83 option.

Interchange Number: 29
Usage: 1970 full-size Chevrolet
Main Section: Upper, 3972818; lower, 3972819
Extensions/Headlamp Bezels: RH, 3955082; LH, 3955081
Notes: A handful (less than 100) of Impalas were built with headlamp washers. They used
Special bezels with part numbers: RH, 3962364; LH, 3962363. Had nozzle mounting holes over each outboard headlamp. Built in the first 30 days of 1970 model year.

Interchange Number: 30
Usage: 1962 Chevy II
Main Section: 3792544
Extensions/Headlamp Bezels: RH, 3790350; LH, 3790349
Notes: RH bezels fit 1962–64 Chevy II.

Interchange Number: 31
Usage: 1963 Chevy II
Main Section: 383312
Extensions/Headlamp Bezels: RH, 3790350; LH, 3790349
Notes: RH bezels fit 1962–64 Chevy II.

Interchange Number: 32
Usage: 1964 Chevy II
Main Section: 3859082
Extensions/Headlamp Bezels: RH, 3790350; LH, 3790349
Notes: RH bezels fit 1962–64 Chevy II.

Interchange Number: 33
Usage: 1965 Chevy II
Main Section: 3867837
Extensions/Headlamp Bezels: RH, 3865310; LH, 3865309
Notes: Extensions are moldings.

Interchange Number: 34
Usage: 1966 Chevy II
Main Section: 3885299
Extensions/Headlamp Bezels: 3866885 (fits either side)

Interchange Number: 35
    Usage: 1967 Chevy II
    Main Section: 3886428
    Extensions/Headlamp Bezels: RH, 3892282; LH, 3892281
    Notes: Paint black for application on 1967 Nova SS models.

Interchange Number: 36
    Usage: 1968–72 Nova
    Main Section: 3949721

Notes: (1) Extension differed each year. 1968 part numbers: RH, 3914760; LH, 3914759. 1969–72 part numbers: RH, 3949790; LH, 3949789. If the headlamp washers were ordered (1969 only), then part numbers: RH, 3957034; LH, 3957033 were used. (2) Production grille and extensions: To use on SS 350 or 396, paint grille and extensions black.

Chapter 12

Trim and Exterior Parts

Molding

General Notes
There are many different types of molding used on cars. Thus, to help you more easily find the type of molding you need, I have grouped together the different types.

They include, in this order: windshield molding, drip rail molding, rear quarter window molding, wheel lip molding, rocker panel molding, and hood molding. When interchanging a molding, it is always a good idea to include all holding clips. Also, note that the range of molding available for interchange varies and that bodystyle may affect some interchange situations.

When interchanging *used* molding, inspect it carefully for signs of pitting, scratches, or general abuse. Perhaps the molding was removed and then not replaced correctly. Molding is easily bent, so remove it carefully.

Windshield Molding

Model Identification

Interchange

Interchange Number: 1
Part Number(s): 7638868
Usage: 1967–69 Camaro; 1967–69 Pontiac Firebird; both hardtop

Interchange Number: 2
Part Number(s): 7638870
Usage: 1967–69 Camaro; 1967–69 Pontiac Firebird; convertible only

Interchange Number: 3
Part Number(s): 9808500
Usage: 1970–75 Camaro; 1970–75 Pontiac Firebird

Interchange Number: 4
Part Number(s): RH, 4430502; LH, 4430503
Usage: 1964–67 Chevelle; 1964–67 Pontiac LeMans; 1964–67 Buick Skylark; 1964–67 Olds Cutlass; 1964–67 El Camino; all two- or four-door sedan, or station wagon

Interchange Number: 5
Part Number(s): RH, 4541648; LH, 4541649
Usage: 1966–67 Chevelle; 1966–67 Pontiac LeMans; 1966–67 Olds Cutlass; 1966–67 Buick Skylark; all two-door hardtop or convertible
Notes: Will not fit El Camino or two-door pillar coupe. See Interchange number 4 this section for interchange.

Interchange Number: 6
Part Number(s): 7726034
Usage: 1968–72 Chevelle; 1968–72 Pontiac LeMans; 1968–72 Olds Cutlass; 1968–72 Buick Skylark; all two-door sedan or two-door hardtop, or El Camino

Interchange Number: 7
Part Number(s): 7726036
Usage: 1968–72 Chevelle; 1968–72 Pontiac LeMans; 1968–72 Buick Skylark; 1968–72 Olds Cutlass; convertible only

Interchange Number: 8
Usage: 1959 full-size Chevrolet; 1959 El Camino; 1959 full-size Pontiac; 1959–60 full-size Oldsmobile; 1959–60 full-size Buick; all sedan or station wagon
Notes: Interchange 10 will fit.

Interchange Number: 9
Usage: 1959–60 full-size Chevrolet, Pontiac, Oldsmobile, or Buick; all two- or four-door hardtop or convertible

Interchange Number: 10
Usage: 1960 full-size Chevrolet;1960 El Camino; 1960 full-size Pontiac; all sedan or station wagon

Interchange Number: 11
Part Number(s): 4807561
Usage: 1962–64 full-size Chevrolet, Pontiac, Oldsmobile, or Buick; all sedan or station wagon

Interchange Number: 12
Part Number(s): 4838489
Usage: 1962–64 full-size Chevrolet, Pontiac, Oldsmobile, or Buick; all two-door hardtop or convertible

Interchange Number: 13
Part Number(s): 4467600
Usage: 1965–68 full-size Chevrolet, Pontiac, Oldsmobile, or Buick; all sedan or station wagon

Interchange Number: 14
Part Number(s): 4467604
Usage: 1965–68 full-size Chevrolet, Pontiac, Oldsmobile, or Buick; all hardtop or convertible

Interchange Number: 15
Part Number(s): 8711813
Usage: 1969–70 full-size Chevrolet, Pontiac, Oldsmobile, or Buick; all hardtop or convertible

Interchange Number: 16
Part Number(s): 4842066
Usage: 1962–67 Chevy II, all except two-door hardtop or convertible

Interchange Number: 17
Part Number(s): 4842319
Usage: 1962–67 Chevy II two-door hardtop or convertible

Interchange Number: 18
Part Number(s): RH, 7738570; LH, 7738571
Usage: 1968–74 Nova; 1971–74 Pontiac Ventura II; 1974 Olds Omega; 1974 Buick Apollo; all two-door or hatchback

Interchange Number: 19
Part Number(s): RH, 7639558; LH, 7639559
Usage: 1967–69 Camaro; 1967–69 Pontiac Firebird; both hardtop

Interchange Number: 20
Part Number(s): RH, 7639560; LH, 7639561
Usage: 1967–69 Camaro; 1967–69 Pontiac Firebird; convertible only

Interchange Number: 21
Part Number(s): RH, 9868730; LH, 9898691
Usage: 1970–75 Camaro; 1970–75 Pontiac Firebird
Notes: LH unit only used on original 1970 Camaro and Firebird. 1972–75 LH trim fits.

Interchange Number: 22
Part Number(s): RH, 4430500; LH, 4430501
Usage: 1964–67 Chevelle; 1964–67 Pontiac LeMans; 1964–67 Buick Skylark; 1964–67 Olds Cutlass; 1964–67 El Camino; all bodystyles, including convertible

Interchange Number: 23
Part Number(s): RH, 7725634; LH, 7725635
Usage: 1968–72 Chevelle; 1968–72 Pontiac LeMans; 1968–72 Buick Skylark; 1968–72 Olds Cutlass; all two-door sedan, hardtop, or El Camino or convertible
Notes: Four-door sedan will not interchange.

Interchange Number: 25
Usage: 1959 full-size Chevrolet; 1959 El Camino; 1959 full-size Pontiac; 1959–60 full-size Oldsmobile; 1959–60 full-size Buick; all sedan or station wagon

Interchange Number: 27
Usage: 1959–60 full-size Chevrolet; 1959–60 full-size Pontiac; 1959–60 full-size Oldsmobile; 1959–60 full-size Buick; all two- or four-door hardtop or convertible

Interchange Number: 28
Usage: 1960 full-size Chevrolet; 1960 El Camino; 1960 full-size Pontiac; all sedan or station wagon

Interchange Number: 29
Usage: 1962–64 full-size Chevrolet, Pontiac, Oldsmobile, or Buick; all two- or four-door sedan

Interchange Number: 30
Part Number(s): RH, 4873358; LH, 4873359
Usage: 1963–64 full-size Chevrolet, Pontiac, Oldsmobile, or Buick; all two-door hardtop or convertible

Interchange Number: 31
Part Number(s): RH, 7685034; LH, 7685035
Usage: 1965–67 full-size Chevrolet, Pontiac, Oldsmobile, or Buick; all sedan or station wagon

Interchange Number: 32
Part Number(s): RH, 7685038; LH, 7685039
Usage: 1965–67 full-size Chevrolet, Pontiac, Oldsmobile, or Buick; all two- or four-door hardtop

Interchange Number: 33
Part Number(s): RH, 7600994; LH, 7600995
Usage: 1966–67 full-size Chevrolet, Pontiac, Oldsmobile, or Buick; convertible only
Notes: Pillar finishing molding.

Interchange Number: 34
Part Number(s): RH, 7608398; LH, 7608399
Usage: 1966 full-size Chevrolet, Pontiac, Oldsmobile, or Buick; all two- or four-door hardtop with vinyl top
Notes: Pillar finishing molding.

Interchange Number: 35
Part Number(s): RH, 7765228; LH, 7765229
Usage: 1968 full-size Chevrolet, Pontiac, Oldsmobile, or Buick; all two- or four-door hardtop

Interchange Number: 36
Part Number(s): RH, 7758553; LH, 7758554
Usage: 1968 full-size Chevrolet, Pontiac, Oldsmobile, or Buick; convertible only

Interchange Number: 37
Part Number(s): RH, 8712722; LH, 8712723
Usage: 1969–70 full-size Chevrolet, Pontiac, Oldsmobile, or Buick; all two- or four-door hardtop

Interchange Number: 38
Part Number(s): RH, 8715890; LH, 8715891
Usage: 1969–70 full-size Chevrolet, Pontiac, Oldsmobile, or Buick; convertible only

Interchange Number: 39
Part Number(s): RH, 4842155; LH, 4842156
Usage: 1962–67 Chevy II, all except two-door hardtop or convertible

Interchange Number: 40
Part Number(s): RH, 4842157; LH, 4842158
Usage: 1962–67 Chevy II two-door hardtop or convertible

Interchange Number: 41
Part Number(s): RH, 7639926; LH, 7639927
Usage: 1967–69 Camaro; 1967–69 Pontiac Firebird; both hardtop

Interchange Number: 42
Part Number(s): RH, 7648736; LH, 7648737
Usage: 1967–69 Camaro; 1967–69 Pontiac Firebird; convertible only

Interchange Number: 43
Part Number(s): 4430558
Usage: 1964–67 Chevelle; 1964–67 Pontiac LeMans; 1964–67 Buick Skylark; 1964–67 Olds Cutlass
Notes: For first design (early) in 1966 four-door models. Fits all 1964–65 and 1967 Chevelles.

Interchange Number: 44
Part Number(s): 7726034
Usage: 1968–72 Chevelle; 1968–72 Pontiac LeMans; 1968–72 Olds Cutlass; 1968–72 Buick Skylark; all with concealed wipers
Notes: Be careful when interchanging for low-grade models like Chevelle (Deluxe); Pontiac Tempest, or Buick special. These models were not standard with concealed wipers and may not have the correct trim.

Interchange Number: 45
Part Number(s): 7737629
Usage: 1968–72 Chevelle; 1968–72 Pontiac LeMans; 1968–72 Buick Skylark; 1968–72 Olds Cutlass
Notes: Base models only. Not for SS-equipped models. Used with non-concealed wipers only.

Interchange Number: 46
Usage: 1959 full-size Chevrolet;1959 El Camino; 1959 full-size Pontiac; 1959–60 full-size
Oldsmobile; 1959–60 full-size Buick; all sedan or station wagon

Interchange Number: 47
Usage: 1959–60 full-size Chevrolet, Pontiac, Oldsmobile, or Buick; all two- or four-door hardtop or convertible

Interchange Number: 48
Usage: 1960 full-size Chevrolet;1960 El Camino; 1960 full-size Pontiac; all sedan or station wagon

Special drip rail moldings are used with vinyl tops.

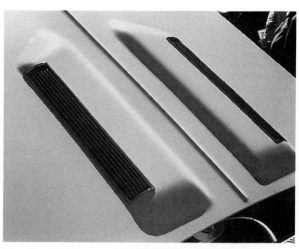
Simulated air vents on a 1967 Chevelle SS 396.

Interchange Number: 49
Part Number(s): 4873368
Usage: 1962–64 full-size Chevrolet, Pontiac, Oldsmobile, or Buick; all sedan or station wagon

Interchange Number: 50
Usage: 1963–64 full-size Chevrolet, Pontiac, Oldsmobile, or Buick; all two-door hardtop or convertible

Interchange Number: 51
Part Number(s): RH, 4474570; LH, 4474571
Usage: 1965–67 full-size Chevrolet, Pontiac, Oldsmobile, or Buick; convertible only

Interchange Number: 52
Part Number(s): RH, 4467229; LH, 4467230
Usage: 1965–67 full-size Chevrolet, Pontiac, Oldsmobile, or Buick; all except convertible

Interchange Number: 53
Part Number(s): 8738876
Usage: 1968 full-size Chevrolet, Pontiac, Oldsmobile, or Buick; all models and bodystyles

Interchange Number: 54
Part Number(s): 8712542
Usage: 1969–70 full-size Chevrolet, Pontiac, Oldsmobile, or Buick; all models and bodystyles

Interchange Number: 55
Part Number(s): 4842068
Usage: 1962–67 Chevy II

Interchange Number: 56
Part Number(s): RH, 8780430; LH, 8780431
Usage: 1968–74 Nova; 1971–74 Pontiac Ventura II; 1974 Olds Omega; 1974 Buick Apollo

Interchange Number: 57
Part Number(s): RH, 9841146; LH, 9841147
Usage: 1970–71 Camaro; 1970–71 Pontiac Firebird
Notes: 1972–75 is rumored to fit.

Drip Rail Molding

Model Identification

Interchange

Interchange Number: 1
    Usage: 1967–69 Camaro; 1967–69 Pontiac Firebird; both hardtop

Interchange Number: 2
    Usage: 1970–73 Camaro; 1970–73 Pontiac Firebird; both without vinyl top

Interchange Number: 3
    Usage: 1970–73 Camaro; 1970–73 Pontiac Firebird; both with vinyl top

Interchange Number: 4
    Part Number(s): RH, 4407700; LH, 4407701
    Usage: 1964–65 Chevelle two-door sedan

Interchange Number: 5
    Part Number(s): *Front:* RH, 4456072, LH, 4456073; *Rear:* RH, 44056076, LH, 44056077
    Usage: 1964–65 Chevelle; 1964–65 Pontiac LeMans; 1964–65 Olds Cutlass; 1964–65 Buick Skylark; all two-door hardtop

Interchange Number: 6
    Part Number(s): RH, 7643206; LH, 7643205
    Usage: 1964–67 El Camino

Interchange Number: 7
    Part Number(s): RH, 4541586; LH, 4541587
    Usage: 1966–67 Chevelle two-door sedan

Interchange Number: 8
    Part Number(s): RH, 4547733; LH, 4547734
    Usage: 1966–67 Chevelle; 1966–67 Olds Cutlass; 1966–67 Pontiac LeMans; 1966–67 Buick Skylark; all two-door hardtop

Interchange Number: 9
    Part Number(s): RH, 7723584; LH, 7723585
    Usage: 1968–69 Chevelle two-door sedan or two-door hardtop without vinyl top

Interchange Number: 10
    Part Number(s): RH, 7753596; LH, 7753597
    Usage: 1968–70 Chevelle two-door hardtop or convertible with vinyl top

Interchange Number: 11
    Part Number(s): RH, 7723362; LH, 7723363
    Usage: 1968–72 El Camino

Interchange Number: 12
    Part Number(s): RH, 4753283; LH, 4753284
    Usage: 1959–60 full-size Chevrolet, Pontiac, or Oldsmobile; all two-door or four-door sedan

Interchange Number: 13
    Usage: 1959–60 full-size Chevrolet, Pontiac, or Oldsmobile; all two-door hardtop

Interchange Number: 14
    Usage: 1959–60 El Camino
    Notes: No other interchange.

Interchange Number: 15
> Part Number(s): *front:* RH, 4809565, LH, 4809566; *Rear:* RH, 4808264; LH, 4808265
> Usage: 1961 full-size Pontiac; 1961 full-size Oldsmobile; 1961–62 full-size Chevrolet; all two-door or four-door sedan

Interchange Number: 16
> Usage: 1961 full-size Chevrolet, Pontiac or Oldsmobile; all two-door hardtop

Interchange Number: 17
> Part Number(s): RH, 4874466; LH, 4874467
> Usage: 1962–64 full-size Chevrolet; 1962–64 full-size Pontiac; 1962–64 full-size Oldsmobile; all two- or four-door sedan

Interchange Number: 18
> Part Number(s): RH, 4839213; LH, 4839214
> Usage: 1963–64 full-size Chevrolet; 1963–64 Pontiac Catalina or Bonneville; 1963–64 full-size Olds Delta 88, S88 or J88; all two-door hardtop

Interchange Number: 19
> Part Number(s): RH, 4474394; LH, 4474395
> Usage: 1965–66 full-size Chevrolet; 1965–66 full-size Pontiac; both two-door sedan

Interchange Number: 20
> Part Number(s): RH, 4481690; LH, 4481691
> Usage: 1965–66 full-size Chevrolet; 1965–66 full-size Pontiac, except Grand Prix; 1965 full-size Olds Delta 88, J88; 1965–66 Buick LeSabre or Wildcat; all two-door hardtop.
> Notes: Not Caprice.

Interchange Number: 21
> Part Number(s): *Front:* RH, 4545368, LH, 4545367; *Rear:* RH, 7580648, LH, 7580649
> Usage: 1966–67 Caprice two-door hardtop
> Notes: No other interchange.

Interchange Number: 22
> Part Number(s): RH, 7650000; LH, 7650001
> Usage: 1967–68 full-size Chevrolet; 1967–68 full-size Pontiac; 1967–68 full-size Oldsmobile except Delta 98;1967–68 Buick LeSabre or Wildcat; all two-door hardtop
> Notes: Not Caprice or 1968 Impala Custom.

Interchange Number: 23
> Part Number(s): RH, 7648328; LH, 7648329
> Usage: 1967–68 full-size Chevrolet; 1967–68 full-size Pontiac; both two-door sedan

Interchange Number: 24
> Part Number(s): *Front:* RH, 7761578, LH, 7761579; *Rear:* RH, 7761580, LH, 7761581
> Usage: 1968 Caprice; 1968 Impala Custom; both two-door hardtop

Interchange Number: 25
> Part Number(s): RH, 8784783; LH, 8784782
> Usage: 1969 full-size Chevrolet two-door sedan

Interchange Number: 26
> Part Number(s): *Windshield:* RH, 8719410, LH, 8719411; *front:* LH, 8784782, LH, 8784783; *Rear:* RH, 8715173, LH, 8715172 LH
> Usage: 1969 full-size Chevrolet two-door hardtop, except Impala Custom or Caprice
> Notes: Rear portions were also used on 1970 models. See interchange number 28.

Interchange Number: 27
> Part Number(s): *Windshield:* RH, 8784784, LH, 8784785; *front:* RH, 8712748, LH, 8712747; *rear:* RH, 8714837, LH, 8714836
> Usage: 1969–70 Caprice two-door hardtop or Impala Custom and Impala convertible
> Notes: Windshield pillars were used on all 1970 full-size models. See interchange number 28.

Interchange Number: 28
> Part Number(s): *Windshield:* RH, 8784784, LH, 8784785; *front:* 8713316, LH 8713317, LH; *Rear:* RH, 8715173, LH, 8715172
> Usage: 1970 Impala two-door hardtop, except Custom
> Notes: Windshield pillars can be found on 1970 Impala Custom and Caprice, including four-door hardtop. Sedans will not interchange. Rear moldings were used on 1969 models. See interchange number 26.

Interchange Number: 29
> Part Number(s): RH, 4845410; LH, 4845411
> Usage: 1962–65 Chevy II two- or four-door sedan

Interchange Number: 30
> Part Number(s): *Front:* RH, 4844714, LH, 4844715; *Rear:* RH, 4844712, LH, 4844713
> Usage: 1962–65 Chevy II two-door hardtop

Interchange Number: 31
> Usage: 1966–67 Chevy II two-door sedan

Interchange Number: 32
> Part Number(s): RH, 7582513; LH, 7582514
> Usage: 1966–67 Chevy II two-door hardtop

Interchange Number: 33
> Part Number(s): *Front:* RH, 7738095, LH, 7738096; *Rear:* RH, 7741463, LH, 7741464
> Usage: 1968–72 Nova; 1971–72 Pontiac Ventura II two-door sedan

Rear Quarter Window Molding

Model Identification

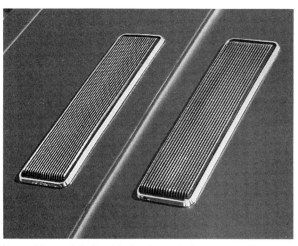

Nova SS models for 1968–72 used these vents.

Interchange

Interchange Number: 1
Part Number(s): 7639859
Usage: 1967–69 Camaro; 1967–69 Pontiac Firebird; both hardtop

Interchange Number: 2
Part Number(s): 8798351
Usage: 1970–74 Camaro; 1970–74 Pontiac Firebird

Interchange Number: 3
Part Number(s): RH, 4430550; LH, 4430551
Usage: 1964–65 Chevelle; 1964–65 Pontiac LeMans; 1964–65 Olds Cutlass; 1964–65 Buick Skylark
Notes: Chevelle is two- or four-door sedan; others are four-door sedan only

Interchange Number: 4
Part Number(s): RH, 4430552; LH, 4430553
Usage: 1964–65 Chevelle;1964–65 Buick Skylark; 1964–65 Pontiac LeMans; 1964–65 Olds Cutlass; all two-door hardtop

Interchange Number: 5
Part Number(s): RH, 4408581; LH, 4408580
Usage: 1964–67 El Camino

Interchange Number: 6
Part Number(s): RH, 4542514; LH, 4542515
Usage: 1966–67 Chevelle; 1966–67 Pontiac LeMans; 1966–67 Olds Cutlass; 1966–67 Buick Skylark; all two- or four-door sedan

Interchange Number: 7
Part Number(s): RH, 7580180; LH, 7580181
Usage: 1966–67 Chevelle; 1966–67 Pontiac LeMans; 1966–67 Olds Cutlass; 1966–67 Buick Skylark; all two-door hardtop

Interchange Number: 8
Part Number(s): RH, 7727134; LH, 7727135
Usage: 1968–72 Chevelle; 1968–72 Pontiac LeMans; all two-door sedan or two-door hardtop
Notes: Interchange includes side molding.

Interchange Number: 9
Part Number(s): RH, 8775846; LH, 8775847
Usage: 1968–72 El Camino; 1971–72 GMC Sprint

Interchange Number: 10
Usage: 1959–60 full-size Chevrolet, except Impala; 1959–60 Olds Eighty-Eight; 1959–60 full-size Pontiac; all two- or four-door sedan

Interchange Number: 11
Part Number(s): 4756111
Usage: 1959–60 Impala; 1959–60 Olds Eighty-Eight; 1959–60 full-size Pontiac; all two-door hardtop or four-door sedan
Notes: Four-door hardtop will not interchange.

Interchange Number: 12
Usage: 1959–60 El Camino

Interchange Number: 13
Part Number(s): RH, 4810470; LH, 4810471
Usage: 1961 full-size Chevrolet; 1961 Olds Eighty-Eight; 1961 full-size Pontiac; all two-door or four-door sedan

Interchange Number: 14
Part Number(s): RH, 4808114; LH, 4808115
Usage: 1961 full-size Chevrolet; 1961 Olds Eighty-Eight; 1961 full-size Pontiac; all two-door hardtop

Interchange Number: 15
Part Number(s): RH, 4841990; LH, 4841991
Usage: 1962–64 full-size Chevrolet; 1962–64 Olds Eighty-Eight; 1962–64 full-size Pontiac; 1963–64 Buick LeSabre; all two- or four-door sedan

Interchange Number: 16
Part Number(s): RH, 4838508; LH, 4838509
Usage: 1962–64 full-size Chevrolet; 1962–64 Olds Eighty-Eight; 1962–64 full-size Pontiac; 1963–64 Buick LeSabre; all two-door hardtop

Interchange Number: 17
Part Number(s): 4481668
Usage: 1963–64 Buick LeSabre; 1965–66 full-size Chevrolet; 1965–66 Olds Eighty-Eight; 1965–66 full-size Pontiac; all two- or four-door sedan

Interchange Number: 18
Part Number(s): LH, 4478769
Usage: 1963–64 Buick LeSabre; 1965–66 full-size Chevrolet; 1965–66 Olds Eighty-Eight; 1965–66 full-size Pontiac; all two-door hardtop, except Caprice

Interchange Number: 19
Part Number(s): RH, 4547616; LH, 4547617
Usage: 1966–67 Caprice two-door hardtop
Notes: No other interchange.

Interchange Number: 20
Part Number(s): RH, 7646717; LH, 7646718
Usage: 1967–68 full-size Chevrolet; 1967–68 Olds Eighty-Eight; 1967–68 full-size Pontiac; 1967–68 Buick LeSabre; all two-door hardtop, except Caprice or Impala Custom

Interchange Number: 21
Part Number(s): RH, 7648027; LH, 7648028
Usage: 1967–68 full-size Chevrolet; 1967–68 Olds Eighty-Eight; 1967–68 full-size Pontiac; 1967–68 Buick LeSabre; all two- or four-door sedan

Interchange Number: 22
Part Number(s): RH, 7730310; LH, 7730311
Usage: 1968 Caprice; 1968 Impala Custom; both two-door hardtop
Notes: No other interchange.

Interchange Number: 23
Part Number(s): 8715509
Usage: 1969–70 full-size Chevrolet; 1969–70 Olds Eighty-Eight; 1969–70 full-size Pontiac; 1969–70 Buick LeSabre; all two-door hardtop, except Caprice or Impala Custom

Interchange Number: 24
Part Number(s): RH, 8775840; LH, 8775841
Usage: 1969–70 full-size Chevrolet; 1969–70 Olds Eighty-Eight; 1969–70 full-size Pontiac; 1969–70 Buick LeSabre; all four-door sedan
Notes: Will fit 1969 two-door sedan.

Interchange Number: 25
Part Number(s): RH, 8775844; LH, 8775845
Usage: 1969–70 Caprice or Impala Custom; both two-door hardtop
Notes: No Other interchange.

Interchange Number: 26
Part Number(s): RH, 4843563; LH, 4843564
Usage: 1962–64 Chevy II two- or four-door sedan

Interchange Number: 27
Part Number(s): RH, 4846228; LH, 4846229
Usage: 1962–65 Chevy II two-door hardtop

Interchange Number: 28
Part Number(s): RH, 4500523; LH, 4500524
Usage: 1965 Chevy II two- or four-door sedan

Interchange Number: 29
Part Number(s): 4541891
Usage: 1966–67 Chevy II two- or four-door sedan

Interchange Number: 30
Part Number(s): RH, 7581305; LH, 7581304
Usage: 1966–67 Chevy II two-door hardtop

Interchange Number: 31
Part Number(s): RH, 7741473; LH, 7741472
Usage: 1968–74 Nova; 1971–74 Pontiac Ventura II; 1973–74 Olds Omega; 1973–74 Buick Apollo; all two-door hardtop
Notes: Hatchback or bodystyles will not interchange.

Interchange Number: 32
Part Number(s): RH, 8775872; LH, 8775873
Usage: 1967–69 Camaro; 1967–69 Pontiac Firebird; both hardtop

Interchange Number: 33
Part Number(s): RH, 4430550; LH, 4430551
Usage: 1964–65 Chevelle; 1964–65 Pontiac LeMans; 1964–65 Olds Cutlass; 1964–65 Buick Skylark
Notes: Chevelle is two- or four-door sedan. Others are four-door sedan.

Interchange Number: 34
Part Number(s): RH, 4430546; LH, 4430547
Usage: 1964–65 Chevelle;1964–65 Buick Skylark; 1964–65 Pontiac LeMans; 1964–65 Olds Cutlass; all two-door hardtop

Interchange Number: 35
Part Number(s): RH, 7695648; LH, 7695647
Usage: 1964–67 El Camino

Interchange Number: 36
Part Number(s): RH, 4758874; LH, 4758875
Usage: 1959–60 full-size Chevrolet, except Impala; 1959–60 Olds Eighty-Eight; 1959–60 full-size Pontiac; all two- or four-door sedan

Interchange Number: 37
Part Number(s): RH, 4756720; LH, 4756721
Usage: 1959–60 Impala; 1959–60 Olds Eighty Eight; 1959–60 full-size Pontiac; all two-door hardtop or four-door sedan
Notes: Four-door hardtop will not interchange.

Interchange Number: 38
Usage: 1959–60 El Camino

Interchange Number: 39
Part Number(s): RH, 4812946; LH, 48122947
Usage: 1961 full-size Chevrolet; 1961 Olds Eighty-Eight; 1961 full-size Pontiac; all two- or four-door sedan, except Impala four-door sedan

Interchange Number: 40
Usage: 1962–64 full-size Chevrolet; 1962–64 Olds Eighty-Eight; 1962–64 full-size Pontiac; 1963–64 Buick LeSabre; all two- or four-door sedan

Interchange Number: 41
Usage: 1962–64 full-size Chevrolet; 1962–64 Olds Eighty-Eight; 1962–64 full-size Pontiac; 1963–64 Buick LeSabre; all two-door hardtop

Interchange Number: 42
Part Number(s): RH, 4537486; LH, 4537487
Usage: 1963–64 Buick LeSabre; 1965–66 full-size Chevrolet; 1965–66 Olds Eighty-Eight; 1965–66 full-size Pontiac; all two- or four-door sedan

Interchange Number: 43
Part Number(s): RH, 4478990; LH, 4478991
Usage: 1963–64 Buick LeSabre; 1965–66 full-size Chevrolet; 1965–66 Olds Eighty-Eight; 1965–66 full-size Pontiac; all two-door hardtop, except Caprice

Interchange Number: 44
Part Number(s): RH, 4547910; LH, 4547911
Usage: 1966–67 Caprice two-door hardtop
Notes: No other interchange.

Interchange Number: 45
Part Number(s): RH, 7647558; LH, 7647559
Usage: 1967–68 full-size Chevrolet; 1967–68 Olds Eighty-Eight; 1967–68 full-size Pontiac; 1967–68 Buick LeSabre; all two-door hardtop, except Caprice or Impala Custom

Interchange Number: 46
Part Number(s): RH, 7726248; LH, 7726249
Usage: 1968 Caprice; 1968 Impala Custom; both Two-door hardtop
Notes: No other interchange.

Interchange Number: 47
Part Number(s): RH, 8715868; LH, 8715869
Usage: 1969–70 full-size Chevrolet; 1969–70 Olds Eighty-Eight; 1969–70 full-size Pontiac; 1969–70 Buick LeSabre; all two-door hardtop, except Caprice or Impala Custom

Interchange Number: 48
Part Number(s): RH, 4846230; LH, 4846231
Usage: 1962–65 Chevy II two-door hardtop

Interchange Number: 49
Part Number(s): RH, 4545265; LH, 4545266
Usage: 1966–67 Chevy II two- or four-door sedan

Interchange Number: 50
Part Number(s): RH, 7581308; LH, 7581307
Usage: 1966–67 Chevy II two-door hardtop

Interchange Number: 51
Part Number(s): RH, 7639866; LH, 7639867
Usage: 1967–69 Camaro; 1967–69 Pontiac Firebird; both hardtop

Interchange Number: 52
Part Number(s): RH, 8799269; LH, 8799268
Usage: 1970–74 Camaro; 1970–74 Pontiac Firebird

Interchange Number: 53
Part Number(s): 4430539
Usage: 1964–65 Chevelle; 1964–65 Pontiac LeMans; 1964–65 Olds Cutlass; 1964–65 Buick Skylark
Notes: Chevelle is two- or four-door sedan. Others are four-door sedan only.

Interchange Number: 54
Part Number(s): 4430548
Usage: 1964–65 Chevelle;1964–65 Buick Skylark; 1964–65 Pontiac LeMans; 1964–65 Olds Cutlass; all two-door hardtop

Interchange Number: 55
Part Number(s): RH, 4408577; LH, 4408576
Usage: 1964–67 El Camino

Interchange Number: 56
Part Number(s): RH, 4542514; LH, 4542515
Usage: 1966–67 Chevelle; 1966–67 Pontiac LeMans; 1966–67 Olds Cutlass; 1966–67 Buick Skylark; all two- or four-door sedan

Interchange Number: 57
Part Number(s): RH, 7581670; LH, 7581671
Usage: 1966–67 Chevelle; 1966–67 Pontiac LeMans; 1966–67 Olds Cutlass; 1966–67 Buick Skylark; all two-door hardtop

Interchange Number: 58
Part Number(s): RH, 7725807; LH, 7725808
Usage: 1968–72 Chevelle; 1968–72 Pontiac LeMans; all two-door sedan or two-door hardtop

Interchange Number: 59
Part Number(s): 7741450
Usage: 1968–72 El Camino; 1971–72 GMC Sprint

Interchange Number: 60
Part Number(s): 4756271
Usage: 1959–60 full-size Chevrolet, except Impala; 1959–60 Olds Eighty-Eight; 1959–60 full-size Pontiac; all two- or four-door sedan

Interchange Number: 61
Part Number(s): 4756577
Usage: 1959–60 Impala; 1959–60 Oldsmobile Eighty Eight; 1959–60 full-size Pontiac; all two-door hardtop or four-door sedan
Notes: Four-door hardtop will not interchange.

Interchange Number: 62
Usage: 1959–60 El Camino

Interchange Number: 63
Part Number(s): 4842160
Usage: 1961 full-size Chevrolet; 1961 Olds Eighty-Eight; 1961 full-size Pontiac; all two- or four-door sedan

Interchange Number: 64
Part Number(s): RH, 4807728; LH, 4807729
Usage: 1961 full-size Chevrolet; 1961 Olds Eighty-Eight; 1961 full-size Pontiac; all two-door hardtop

Interchange Number: 65
Usage: 1962–64 full-size Chevrolet; 1962–64 Olds Eighty-Eight; 1962–64 full-size Pontiac; 1963–64 Buick LeSabre; all two- or four-door sedan

Interchange Number: 66
Part Number(s): 4839944
Usage: 1962–64 full-size Chevrolet; 1962–64 Olds Eighty-Eight; 1962–64 full-size Pontiac; 1963–64 Buick LeSabre; all two-door hardtop

Interchange Number: 67
  Part Number(s): RH, 4481975; LH, 4481976
  Usage: 1963–64 Buick LeSabre; 1965–66 full-size Chevrolet; 1965–66 Olds Eighty-Eight; 1965–66 full-size Pontiac; all two- or four-door sedan

Interchange Number: 68
  Part Number(s): RH, 4478793; LH, 4478794
  Usage: 1963–64 Buick LeSabre; 1965–66 full-size Chevrolet; 1965–66 Olds Eighty-Eight; 1965–66 full-size Pontiac; all two-door hardtop, except Caprice

Interchange Number: 69
  Part Number(s): 4547912
  Usage: 1966–67 Caprice two-door hardtop
  Notes: No other interchange.

Interchange Number: 70
  Part Number(s): 7660862
  Usage: 1963–64 Buick LeSabre; 1967–68 full-size Chevrolet; 1967–68 Olds Eighty-Eight; 1967–68 full-size Pontiac; all two-door hardtop, except Caprice or Impala Custom

Interchange Number: 71
  Part Number(s): RH, 7646796; LH, 7646797
  Usage: 1967–68 full-size Chevrolet; 1967–68 Olds Eighty-Eight; 1967–68 full-size Pontiac; 1967–68 Buick LeSabre; all two- or four-door sedan

Interchange Number: 72
  Part Number(s): 7726250
  Usage: 1968 Caprice; 1968 Impala Custom; both two-door hardtop
  Notes: No other interchange.

Interchange Number: 73
  Part Number(s): RH, 8775837; LH, 8775838
  Usage: 1969–70 full-size Chevrolet; 1969–70 Olds Eighty-Eight; 1969–70 full-size Pontiac; 1969–70 Buick LeSabre; all two- or four-door sedan

Interchange Number: 74
  Part Number(s): RH, 9811304; LH, 9811305
  Usage: 1969–70 full-size Chevrolet; 1969–70 Olds Eighty-Eight; 1969–70 full-size Pontiac; 1969–70 Buick LeSabre; all two-door hardtop

Interchange Number: 75
  Part Number(s): RH, 4849308; LH, 4849309
  Usage: 1962–64 Chevy II two- or four-door sedan

Interchange Number: 76
  Part Number(s): RH, 4846232; LH, 4846233
  Usage: 1962–65 Chevy II two-door hardtop

Interchange Number: 77
  Part Number(s): RH, 4500525; LH, 4500526
  Usage: 1965 Chevy II two- or four-door sedan

Interchange Number: 78
  Part Number(s): RH, 4545263; LH, 4545264
  Usage: 1966–67 Chevy II two- or four-door sedan

Interchange Number: 79
  Part Number(s): 7581305
  Usage: 1966–67 Chevy II two-door hardtop

Interchange Number: 80
  Part Number(s): RH, 7722529; LH, 7722528
  Usage: 1968–74 Nova; 1971–74 Pontiac Ventura II; 1973–74 Olds Omega; 1973–74 Buick Apollo; all two-door hardtop
  Notes: Hatchback or bodystyles will not interchange.

Wheel Lip Molding

Wheel lip moldings are unique accessories, therefore, their is little interchange available. Most of the trim included in this section changes every year with each model, and in some cases, with the sub-models. For example, the Chevelle Super Sport used a different trim than other two-door Chevelles due to differences in color and style.

The only interchange I was able to find for this section was rear wheel trim for the 1967 Camaro, which is also available on the 1967–68 Pontiac Firebird. The 1969 Camaro and 1969 Pontiac Firebird rear wheel-well trim will interchange as well.

At the front fenders, the 1967 and 1968 Camaro Rallye Sport models used the same front wheel-well trim. However, the Pontiac Firebird's will not fit a Camaro. Second-generation Camaros from 1970–72 also used the same molding front and rear. But rear wheel moldings will not fit the front fenders, nor will Firebird or later models interchange.

Chevy II models are more interchangeable. The 1966 and 1967 model years used the same moldings, but interchange is limited to Nova SS models. In only two interchanges were found for the Chevelle. The moldings used with the 1970 El Camino can also be found on the 1970–72 Concours or El Caminos. And 1970–72 Chevelle Malibus all used the same trim, including all SS models. No interchange was found for Impala models.

Rocker Panel Molding

Model Identification

Interchange

Interchange Number: 1
Part Number(s): 3904540 (fits either side)
Usage: 1967–69 Camaro

Interchange Number: 2
Part Number(s): RH, 481539; LH, 481540
Usage: 1970–75 Camaro; 1970–75 Pontiac Firebird Espirit
Notes: Other Pontiac Firebird models will not interchange.

Interchange Number: 3
Part Number(s): RH, 3843904; LH, 3843903
Usage: 1964 Chevelle, all except SS or El Camino

Interchange Number: 4
Part Number(s): RH, 3846278; LH, 3846277
Usage: 1964 Chevelle SS or El Camino
Notes: Other Chevelle models will not interchange.

Interchange Number: 5
Part Number(s): RH, 3865362; LH, 3865361
Usage: 1965 Chevelle

Interchange Number: 6
Part Number(s): RH, 3886232; LH, 3886231
Usage: 1966 Chevelle, all including El Camino, SS 396, and station wagon

Interchange Number: 7
Part Number(s): RH, 3904585; LH, 3904586
Usage: 1967 Chevelle, all except SS 396 or Concours

Interchange Number: 8
Part Number(s): RH, 3904584; LH, 3904583
Usage: 1967 Chevelle SS 396 or Concours

Interchange Number: 9
Part Number(s): RH, 3928426; LH, 3928425
Usage: 1968 Chevelle, all two-door models except El Camino

Interchange Number: 10
Part Number(s): 3952496 (fits either side)
Usage: 1968–69 El Camino

Interchange Number: 11
Part Number(s): 3952495 (fits either side)
Usage: 1969 Chevelle, all two-door models except El Camino

Interchange Number: 12
Part Number(s): 3980807 (fits either side)
Usage: 1970 Chevelle, all two-door models except El Camino

Interchange Number: 13
Part Number(s): RH, 3770176; LH, 3770175
Usage: 1959–60 Impala

Interchange Number: 14
Part Number(s): 3782370 (fits either side)
Usage: 1961 Biscayne two- or four-door; 1961 Brookline station wagon

Interchange Number: 15
Part Number(s): RH, 3780520; LH, 3780519
Usage: 1961 Bel Air two- or four-door; 1961 Parkwood station wagon; 1961 Impala two- or four-door; 1961 Nomad station wagon

Interchange Number: 16
Part Number(s): RH, 3797802; LH, 3797801
Usage: 1962 Impala two- or four-door or station wagon

Interchange Number: 17
Part Number(s): 3844288 (fits either side)
Usage: 1964 Bel Air; 1964 Impala

Interchange Number: 18
Part Number(s): 3862227 (fits either side)
Usage: 1965 Biscayne or Bel Air

Interchange Number: 19
Part Number(s): RH, 3865332; LH, 3865331
Usage: 1965 Impala

Interchange Number: 20
Part Number(s): RH, 3886228; LH, 3886227
Usage: 1966 Caprice, 1966 Impala, all except station wagon

Interchange Number: 21
Part Number(s): RH, 3904650; LH, 3904649
Usage: 1967 Impala

Interchange Number: 22
Part Number(s): 3927546 (fits either side)
Usage: 1968 full-size Chevrolet

Interchange Number: 23
    Part Number(s): RH, 3953846; LH, 3953845
    Usage: 1969 Impala, all except station wagon

Interchange Number: 24
    Part Number(s): 3927546 (fits either side)
    Usage: 1969 Biscayne or Bel Air, all except station wagon

Interchange Number: 25
    Part Number(s): *With skirts:* RH, 3980816; LH, 3980815
    Without skirts: RH, 3980818; LH, 3980817
    Usage: 1970 Impala; 1970 Caprice; includes Impala Custom; all two- or four-door
    Notes: Came with fender skirts as optional equipment.

Interchange Number: 26
    Part Number(s): RH, 3885382; LH, 3885381
    Usage: 1966–67 Chevy II Nova, except Nova SS

Interchange Number: 27
    Part Number(s): RH, 3885386; LH, 3885385
    Usage: 1966–67 Chevy II Nova SS

Interchange Number: 28
    Part Number(s): RH, 3927548; LH, 3927547
    Usage: 1968–74 Nova
    Notes: Molding was not standard affair on all. Was part of exterior decor package.

Interchange Number: 29
    Part Number(s): RH, 3792280; LH, 3792279
    Usage: 1962–63 Chevy II

Interchange Number: 30
    Part Number(s): 3850818 (fits either side)
    Usage: 1964 Chevy II, except Nova or Nova SS

Interchange Number: 31
    Part Number(s): RH, 3850882; LH, 3850881
    Usage: 1964 Nova or Nova SS

Interchange Number: 32
    Part Number(s): RH, 3885382; LH, 3885381
    Usage: 1966–67 Nova, except Nova SS

Molding, Hood

Model Identification

Interchange

Interchange Number: 1
    Part Number(s): 3914781 (fits either side)
    Description: Simulated air vents
    Usage: 1967 Camaro with 350 or 396ci

Interchange Number: 2
    Part Number(s): RH, 3909010; LH, 3930909
    Description: Simulated air vents (four intakes)
    Usage: 1968–69 Camaro with SS 350 or SS 396

Interchange Number: 3
    Part Number(s): RH, 3891432; LH, 3891431
    Description: Simulated air vents
    Usage: 1966 Chevelle SS 396

Interchange Number: 4
    Part Number(s): 3904582 (fits either side)
    Description: Simulated air vents
    Usage: 1967 Chevelle SS 396

Interchange Number: 5
    Part Number(s): RH, 3915490; LH, 3915489
    Description: Hood vents
    Usage: 1968 El Camino SS 396;
    1968–69 Chevelle SS 396

Interchange Number: 6
    Part Number(s): 3905741
    Description: Hood vents
    Usage: 1967 Impala SS 427

Interchange Number: 7
    Part Number(s): 3927442
    Description: Simulated air vents
    Usage: 1968–72 Nova with SS 350 or SS 396
    Notes: Similar to interchange number 1 but uses Bezel.

Spoilers and Racks

Model Identification

Camaro front spoiler for 1970. *Year One*

Interchange

Interchange Number: 1
    Part Number(s): 3949798
    Description/Location: Spoiler (lip style), rear deck
    Usage: 1967–69 Camaro

Interchange Number: 2
    Part Number(s): 3938689
    Description/Location: Spoiler (air foil style), front valance
    Usage: 1969 Camaro
    Notes: Will fit 1967–69 Camaro with a little modification.

Interchange Number: 3
    Part Number(s): 3974538
    Description/Location: Spoiler (lip style), rear deck
    Usage: 1970 Camaro
    Notes: This is single-piece design; the three-piece design (foil type) was first used in May 1970.

Camaro front spoiler, 1967–69.

Interchange Number: 4
    Part Number(s): *Center:* 480161; *RH extension:* 3990476; *LH extension:* 3990475
    Description/Location: Spoiler (foil style), rear deck
    Usage: 1970–75 Camaro; 1970–75 Pontiac Firebird
    Notes: This is a three-piece design.

Interchange Number: 5
    Part Number(s): 3982047
    Description/Location: Spoiler (foil style), front valance
    Usage: 1970–72 Camaro

Interchange Number: 6
    Part Number(s): 993782
    Description/Location: Ski rack, rear deck lid mount
    Usage: 1968–72 Chevelle; 1969 Camaro; 1969–72 full-size Chevrolet; 1969–72 Nova; 1970–72 Buick Skylark; 1970–72 full-size Buick; 1970–72 full-size Oldsmobile; 1970–72 full-size Pontiac

Interchange Number: 7
    Part Number(s): 3900396
    Description/Location: Ski rack, rear deck lid mount
    Usage: 1966–67 Chevelle

Convertible Lift Assembly

Lift cylinders are widely interchangeable. Since GM made the parts, they can be found in a variety of makes and models. However, be aware that there are two distinct types of cylinders: manual and power. The two are not interchangeable. Parts from a power top are easily identified by the hydraulic lines running to the convertible top motor.

Model Identification

Interchange

Interchange Number: 1
Part Number(s): 4412503
Type: Manual
Usage: 1964–67 Chevelle; 1964–67 Buick Skylark; 1964–67 Pontiac LeMans; 1964–67 Pontiac Firebird; 1967–69 Camaro

Interchange Number: 2
Part Number(s): 7704518
Type: Power
Usage: 1967–69 Camaro; 1967–69 Firebird

Interchange Number: 3
Part Number(s): 4407818
Type: Power
Usage: 1964–67 Chevelle;1964–67 Pontiac LeMans; 1964–67 Olds Cutlass; 1964–67 Buick Skylark

Interchange Number: 4
Part Number(s): 9812594
Type: Power
Usage: 1968–72 Chevelle; 1968–72 Pontiac LeMans; 1968–72 Olds Cutlass; 1968–72 Buick Skylark

Interchange Number: 5
Part Number(s): 77779370
Type: Manual (counterbalanced)
Usage: 1968–70 Chevelle; 1968–70 Pontiac LeMans

Interchange Number: 6
Part Number(s): 4512194
Type: Power
Usage: 1965–69 full-size Chevrolet, Pontiac, Oldsmobile, or Buick
Notes: Interchange number 8 will fit.

Interchange Number: 7
Part Number(s): 4888520
Type: All
Usage: 1962–64 full-size Chevrolet; 1962–64 full-size Buick; 1962–64 full-size Oldsmobile; 1963–64 full-size Pontiac

Interchange Number: 8
Part Number(s): 9812596
Type: Power
Usage: 1970 full-size Chevrolet, Pontiac, Oldsmobile, or Buick

Interchange Number: 9
Part Number(s): 7704518
Type: Power
Usage: 1962–63 Chevy II Nova; full-size Pontiac; 1970 full-size Buick; 1970 full-size Oldsmobile

Convertible Top Latch

Model Identification

Interchange

Interchange Number: 1
Part Number(s): RH, 7762250; LH, 7762251
Usage: 1967 Pontiac Firebird; 1967–69 Camaro

Interchange Number: 2
Part Number(s): RH, 4484803; LH, 4484804
Usage: 1964–65 Chevelle; 1964–65 Olds Cutlass; 1964–65 Buick Skylark; 1964–65 Pontiac LeMans

Interchange Number: 3
Part Number(s): RH, 7590745; LH, 7590746
Usage: 1966–67 Chevelle; 1966–67 Olds Cutlass; 1966–67 Pontiac LeMans; 1966–67 Buick Skylark

Interchange Number: 4
Part Number(s): RH, 7762242; LH, 7762243
Usage: 1968–70 Chevelle; 1968–70 Olds Cutlass; 1968–70 Pontiac LeMans; 1968–70 Buick Skylark

Interchange Number: 5
Part Number(s): RH, 4506908; LH, 4506909
Usage: 1965 full-size Chevrolet, Pontiac, Oldsmobile, or Buick

Interchange Number: 6
Part Number(s): RH, 7762258; LH, 7762259
Usage: 1968–70 full-size Chevrolet, Pontiac, Oldsmobile, or Buick

Interchange Number: 7
Part Number(s): RH, 7614582; LH, 4506909
Usage: 1966–67 full-size Chevrolet, Pontiac, Oldsmobile, or Buick
Notes: Driver's side latch will fit interchange number 6.

Interchange Number: 8
Part Number(s): RH, 4813716; LH, 4813717
Usage: 1961–63 Olds F-85; 1961–64 full-size Chevrolet; 1961–64 full-size Pontiac; 1961–64 full-size Buick; 1961–64 full-size Oldsmobile; 1962–63 Chevy II Nova

Interchange Number: 9
Usage: 1959–60 full-size Chevrolet, Pontiac, Oldsmobile, or Buick

Interchange Number: 10
Usage: 1961 full-size Chevrolet, Pontiac, Oldsmobile, or Buick

Chapter 13

Glass and Mirrors

General Notes

The major factors in interchanging glass are fit and bodystyle. Bodystyle can affect the usage of glass, particularly door glass, windshield, and even back window glass. Also, because door and quarter window glass is unique to each side on some models, you will need to avoid swapping sides when replacing.

Another factor that differentiates glass is whether it is tinted. Around 80 percent of cars from this era came with some sort of tinted glass. However, note that tint does not affect interchange.

All glass is date stamped, along with a pattern number and code that indicates whether the glass is tinted. Tinted glass was standard on air conditioned cars—unless the customer specifically requested that it not be. There were two types of tinted glass: Option AO1, where *all* windows were tinted, and Option AO2, where only the windshield was tinted.

Unless all of the glass in a vehicle is changed, tinted glass should not be used to replace non-tinted glass, or vice versa. The one exception is that a tinted windshield can be used in place of a non-tinted windshield, thus matching the AO2 option.

Windshield Glass

Model Identification

Example of the glass code.

Interchange

Interchange Number: 1
Usage: 1967–69 Camaro; 1967–69 Pontiac Firebird; both hardtop
Notes: Will not fit convertible.

Interchange Number: 2
Usage: 1967–69 Camaro; 1967–69 Pontiac Firebird; convertible only

Interchange Number: 3
Usage: 1970–75 Camaro; 1970–75 Pontiac Firebird
Notes: Four different windshields were used in the 1970 model year. Early models (up to approximately 5-1-70) used a roof mount rearview mirror. After this date a windshield mounted mirror was used. To use 1971–75 glass in a 1970 Camaro, mirror will have to be swapped also. If the car was equipped with a radio, the car came with a built-in radio antenna.

Interchange Number: 4
Usage: 1964–65 Chevelle; 1964–65 Pontiac LeMans; 1964–65 Buick Skylark; 1964–65 Olds Cutlass; 1964–67 El Camino; 1966–67 Chevelle, except two-door hardtop and convertible; 1966–67 Pontiac LeMans, except two-door hardtop and convertible; 1966–67 Olds Cutlass, all but two-door hardtop or convertible; 1966–67 Buick Skylark, all but two-door hardtop or convertible
Notes: Read usage carefully for 1966–67 models.

Interchange Number: 5
Usage: 1966–67 Chevelle; 1966–67 Pontiac LeMans; 1966–67 Olds Cutlass; 1966–67 Buick Skylark; all two-door hardtop or convertible

Interchange Number: 6
Usage: 1968–72 Chevelle; 1968–72 Pontiac LeMans; 1968–72 Olds Cutlass; 1968–72 Buick Skylark; 1968–72 El Camino; 1969–72 Pontiac Grand Prix; 1970–72 Monte Carlo; 1971–72 GMC Sprint; all two-door sedan or hardtop
Notes: Watch for 1970–72 windshields with built-in radio antenna.

Interchange Number: 7
Usage: 1968–72 Chevelle; 1968–72 Pontiac LeMans; 1968–72 Olds Cutlass; 1968–72 Buick Skylark; convertible only
Notes: Watch for 1970–72 windshields with built-in radio antenna.

Interchange Number: 8
Usage: 1959 full-size Pontiac; 1959–60 full-size Chevrolet; 1959–60 full-size Oldsmobile; 1959–60 full-size Buick; all sedan or station wagon

Interchange Number: 9
Usage: 1959–60 full-size Chevrolet; 1959–60 full-size Pontiac; 1959–60 Oldsmobile Holiday; 1959–60 full-size Buick, all but Riviera or Electra; all two- or four-door hardtop or convertible

Interchange Number: 10
Usage: 1961 full-size Chevrolet, Pontiac, or Oldsmobile; 1961 Buick LeSabre; all except convertible

Interchange Number: 11
Usage: 1961–62 full-size Chevrolet, Pontiac, Oldsmobile, or Buick convertible; 1961–62 full-size Chevrolet, Buick, Oldsmobile or Pontiac two-door hardtop

Interchange Number: 12
Usage: 1963–64 full-size Chevrolet, Pontiac, Oldsmobile, or Buick; all convertible or two-door hardtop

Interchange Number: 13
Usage: 1963–64 full-size Chevrolet, Pontiac, Oldsmobile, or Buick; all two- or four-door sedan or station wagon

Interchange Number: 14
Usage: 1965–68 full-size Chevrolet, Pontiac, Oldsmobile, or Buick; all hardtop or convertible

Interchange Number: 15
Usage: 1965–68 full-size Chevrolet, Pontiac, Oldsmobile, or Buick; all sedan or station wagon

Interchange Number: 16
Usage: 1969–70 full-size Chevrolet, Pontiac, Oldsmobile, or Buick; all two-door hardtop or convertible
Notes: Watch for hidden radio antenna when swapping 1970 windshields.

Interchange Number: 17
Usage: 1969–70 full-size Chevrolet, Pontiac, Oldsmobile, or Buick; all sedan or station wagon

Interchange Number: 18
Usage: 1962–67 Chevy II two- or four-door sedan or station wagon

Interchange Number: 19
Usage: 1962–64 Chevy II convertible; 1962–67 Chevy II two-door hardtop

Interchange Number: 20
Usage: 1968–72 Nova two-door; 1971–72 Pontiac Ventura II two-door
Notes: Four-door models will not fit, nor will later models. Watch for hidden radio antenna when swapping 1970–72 windshields.

Door Window Glass

Model Identification

Interchange

Interchange Number: 1

    Usage: 1967 Camaro; 1967 Pontiac Firebird

    Notes: Wing window interchanges as well.

Interchange Number: 2

    Usage: 1968–69 Camaro; 1968–69 Pontiac Firebird

    Notes: No wing window.

Interchange Number: 3

    Usage: 1970–71 Camaro; 1970–71 Pontiac Firebird

    Notes: On early 1971 Camaro (up to approximately 12-1-70).

Interchange Number: 4

    Usage: 1964–65 Pontiac LeMans; 1964–65 Olds Cutlass; 1964–65 Buick Skylark; 1964–67 Chevelle; all two-door sedans

Interchange Number: 5

    Usage: 1964 Chevelle; 1964 Pontiac LeMans; 1964 Olds Cutlass; 1964 Buick Skylark; all two-door hardtop

Interchange Number: 6

    Usage: 1964 Chevelle; 1964 Pontiac LeMans; 1964 Olds Cutlass; 1964 Buick Skylark; convertible only

    Notes: Interchange number 5 is reported to fit

Interchange Number: 7

    Usage: 1964–67 El Camino

    Notes: No other interchange.

Interchange Number: 8

    Usage: 1965 Chevelle; 1965 Pontiac LeMans; 1965 Olds Cutlass; 1965 Buick Skylark; all two-door hardtop

Interchange Number: 9

    Usage: 1965 Chevelle; 1965 Pontiac LeMans; 1965 Olds Cutlass; 1965 Buick Skylark; convertible only

Interchange Number: 10

    Usage: 1966–67 Chevelle two-door hardtop or convertible

    Notes: No other model interchange.

Interchange Number: 11

    Usage: 1968–69 Chevelle; 1968–72 Pontiac LeMans; 1968–72 Olds Cutlass; 1968–72 Buick Skylark; all two-door sedan

    Notes: Have wing windows.

Interchange Number: 12

    Usage: 1968 Chevelle; 1968 Pontiac LeMans; 1968 Olds Cutlass; 1968 Buick Skylark; all two-door hardtop or convertible

    Notes: Have wing window.

Interchange Number: 13
Usage: 1969 Chevelle; 1969 Pontiac LeMans; 1969 Olds Cutlass; 1969 Buick Skylark; all two-door hardtop or convertible
Notes: No wing window.

Interchange Number: 14
Usage: 1968–72 El Camino; 1971–72 GMC Sprint
Notes: Door has wing window.

Interchange Number: 15
Usage: 1970–72 Chevelle; 1970–72 Pontiac LeMans; 1970–72 Olds Cutlass; 1970–72 Buick Skylark; 1970–72 Monte Carlo; 1970–72 Pontiac Grand Prix; all two-door hardtop or convertible where applicable

Interchange Number: 16
Usage: 1962–67 Chevy II two-door sedan

Interchange Number: 17
Usage: 1962–64 Chevy II convertible; 1962–67 Chevy II two-door hardtop

Interchange Number: 18
Usage: 1968–72 Nova; 1968–72 Pontiac Ventura II; both two-door sedan

Interchange Number: 19
Usage: 1959–60 full-size Chevrolet, Pontiac, Oldsmobile, or Buick; 1959–60 El Camino; all two-door sedan or delivery wagon

Interchange Number: 20
Usage: 1959–60 full-size Chevrolet, Pontiac, Oldsmobile, or Buick; all two-door hardtop

Interchange Number: 21
Usage: 1959–60 full-size Chevrolet, Pontiac, Oldsmobile, or Buick; convertible only

Interchange Number: 22
Usage: 1961–62 full-size Chevrolet, Pontiac, Oldsmobile, or Buick; all two-door sedan or wagon

Interchange Number: 23
Usage: 1961 full-size Chevrolet, Pontiac, Oldsmobile, or Buick; 1962 Bel Air; all two-door hardtop
Notes: 1962 Impala will not fit.

Interchange Number: 24
Usage: 1963 full-size Buick; 1963–64 full-size Chevrolet; 1963–64 full-size Pontiac; all two-door sedan

Interchange Number: 25
Usage: 1965–66 full-size Chevrolet; 1963–64 full-size Pontiac; all two-door sedan

Interchange Number: 26
Usage: 1965 full-size Chevrolet, Pontiac, Oldsmobile, or Buick; all two-door hardtop

Interchange Number: 27
Usage: 1965 full-size Chevrolet, Pontiac, Oldsmobile, or Buick; convertible only

Interchange Number: 28
Usage: 1966 Impala; 1966 full-size Pontiac; 1966 full-size Buick; 1966 full-size Oldsmobile; all two-door hardtop
Notes: Caprice will *not* interchange.

Interchange Number: 29
Usage: 1966 full-size Chevrolet; 1966 full-size Pontiac; 1966 Pontiac Grand Prix; 1966 full-size Buick; 1966 full-size Oldsmobile; convertible only, except Grand Prix which is two-door hardtop

Interchange Number: 30
Usage: 1966 Caprice two-door hardtop
Notes: No other interchange. Usually all glass is tinted.

Interchange Number: 31
Usage: 1967–68 full-size Chevrolet; 1967–68 full-size Pontiac; both two-door sedan

Interchange Number: 32
Usage: 1967–68 Impala; 1967–68 full-size Pontiac; 1967–68 full-size Oldsmobile; 1968 full-size Buick; all two-door hardtop
Notes: Caprice, 1968 Impala Custom, 1967–68 Pontiac Grand Prix, and 1967–68 Delta 98 *will* interchange.

Interchange Number: 33
Usage: 1963 full-size Buick; 1963–64 full-size Pontiac; 1967–68 Impala; 1967–68 full-size Oldsmobile; convertible only

Interchange Number: 34
Usage: 1967 Caprice two-door hardtop
Notes: No other interchange. Most glass is tinted.

Interchange Number: 35
Usage: 1968 Impala Custom two-door hardtop
Notes: No other interchange.

Interchange Number: 36
Usage: 1968 Caprice two-door hardtop
Notes: No other formal interchange. Glass from 1968 Pontiac Grand Prix is rumored to fit.

Interchange Number: 37
Usage: 1969 full-size Chevrolet two-door sedan
Notes: No other interchange. Glass is usually non-tinted.

Interchange Number: 38
Usage: 1969 full-size Chevrolet; 1969 full-size Pontiac; 1969 full-size Buick; 1969 full-size Oldsmobile except Delta 98; all two-door hardtop or convertible
Notes: Interchange includes Caprice two-door hardtop and Impala Custom.

Interchange Number: 39
Usage: 1970 full-size Chevrolet; 1970 full-size Pontiac; 1970 full-size Buick; 1970 full-size Oldsmobile except Delta 98; all two-door hardtop or convertible
Notes: Interchange includes Caprice two-door hardtop and Impala Custom.

Interchange Number: 40
Usage: 1962–63 Olds Delta 88; 1962–64 Impala; 1962–64 Buick LeSabre; 1962–64 Pontiac Catalina; all two-door hardtop

Interchange Number: 41
Usage: 1961–64 Impala; 1961–64 Buick LeSabre; 1961–64 Pontiac Catalina; 1961–64 Olds Eighty-eight; convertible only

Wing Window Glass

Model Identification

Interchange

Interchange Number: 1
Usage: 1967 Camaro; 1967 Pontiac Firebird, both two-door hardtop or convertible

Interchange Number: 2
Usage: 1964–67 Chevelle; 1964–67 El Camino; 1964–67 Pontiac LeMans; 1964–67 Olds Cutlass; 1964–67 Buick Skylark; all two- or four-door sedan or station wagon
Notes: Also will fit 1964–65 hardtop or convertible. But will not fit 1966–67 hardtop or convertible.

Interchange Number: 3
Usage: 1966–67 Chevelle; 1966–67 Pontiac LeMans; 1966–67 Olds Cutlass; 1966–67 Buick Skylark; all two-door hardtop or convertible

Interchange Number: 4
Usage: 1968–69 Chevelle; 1968–72 El Camino; 1968–72 Pontiac LeMans; 1968–72 Olds Cutlass; 1968–72 Buick Skylark; 1971–72 GMC Sprint; all two-door sedans

Interchange Number: 5
Usage: 1968 Chevelle; 1968 Pontiac LeMans; 1968 Olds Cutlass; 1968 Buick Skylark; all two-door hardtops or convertibles

Interchange Number: 6
Usage: 1959–60 full-size Chevrolet, Pontiac, Oldsmobile, or Buick; 1959–60 El Camino; all two- or four-door sedans or station wagons

Interchange Number: 7
Usage: 1959–60 full-size Chevrolet, Pontiac, Oldsmobile, or Buick; all two-door hardtop or convertible

Interchange Number: 8
Usage: 1961–62 full-size Chevrolet, Pontiac, Oldsmobile, or Buick; all two- or four-door sedan or station wagon

Interchange Number: 9
Usage: 1961–62 full-size Chevrolet, Pontiac, Oldsmobile, or Buick; all two-door hardtop or convertible
Notes: Four-door hardtop will fit.

Interchange Number: 10
Usage: 1963–64 full-size Chevrolet, Pontiac, Oldsmobile, or Buick; all two- or four-door sedan or station wagon

Interchange Number: 11
Usage: 1963–64 full-size Chevrolet, Pontiac, Oldsmobile, or Buick; all two-door hardtop or convertible
Notes: 1963–64 four-door hardtop will not interchange.

Interchange Number: 12
Usage: 1965–68 full-size Chevrolet; 1965–68 full-size Pontiac; 1965–68 full-size Oldsmobile except Olds Delta 98 four-door sedan; 1965–68 full-size Buick; all two- or four-door sedan or station wagon

Interchange Number: 13
Usage: 1965–68 full-size Chevrolet; 1965–68 full-size Pontiac; 1965–68 full-size Oldsmobile except Delta 98 four-door sedan; 1965–68 full-size Buick; all two- or four-door hardtop or convertible

Interchange Number: 14
Usage: 1962 Chevy II
Notes: Later models will not interchange.

Interchange Number: 15
Usage: 1963–67 Chevy II
Notes: All bodystyles will not fit 1962 Chevy II.

Interchange Number: 16
Usage: 1968–72 Nova; 1971–72 Pontiac Ventura II

Quarter Window Glass

Model Identification

Interchange

Interchange Number: 1
Usage: 1967 Camaro; 1967 Pontiac Firebird; both hardtop

Interchange Number: 2
Usage: 1968–69 Camaro; 1968–69 Pontiac Firebird; both hardtop

Interchange Number: 3
Usage: 1968–69 Camaro; 1968–69 Pontiac Firebird; convertible only

Interchange Number: 4
Usage: 1964–65 Chevelle two-door sedan
Notes: No other formal interchange.

Interchange Number: 5
Usage: 1964–65 Chevelle two-door hardtop
Notes: No other formal interchange.

Interchange Number: 6
Usage: 1964–65 Chevelle; 1964–65 Pontiac LeMans; 1964–65 Buick Skylark; 1964–65 Olds Cutlass; convertible only

Interchange Number: 7
Usage: 1966–67 Chevelle two-door sedan
Notes: No other formal interchange.

Interchange Number: 8
Usage: 1966–67 Chevelle; 1966–67 Pontiac LeMans; 1966–67 Olds Cutlass; 1966–67 Buick Skylark; all two-door hardtop

Interchange Number: 9
Usage: 1966–67 Chevelle two-door; 1966–67 Pontiac LeMans; 1966–67 Olds Cutlass; 1966–67 Buick Skylark; convertible only

Interchange Number: 10
Usage: 1968–69 Chevelle; 1968–69 Pontiac LeMans; both two-door sedan

Interchange Number: 11
Usage: 1968–69 Chevelle two-door hardtop
Notes: No other formal interchange.

Interchange Number: 12
Usage: 1968–72 Chevelle two-door; 1968–72 Pontiac LeMans; 1968–72 Olds Cutlass; 1968–72 Buick Skylark; convertible only

Interchange Number: 13
Usage: 1970–72 Chevelle; 1970–72 Buick Skylark; both two-door hardtop

Interchange Number: 14
Usage: 1959–60 full-size Chevrolet, Pontiac, Oldsmobile, or Buick; all two-door sedan

Interchange Number: 15
Usage: 1959–60 full-size Chevrolet; 1959–60 full-size Pontiac; 1959–60 full-size Buick; 1959–60 full-size Oldsmobile; all two-door hardtop

Interchange Number: 16
Usage: 1959–60 full-size Chevrolet, Pontiac, Oldsmobile, or Buick; convertible only

Interchange Number: 17
Usage: 1961 full-size Oldsmobile; 1961–63 full-size Buick; 1961–64 full-size Chevrolet; 1961–64 full-size Pontiac; all two-door sedan
Notes: Used with manual lift windows only.

Interchange Number: 18
Usage: 1961 full-size Chevrolet, Pontiac, Oldsmobile, or Buick; 1962 Bel Air; all two-door hardtop
Notes: Will not fit 1962 Impala.

Interchange Number: 19
Usage: 1961 full-size Oldsmobile except Delta 98; 1961–63 full-size Buick; 1961–64 full-size Chevrolet; 1961–64 full-size Pontiac; convertible only

Interchange Number: 20
Usage: 1962–64 full-size Chevrolet; 1963 full-size Pontiac; all two-door sedan with power windows
Notes: Can be adapted to 1961–64 full-size Chevrolet two-door sedan if converting to power windows.

Interchange Number: 21
Usage: 1965–66 full-size Chevrolet; 1965 66 full-size Pontiac; both two-door sedan

Interchange Number: 22
Usage: 1965–66 full-size Chevrolet; 1965–66 full-size Pontiac; both two-door hardtop

Interchange Number: 23
Usage: 1965–66 full-size Chevrolet, Pontiac, Oldsmobile, or Buick; convertible only

Interchange Number: 24
Usage: 1967–68 full-size Chevrolet; 1967–68 full-size Pontiac; both two-door sedan

Interchange Number: 25
Usage: 1967–68 full-size Chevrolet; 1967–68 full-size Pontiac; 1967–68 full-size Oldsmobile except Delta 98; all two-door hardtop
Notes: Will not fit Caprice or 1968 Impala Custom.

Interchange Number: 26
Usage: 1967 Caprice two-door hardtop
Notes: No other interchange. Glass is usually tinted.

Interchange Number: 27
Usage: 1967–68 full-size Chevrolet; 1967–68 full-size Pontiac; 1967–68 full-size Buick; 1967–68 full-size Oldsmobile except Delta 98; convertible only

Interchange Number: 28
Usage: 1968 Caprice; 1968 Impala Custom; both two-door hardtop.
Notes: No other formal interchange. Glass usually tinted.

Interchange Number: 29
Usage: 1969 full-size Chevrolet two-door sedan
Notes: No other interchange. Glass is usually non-tinted.

Interchange Number: 30
Usage: 1969–70 Impala two-door hardtop, except Impala Custom
Notes: Will not fit Caprice.

Interchange Number: 31
Usage: 1969–70 Impala Custom; 1969–70 Caprice; both two-door hardtop
Notes: Glass is usually tinted.

Interchange Number: 32
Usage: 1969–70 full-size Chevrolet; 1969–70 full-size Pontiac; 1969–70 full-size Buick except Electra; 1969–70 full-size Oldsmobile except Delta 98; convertible only

Interchange Number: 33
Usage: 1962–65 Chevy II two-door sedan
Notes: 1966–67 glass will not interchange.

Interchange Number: 34
Usage: 1962–63 Chevy II convertible

Interchange Number: 35
Usage: 1966–67 Chevy II two-door sedan
Notes: Earlier model glass will not interchange.

Interchange Number: 36
Usage: 1966–67 Chevy II two-door hardtop
Notes: Earlier model glass will not interchange.

Interchange Number: 37
Usage: 1968–72 Nova; 1971–72 Pontiac Ventura II; both two-door hardtop

Interchange Number: 38
Usage: 1967 Camaro; 1967 Pontiac Firebird; both convertible only

Interchange Number: 39
Usage: 1962–65 Chevy II two-door hardtop

Rear Window Glass

Model Identification

Interchange

Interchange Number: 1
Usage: 1967–69 Camaro; 1967–69 Pontiac Firebird; both hardtop
Notes: Convertible used plastic window.

Interchange Number: 2
Usage: 1970–73 Camaro; 1970–73 Pontiac Firebird
Notes: Watch for window with rear defroster. Rarely ordered in Camaro or Firebird.

Interchange Number: 3
Usage: 1964–65 Chevelle two- or four-door sedan

Interchange Number: 4
Usage: 1964–65 Chevelle two-door hardtop

Interchange Number: 5
Usage: 1964–67 El Camino

Interchange Number: 6
Usage: 1966–67 Chevelle two- or four-door sedan

Interchange Number: 7
Usage: 1966–67 Chevelle; 1966–67 Pontiac LeMans; 1966–67 Olds Cutlass; 1966–67 Buick Skylark; all two-door hardtop

Interchange Number: 8
Usage: 1968–72 Chevelle; 1969–70 Pontiac Grand Prix; 1970–72 Monte Carlo; all two-door hardtop or two-door sedan
Notes: Watch for rear defroster 1970–72.

Interchange Number: 9
Usage: 1968–72 El Camino; 1971–72 GMC Sprint

Interchange Number: 10
Usage: 1959–60 full-size Chevrolet, Pontiac, Oldsmobile, or Buick; all two- or four-door sedan
Notes: Includes El Camino.

Interchange Number: 11
Usage: 1959–60 full-size Chevrolet, Pontiac, Oldsmobile, or Buick; all two-door hardtop

Interchange Number: 12
Usage: 1961 full-size Chevrolet, Pontiac, Oldsmobile, or Buick; all two-door sedan

Interchange Number: 13
Usage: 1961 full-size Chevrolet, Pontiac, Oldsmobile, or Buick; 1962 Bel Air; all two-door hardtop
Notes: Will not fit 1962 Impala.

Interchange Number: 14
Usage: 1962–64 full-size Chevrolet, Pontiac, Oldsmobile, or Buick; all two- or four-door sedan

Interchange Number: 15
Usage: 1962–64 full-size Chevrolet; 1962–64 Pontiac Catalina; 1962–64 full-size Buick (LeSabre); 1962–64 full-size Oldsmobile D88, J88, S88 only; all two-door hardtop

Interchange Number: 16
Usage: 1965–66 full-size Chevrolet, Pontiac, Oldsmobile, or Buick; all two- or four-door sedan

Interchange Number: 17
Usage: 1965–66 full-size Chevrolet; 1965–66 full-size Pontiac; 1965–66 full-size Buick; 1965–66 full-size Oldsmobile except Delta 98; all two-door hardtop

Interchange Number: 18
Usage: 1965–70 full-size Chevrolet, Pontiac, Oldsmobile, or Buick; convertible only

Interchange Number: 19
Usage: 1967–68 full-size Chevrolet, Pontiac, Oldsmobile, or Buick; all two- or four-door sedan

Interchange Number: 20
Usage: 1966–67 Caprice two-door hardtop
Notes: No other formal interchange. Glass is usually tinted.

Interchange Number: 21
Usage: 1967–68 full-size Chevrolet, Pontiac, Oldsmobile, or Buick; all two-door hardtop
Notes: Will not fit 1968 Impala Custom or Caprice.

Interchange Number: 22
    Usage: 1968 Impala Custom or 1968 Caprice; both two-door hardtop
    Notes: No other interchange. Glass is usually tinted.

Interchange Number: 23
    Usage: 1969–70 full-size Chevrolet, Pontiac, Oldsmobile, or Buick; all two- or four-door sedan

Interchange Number: 24
    Usage: 1969–70 full-size Chevrolet except Impala Custom or Caprice; 1969–70 full-size Pontiac; 1969–70 full-size Buick; 1969–70 full-size Oldsmobile except Royale or Delta 98; all two-door hardtop

Interchange Number: 25
    Usage: 1969–70 Impala Custom; 1969–70 Caprice; both two-door hardtop
    Notes: Glass is usually tinted.

Interchange Number: 26
    Usage: 1962–64 Chevy II two- or four-door sedan

Interchange Number: 27
    Usage: 1962–65 Chevy II two-door hardtop

Interchange Number: 28
    Usage: 1965 Chevy II two- or four-door sedan

Interchange Number: 29
    Usage: 1966–67 Chevy II two-door hardtop

Interchange Number: 30
    Usage: 1966–67 Chevy II two- or four-door sedan

Interchange Number: 31
    Usage: 1968–74 Nova; 1971–74 Pontiac Ventura II; both two-door sedan
    Notes: Hatchback or four-door models will not interchange.

Mirrors

Mirrors, Exterior
    This section covers three types of exterior mirrors: the standard left-hand door mirror, the optional remote-control

The bow-tie mirror in 1963–65 models.

left-hand door mirror, and the optional remote-control right-hand door mirror which was available on some models as extra equipment. When available, the remote right-hand mirror option is listed under "Notes" in the interchange chart.
    The entire mirror assembly is included in the interchange, including the mounting brackets.

Model Identification

Example of the 1959–62 mirror.

Standard mirror in 1969.

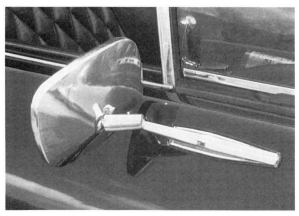

Passenger's side mirror matched the driver's side, as does the 1969–70 mirror on this El Camino.

1968–69
    Standard 7
    Remote 15
    RH door 7
1970
    Standard 20
    Remote 18
    RH door 18

Chevelle ....*Interchange Number*
1964–65
    Standard 2
    Remote 9
    RH door ....na
1966–67
    Standard 3
    Remote 13
    RH door ....na
March 1967–68
    Standard 4
    Remote 15
    RH door 4
1969
    Standard 7
    Remote 15
    RH door 7
1970
    except El Camino 8

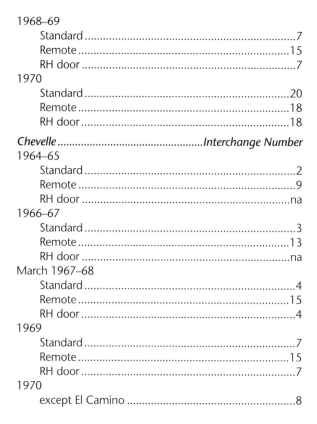

Inside mirror for 1959–64 models.

Inside mirror without lamp, used from 1965 to 1970.

    El Camino 7
    Remote 15, 19
    RH door 7, 8, 19

Impala ....*Interchange Number*
1959–62
    Standard 1
    Remote ....na
    RH door ....na
1963–65
    Standard 2
    Remote 10
    RH door ....na
1966
    Standard 5
    Remote 11, 12
    RH door ....na
1967
    Standard 6
    Remote 14
    RH door 6
1968
    Standard 4
    Remote 15
    RH door 7
1969–70
    Standard 7, 8
    Remote 15
    RH door 7

Chevy II/Nova ....*Interchange Number*
1962
    Standard 1
1963–65
    Standard 2
    Remote 10
1966–67
    Standard 3
    Remote 13
    RH door ....na
1968–69
    Standard 4
    Remote 16
    RH door 4

1970

Interchange

Interchange Number: 1
Part Number(s): 3796398
Usage: 1959–62 full-size Chevrolet; 1962 Chevy II
Notes: Part of the code 147 Comfort and Convenience option.

Interchange Number: 2
Part Number(s): 3821956
Usage: 1963–65 full-size Chevrolet; 1963–65 Chevy II; 1964–65 Chevelle
Notes: Part of ZO1 Comfort and Convenience option group. Interchange 4 will fit but has no bow-tie symbol on the back.

Interchange Number: 3
Part Number(s): 3874240
Usage: 1966–67 Chevy II; 1966–67 Chevelle; 1967 Camaro
Notes: Interchange number 4 will fit, but does not have Chevy emblem in back. Mirror standard item.

Interchange Number: 4
Part Number(s): 3909197
Usage: Late 1967 to 1968 Chevelle; 1968 full-size Chevrolet, except Impala two-door hardtop; 1968–69 Nova
Notes: (1) RH matching mirror was available as part number 3901862. (2) Replacement mirror for cars in interchange numbers 2 and 3.

Interchange Number: 5
Part Number(s): 3863608
Usage: 1965–66 full-size Chevrolet

Interchange Number: 6
Part Number(s): RH, 3901862; LH, 3901861
Usage: 1967 full-size Chevrolet
Notes: No other interchange. Dual mirrors standard.

Interchange Number: 7
Part Number(s): 3914753
Usage: 1968 Pontiac Firebird; 1968–69 Camaro; 1969 Chevelle; 1969–70 full-size Chevrolet; 1970–72 Chevelle station wagon or El Camino
Notes: (1) Will not fit 1970 Chevelle two-door or sedan. (2) RH matching mirror was available, part number 3914754, used on same models.

Interchange Number: 8
Part Number(s): 3965921
Usage: 1970 Impala; 1970–71 Nova; 1970–72 Chevelle, all except station wagon or El Camino or 1971–72 SS models
Notes: Mirror fits either side of car. On Nova or Impala, mirror is used only as RH mirror with remote-control LH mirror.

Interchange Number: 9
Part Number(s): 910792
Usage: 1964–65 Chevelle
Notes: Round head mirror. Remote control.

Interchange Number: 10
Part Number(s): 911146
Usage: 1964–65 full-size Chevrolet; 1964–65 Chevy II; both with remote control.
Notes: Interchange with controls.

Interchange Number: 11
Part Number(s): 911137
Usage: 1966 full-size Chevrolet with remote control, except Impala
Notes: Was used on Impala station wagon.

Interchange Number: 12
Part Number(s): 3892175
Usage: 1966 Impala remote control, except station wagon
Notes: Unique shaped. Mounts with Phillips head screw in top of base arm.

Interchange Number: 13
Part Number(s): 3899857
Usage: 1966–67 Chevelle; 1966–67 Chevy II; 1967 Camaro; all with remote control
Notes: Interchange with mounting bracket.

Interchange Number: 14
Part Number(s): 916500
Usage: 1967 full-size Chevrolet with remote control
Notes: Large face round mirror. Held on with two Phillips head screws in base. Passenger's side mirror found in interchange number 6.

Interchange Number: 15
Part Number(s): 3921832
Usage: 1968–69 Camaro; 1968–70 full-size Chevrolet; 1968–72 Chevelle; all with remote control
Notes: Passenger's side non-remote, same as in interchange number 7.

Interchange Number: 16
Part Number(s): 3934582
Usage: 1968 Nova with remote control

Interchange Number: 17
Part Number(s): 3950765
Usage: 1969–71 Nova with remote control

Interchange Number: 18
Part Number(s): RH, 9626972; LH, 9865801
Usage: 1970–72 Camaro
Notes: Racing (bullet type) mirrors. Used in pairs. LH remote, RH manual.

Interchange Number: 19
Part Number(s): RH, 9878202; LH, 9878201
Usage: 1970–72 Chevelle racing (bullet type) mirrors
Notes: LH remote, RH manual.

Interchange Number: 20
Part Number(s): 9814436
Usage: 1970–75 Camaro; 1970–75 Pontiac Firebird; both with standard non-remote mirror
Notes: Passenger mirror not available.

Chapter 14

Emblems

This section covers the various exterior emblems worn by Chevrolet models between 1959 and 1970. Interchange is given for the following emblems, listed in the same order: grille, hood or header, fender, rear quarter panel, and rear deck or rear panel. Note that the same emblems can be found on many models, which means a large interchange.

Grille Emblem

Model Identification

Interchange

Interchange Number: 1
Part Number(s): 3907915
Type: RS medallion
Usage: 1967–68 Camaro RS, unless equipped with SS package

Interchange Number: 2
Part Number(s): 3918871
Type: SS
Usage: 1967 Camaro; 1968–69 Nova SS

Interchange Number: 3
Part Number(s): 3893819
Type: Medallion
Usage: 1967 Camaro, except when equipped with RS or SS trim

Interchange Number: 4
Part Number(s): 3916655
Type: Medallion
Usage: 1968 Camaro without RS, SS, or Z-28

Interchange Number: 5
Part Number(s): 3919194
Type: SS
Usage: 1968 Camaro SS without RS
Notes: For cars without hideaway headlamps only.

Interchange Number: 6
Part Number(s): 3921860
Type: SS
Usage: 1968 Camaro SS with RS

Interchange Number: 7
Part Number(s): 3943219
Type: Bow-tie (blue)
Usage: 1969 Camaro except with SS, RS, or Z-28

Interchange Number: 8
Part Number(s): 3958642
Type: Z-28
Usage: 1969 Camaro Z-28

Interchange Number: 9
Part Number(s): 3958641
Type: RS
Usage: 1969 Camaro RS without SS

Interchange Number: 10
Part Number(s): 3958640
Type: SS
Usage: 1969 Camaro SS with RS

Interchange Number: 11
Part Number(s): 3958638
Type: SS
Usage: 1969 Camaro SS without RS

Interchange Number: 12
Part Number(s): 3981921
Type: SS
Usage: 1970–71 Camaro with SS

Interchange Number: 13
Part Number(s): 3875758
Type: Medallion
Usage: 1965 Chevelle

Interchange Number: 14
Part Number(s): 3891434
Type: SS 396
Usage: 1966 Chevelle SS 396

Interchange Number: 15
Part Number(s): 3904590
Type: SS 396
Usage: 1967 Chevelle SS 396

Interchange Number: 16
Part Number(s): 3920802
Type: SS 396
Usage: 1968 Chevelle SS 396, or El Camino SS 396

Interchange Number: 17
Part Number(s): 3942781
Type: SS 396
Usage: 1969 Chevelle SS 396, or El Camino SS 396

Interchange Number: 18
Part Number(s): 3977563
Type: SS
Usage: 1970 Chevelle SS, or El Camino SS

Interchange Number: 19
Part Number(s): 3779608
Type: Medallion V-8
Usage: 1961 full-size Chevrolet V-8

Interchange Number: 20
Part Number(s): 3820185
Type: Medallion
Usage: 1962 full-size Chevrolet

Interchange Number: 21
Part Number(s): 3839351
Type: Script (Chevrolet)
Usage: 1964 full-size Chevrolet

Interchange Number: 22
Type: Script (Chevrolet)
Usage: 1965 full-size Chevrolet

Interchange Number: 23
Part Number(s): 3874556
Type: Script (Chevrolet) with bow-tie bar
Usage: 1966 Biscayne, Bel Air, or Impala

Interchange Number: 24
Part Number(s): 3891436
Type: Impala SS
Usage: 1966 Impalas SS

Interchange Number: 25
Part Number(s): 3899549
Type: Script (Chevrolet)
Usage: 1967 full-size Chevrolet, all but SS

Interchange Number: 26
Part Number(s): 3899599
Type: Impala SS
Usage: 1967 Impala SS

Interchange Number: 27
Part Number(s): 3920851
Type: Script "Impala" with "Super Sport" name bar
Usage: 1968 Impala SS, except SS 427

Interchange Number: 28
 Part Number(s): 3920800
 Type: SS 427
 Usage: 1968 Impala SS 427

Interchange Number: 27
 Part Number(s): 3941242
 Type: Bow-tie (blue)
 Usage: 1969 full-size Chevrolet, all except SS

Interchange Number: 28
 Part Number(s): 3949280
 Type: SS
 Usage: 1969 Impala SS 427

Interchange Number: 29
 Part Number(s): 3977571
 Type: Bow-tie
 Usage: 1970 Impala

Interchange Number: 30
 Part Number(s): 3863613
 Type: Bow-tie medallion
 Usage: 1965 Chevy II

Interchange Number: 31
 Part Number(s): 3874540
 Type: "Chevy II" name badge
 Usage: 1966 Chevy II, all except SS

Interchange Number: 32
 Part Number(s): 3875713
 Type: SS (circle)
 Usage: 1966 Nova SS

Interchange Number: 33
 Part Number(s): 3904672
 Type: "Chevy II" name badge
 Usage: 1967 Chevy II, all except Nova SS

Interchange Number: 34
 Part Number(s): 3904655
 Type: "Nova SS" name badge
 Usage: 1967 Nova SS

Interchange Number: 35
 Part Number(s): 3981924
 Type: "Z-28" name badge
 Usage: 1970 Camaro Z-28

Interchange Number: 36
 Part Number(s): 3981924
 Type: "Z-28" name badge
 Usage: 1970 Camaro Z-28

Interchange Number: 37
 Part Number(s): 3876137
 Type: "Chevelle" name badge
 Usage: 1966 Chevelle, except SS 396 or El Camino

Interchange Number: 38
 Part Number(s): 3880824
 Type: "El Camino" name badge
 Usage: 1966 El Camino

Interchange Number: 39
 Part Number(s): 3907069
 Type: Medallion with bow-tie; mounts on upper grille
 Usage: 1967 Chevelle except SS 396

Interchange Number: 40
 Part Number(s): 3920850
 Type: Medallion with bow-tie
 Usage: 1968 Chevelle except SS 396

Interchange Number: 41
 Part Number(s): 3952427
 Type: Bow-tie
 Usage: 1969 Chevelle except SS 396

Interchange Number: 42
 Part Number(s): 3977585
 Type: Bow-tie
 Usage: 1970 Chevelle Malibu except SS

Interchange Number: 43
 Part Number(s): 3979918
 Type: "Chevelle" nameplate on LH corner of grille
 Usage: 1970–71 El Camino, except SS 396 or SS 454;
  1970–71 Chevelle station wagon

Interchange Number: 44
 Part Number(s): 3920851
 Type: "Impala Super Sport" nameplate
 Usage: 1968 Impala SS, except SS 427

Hood or Header Panel Emblems

Model Identification

Interchange

Interchange Number: 1
Type/Location: Header panel
Usage: 1967 Camaro
Notes: Two emblems used script "Chevrolet" (part number 3910000) placed above Camaro nameplate (part number 3912192).

Interchange Number: 2
Part Number(s): 3916654
Type/Location: Script "Camaro, by Chevrolet"
Usage: 1968–69 Camaro

Interchange Number: 3
Part Number(s): 3982037
Type/Location: Medallion "C" crest, on header panel
Usage: 1970 Camaro

Interchange Number: 4
Part Number(s): 3844091
Type/Location: "C-H-E-V-R-O-L-E-T" letters, on hood
Usage: 1964 Chevelle

Interchange Number: 5
Part Number(s): 3862174
Type/Location: "C-H-E-V-R-O-L-E-T" letters, on hood
Usage: 1965 Chevelle

Interchange Number: 6
Part Number(s): 3904589
Type/Location: "Chevelle" nameplate, on hood
Usage: 1967 Chevelle, all except El Camino

Interchange Number: 7
Part Number(s): 3904588
Type/Location: "El Camino" nameplate, on hood
Usage: 1967 El Camino

Interchange Number: 8
Part Number(s): 3920825
Type/Location: "Chevelle" script nameplate, on hood
Usage: 1968–69 Chevelle, all except El Camino or station wagon
Notes: Use in conjunction with "By Chevrolet" block letters on 1969 models. Also used on the fenders in 1968 models.

Interchange Number: 9
Part Number(s): 3920867
Type/Location: "El Camino" script, on hood
Usage: 1968–69 El Camino

Interchange Number: 10
Type/Location: "Cowl Induction," on hood dome
Usage: 1970–72 Chevelle SS with ZL2 hood; Also used on El Camino SS with ZL2 hood
Notes: Cowl, part number 3968567; induction, part number 3968568.

Interchange Number: 11
Part Number(s): 3759106
Type/Location: "Chevrolet" script, on hood
Usage: 1959 full-size Chevrolet
Notes: Use in conjunction with V medallion part number 3760526. On all V-8 equipped cars.

Interchange Number: 12
Part Number(s): 3770391 to 3770399
Type/Location: "C-H-E-V-R-O-L-E-T" block letters, on hood
Usage: 1960–61 full-size Chevrolet
Notes: Each letter has different part number. Letter "E" not interchangeable. One fits the right side (C-H-E-V-R-O-L-E-T) and the other the left side (C-H-E-V-R-O-L-E-T). So mark location when interchanging.

Interchange Number: 13
Part Number(s): 3799051
Type/Location: Chevrolet name imprint on molding on forward edge of hood
Usage: 1962 full-size Chevrolet
Notes: Use in conjunction with bow-tie medallion, part number 3816345.

Interchange Number: 14
Part Number(s): 3821976
Type/Location: Chevrolet name imprint on molding on forward edge of hood
Usage: 1963 full-size Chevrolet
Notes: Use in conjunction with bow-tie medallion, part number 3819741.

Interchange Number: 15
Part Number(s): 3842091
Type/Location: Bow-tie medallion imprint on molding on forward edge of hood
Usage: 1964 full-size Chevrolet

Interchange Number: 16
Part Number(s): 3941255
Type/Location: "Chevrolet" script, on header
Usage: 1969 Biscayne or Bel Air

Interchange Number: 17
Part Number(s): 3941261 to 3941269
Type/Location: "C-H-E-V-R-O-L-E-T" block letters, on center of header panel
Usage: 1969 Impala

Interchange Number: 18
Part Number(s): 3792812
Type/Location: "Chevrolet" nameplate with bow-tie medallion, on front of hood
Usage: 1962 Chevy II

Interchange Number: 19
Part Number(s): 3793377
Type/Location: "Chevrolet" nameplate with bow-tie medallion, on front of hood
Usage: 1963 Chevy II

Interchange Number: 20
Part Number(s): 3881472
Type/Location: Odd-shaped medallion with bow-tie symbol, on front of hood
Usage: 1966 Chevy II

Interchange Number: 21
Part Number(s): 3919092
Type/Location: "Chevy II" nameplate, on front of hood
Usage: 1968 Nova

Interchange Number: 22
>Part Number(s): 3953840
>Type/Location: "Nova" nameplate, on front of hood
>Usage: 1969–70 Nova

Fender Emblems

Model Identification

Interchange

Interchange Number: 1

Part Number(s): 3904573
Type/Location: "RS" lettering, on front edge of fender
Usage: 1967 Camaro RS without SS

Interchange Number: 2

Part Number(s): 3917718
Type/Location: "SS" lettering, on front edge of fender
Usage: 1967 Camaro with SS, or with RS and SS

Interchange Number: 3

Part Number(s): 3907901
Type/Location: "Camaro" nameplate, at rear of fender
Usage: 1967 Camaro

Interchange Number: 4

Part Number(s): 3840318
Type/Location: Flying "V" emblem used in correlation with engine displacement badge; location varies according to model
Usage: 1964–67 Chevelle;1964–67 Chevy II; 1964–67 full-size Chevrolet;1967 Camaro

Notes: Used with all V-8 engines except 396 or 427ci versions. Used to signify 327 or 409ci in 1964 without engine call-outs.

Interchange Number: 5

Part Number(s): 3863853
Type/Location: "327" displacement badge; used in conjunction with flying "V"
Usage: 1965–67 Chevelle;1965–67 Chevy II; 1965–67 full-size Chevrolet; 1967 Camaro; all with 327ci any output level

Interchange Number: 6

Part Number(s): 3871057
Type/Location: "396 with turbo flags"; location varies with model
Usage: 1965–67 Chevelle; 1965–67 full-size Chevrolet; 1967 Camaro; all with 396ci regardless of output

Interchange Number: 7

Part Number(s): 3876435
Type/Location: "427 with turbo flags"; location varies with model
Usage: 1966–67 Chevelle; 1966–67 full-size Chevrolet; 1967 Camaro; all with 427ci regardless of output

Interchange Number: 8

Part Number(s): 3916660
Type/Location: "Camaro" script, on front fender
Usage: 1968–69 Camaro, all except with RS

Interchange Number: 9

Part Number(s): 3916692
Type/Location: "Rallye Sport" nameplate, on front fender
Usage: 1968 Camaro RS without SS

Interchange Number: 10

Part Number(s): 3987377
Type/Location: "SS" individual letters, on front fender
Usage: 1968–72 Camaro SS with or without RS

Interchange Number: 11

Part Number(s): RH, 3947012; LH, 3947011
Type/Location: "Z/28" badge; unique to each side
Usage: 1968 Camaro Z-28

Interchange Number: 12

Part Number(s): RH, 3927482; LH, 3927481
Type/Location: "302 " engine; unique to each side
Usage: 1968 Camaro Z-28

Interchange Number: 13

Part Number(s): RH, 3927484; LH, 3927483
Type/Location: "327 " engine call-out; unique to each side
Usage: 1968 Camaro

Interchange Number: 14

Part Number(s): RH, 3927486; LH, 3927485
Type/Location: "350 " engine call-out; unique to each side
Usage: 1968 Camaro

Interchange Number: 15

Part Number(s): RH, 3927488; LH, 3927487
Type/Location: "396 " engine call-out; unique to each side
Usage: 1968 Camaro SS

Interchange Number: 16
Part Number(s): 3953633
Type/Location: "Rallye Sport" script
Usage: 1969 Camaro RS without SS, Z-28, Z-11, or Z-10 pace car replicas

Interchange Number: 17
Part Number(s): RH, 3957936; LH, 3957935
Type/Location: "Z/28 " name badge; unique to each side
Usage: 1969 Camaro Z -28

Interchange Number: 18
Part Number(s): 3953625
Type/Location: "327" engine call-out
Usage: 1969 Camaro

Interchange Number: 19
Part Number(s): RH, 3928670; LH, 3928669
Type/Location: "350" engine call-out; unique to each side
Usage: 1969 Camaro

Interchange Number: 20
Part Number(s): 3953629
Type/Location: "396" engine call-out
Usage: 1969 Camaro SS 396

Interchange Number: 21
Part Number(s): 3957933
Type/Location: "307" engine call-out
Usage: 1969 Camaro, except SS or Z-28

Interchange Number: 22
Part Number(s): RH, 3957936; LH, 3957935
Type/Location: "302" engine call-out; unique to each side
Usage: 1969 Camaro Z-28; used without ZL-2 hood

Interchange Number: 23
Part Number(s): 3981851
Type/Location: "Camaro" script
Usage: 1970–74 Camaro, all except RS

Interchange Number: 24
Part Number(s): 3981852
Type/Location: "Rallye Sport" nameplate
Usage: 1970–74 Camaro RS

Interchange Number: 25
Part Number(s): 3981856
Type/Location: "Z/28" badge
Usage: 1970–72 Camaro Z-28

Interchange Number: 26
Part Number(s): 3988829
Type/Location: "396" engine call-out
Usage: 1970–72 Camaro SS

Interchange Number: 27
Part Number(s): 3988830
Type/Location: "350" engine call-out
Usage: 1970–75 Camaro

Interchange Number: 28
Part Number(s): 3849498
Type/Location: "C-H-E-V-E-L-L-E" block letter nameplate
Usage: 1964 Chevelle

Interchange Number: 29
Part Number(s): 3840317
Type/Location: "V" symbol for 283ci V-8
Usage: 1964 Chevelle; 1964 full-size Chevrolet; all with 283ci V-8

Interchange Number: 30
Part Number(s): 3865833
Type/Location: "283" engine call-out used in conjunction with flying "V" symbol
Usage: 1965 Chevy II; 1965 Chevelle; 1965–66 full-size Chevrolet; all with 283ci V-8

Interchange Number: 31
Part Number(s): Varies with displacement
Type/Location: Displacement badge bezel insert
Usage: 1968 Chevelle; 1968 full-size Chevrolet
Notes: Displacements included 327, 307, 396, and 427ci. All are interchangeable with these models, as are the bezels. A few early models did come with bezels that read "SS 396."

Interchange Number: 32
Part Number(s): 3953658
Type/Location: "SS" individual letters
Usage: 1969 Impala SS 427; 1969–72 Chevelle

Interchange Number: 33
Part Number(s): 3953679
Type/Location: "396" engine call-out
Usage: 1969–70 Chevelle SS

Interchange Number: 34
Part Number(s): 3981833
Type/Location: "454" engine call-out
Usage: 1970–72 Chevelle SS

Interchange Number: 35
Part Number(s): 3759111
Type/Location: "El Camino" script
Usage: 1959–60 El Camino

Interchange Number: 36
Part Number(s): RH, 3756818; LH, 3756817
Type/Location: "Bel Air" script
Usage: 1959 Bel Air

Interchange Number: 37
Part Number(s): 3752641
Type/Location: "Biscayne" script
Usage: 1960 Biscayne

Interchange Number: 38
Part Number(s): 3776911
Type/Location: "Bel Air" script
Usage: 1960 Bel Air

Interchange Number: 39
Part Number(s): 3791999
Type/Location: "V" emblem
Usage: 1962–63 full-size Chevrolet V-8, except 1962 Impala

Interchange Number: 40
Part Number(s): RH, 3813428; LH, 3813427
Type/Location: "Flying cross flags" Impala emblem
Usage: 1962 Impala

Interchange Number: 41
Part Number(s): 3840319
Type/Location: "409" call-out with flying cross flags
Usage: 1964–65 Impala
Notes: Interchange number 4 was also used.

Interchange Number: 42
Part Number(s): 3873792
Type/Location: "Caprice" script
Usage: 1966–69 Caprice

Interchange Number: 43
Part Number(s): 3862173
Type/Location: "I-M-P-A-L-A" block letters
Usage: 1965–66 Impala, all but SS
Notes: Individual letters.

Interchange Number: 44
Part Number(s): 3866070
Type/Location: "Super Sport" script
Usage: 1965–66 Impala SS

Interchange Number: 45
Part Number(s): 3862208
Type/Location: "Impala" in circle; used in conjunction
    with letters in interchange number 43
Usage: 1965–66 Impala, all but SS

Interchange Number: 46
Part Number(s): 3899599
Type/Location: "Impala Super Sport"
Usage: 1967 Impala SS
Notes: Emblem on grille will fit.

Interchange Number: 47
Part Number(s): 3928469
Type/Location: "Biscayne" script
Usage: 1968–69 Biscayne

Interchange Number: 48
Part Number(s): 3917489
Type/Location: "Impala" script
Usage: 1968–69 Impala, all except SS

Interchange Number: 49
Part Number(s): 3917490
Type/Location: "Super Sport" script
Usage: 1968 Impala SS

Interchange Number: 50
Part Number(s): 3920888
Type/Location: "Custom" badge
Usage: 1968–69 Impala Custom

Interchange Number: 51
Part Number(s): 3920868
Type/Location: "Bel Air" script
Usage: 1968–69 Bel Air

Interchange Number: 52
Part Number(s): 3963266
Type/Location: "Biscayne" script
Usage: 1970 Biscayne

Interchange Number: 53
Part Number(s): 3963268
Type/Location: "Impala" script
Usage: 1970 Impala

Interchange Number: 54
Part Number(s): 3963267
Type/Location: "Bel Air" script
Usage: 1970 Bel Air

Interchange Number: 55
Part Number(s): 3950773
Type/Location: "327" engine call-out bezel
Usage: 1969 full-size Chevrolet

Interchange Number: 56
Part Number(s): 3950774
Type/Location: "396" engine call-out bezel
Usage: 1969 full-size Chevrolet

Interchange Number: 57
Part Number(s): 3949287
Type/Location: "350" engine call-out bezel
Usage: 1969 full-size Chevrolet

Interchange Number: 58
Part Number(s): 3949288
Type/Location: "427" engine call-out bezel
Usage: 1969 full-size Chevrolet

Interchange Number: 59
Part Number(s): RH, 3974224; LH, 3974223
Type/Location: "350" engine call-out; unique to each
    side
Usage: 1970 full-size Chevrolet; 1970–72 Chevelle, all
    except El Camino

Interchange Number: 60
Part Number(s): RH, 3970620; LH, 3970619
Type/Location: "454" engine call-out
Usage: 1970–72 full-size Chevrolet

Interchange Number: 61
Part Number(s): RH, 3974226; LH, 3974225
Type/Location: "400" engine call-out
Usage: 1970–72 full-size Chevrolet; 1970–71 Chevelle;
    1970–71 Monte Carlo
Notes: Not for El Camino or 1972 Caprice except 1972
    Estate station wagon. Not for 1971 models with
    400ci 4bbl.

Interchange Number: 62
Part Number(s): RH, 3929994; LH, 3929993
Type/Location: "307" engine call-out lamp bezel
Usage: 1968–69 Nova
Notes: ID insert is the same as used in Chevelle and full-
    size Chevrolet.

Interchange Number: 63
Part Number(s): RH, 3929996; LH, 3929995
Type/Location: "327" engine call-out lamp bezel
Usage: 1968 Nova
Notes: ID insert is the same as used in Chevelle and full-
    size Chevrolet.

Interchange Number: 64
Part Number(s): RH, 3929998; LH, 3929997
Type/Location: "350" engine call-out lamp bezel
Usage: 1968–69 Nova

Interchange Number: 65
    Part Number(s): RH, 3937593; LH, 3937593
    Type/Location: "396" engine call-out lamp bezel
    Usage: 1968–69 Nova

Interchange Number: 66
    Part Number(s): 3953676
    Type/Location: "Nova" Script nameplate
    Usage: 1969–72 Nova

Interchange Number: 67
    Part Number(s): 3920825
    Type/Location: "Chevelle" script nameplate
    Usage: 1968 Chevelle except SS 396, El Camino, or
      Malibu

Interchange Number: 68
    Part Number(s): 3920864
    Type/Location: "Malibu" script nameplate
    Usage: 1968 Chevelle Malibu

Interchange Number: 69
    Part Number(s): 3974320
    Type/Location: "Malibu" nameplate
    Usage: 1970 Chevelle Malibu

Interchange Number: 70
    Part Number(s): 3972937
    Type/Location: "El Camino" nameplate
    Usage: 1970–72 El Camino

Interchange Number: 71
    Part Number(s): 3974354
    Type/Location: "350" call-out
    Usage: 1970–72 El Camino

Interchange Number: 72
    Part Number(s): 3871637
    Type/Location: Malibu SS
    Usage: 1965 Malibu SS 396. Also used on rear quarter
      panels of 1965 Malibu SS.

Rear Quarter Panel Emblems

Model Identification

Interchange

Interchange Number: 1
Part Number(s): 3853533
Type/Location: Malibu SS
Usage: 1964 Malibu SS

Interchange Number: 2
Part Number(s): 3871637
Type/Location: Malibu SS
Usage: 1965 Malibu SS
Notes: Also used on front of Z-16 car.

Interchange Number: 3
Part Number(s): 4227377
Type/Location: Super Sport
Usage: 1966 Chevelle SS 396

Interchange Number: 4
Part Number(s): 4229717
Type/Location: Super Sport
Usage: 1967 Chevelle SS 396

Interchange Number: 5
Part Number(s): 3853534
Type/Location: Malibu
Usage: 1964 Malibu, except SS

Interchange Number: 6
Part Number(s): 3871638
Type/Location: Malibu
Usage: 1965 Malibu, except SS

Interchange Number: 7
Part Number(s): 4229716
Type/Location: Malibu
Usage: 1966–67 Malibu

Interchange Number: 8
Part Number(s): 3852952
Type/Location: El Camino
Usage: 1964 El Camino

Interchange Number: 9
Part Number(s): 3871635
Type/Location: El Camino
Usage: 1965 El Camino

Interchange Number: 10
Part Number(s): 4227313
Type/Location: El Camino
Usage: 1966 El Camino

Interchange Number: 11
Part Number(s): 4229728
Type/Location: El Camino
Usage: 1967 El Camino

Interchange Number: 12
Part Number(s): 7795052
Type/Location: El Camino
Usage: 1968–70 El Camino

Interchange Number: 13
Part Number(s): 8701037
Type/Location: Malibu
Usage: 1969 Malibu

Interchange Number: 14
Part Number(s): 3774631
Type/Location: "Impala" script on molding
Usage: 1960 Impala two-door

Interchange Number: 15
Part Number(s): 3774633
Type/Location: Racing flags
Usage: 1960 Impala

Interchange Number: 16
Part Number(s): 3787463
Type/Location: "Biscayne" script
Usage: 1961 Biscayne

Interchange Number: 17
Part Number(s): 3787464
Type/Location: "Bel Air" script
Usage: 1961 Bel Air

Interchange Number: 18
Part Number(s): 3787465
Type/Location: "Impala" script
Usage: 1961 Impala

Interchange Number: 19
Part Number(s): 4837369
Type/Location: Racing flags medallion
Usage: 1961 Impala, including Nomad

Interchange Number: 20
Part Number(s): 3817133
Type/Location: "Bel Air" script
Usage: 1962 Bel Air

Interchange Number: 21
Part Number(s): 3817132
Type/Location: "Impala" script
Usage: 1962 Impala, except SS

Interchange Number: 22
Part Number(s): 3813889
Type/Location: "Impala SS" script
Usage: 1962 Impala SS
Notes: Casting part number 3813889.

Interchange Number: 23
Part Number(s): 3822641
Type/Location: Deer in circle; Impala emblem
Usage: 1962 Impala, except SS

Interchange Number: 24
Part Number(s): 3831847
Type/Location: "Bel Air" script
Usage: 1963 Bel Air

Interchange Number: 25
Part Number(s): 3832299
Type/Location: Deer in circle; Impala emblem
Usage: 1963 Impala, except SS

Interchange Number: 26
Part Number(s): 3827300
Type/Location: "SS"
Usage: 1963 Impala SS

Interchange Number: 27
Type/Location: "Impala" imprint on molding
Usage: 1963 Impala two-door
Notes: Molding was available in either black or white.

Interchange Number: 28
    Type/Location: "Impala SS" imprint on molding
    Usage: 1963 Impala SS two-door
    Notes: Regular Impala molding will not interchange, but will fit.

Interchange Number: 29
    Part Number(s): 3851721
    Type/Location: "Biscayne" script
    Usage: 1964 Biscayne

Interchange Number: 30
    Part Number(s): 3851722
    Type/Location: "Bel Air" Script.
    Usage: 1964 Bel Air

Interchange Number: 31
    Part Number(s): 3853942
    Type/Location: "Impala" bold letter name badge
    Usage: 1964 Impala, all except station wagon

Interchange Number: 32
    Part Number(s): 3852381
    Type/Location: Deer in circle; Impala emblem
    Usage: 1964 Impala

Interchange Number: 33
    Part Number(s): 3851724
    Type/Location: "SS" Individual letters
    Usage: 1964 Impala

Interchange Number: 34
    Part Number(s): 4229780
    Type/Location: "Biscayne" script
    Usage: 1967 Biscayne

Interchange Number: 35
    Part Number(s): 4229657
    Type/Location: "Bel Air" script
    Usage: 1967 Bel Air

Interchange Number: 36
    Part Number(s): 4229431
    Type/Location: "Impala" script
    Usage: 1967 Impala, all except Impala SS

Interchange Number: 37
    Type/Location: "Nova" script
    Usage: 1962 Chevy II Nova

Interchange Number: 38
    Part Number(s): 3852497
    Type/Location: "Chevy II" name badge
    Usage: 1962–64 Chevy II, except Nova or Nova SS

Interchange Number: 39
    Part Number(s): 3870976
    Type/Location: "Nova SS" script
    Usage: 1963–65 Nova SS

Interchange Number: 40
    Part Number(s): 3870999
    Type/Location: "Chevy II" nameplate
    Usage: 1965–67 Chevy II, except Nova or Nova SS

Interchange Number: 41
    Part Number(s): 3871501
    Type/Location: "Nova" script
    Usage: 1963–65 Chevy II Nova, except Nova SS

Interchange Number: 42
    Part Number(s): 4227012
    Type/Location: "Super Sport" script
    Usage: 1966–67 Nova SS

Interchange Number: 43
    Part Number(s): 4226981
    Type/Location: "Nova " nameplate
    Usage: 1966–67 Nova, except SS

Interchange Number: 44
    Type/Location: "Nova " script
    Usage: 1968 Nova

Rear Deck or Rear Panel Emblems

Model Identification

Interchange

Interchange Number: 1
Part Number(s): 4229839
Type/Location: "Camaro" script
Usage: 1967 Camaro

Interchange Number: 2
Part Number(s): 7795106
Type/Location: "Camaro" script
Usage: 1968–69 Camaro; all models also used Camaro script the front header

Interchange Number: 3
Part Number(s): 8701129
Type/Location: "RS" center of tail
Usage: 1969 Camaro RS

Interchange Number: 4
Part Number(s): 8701333
Type/Location: "Z/28" center of tail end
Usage: 1969 Camaro Z-28

Interchange Number: 5
Part Number(s): 8701158
Type/Location: Bow-tie (blue)
Usage: 1969 Camaro except with RS, SS, or Z-28

Interchange Number: 6
Part Number(s): 8704053
Type/Location: "Camaro by Chevrolet"
Usage: 1970 Camaro
Notes: When interchanging 1971 and up deck lids, be sure to swap to the 1970 emblem.

Interchange Number: 7
Part Number(s): 3981889
Type/Location: "Z/28" center of tail end
Usage: 1970–71 Camaro Z-28

Interchange Number: 8
Part Number(s): 3853422
Type/Location: "C-H-E-V-R-O-L-E-T"
Usage: 1964–65 Chevelle and El Camino

Interchange Number: 9
Type/Location: "SS"
Usage: 1964 Chevelle SS

Interchange Number: 10
Part Number(s): 3871645
Type/Location: "Malibu SS"
Usage: 1965 Chevelle SS except SS 396

Interchange Number: 11
Part Number(s): 4229439
Type/Location: "Chevelle"
Usage: 1966 Chevelle SS 396; 1966–67 Chevelle (except Malibu); or 1967 SS 396

Interchange Number: 12
Part Number(s): 4227199
Type/Location: "SS 396"
Usage: 1966 Chevelle SS 396

Interchange Number: 13
Part Number(s): 4229992
Type/Location: "SS 396"
Usage: 1967 Chevelle SS 396

Interchange Number: 14
Type/Location: "SS 396"
Usage: 1968 Chevelle SS 396

Interchange Number: 15
Part Number(s): 8701218
Type/Location: "Chevelle by Chevrolet"
Usage: 1969 Chevelle, all except station wagon or El Camino

Interchange Number: 16
Part Number(s): 8791686
Type/Location: "Chevelle by Chevrolet"
Usage: 1970 Chevelle, all except station wagon or El Camino

Interchange Number: 17
Part Number(s): 3767506
Type/Location: Nameplate
Usage: 1960 full-size Chevrolet, all except Impala

Interchange Number: 18
Part Number(s): 3767507
Type/Location: Cross flags
Usage: 1960 Impala

Interchange Number: 19
Part Number(s): 3767503
Type/Location: "V" plate under nameplate
Usage: 1960 full-size Chevrolet, all except station wagon or pickup

Interchange Number: 20
Part Number(s): 3779728
Type/Location: "283" V-8 engine call-out
Usage: 1961 full-size Chevrolet

Interchange Number: 21
Part Number(s): 3779729
Type/Location: "343" V-8 engine call-out
Usage: 1961 full-size Chevrolet

Interchange Number: 22
Part Number(s): 3816347
Type/Location: Chevy bow-tie medallion "V"
Usage: 1962 full-size Chevrolet

Interchange Number: 23
Part Number(s): First, 4878296; second, 4872582
Type/Location: "Impala" imprint on molding
Usage: 1962 Impala, except SS
Notes: Early models used a satin finish molding while later models used a brushed aluminum finish molding.

Interchange Number: 24
Part Number(s): First, 4878294; second, 4872584
Type/Location: "Impala SS" imprint on molding
Usage: 1962 Impala SS

Notes: Early models used a satin finish molding while later models used a brushed aluminum finish molding.

Interchange Number: 25
Part Number(s): 3820220
Type/Location: Multicolor emblem with bow-tie symbol
Usage: 1963 full-size Chevrolet

Interchange Number: 26
Part Number(s): 3853124
Type/Location: "B-E-L A-I-R " block letters
Usage: 1964 Bel Air

Interchange Number: 27
Part Number(s): 3853122
Type/Location: "Impala" imprint on molding
Usage: 1964 Impala, except Impala SS

Interchange Number: 28
Part Number(s): 3853123
Type/Location: "Impala SS" imprint on molding
Usage: 1964 Impala SS

Interchange Number: 29
Part Number(s): 4413013
Type/Location: "Impala SS " upper rear deck emblem
Usage: 1964 Impala SS

Interchange Number: 30
Part Number(s): 3870722
Type/Location: Multicolor emblem with bow-tie
Usage: 1965 full-size Chevrolet

Interchange Number: 31
Part Number(s): 4227047
Type/Location: Multicolor emblem with bow-tie
Usage: 1966 full-size Chevrolet,
except station wagon

Interchange Number: 32
Part Number(s): 4227048
Type/Location: "Caprice" script
Usage: 1966 Caprice, all including station wagon

Interchange Number: 33
Part Number(s): 4227044
Type/Location: "Chevrolet" script
Usage: 1966 full-size Chevrolet, except Caprice

Interchange Number: 34
Part Number(s): 4229977
Type/Location: "Chevrolet" script
Usage: 1967 full-size Chevrolet, except Impala SS or Caprice

Interchange Number: 35
Part Number(s): 4229592
Type/Location: "Impala SS" emblem
Usage: 1967 Impala SS

Interchange Number: 36
Part Number(s): 4229550
Type/Location: "Caprice" script
Usage: 1967 Caprice, all including station wagon

Interchange Number: 37
Part Number(s): 7731109
Type/Location: "Caprice by Chevrolet" script
Usage: 1968 Caprice

Interchange Number: 38
Part Number(s): 7731108
Type/Location: "Chevrolet" script
Usage: 1968 full-size Chevrolet, except Impala, Caprice, and Impala SS

Interchange Number: 39
Part Number(s): 7752253
Type/Location: "Impala by Chevrolet" script
Usage: 1968 Impala, except Impala SS 427

Interchange Number: 40
Part Number(s): 7752254
Type/Location: "SS 427"
Usage: 1968 Impala SS 427

Interchange Number: 41
Part Number(s): 8701219
Type/Location: "Chevrolet" script
Usage: 1969–70 full-size Chevrolets, except Caprice or Impala SS
Notes: Station wagon used a different emblem and will not interchange.

Interchange Number: 42
Part Number(s): 8701019
Type/Location: "Caprice by Chevrolet" script
Usage: 1969 Caprice

Interchange Number: 43
Part Number(s): 8702629
Type/Location: "Caprice by Chevrolet" script
Usage: 1970 Caprice

Interchange Number: 44
Part Number(s): 3790800
Type/Location: Multicolor bow-tie emblem
With "C-H-E-V-R-O-L-E-T" above
Usage: 1962 Chevy II
Notes: Station wagon used a different emblem and will not interchange.

Interchange Number: 45
Part Number(s): 3793409
Type/Location: Multicolor bow-tie emblem
With "C-H-E-V-R-O-L-E-T" above
Usage: 1963 Chevy II
Notes: Similar to 1962 unit in looks, but mounts With six 3/16 inch nuts instead of four used in 1962.

Interchange Number: 46
Part Number(s): 3877190
Type/Location: "C-H-E-V-R-O-L-E-T"
Usage: 1964 Chevy II, except Nova or Nova SS
Notes: Station wagon will not interchange.

Interchange Number: 47
Part Number(s): 3848421
Type/Location: "Nova"
Usage: 1964 Chevy II Nova, except station wagon

Interchange Number: 48
Type/Location: "C-H-E-V-R-O-L-E-T"
Usage: 1965 Chevy II, except station wagon or Nova

Interchange Number: 49
Part Number(s): 3871604

Type/Location: Bow-tie and "C-H-E-V-R-O-L-E-T"
Usage: 1965 Chevy II Nova, Nova SS, or Chevy II with decor package

Interchange Number: 50
Part Number(s): 4545266
Type/Location: "SS" imprint on molding
Usage: 1966 Nova SS

Interchange Number: 51
Part Number(s): 4227229
Type/Location: "Chevy II imprint on molding
Usage: 1966 Chevy II Nova, except SS

Interchange Number: 52
Part Number(s): 4229497
Type/Location: "Nova SS" imprint on molding
Usage: 1967 Nova SS

Interchange Number: 53
Part Number(s): 4229497
Type/Location: "Chevy II" imprint on molding
Usage: 1967 Chevy II Nova, except SS or station wagon

Interchange Number: 54
Part Number(s): 4229499
Type/Location: Triangular-shaped emblem
Usage: 1967 Chevy II, except Nova or Nova SS or station wagon

Interchange Number: 55
Part Number(s): 7745749
Type/Location: "Chevy II" nameplate
Usage: 1968 Nova

Interchange Number: 56
Part Number(s): 7795107
Type/Location: "SS"
Usage: 1968–69 Nova SS

Interchange Number: 57
Part Number(s): 8701089
Type/Location: "Nova by Chevrolet" script
Usage: 1969–72 Nova

Interchange Number: 58
Part Number(s): 8702427
Type/Location: "SS"
Usage: 1970–72 Nova SS

Interchange Number: 59
Part Number(s): 8701130
Type/Location: "SS"
Usage: 1969 Camaro SS 350 or SS 396 or RS with SS package; 1969 Z-11 or Z-10 pace car replicas

Interchange Number: 60
Part Number(s): 8701130
Type/Location: "Malibu SS 396"
Usage: 1965 Chevelle SS 396

Interchange Number: 61
Part Number(s): 4227111
Type/Location: "Chevelle"
Usage: 1966 Malibu
Notes: Will not fit other models or station wagon.

Interchange Number: 62
Part Number(s): 4229502
Type/Location: "Malibu"
Usage: 1967 Malibu

Interchange Number: 63
Part Number(s): 7740129
Type/Location: "Chevelle"
Usage: 1968 Chevelle, except Concours or El Camino
Notes: Station wagon will fit.

Interchange Number: 64
Part Number(s): 8701346
Type/Location: "SS 396"
Usage: 1969 Chevelle 396, except El Camino

Interchange Number: 65
Part Number(s): 7795089
Type/Location: "Chevrolet" script
Usage: 1968–69 El Camino (tailgate) without SS 396

Interchange Number: 66
Part Number(s): 8701343
Type/Location: "C-H-E-V-R-O-L-E-T" block letters
Usage: 1970–72 El Camino (tailgate) without SS

Interchange Number: 67
Part Number(s): 7795093
Type/Location: "SS" emblem
Usage: 1968–70 El Camino with SS 396

Interchange Number: 68
Part Number(s): 8791686
Type/Location: "MALIBU" block letters
Usage: 1970 Malibu without SS

Interchange Number: 69
Part Number(s): 8701343
Type/Location: Bow-tie medallion on upper tailgate
Usage: 1968–72 El Camino

Interchange Number: 70
Part Number(s): 3853422
Type/Location: C-H-E-V-R-O-L-E-T block letters
Usage: 1964–67 El Camino

Interchange Number: 71
Part Number(s): 3871647
Type/Location: Bow-tie medallion
Usage: 1964–67 El Camino

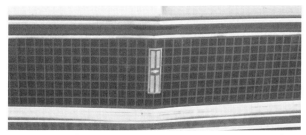

The 1967 Camaro grille emblem, except when equipped with SS or RS packages.

"SS" was used with all 1970 SS Chevelle packages.

The 1969 Camaro SS grille emblem with RS package.

The 1970 Camaro Z-28 grille emblem. *Year One*

This emblem was used on the 1968 Chevelle SS 396.

Grille emblem for 1964 Impalas.

The 1966 Impala SS used this grille emblem.

A 1969 Camaro header emblem.

Full-size script on grille for 1967.

Hood emblems were used on the 1970–72 Chevelle SS with the ZL-2 option.

Nova SS grille emblem, 1969–72.

Camaro nameplate used on front fenders for 1967.

The 1967 Chevy II grille emblem.

Rallye Sport nameplate for 1969.

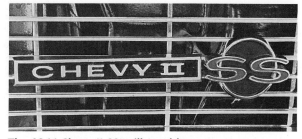

The 1966 Chevy II SS grille emblem.

Z-28 emblem for 1969.

Engine callout on a 1969 Camaro.

Emblem signifying the V-8 engine.

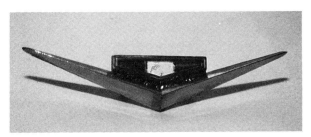

"V" emblem indicated a V-8 engine for 1962–63.

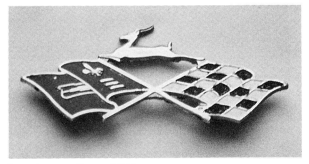

Impala cross flags, 1962.

Used with various engine sizes on Impalas.

Engine callouts for 409ci Impalas.

Impala Super Sport script on a 1965 model.

Impala emblem for 1965.

The 1968 Chevelle, Impala used engine callout bezels.

The 1969 Impala turn-lamp engine callouts.

The 1970 Chevelle, Impala 350ci engine callout.

Nova SS rear quarter emblems for 1964–65.

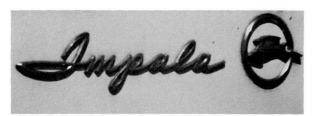

Impala script for 1962.

Nova rear quarter emblems for 1966–67.

Block letters on 1964 Impala SS.

Camaro rear bow-tie medallion, 1969.

Nameplate for 1967 Impala.

Camaro Z-28 emblem, 1969.

Nova SS quarter panel script for 1966–67.

Camaro deck lid script, 1969.

The 1962 Chevy 300 series used this nameplate on the rear quarters.

The 1969 Camaro with SS or RS and SS packages used this emblem.

The 1964 Malibu SS circle medallion.

Chevelle deck lid lettering for 1964.

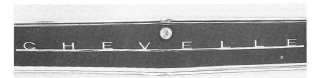

Chevelle nameplate used with 1966 SS 396 models.

Chevelle SS 396 emblem for 1966.

A 1967 Chevelle SS 396 tail-end emblem.

Chevelle script on deck lid, 1968.

Rear deck emblem for 1965 Impala SS.

SS 396 nameplate used on the 1968 Chevelle.

Chevelle emblem on deck lid for 1968.

The 1970 Chevelle used this rear deck emblem.

Deck lid emblem for 1967 Impala.

Impala deck lid emblem for 1968.

Nova SS rear panel emblem, 1969–70 models.

A 1970 Camaro Z-28 rear deck emblem. *Year One*

Nova SS rear deck emblem for 1965.

Chapter 15

Dash and Interior Parts

Instrument Panel
This interchange covers the bare instrument panel, striped of all gauges, pads, and controls. Interchange is quite large and, in some cases, will even cross makes.

Model Identification

Interchange

Interchange Number: 1
    Part Number(s): 7653486
    Usage: 1967–68 Camaro; 1967–68 Pontiac Firebird
    Notes: Cars with a/c use special panel with provisions for outlets.

Interchange Number: 2
    Part Number(s): 8716458
    Usage: 1969 Camaro

Interchange Number: 3
    Part Number(s): RH, 3994524; LH, 3994523
    Usage: 1970–75 Camaro

Interchange Number: 4
    Usage: 1964–65 Chevelle

Interchange Number: 5
    Usage: 1966–67 Chevelle
    Notes: (1) Models differ and will not interchange due to the way trim mounts:
        part number 3897575—Chevelle standard;
        part number 3897577—Chevelle Deluxe;
        part number 3897579—Malibu, SS 396, and Concours
    (2) Air conditioned cars used a different panel and will not interchange with cars without a/c or vice versa.

Interchange Number: 6
　　Part Number(s): 8716960
　　Usage: 1968 Chevelle without a/c; 1968–69 El Camino without a/c; 1969 Chevelle without a/c except two-door hardtop or convertible

Interchange Number: 7
　　Part Number(s): 8716961
　　Usage: 1968–69 Chevelle with a/c; 1968–69 El Camino with a/c; 1969 Chevelle two-door hardtop or convertible with or without air conditioning

Interchange Number: 8
　　Part Number(s): 3999456
　　Usage: 1970–72 Chevelle SS; 1970–72 El Camino SS; 1970–72 Chevelle with Rallye instrumentation (round gauges); 1970–72 Monte Carlo

Interchange Number: 9
　　Part Number(s): 3965419
　　Usage: 1970–72 Chevelle, except SS or with gauge package
　　Notes: Use only with rectangular gauges.

Interchange Number: 10
　　Part Number(s): 7654005
　　Usage: 1967 Bel Air or Biscayne without a/c
　　Notes: Will not fit Impala.

Interchange Number: 11
　　Part Number(s): 7654006
　　Usage: 1967 Bel Air or Biscayne with a/c
　　Notes: Will not fit Impala.

Interchange Number: 12
　　Part Number(s): 7654007
　　Usage: 1967 Impala or Caprice without a/c

Interchange Number: 13
　　Part Number(s): 7654008
　　Usage: 1967 Impala or Caprice with a/c

Interchange Number: 14
　　Part Number(s): 7727706
　　Usage: 1968 Bel Air or Biscayne without a/c
　　Notes: Will not fit Impala.

Interchange Number: 15
　　Part Number(s): 7727707
　　Usage: 1968 Bel Air or Biscayne with a/c
　　Notes: Will not fit Impala.

Interchange Number: 16
　　Part Number(s): 8806233
　　Usage: 1969–70 full-size Chevrolet with or without a/c

Interchange Number: 17
　　Usage: 1962–65 Chevy II
　　Notes: Used with or without a/c

Interchange Number: 18
　　Usage: 1966–67 Chevy II
　　Notes: Used with or without a/c

Interchange Number: 19
　　Part Number(s): 8727173
　　Usage: 1968 Nova without a/c

Interchange Number: 20
　　Part Number(s): 8727174
　　Usage: 1968 Nova with a/c

Interchange Number: 21
　　Part Number(s): 9662943
　　Usage: 1969–72 Nova; 1971–75 Pontiac Ventura II; both without a/c

Interchange Number: 22
　　Part Number(s): 9662944
　　Usage: 1969–72 Nova; 1971–75 Pontiac Ventura II; both with a/c

Interchange Number: 23
　　Usage: 1959–60 full-size Chevrolet
　　Notes: Those with a/c used a special panel, with provisions for outlets.

Interchange Number: 24
　　Usage: 1961–62 full-size Chevrolet
　　Notes: Those with a/c used a special panel, with provisions for outlets.

Interchange Number: 25
　　Usage: 1963–64 full-size Chevrolet
　　Notes: Those with a/c used a special panel, with provisions for outlets.

Interchange Number: 26
　　Usage: 1965 full-size Chevrolet
　　Notes: Those with a/c used a special panel, with provisions for outlets.

Interchange Number: 27
　　Usage: 1966 full-size Chevrolet
　　Notes: Those with a/c used a special panel, with provisions for outlets.

Interchange Number: 28
　　Part Number(s): 7739834
　　Usage: 1968 Impala without a/c; 1968 Caprice without a/c
　　Notes: Other models will not fit.

Interchange Number: 29
　　Part Number(s): 7739835
　　Usage: 1968 Impala with a/c; 1968 Caprice with a/c
　　Notes: Other models will not fit.

Glovebox Compartment

Model Identification

Interchange

Interchange Number: 1
    Part Number(s): 3891671
    Usage: 1967–68 Camaro without a/c

Interchange Number: 2
    Part Number(s): 3891766
    Usage: 1967–68 Camaro with a/c

Interchange Number: 3
    Part Number(s): 3939609
    Usage: 1968–75 Nova; 1969 Camaro; 1971–75 Pontiac Ventura II; 1975 Buick Apollo; 1975 Olds Omega; all without a/c

Interchange Number: 4
    Part Number(s): 3939611
    Usage: 1968–75 Nova; 1969 Camaro; 1971–75 Pontiac Ventura II; 1975 Buick Apollo; 1975 Olds Omega, all with a/c

Interchange Number: 5
    Part Number(s): 3975883
    Usage: 1970–75 Camaro without a/c

Interchange Number: 6
    Part Number(s): 3975884
    Usage: 1970–75 Camaro with a/c

Interchange Number: 7
    Part Number(s): 3752776
    Usage: 1959–60 full-size Chevrolet without a/c
    Notes: Stapled cardboard.

Interchange Number: 8
    Part Number(s): 3752777
    Usage: 1959–60 full-size Chevrolet with a/c

Interchange Number: 9
    Part Number(s): 3785539
    Usage: 1961–62 full-size Chevrolet without a/c

Interchange Number: 10
    Part Number(s): 3785558
    Usage: 1961–62 full-size Chevrolet with a/c

Interchange Number: 11
    Part Number(s): 3841767
    Usage: 1963–64 full-size Chevrolet without a/c

Interchange Number: 12
    Part Number(s): 3841897
    Usage: 1963–64 full-size Chevrolet with a/c

Interchange Number: 13
    Part Number(s): 3861659
    Usage: 1965–66 full-size Chevrolet without a/c

Interchange Number: 14
    Part Number(s): 3870231
    Usage: 1965–66 full-size Chevrolet with a/c except those with auto temperature control

Interchange Number: 15
    Part Number(s): 3875851
    Usage: 1965–66 full-size Chevrolet with auto temp a/c

Interchange Number: 16
    Part Number(s): 3895189
    Usage: 1967 full-size Chevrolet without a/c

Interchange Number: 17
    Part Number(s): 3919981
    Usage: 1967 full-size Chevrolet with a/c
    Notes: Interchange number 18 will fit as a replacement unit.

Interchange Number: 18
    Part Number(s): 3919981
    Usage: 1968 full-size Chevrolet without a/c, except two-door hardtop, convertible, or Caprice

Interchange Number: 19
    Part Number(s): 3934138
    Usage: 1968 full-size Chevrolet two-door hardtop, convertible, or Caprice. All 1968 full-size Chevrolet models with a/c.

Interchange Number: 20
    Part Number(s): 3939657

Usage: 1969–70 full-size Chevrolet without a/c

Interchange Number: 21
Part Number(s): 3921085
Usage: 1969–70 full-size Chevrolet with a/c

Interchange Number: 22
Part Number(s): 3791661
Usage: 1962–65 Chevy II

Interchange Number: 23
Part Number(s): 3876693
Usage: 1966–67 Chevy II

Interchange Number: 24
Part Number(s): 3386294
Usage: 1964–65 Chevelle

Interchange Number: 25
Part Number(s): 3878159
Usage: 1966–67 Chevelle without a/c

Interchange Number: 26
Part Number(s): 3885196
Usage: 1966–67 Chevelle with a/c

Interchange Number: 27
Part Number(s): 3939635
Usage: 1968–69 Chevelle without a/c

Interchange Number: 28
Part Number(s): 3930197
Usage: 1968–69 Chevelle with a/c

Interchange Number: 29
Usage: 1970–72 Chevelle;1970–72 Monte Carlo

Glovebox Door

This section refers to the glovebox outer door assembly. Besides model usage, another factor that will influence interchange in some models is whether or not air conditioning is used. Also, the 1969 Camaro with the Deluxe interior used a different door than those with the standard interior.

Model Identification

Interchange

Interchange Number: 1
Part Number(s): 3891663
Usage: 1967 Camaro; 1967 Pontiac Firebird; both with or without a/c

Interchange Number: 2
Part Number(s): 3921873
Usage: 1968 Camaro with or without a/c

Interchange Number: 3
Part Number(s): 3991755
Usage: 1969 Camaro with standard interior only; 1969–75 Nova; 1971–75 Pontiac Ventura; 1973–75 Buick Apollo; 1973–75 Olds Omega; all with or without a/c

Interchange Number: 4
Part Number(s): Inner, 3999447; outer, 6264757
Usage: 1970–75 Camaro with all trim levels and with or without a/c
Notes: This is the 1975 part number and will fit. When used on 1970 Camaro without Deluxe interior, bright trim must be painted black.

Interchange Number: 5
Usage: 1964–65 Chevelle; 1964–65 El Camino; both with or without a/c

Interchange Number: 6
Part Number(s): 3871013
Usage: 1966–67 Chevelle; 1966–67 El Camino; both with or without a/c

Interchange Number: 7
Part Number(s): 3927641
Usage: 1968–69 Chevelle; 1968–69 El Camino; both without a/c

Interchange Number: 8
   Part Number(s): 3930193
   Usage: 1968–69 Chevelle; 1968–69 El Camino; both
      with a/c

Interchange Number: 9
   Part Number(s): Inner, 3991762; outer, 3957090
   Usage: 1970–72 Chevelle; 1970–72 El Camino; both
      with or without a/c

Interchange Number: 10
   Usage: 1959–60 full-size Chevrolet

Interchange Number: 11
   Usage: 1961–62 full-size Chevrolet without a/c

Interchange Number: 12
   Usage: 1961–62 full-size Chevrolet with a/c

Interchange Number: 13
   Usage: 1963–64 full-size Chevrolet without a/c

Interchange Number: 14
   Usage: 1963–64 full-size Chevrolet with a/c

Interchange Number: 15
   Part Number(s): 3873775
   Usage: 1965 Impala with or without a/c

Interchange Number: 16
   Part Number(s): 3873774
   Usage: 1965 Bel Air or Biscayne with or without a/c

Interchange Number: 17
   Part Number(s): 3875791
   Usage: 1966 Biscayne with or without a/c

Interchange Number: 18
   Part Number(s): 3875793
   Usage: 1966 Bel Air; 1966 Impala except Impala SS;
      both with or without a/c

Interchange Number: 19
   Part Number(s): 3891473
   Usage: 1966 Impala SS with or without a/c
   Notes: Interchange number 17 can be modified to fit by
      drilling the required holes.

Interchange Number: 20
   Part Number(s): 3892181
   Usage: 1966 Caprice with or without a/c

Interchange Number: 21
   Part Number(s): 3892127
   Usage: 1967 full-size Chevrolet with or without a/c

Interchange Number: 22
   Part Number(s): 3913691
   Usage: 1968 full-size Chevrolet without a/c

Interchange Number: 23
   Part Number(s): 3927617
   Usage: 1968 full-size Chevrolet with a/c

Interchange Number: 24
   Part Number(s): 3935947
   Usage: 1969–70 full-size Chevrolet without a/c

Interchange Number: 25
   Part Number(s): 3935971
   Usage: 1969–70 full-size Chevrolet with a/c

Interchange Number: 26
   Part Number(s): 3791663
   Usage: 1962–65 Chevy II with or without a/c

Interchange Number: 27
   Part Number(s): 3893899
   Usage: 1966–67 Chevy II, all but 1967 Nova; all with or
      without a/c

Interchange Number: 28
   Part Number(s): 3898101
   Usage: 1967 Nova with or without a/c
   Notes: Interchange number 27 can be modified to fit.

Interchange Number: 29
   Part Number(s): 3916699
   Usage: 1968 Nova with or without a/c

Interchange Number: 30
   Part Number(s): 3945905
   Usage: 1969 Camaro with Deluxe interior and with or
      without a/c

Sun Visor

Sun visors were covered in vinyl trim. The color depended on the type and color of the interior, and usually matched the headliner. However, no interchange is given for color. Interchange is based on either black or white.

The major factor is the intended use of a particular visor. They can always be repainted or recovered. And in most cases, the visor is reversible, meaning it can fit either side of the car.

Bodystyle has little effect on their interchangeability, with one exception: the convertible. Convertibles used special visors; those from a hardtop model will not fit. Also, beginning in 1968, the El Camino and station wagon used a different set of visors that will not fit other bodystyles.

All visors are a GM part, and can be found in a variety of makes and models.

Model Identification

Interchange

Interchange Number: 1
    Part Number(s): 7666115
    Usage: 1967 Camaro; 1967 Pontiac Firebird; both hardtop

Interchange Number: 2
    Part Number(s): 7661222
    Usage: 1967–68 Camaro; 1967–68 Pontiac Firebird; convertible only

Interchange Number: 3
    Part Number(s): 7766101
    Usage: 1968 Camaro; 1968 Pontiac Firebird; both hardtop

Interchange Number: 4
    Part Number(s): 8765281
    Usage: 1969 Camaro; 1969 Pontiac Firebird; both hardtop

Interchange Number: 5
    Part Number(s): 8765289
    Usage: 1969 Camaro; 1969 Pontiac Firebird; convertible only

Interchange Number: 6
    Part Number(s): 9818936
    Usage: 1970 Camaro; 1970 Pontiac Firebird; both hardtop

Interchange Number: 7
    Part Number(s): 4442047
    Usage: 1964 Chevelle; 1964 Olds Cutlass; 1964 Buick Skylark; 1964 Pontiac LeMans; all except convertible

Interchange Number: 8
    Part Number(s): 4497471
    Usage: 1964 Chevelle; 1964 Olds Cutlass; 1964 Buick Skylark; 1964 Pontiac LeMans; convertible only

Interchange Number: 9
    Part Number(s): 4481246
    Usage: 1965 Chevelle; 1965 Olds Cutlass; 1965 Buick Skylark; 1965 Pontiac LeMans; all except convertible

Interchange Number: 10
    Part Number(s): 4480644
    Usage: 1965 Chevelle; 1965 Olds Cutlass; 1965 Buick Skylark; 1965 Pontiac LeMans; convertible only

Interchange Number: 11
    Part Number(s): 7631361
    Usage: 1966 Chevelle; 1966 Olds Cutlass; 1966 Buick Skylark; 1966 Pontiac LeMans; all except convertible

Interchange Number: 12
    Part Number(s): 7630473
    Usage: 1966 Chevelle; 1966 Olds Cutlass; 1966 Buick Skylark; 1966 Pontiac LeMans; convertible only

Interchange Number: 13
    Part Number(s): 7666339
    Usage: 1967 Chevelle; 1967 Olds Cutlass; 1967 Buick Skylark; 1967 Pontiac LeMans; all except convertible

Interchange Number: 14
 Part Number(s): 7630473
 Usage: 1967 Chevelle; 1967 Olds Cutlass; 1967 Buick Skylark; 1967 Pontiac LeMans; convertible only

Interchange Number: 15
 Part Number(s): 7769129
 Usage: 1965 Pontiac LeMans (not base Tempest); 1968 Malibu; 1968 Olds Cutlass (not base F-85); 1968 Buick Skylark (not base Special); all except convertible, El Camino, or Chevelle station wagon

Interchange Number: 16
 Part Number(s): 7769157
 Usage: 1968 Chevelle (not Malibu); 1968 Olds F-85; 1968 Buick Special; 1968 Pontiac Tempest; 1968 Nova; all except convertible

Interchange Number: 17
 Part Number(s): 7772866
 Usage: 1965 Pontiac LeMans (not base Tempest); 1968 Malibu; 1968 Olds Cutlass (not base F-85); 1968 Buick Skylark (not base Special); convertible only

Interchange Number: 18
 Part Number(s): 8765321
 Usage: 1969 Malibu; 1969 Pontiac LeMans (not base Tempest); all except convertible, El Camino, or station wagon

Interchange Number: 19
 Part Number(s): 8765296
 Usage: 1969–70 Chevelle; 1969–70 Olds Cutlass (not base F-85); 1969–70 Buick Skylark (not base special); 1969–70 Pontiac LeMans (not base Tempest); convertible only

Interchange Number: 20
 Part Number(s): 8743228
 Usage: 1969 Chevelle (except Malibu); 1969 Olds Cutlass F-85; 1969 Buick Special; 1969 Tempest; 1969 Nova; all except Convertible, El Camino, or Chevelle station wagon

Interchange Number: 21
 Part Number(s): 8765304
 Usage: 1968–69 El Camino; 1968–69 Chevelle Concours; 1969 Chevelle station wagon

Interchange Number: 22
 Part Number(s): 8802658
 Usage: 1970 Malibu; 1970 Monte Carlo; 1970 El Camino Custom; 1970 Pontiac LeMans; all except station wagon or convertible

Interchange Number: 23
 Part Number(s): 8802667
 Usage: 1970 base Chevelle; all except station wagon or convertible

Interchange Number: 24
 Part Number(s): 8802576
 Usage: 1970 Nova; 1970 Chevelle station wagon

Interchange Number: 25
 Part Number(s): 9812146
 Usage: 1970 El Camino

Interchange Number: 26
 Usage: 1959 full-size Chevrolet, Pontiac, Oldsmobile, or Buick; all except convertible

Interchange Number: 27
 Usage: 1959 full-size Chevrolet, Pontiac, Oldsmobile, or Buick; convertible only

Interchange Number: 28
 Usage: 1960–63 full-size Chevrolet, Pontiac, Oldsmobile, or Buick; all except convertible

Interchange Number: 29
 Usage: 1960–63 full-size Chevrolet, Pontiac, Oldsmobile, or Buick; convertible only

Interchange Number: 30
 Usage: 1964 full-size Chevrolet, Pontiac, Oldsmobile, or Buick; all except convertible

Interchange Number: 31
 Usage: 1964 full-size Chevrolet, Pontiac, Oldsmobile, or Buick; convertible only

Interchange Number: 32
 Usage: 1965 full-size Chevrolet, Pontiac, Oldsmobile, or Buick; all except convertible

Interchange Number: 33
 Usage: 1965 full-size Chevrolet, Pontiac, Oldsmobile, or Buick; convertible only

Interchange Number: 34
 Usage: 1966 full-size Chevrolet, Pontiac, Oldsmobile, or Buick; all except Convertible Caprice or station wagon

Interchange Number: 35
 Usage: 1966 full-size Chevrolet, Pontiac, Oldsmobile, or Buick; convertible only

Interchange Number: 36
 Part Number(s): 7665430
 Usage: 1967 Impala, all but convertible or Caprice

Interchange Number: 37
 Part Number(s): 7706362
 Usage: 1967–68 Impala; 1968 full-size Oldsmobile, Pontiac, or Buick; convertible only

Interchange Number: 38
 Part Number(s): 7636113
 Usage: 1967–68 Caprice; 1968 Impala two-door hardtop; 1967–68 Delta 98 sedan
 Notes: Impala sedan or station wagon will not interchange, nor will convertible. But Caprice models except for station wagon will fit.

Interchange Number: 39
 Part Number(s): 7706362
 Usage: 1968 Impala; 1968 full-size Oldsmobile, Pontiac, or Buick; convertible only

Interchange Number: 40
 Part Number(s): 8774777
 Usage: 1969 Biscayne
 Notes: Will not fit Bel Air, Impala, or Caprice.

Interchange Number: 41
Part Number(s): 877482
Usage: 1969 Bel Air
Notes: Will not fit Biscayne, Impala, or Caprice.

Interchange Number: 42
Part Number(s): 8774852 or 8774862
Usage: 1969 Impala two-door hardtop; 1969 full-size Oldsmobile, Buick, or Pontiac; all two-door hardtop; and 1969 Caprice
Notes: Part number 8774862 used with Caprice or Impalas with insulation package only.

Interchange Number: 43
Part Number(s): 8765332
Usage: 1969–70 Impala; 1969–70 full-size Oldsmobile, Buick, or Pontiac; convertible only

Interchange Number: 44
Part Number(s): 9812151
Usage: 1970 Biscayne; 1970 Bel Air
Notes: Will not fit Bel Air, Impala, or Caprice.

Interchange Number: 45
Part Number(s): 8806525
Usage: 1970 Impala; 1970 Caprice; all except convertible or sedan

Interchange Number: 46
Usage: 1962–65 Chevy II, except convertible

Interchange Number: 47
Usage: 1962–63 Chevy II convertible

Impala 1959–62 used this handle.

Inside Door Handle

Interchange

Interchange Number: 1
Part Number(s): 3764017
Usage: 1959–64 full-size Chevrolet, except 1960–64 Impala; 1962–65 Chevy II, except Nova; 1964–65 Chevelle, except Malibu; 1964–65 El Camino

Interchange Number: 2
Part Number(s): RH, 4787463; LH, 4787464
Usage: 1960–67 Impala; 1964–67 Bonneville Brougham; 1965–67 Olds Cutlass (except base F-85); 1966–67 Caprice; 1966–67 full-size Oldsmobile, except Toronado. 1966–67 full-size
Notes: Each side is unique. Front and rear will interchange.

Interchange Number: 3
Part Number(s): 4753532
Usage: 1960–61 full-size Pontiac S-88; 1961–64 Olds F-85 (four-door only); 1962–64 Chevy II (Nova only); 1964 Chevy II; 1964 Chevelle (Malibu only)

Interchange Number: 4
Part Number(s): 4468414
Usage: 1965–67 Chevelle; 1965–67 Bel Air; 1965–67 Biscayne; 1965–67 Pontiac LeMans; 1965–67 Pontiac GTO; 1965–67 full-size Pontiac, all except Grand Prix; 1965–67 Buick LeSabre; 1965–67 Buick Wildcat, all except Convertible; 1966–67 Buick Skylark; 1966–67 Chevy II; 1967 Camaro (with Standard interior); 1967 Pontiac Firebird (with standard interior)

Interchange Number: 5
Part Number(s): RH, 7712035; LH, 7712036
Usage: 1967 Camaro with Deluxe interior; 1967 Pontiac Firebird with Deluxe interior

Interchange Number: 6
Part Number(s): 7743520
Usage: 1968–70 Camaro; 1968–70 Pontiac Firebird; 1968–72 Chevelle; 1968–72 Buick Skylark; 1968–72 Pontiac LeMans; 1968–72 Pontiac GTO; 1968–72 Nova; 1968–72 Olds Cutlass; 1968–70 full-size Chevrolet; 1968–72 El Camino; 1971–72 GMC Sprint; 1971–72 Pontiac Ventura II

Window Regulator Handle (Inside Front Door)

Inside door window regulator handles are greatly interchangeable with a variety of GM makes and models. Some came with a knob that was color keyed to the interior trim. There is no mention of color in this interchange, and all part numbers are for black colored knobs. However, most models offered the same color choices for various bodystyles, so finding the correct color should be fairly easy. Window handles are also interchangeable from side to side, and usually those on the rear door will fit the front door as well.

Model Identification

Camaro	Interchange Number
1967	
Standard interior	4
Deluxe interior	6
1968	8
1969–70	9

Chevelle	Interchange Number
1964	
except Malibu	1
Malibu	10
1965–66	4
1967	
except 300 models	6
300 models	4
1968	8
1969–70	9

Impala	Interchange Number
1959–60	
except Impala	1
Impala	2
1962–64	
except Biscayne	2
Biscayne	1

Chevy II/Nova	Interchange Number
1962	
except Nova	3
Nova	10
1963–64	
except Nova	1
Nova	10
1965–66	4

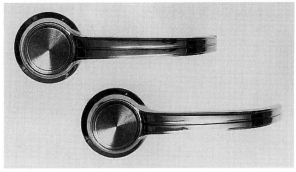

Chevelle door handle used in 1965–67. *Year One*

Biscayne used this window regulator from 1959 to 1964.

Impala window regulator handle for 1959–64.

Window regulator handle for 1965–66.

1967	6
1968	8
1969–70	9

Interchange

Interchange Number: 1
    Part Number(s): 4619388

The window regulator handle used in most 1967 models.

Usage: 1959–60 full-size Chevrolet except Impala; 1961–64 Biscayne; 1963–64 Chevy II except for Nova; 1964 Chevelle except Malibu

Notes: Black knob.

Interchange Number: 2
Part Number(s): 4619387
Usage: 1959–64 Impala; 1961–64 Bel Air
Notes: Black knob with charcoal insert.

Interchange Number: 3
Part Number(s): 6275958
Usage: 1962 Chevy II except Nova

Interchange Number: 4
Part Number(s): 4472076
Usage: 1965–66 Biscayne; 1965–66 Bel Air; 1965–67 Chevy II; 1967 Camaro; 1965–67 Chevelle (1967 300 models only)
Notes: Front doors only.

Interchange Number: 5
Part Number(s): 4468651
Usage: 1965–66 Impala; 1965–66 full-size Oldsmobile except Starfire or Toronado; 1965–66 full-size Pontiac; 1965–66 Pontiac LeMans; 1965–66 full-size Buick; 1966 Buick Skylark

Interchange Number: 6
Part Number(s): 7680653
Usage: 1967 full-size Chevrolet; 1967 Chevelle; 1967 Chevy II; 1967 Corvair; 1967 Olds Cutlass; 1967 full-size Oldsmobile, except Toronado

Window regulator handle for 1969–70.

A 1969–70 style lock knob.

Notes: Front door only on Olds Cutlass and Chevelle. Color keyed knob. Other colors available.

Interchange Number: 7
Part Number(s): 7680654
Usage: 1967 Camaro with Deluxe interior trim; 1967 Pontiac Firebird with standard trim

Interchange Number: 8
Part Number(s): 7752485
Usage: 1968 Camaro; 1968 Chevelle; 1968 full-size Chevrolet, Pontiac, Oldsmobile, or Buick; 1968 Olds Cutlass; 1968 Pontiac LeMans; 1968 Pontiac Firebird; 1968 Buick Skylark; 1968 El Camino; 1968 Nova
Notes: Color keyed knobs.

Interchange Number: 9
Part Number(s): 8732961
Usage: 1969–70 Camaro; 1969–71 Chevelle; 1969–70 full-size Chevrolet, Pontiac, Oldsmobile, or Buick; 1969–70 Pontiac Firebird; 1969–71 Olds Cutlass; 1969–71 Pontiac LeMans; 1969–71 Buick Skylark; 1969–71 El Camino; 1969–72 Nova; 1971–72 Pontiac Ventura II

Interchange Number: 10
Part Number(s): 4807923
Usage: 1962–64 Chevy II Nova; 1963–64 Nova SS; 1964 Chevelle Malibu

Console

There are many different components involved in the console swap. This includes the lower and upper parts, along with the compartment door and trim. Of these, only the upper and lower parts are given in this interchange, although most other parts usually will interchange with them.

Probably the biggest consideration in console interchange is transmission type because some units were molded in color, but consoles can always be repainted to match your existing interior.

Model Identification

Interchange

Interchange Number: 1
Part Number(s): Lower, 3918725; upper, 3918724
Usage: 1967 Camaro; 1967 Pontiac Firebird; both without gauge cluster; all transmissions

Interchange Number: 2
Part Number(s): Lower, 6457859; upper, 3918724 upper
Usage: 1967 Camaro; 1967 Pontiac Firebird; both with gauge cluster; all transmissions

Interchange Number: 3
Part Number(s): Lower, 3938644; upper, 3938640
Usage: 1968–69 Camaro

Interchange Number: 4
Part Number(s): Lower, RH, 3975800, LH, 3975799; upper, 3975798
Usage: 1970–72 Camaro, all transmissions
Notes: Floor mounting brackets differ between automatic and manual transmissions.

Interchange Number: 5
Part Number(s): Front, 3858052; rear, 3858053
Usage: 1964–65 Chevelle automatic
Notes: Rear part also fits cars with four-speed.

Interchange Number: 6
Part Number(s): Front, 3858051; rear, 3858053
Usage: 1964–65 Chevelle four-speed
Notes: Rear part also fits cars with automatic.

Interchange Number: 7
Part Number(s): Lower, 3876407; upper front, 3878467; upper rear, 3878156
Usage: 1966–67 Chevelle manual
Notes: Rear upper panel also used on automatic-equipped Chevelle.

Interchange Number: 8
Part Number(s): Lower, 3876408;
Upper front, 3878468; upper rear, 3878156
Usage: 1966–67 Chevelle automatic

Interchange Number: 9
Part Number(s): 6264879
Usage: 1968–72 Chevelle, all transmissions; 1968–72 El Camino; 1970–72 Monte Carlo; 1971–72 GMC Sprint

Interchange Number: 10
Part Number(s): 3827420
Usage: 1963 Impala SS manual

Interchange Number: 11
Part Number(s): Lower, 3827400; upper, 3827417
Usage: 1963 Impala SS automatic

Interchange Number: 12
Part Number(s): 3844146
Usage: 1964 full-size Chevrolet, all transmissions
Notes: Molded in colors black given. Trim bezels differ between transmissions.

Interchange Number: 13
Part Number(s): Lower, 3858908; upper, 3866017
Usage: 1965 Impala SS four-speed

Interchange Number: 14
Part Number(s): Lower, 3858905; upper, 3866834
Usage: 1965 Impala SS automatic

Interchange Number: 15
Part Number(s): Lower, 3895183; upper, 3918228
Usage: 1966–67 full-size Chevrolet manual

Interchange Number: 16
Part Number(s): Lower, 3895181; upper, 3918226
Usage: 1966–67 full-size Chevrolet automatic

Interchange Number: 17
Part Number(s): Lower, 3919966; upper, 3919969
Usage: 1968–69 full-size Chevrolet manual
Notes: Color keyed to interior. Paint as required.

Interchange Number: 18
Part Number(s): Lower, 3919966; upper, 3920056
Usage: 1968–69 full-size Chevrolet automatic
Notes: Color keyed to interior. Paint as required.

Interchange Number: 19
Part Number(s): Front, 3841791; rear, 3841599
Usage: 1963–64 Nova SS automatic
Notes: Rear plate used on cars with manual transmission.

Interchange Number: 20
Part Number(s): Front, 3841598; rear, 3841599
Usage: 1963–64 Nova SS manual
Notes: Rear plate used on cars with automatic transmission.

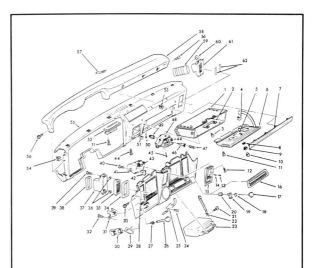

1969 CAMARO INSTRUMENT PANEL—EXPLODED

1.	10.260	COMPARTMENT ASM.	3939609
2.	10.268	STRIKER	3984446
3.	8.977	SCREW (#10–16 x 5/8)	
4.	10.263	BUMPER	4566397
5.	10.266	CASE ASM.	3934137
6.	10.261	DOOR ASM.	3991755
7.	10.252	MOULDING	3939692
8.	10.266	SPL. WASHER	4416740
9.	10.267	ESCUTCHEON	3922831
10.	10.266	CYLINDER	
11.	8.977	SCREW (#10–16 x 3/4)	
12.	8.977	SCREW (#8–18 x 1/2)	
13.	9.772	NUT	3794018
14.	9.772	KNOB	3794017
15.	9.772	LESN. ASM.	3943616
16.	10.256	COVER-RADIO CONTROL HOLE	3945981
17.	RADIO	KNOB ASM.	
18.	RADIO	WASHER	
19.	RADIO	KNOB	
20.	RADIO	SPL. NUT	
21.	RADIO	SCREW (#10–16 x 5/8)	
22.	RADIO	BRACKET	
23.	RADIO	RECEIVER-U63-U69	
24.	8.977	SCREW (#8–18 x 5/8)	
25.	6.518	COVER	3935995
26.	2.486	ROD ASM.	3954210
27.	2.487	NUT	3919021
28.	9.743	CARRIER ASSY.	6482858
29.	*	STRAP	
30.	2.485	SWITCH ASM.-LIGHT	1995176
31.	10.163	SWITCH ASM.	1993464
32.	8.977	SCREW (#8–18 x 3/8)	
33.	8.977	SCREW (#8–28 x 3/4)	
34.	9.260	SEAL	3937172
35.	9.262	DEFLECTOR	9791237
36.	9.262	SPACER, Part of ASM.	3937175
37.	9.262	HOUSING	3939681
38.	9.260	SEAL	3942649
39.	9.260	SCREW ASM.	3937182
40.	RADIO	SCREW (#8–18 x 1/2)	
41.	9.772	CLOCK ASM.	3951213
42.	4.020	CLIP	6481602
43.	9.772	SHIELD ASM.	3951214
44.	8.977	SCREW (#8–18 x 1/2)	
45.	10.263	BUMPER	3765243
46.	9.709	HOUSING ASM.	
47.	9.709	UNIT & KNOB ASM.	
48.	12.009	ASH TRAY & RETAINER ASM.	3965143
49.	9.709	RETAINER	
50.	10.263	BUMPER	3765243
51.	12.009	BUMPER	3935938
52.	9.779	OUTLET	3973729
53.	10.252	SCREW & BRACKET ASM.	3922826
54.	8.921	NUT (#8–18)	
55.	10.230	INSTRUMENT PANEL	
56.	8.977	SCREW (#8–18 x 3/4)	
57.	14.655	CLIP	3939655
58.	14.655	PAD ASM.	
59.	9.260	HOSE	3946929
60.	8.917	NUT (#10–16)	
61.	9.262	OUTLET R.H.	
62.	9.260	SEAL	3929027

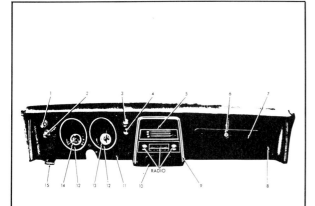

1967-68 CAMARO INSTRUMENT PANEL

1.	10.164	KNOB
2.	2.486	ROD
3.	9.709	LIGHTER UNIT
4.	2.188	SWITCH
5.	8.852	CONTROL ASSY.
6.	10.266	LOCK ASSY.
7.	10.261	DOOR
8.	10.230	PANEL
9.	10.252	PLATE
10.	12.009	TRAY ASSY.
11.	9.743	BEZEL
12.	9.748	LENS
13.	3.108	GAUGE ASSY.
14.	9.761	HEAD ASSY.
15.	4.591	LEVER ASSY.

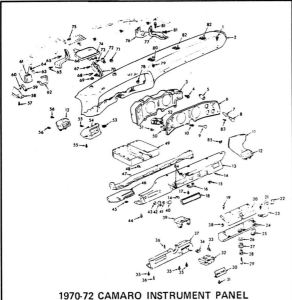

1970-72 CAMARO INSTRUMENT PANEL

1.	8.977	SCREW (8-18 x 5/8)	
2.	14.655	PAD ASSY. w/C.A.C.	
	14.655	PAD ASSY. Except C.A.C.	
3.	N.S.S.	CLUSTER ASSY.	
4.	8.977	SCREW (8-18 x 5/2)	
5.	9.709	RETAINER	3794299
	9.709	RETAINER–Optional	7026954
6.	9.743	CARRIER	3999448
7.	7.412	HOUSING ASSY.	3791036
	9.709	HOUSING ASSY.–Optional	7028056
8.	9.709	UNIT & KNOB	3954207
	9.709	KNOB–Optional	7021700
9.	2.486	ROD ASSY.	3986886
10.	2.487	NUT	3919021
11.	9.262	DUCT – Upper	3967928
12.	9.262	OUTLET ASSY. – Upper	3989237-38
13.	10.230	PANEL ASSY. R.H.	3994524
14.	10.263	BUMPER – Inst. Pnl.	3957096
15.	12.009	BUMPER – Ash Tray	3939670
16.	10.268	STRIKER – Inst. Pnl.	3975839
17.	8.977	SCREW (8 - 18 x 3/4)	
18.	10.256	COVER	3975855
19.	8.977	SCREW (8 - 18 x 7/16)	
20.	10.261	DOOR – Inst. Pnl. 1970-71	3991759
21.	8.977	SCREW (8 - 8 x 7/8)	
22.	10.263	BUMPER – Inst. Pnl.	3820023
23.	10.262	STOP – Inst. Pnl. Door (1970-71)	3984465
24.	10.261	DOOR – Compt. Door	3994525
25.	10.266	CASE	3957092
26.	10.266	WASHER	4416740
27.	10.267	ESCUTCHEON – Inst. Pnl.	3957093
28.	10.266	CYLINDER ASSY.	
29.	2.187	KEY	
30.	12.009	FACE PLATE	3972006
31.	8.967	RIVET	
32.	12.009	ASH TRAY ASSY.	3972005
33.	8.977	SCREW	
34.	12.009	BUMPER	3939670
35.	8.977	SCREW (8-18 x 3/4)	
36.	8.977	SCREW (8-18 x 5/8)	
37.	6.518	COVER ASSY.	3972058
38.	8.977	SCREW (8-18 x 7/16)	
39.	12.009	ASH TRAY ASSY.	3972005
40.	9.649	KNOB	3954238
41.	9.649	WASHER	3961507
42.	9.649	KNOB	
43.	9.667	NUT – Spec. (7/16 - 28)	
44.	8.977	SCREW (8-18 x 5/8)	
45.	8.977	SCREW (8-18 x 5/8)	
46.	RADIO	RADIO	
47.	10.230	REINFORCEMENT R.H. Inst. Pnl.	3984437
48.	8.977	SCREW (8-18 x 3/4)	
49.	10.260	COMPARTMENT ASSY.	3975883
50.	10.163	SWITCH ASSY.	1994098
51.	8.977	SCREW (8-18 x 1/2)	
52.	2.485	SWITCH ASSY.	1995173
53.	8.921	J-NUT (8-18)	
54.	10.230	PANEL ASSY. L.H.	3994523
55.	8.977	SCREW (8-18 x 5/8)	
56.	8.977	SCREW (8-18 x 5/8)	
57.	8.977	SCREW (10-16 x 1/2)	
58.	N.S.	BRACKET	
59.	9.262	BRACKET	3967941
60.	8.967	RIVET (1/8 x 1/4)	
61.	9.262	DUCT – Upper	3967927
62.	9.260	SEAL	3942649
63.	N.S.	REINFORCEMENT	
64.	8.977	SCREW (8-18 x 1/2)	
65.	8.900	SCREW (5/16-18 x 3/4)	
66.	10.260	REINFORCEMENT ASSY. – Ctr., Upr.	3980356
67.	8.977	SCREW (10-16 x 1/2)	
68.	8.977	SCREW (8-18 x 1/4)	
69.	8.921	J-NUT (8-18)	
70.	10.260	REINFORCEMENT ASSY. – Ctr., Upr.	3991784
71.	8.921	J-NUT (10-12)	
72.	9.667	RADIO BRACKET	3973670
73.	8.977	SCREW (8-18 x 1/4)	
74.	RADIO	SPEAKER	
75.	8.900	SCREW (5/16-18 x 7/8)	
76.	N.S.	BRACKET	
77.	10.230	REINFORCEMENT ASSY.	3972078
78.	8.921	J-NUT (8-18)	
79.	8.915	NUT (10-24)	
80.	14.655	CLIP	3980361
81.	8.900	SCREW (5/16-18 x 7/8)	
82.	14.655	CLIP	3980355
83.	8.977	SCREW (8-18 x 5/8)	
84.	8.921	U-NUT (8-18)	
85.	8.921	U-NUT (8-18)	
86.	10.262	STRAP	3975885

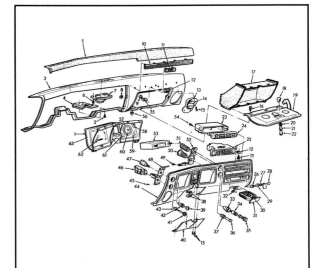

1968 CHEVELLE INSTRUMENT PANEL—EXPLODED

1.	9.743	CASE
2.	8.997	SCREW
3.	10.230	PANEL ASSY.
4.	12.016	RETAINER
5.	14.655	PAD UNIT
6.	8.977	SCREW (1/4–14 x 3/4)
7.	RADIO SPEAKER ASSY.	
8.	8.921	"U" NUT
9.	8.921	NUT (3/16)
10.	10.252	MOULDING
11.	10.254	EMBLEM
12.	8.921	"J" NUT (#8–18)
13.	9.262	BEZEL ASSY.
14.	9.262	DEFLECTOR
15.	8.977	SCREW (#10–16 x 5/8)
16.	N.S.	Part of 10.261 DOOR ASSY.
17.	10.260	COMPARTMENT ASSY.
18.	10.266	CASE ASSY.
19.	10.261	DOOR ASSY.
20.	10.266	WASHER
21.	10.267	ESCUTCHEON
22.	10.266	CYLINDER
23.	9.262	ADAPTER
24.	9.262	DEFLECTOR
25.	9.786	CONTROL ASSY.
26.	RADIO RETAINER	
27.	RADIO WASHER	
28.	RADIO KNOB ASSY.	
29.	RADIO KNOB	
30.	12.009	ASH TRAY ASSY.
31.	10.252	PLATE
32.	12.009	BUMPER
33.	9.709	BEZEL
34.	9.709	HOUSING
35.	9.709	KNOB and UNIT ASSY.
36.	2.188	CYLINDER ASSY.
37.	2.198	BEZEL
38.	8.921	NUT (#10–16)
39.	10.166	BEZEL
40.	6.518	COVER
41.	2.486	ROD ASSY.
42.	10.164	KNOB ASSY.
43.	2.487	NUT ASSY.
44.	9.743	CARRIER ASSY.
45.	8.977	SCREW
46.	2.485	SWITCH ASSY.
47.	10.163	SWITCH ASSY.
48.	9.735	STRAP
49.	8.977	SCREW
50.	2.188	SWITCH ASSY.
51.	9.709	RETAINER
52.	2.485	STRAP
53.	RADIO RECEIVER	
54.	8.977	SCREW (#8–18 x 3/8)
55.	10.252	SCREW and BRACKET ASSY.
56.	8.915	SCREW (#10–24)
	8.932	WASHER (#10)
57.	1.150	GAUGE
58.	3.107	GAUGE
59.	1.803	GAUGE
60.	9.772	CLOCK ASSY.
61.	2.515	GAUGE
62.	9.750	HEAD ASSY.
63.	9.743	CARRIER ASSY.

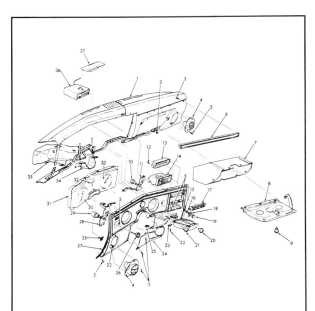

1969 CHEVELLE INSTRUMENT
PANEL—EXPLODED

1. 14.655 PAD UNIT
2. 8.915 NUT (10—24)
3. 8.977 SCREW
4. 9.262 BEZEL L.H. 3937185
   9.262 BEZEL R.H. 3946966
5. 8.977 SCREW (8-18 x 5/8)
6. 10.252 MOULDING
7. 10.260 COMPARTMENT ASSY. 3939635
8. 10.261 DOOR ASSY. 3927641
9. 10.266 CYLINDER 8717640
10. 9.709 RETAINER 3794299
11. 2.485 STRAP 1995164
12. 8.977 SCREW (8-18)
13. 9.262 OUTLET ASSY. 3942682
14. 8.849 CONTROL ASSY. 3949980
15. RADIO NUT
16. RADIO WASHER
17. 9.262 DEFLECTOR 3856472
18. RADIO KNOB
19. RADIO KNOB ASSY.
20. 9.709 UNIT & KNOB ASSY. 7025141
21. 12.009 ASH TRAY & RETAINER ASSY. . 3945901
22. 8.977 SCREW (8-18 x 3/8)
23. 12.009 BUMPER 3939670
24. 6.518 COVER 3939627
25. 8.921 NUT (8-18)
26. 2.486 ROD ASSY. 3986886
27. 9.743 CARRIER ASSY. (Standard) 6482239
   9.743 CARRIER ASSY. (Air Conditioning) 6482247
   9.743 CARRIER ASSY. (Astro
         Ventilation) 6483210
28. 2.188 STRAP 6482453
29. 2.485 SWITCH ASSY. 1995164
30. 9.743 SPEEDOMETER CASE 6482974
31. 9.747 RETAINER 6483281
32. 9.772 CLOCK UNIT 3948956
33. 9.743 CASE (Gen, Oil, Thermo&Gas
         Gauge) 6483003
34. 6.760 BRACKET ASSY. 7804091
35. 4.634 BRACKET ASSY. 3969416
36. RADIO RECEIVER
37. RADIO SPEAKER ASSY.

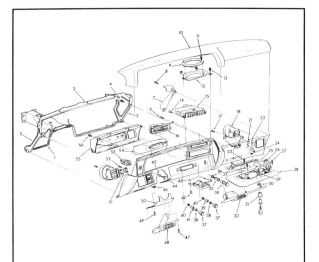

1970 CHEVELLE INSTRUMENT PANEL
(EXC. S.S., MONTE CARLO AND INSTRUMENT GAUGES)

1.	N.S.	REINFORCEMENT ASSY., Lower (Part of 3977631)	
2.	N.S.	REINFORCEMENT ASSY., L.H. (Part of 3977631)	
3.	N.S.	REINFORCEMENT ASSY., Upper (Part of 3977631)	
4.	8.977	SCREW	
5.	N.S.	REINFORCEMENT ASSY., Ctr. (Part of 3977631)	
6.	8.977	SCREW	
7.	10.230	REINFORCEMENT ASSY.	3957070
8.	8.977	SCREW (10–16 x 5/8)	
9.	RADIO	SPEAKER ASSY., Ctr.	7312681
10.	14.655	PAD, Inst. Panel	
11.	8.977	SCREW (8–18 x 3/8)	
12.	8.977	SCREW (10–16 x 1/2)	
13.	RADIO	BRACKER, Ctr.	3961582
14.	8.977	SCREW	
15.	9.262	AIR CONDITION, Ctr.	3963757
16.	8.849	CONTROL ASSY.	3963700
17.	8.900	SCREW (10–24 x 3/4)	
18.	9.262	OUTLET ASSY.	3957085-86
19.	8.977	SCREW	
20.	10.268	STRIKER	3957094
21.	10.263	BUMPER—Stop	3820023
22.	10.230	INSTRUMENT PANEL	
23.	8.977	SCREW	
24.	8.915	NUT ASSY.	
25.	10.261	DOOR—Inner	3957091
26.	10.268	STOP—Door	3957095
27.	8.977	SCREW (8–8 x 3/8)	
28.	10.261	DOOR—Outer	3957090
29.	10.266	CASE ASSY.	3957092
30.	10.266	WASHER	4416740
31.	10.267	ESCUTCHEON	3957093
32.	9.789	OUTLET—Lower R.H.	3967958
33.	8.900	SCREW (8–32 x 3/8)	
34.	9.709	BEZEL	3972040
35.	9.709	HOUSING	3972036
36.	9.709	KNOB ASSY.	3972037
37.	RADIO	KNOB ASSY.	3954238
38.	RADIO	WASHER—Special	3961507
39.	RADIO	SPACER	3954240
40.	RADIO	NUT (7/16–28)	7279805
41.	RADIO	KNOB	3954239
42.	8.977	SCREW (8–18 x 1/2)	
43.	12.009	ASH TRAY ASSY.	3965411
44.	2.486	ROD ASSY.	3954210
45.	2.487	NUT	3961597
46.	8.921	NUT (8–18)	
47.	8.977	SCREW ASSY.	
48.	9.789	OUTLET—Lower L.H.	3967957
49.	8.977	SCREW ASSY. (8–18 x 7/8)	
50.	6.518	COVER	3965459
51.	10.163	SWITCH ASSY.—W/S Wiper	1993464
52.	8.977	SCREW (18 x 3/8)	
53.	2.485	SWITCH ASSY.	1995173
54.	RADIO	RECEIVER	993882
	RADIO	RECEIVER AM/FM	993832
55.	N.S.S.	INSTRUMENT CLUSTER	
	9.748	LENS	6492175
	9.746	BEZEL	6492167
	9.746	COVER	6492178
	9.761	HEAD ASSY.	6492193
	3.108	FUEL GUAGE & BACK PLATE ASSY.	6431324
*		FILTER	
56.	8.977	SCREW (8 - 18 x 5/8)	

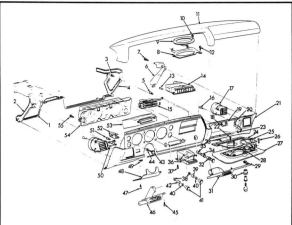

1970-72 MONTE CARLO, S.S. INSTRUMENT PANEL

AND INSTRUMENT GAUGES—EXPLODED

1.	N.S.	REINFORCEMENT ASSY., Lower	
		(Part of 3977631)	
2.	N.S.	REINFORCEMENT ASSY., L.H.	
		(Part of 3977631)	
3.	8.977	SCREW ASSY.	
4.	10.230	REINFORCEMENT ASSY. Ctr....	3957098
5.	8.977	SCREW	
6.	10.230	REINFORCEMENT ASSY.	3957070
7.	8.977	SCREW (10—16 x 5/8)	
8.	RADIO	BRACKET Ctr.	3961582
9.	RADIO	SPEAKER ASSY Ctr...........	7312681
10.	8.977	SCREW (8—18 x 3/8)	
11.	14.655	PAD Inst. Panel	
12.	8.977	SCREW (10—16 x 1/2)	
13.	8.977	SCREW	
14.	9.262	AIR CONDITION Ctr.	3963757
15.	8.849	CONTROL ASSY.	3963700
16.	8.900	SCREW (10—24 x 3/4)	
17.	9.262	OUTLET ASSY	3957085-86
18.	8.977	SCREW	
19.	10.268	STRIKER	3980365
20.	10.263	BUMPER Stop	3820023
21.	10.230	INSTRUMENT PANEL*	
		*NOTE Wood Graining not Serviced Separately.	
22.	8.977	SCREW	
23.	8.915	NUT ASSY.	
24.	10.261	DOOR Inner	3957091
25.	10.268	STOP-Door	3957095
26.	8.977	SCREW (8—8 x 3/8)	
27.	10.261	DOOR Outer	3957090
28.	10.266	CASE ASSY.	3957092
29.	10.266	WASHER	4416740
30.	10.267	ESCUTCHEON	3957093
31.	9.262	OUTLET Lower R.H.	3967958
32.	*	KNOB ASSY.	
33.	8.900	SCREW (8—32 x 3/8)	
34.	9.709	HOUSING	3986869
35.	9.709	BEZEL	3972040
36.	12.009	ASH TRAY ASSY.............	3965457
37.	8.977	SCREW (8—18 x 1/2)	
38.	RADIO	NUT (7/16—28)	7279805
39.	RADIO	SPACER	3973629
40.	RADIO	WASHER Special	3961507
41.	RADIO	KNOB ASSY	3954238
42.	RADIO	KNOB	3973628
43.	2.486	ROD ASSY	3954210
44.	2.487	NUT	3919021
45.	8.977	SCREW ASSY.	
46.	9.262	OUTLET Lower L.H.	3967957
47.	8.977	SCREW (8—18 x 7/8)	
48.	6.518	COVER	3965451
49.	8.921	NUT (8—18)	
50.	10.163	SWITCH ASSY.	1993464
51.	8.977	SCREW (18 x 3/8)	
52.	2.485	SWITCH ASSY.	1995183
53.	RADIO	RECEIVER	993882
	RADIO.	RECEIVER AM/FM	993832
54.	N.S.S.	CLUSTER	
55.	9.260	SCREW ASSY (8—18 x 1/2)	

*Removed From Service

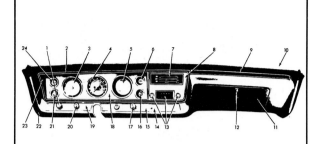

1967 PASS. INSTRUMENT PANEL

1.	2.486	ROD ASSY.
2.	9.743	BEZEL
3.	3.108	GAUGE
4.	9.761	HEAD ASSY.
5.	9.772	CLOCK
6.	9.750	LENS
7.	8.852	CONTROL ASSY.
8.	10.252	PLATE
9.	10.252	PLATE
10.	14.655	PAD ASSY.
11.	10.261	DOOR
12.	10.266	LOCK ASSY.
13.	9.650	RADIO
14.	10.252	PLATE ASSY.
15.	10.252	PLATE ASSY.
16.	1.803	GAUGE
17.	9.709	LIGHTER ASSY.
18.	9.750	LENS
19.	10.252	PLATE ASSY.
20.	10.164	KNOB
21.	1.148	GAUGE ASSY.
22.	10.230	PANEL
23.	9.747	RETAINER
24.	9.750	LENS

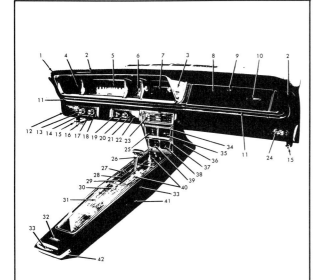

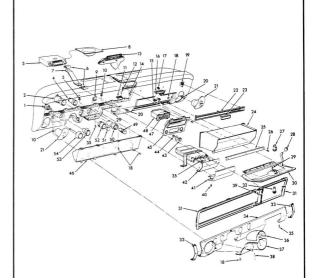

1966 PASS.–INSTRUMENT PANEL
AND CONSOLE (TYPICAL)

1. 14.655 PAD ASSY.
2. 9.743 CONSOLE ASSY.
3. 9.746 BEZEL
4. 3.108 GAUGE ASSY. (GAS)
5. 9.761 HEAD ASSY.
6. 9.772 CLOCK
7. 9.650 RADIO
8. 10.261 DOOR
9. 10.266 LOCK ASSY.
10. 10.261 EMBLEM
11. 10.252 MOULDING
12. 14.655 PAD ASSY.–L.H.
13. 2.486 ROD ASSY.
14. 2.487 BEZEL
15. 9.787 ROD
16. 4.591 LEVER ASSY.
17. 10.164 KNOB
18. 2.487 ESCUTCHEON
19. 2.188 SWITCH
20. 9.709 LIGHTER UNIT
21. 2.198 ESCUTCHEON
22. 14.655 PAD ASSY.–CTR.
23. 8.852 CONTROL ASSY.
24. 14.655 PAD ASSY.
25. 2.515 GAUGE ASSY.
26. 4.006 LEVER ASSY.
27. 4.020 DIAL ASSY.
28. 10.242 BEZEL ASSY., L.H.
29. 10.242 BEZEL ASSY., R.H.
30. 10.266 CASE ASSY.
31. 10.242 DOOR ASSY.
32. 10.261 EMBLEM
33. N.S. COMPARTMENT ASSY.
34. 9.746 HOUSING ASSY.
35. 9.755 VACUUM GAUGE
36. 10.240 CARRIER
37. 9.746 HOUSING ASSY.
38. 1.803 GAUGE
39. 1.148 GAUGE
40. 10.240 PLATE ASSY.
41. N.S. COMPARTMENT ASSY., LOWER
42. 10.275 LENS ASSY.

1968 PASSENGER
INSTRUMENT PANEL–EXPLODED

1. 10.163 SWITCH
2. 2.188 SWITCH ASSY.
3.   RADIO RECEIVER
4. 9.709 RETAINER
5. 9.744 NUT
6. 8.921 "U" NUT (#10–16)
7.   RADIO BRACKET
8.   RADIO SPEAKER ASSY.
9. 8.921 "U" NUT (#8–18)
10. 9.744 NUT
11. 9.744 CLIP
12. 8.977 SCREW (#8–18 x 3/8)
13. 9.779 OUTLET ASSY.
14. 8.977 SCREW (#10–16 x 1-1/4)
15. 10.268 STRIKER
16. N.L. RETAINER
17. 8.921 "J" NUT (#8–18)
18. 8.977 SCREW (#8–18 x 3/4)
19. 8.921 NUT (5/32)
20. 10.263 BUMPER
21. 9.262 BEZEL
22. 10.252 PLATE ASSY.
23. 10.252 PLATE
24. 10.260 COMPARTMENT ASSY.
25. 10.252 MOULDING
26. 8.977 SCREW (#10–16 x 5/8)
27. 10.266 CASE ASSY.
28. 10.263 BUMPER
29. 8.977 SCREW (#10–16 x 1/2)
30. 10.261 DOOR ASSY.
31. 9.743 BEZEL
32. 10.266 CYLINDER
33. 10.230 EXTENSION
34. 10.252 MOULDING
35. 8.977 SCREW (#8–18 x 1/2)
36. 6.518 COVER–Upper
37. 6.518 COVER–Lower
38. 8.977 SCREW (#8–18 x 5/8)
39. 8.977 SCREW (#8–18 x 1)
40. 8.967 RIVET (3/16 x 1/4)
41. 12.009 PLATE ASSY.
42. 12.009 TRAY and RETAINER ASSY.
43.   RADIO KNOB ASSY.
44.   RADIO NUT (7/16)
45. 10.252 PLATE
46. N.L. CLUSTER
47. 8.977 SCREW (#10–16 x 5/8)
48. 8.849 CONTROL ASSY.
49. 9.709 KNOB
50. 9.709 HOUSING
51. 2.188 CYLINDER ASSY.
52. 2.198 BEZEL
53. 10.164 KNOB
54. 2.486 ROD

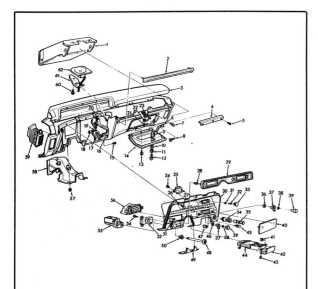

1969-70 PASSENGER INSTRUMENT PANEL—EXPLODED

1.	10.260	COMPARTMENT ASM.	3939657
2.	10.252	MOLDING	
3.	14.655	PAD ASM.	
4.	10.252	MOULDING	3913692
5.	8.977	SCREW (#10—16 x 1/2)	
6.	10.263	STOP BUMPER	4566397
7.	10.263	BUMPER	3765243
8.	8.977	SCREW (#8—18 x 3/4)	
9.	10.266	CASE ASM.	3934137
10.	10.266	WASHER	4416740
11.	10.267	ESCUTCHEON	3922831
12.	10.266	CYLINDER	
13.	8.977	SCREW (#10—16 x 5/8)	
16.	N.L.	BRACKET	
17.	RADIO BRACKET, Radio Receiver		
18.	8.921	"U" NUT (#10—16)	
19.	8.977	SCREW (#10—16 x 5/8)	
20.	8.977	SCREW	
21.	8.977	SCREW ASM. (#8—18 x 3/4)	
22.	10.268	STRIKER	3935997
23.	8.921	"J" NUT (#8—18 x 3/8)	
24.	8.977	SCREW (6 - 20 x 3/8)	
25.	9.772	CLOCK ASM. (16600)	993587
26.	8.929	WASHER (5/16 x 3/4 x 1/16)	
27.	8.977	SCREW (#10—16 x 3/4)	
28.	N.L.	CLIP	
29.	10.252	TRIM PLATE ASM.	
30.	N.L.	CLUSTER ASM.	
31.	9.772	KNOB	3794017
32.	*	NUT	
33.	N.L.	PLUG	
34.	9.709	HOUSING ASM.	
35.	9.709	HEATING UNIT & KNOB ASM.	
36.	RADIO RETAINER		
37.	RADIO KNOB		
38.	RADIO SPRING WASHER		
39.	RADIO KNOB ASM.		
40.	10.256	COVER (15000)	
41.	8.977	SCREW (#8—18 x 1/2)	
42.	12.009	PLATE ASM.	
43.	8.967	RIVET (3/16 x 1/4)	
44.	12.009	ASH TRAY & RETAINER ASM.	3935987
45.	12.009	BUMPER	3935946
46.	RADIO NUT		
47.	9.709	RETAINER	
48.	2.486	ROD ASM.	3937643
49.	6.518	COVER	3950015
50.	2.487	NUT ASM.	3919021
51.	8.977	SCREW (#8—18 x 9/16)	
52.	10.163	SWITCH ASM.	1993463
53.	N.L.	STRAP—GROUND	
54.	8.977	SCREW (#6—20 x 3/8)	
55.	2.485	SWITCH ASM.	1995165
56.	8.849	CONTROL ASM.	3937124
57.	8.917	NUT (3/8—16)	
58.	4.634	BRACKET	3935983
59.	9.262	OUTLET ASM. L.H.	
60.	8.977	SCREW (#10—16 x 3/4)	
61.	RADIO BRACKET		
62.	RADIO SPEAKER ASM.		

*NOTE: Removed from service

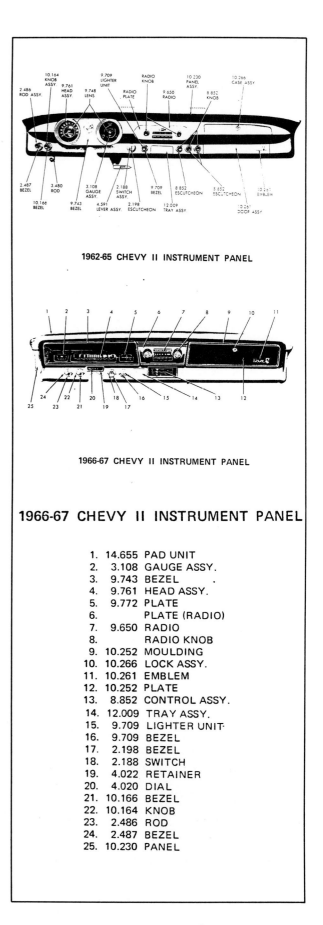

1962-65 CHEVY II INSTRUMENT PANEL

1966-67 CHEVY II INSTRUMENT PANEL

1966-67 CHEVY II INSTRUMENT PANEL

1.	14.655	PAD UNIT
2.	3.108	GAUGE ASSY.
3.	9.743	BEZEL
4.	9.761	HEAD ASSY.
5.	9.772	PLATE
6.		PLATE (RADIO)
7.	9.650	RADIO
8.		RADIO KNOB
9.	10.252	MOULDING
10.	10.266	LOCK ASSY.
11.	10.261	EMBLEM
12.	10.252	PLATE
13.	8.852	CONTROL ASSY.
14.	12.009	TRAY ASSY.
15.	9.709	LIGHTER UNIT
16.	9.709	BEZEL
17.	2.198	BEZEL
18.	2.188	SWITCH
19.	4.022	RETAINER
20.	4.020	DIAL
21.	10.166	BEZEL
22.	10.164	KNOB
23.	2.486	ROD
24.	2.487	BEZEL
25.	10.230	PANEL

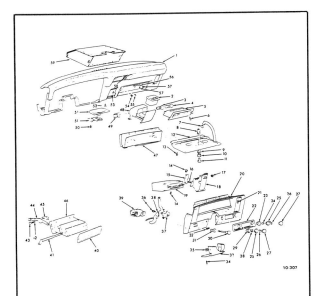

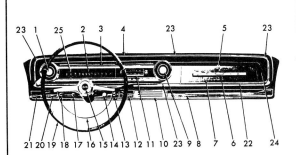

1969-72 CHEVY II INSTRUMENT PANEL—EXPLODED

1.	14.655	PAD ASM.	
2.	12.009	ASH TRAY ASSY...............	3972005
3.	9.709	HOUSING ASSY.	
4.	9.709	KNOB ASSY.	
5.	9.262	CENTER OUTLET	
6.	8.977	SCREW ASM. (#8—18 x 5/8)	
7.	10.263	BUMPER	4566397
8.	10.266	CASE ASM.	3934137
9.	10.266	WASHER	4416740
10.	10.267	ESCUTCHEON	3922831
11.	10.266	CYLINDER	
12.	10.261	DOOR ASM.	3991755
13.	8.977	SCREW ASM. (#10—16 x 3/4)	
14.	8.921	"U" NUT (#10/16)	
15.	*	BRACKET	
16.	8.977	SCREW ASM. (#10—16 x 1/2)	
17.	8.921	NUT (#8—18)	
18.	8.849	CONTROL ASM.	3984626
19.	RADIO RECEIVER ASM.		
20.	9.743	CARRIER	
21.	8.977	SCREW (#8—18 x 3/4)	
22.	RADIO BEZEL		
23.	RADIO SPACER		
24.	RADIO RETAINER		
25.	RADIO KNOB		
26.	RADIO WASHER		
27.	RADIO KNOB		
28.	RADIO NUT		
29.	RADIO SPACER		
30.	2.486	ROD ASM.	3986886
31.	2.487	NUT ASM.	3919021
32.	8.977	SCREW ASM. (#8—18 x 3/4)	
33.	6.518	COVER	3935940
34.	8.977	SCREW ASM. (#8—18 x 3/4)	
35.	8.921	NUT (#8—18)	
36.	8.977	SCREW (#8—18 x 3/8)	
37.	10.163	SWITCH ASM.	1993464
38.	*	STRAP	
39.	2.485	SWITCH ASM.	1995179
40.	9.262	VALVE	3940252
41.	9.262	SHAFT ASM.	3940253
42.	4.312	WASHER	3731921
43.	8.977	SCREW (#10—16 x 3/4)	
44.	9.262	LEVER	3940255
45.	9.262	SPRING	3955903
46.	9.262	CENTER OUTLET	
47.	N.L.	INSTRUMENT CLUSTER	
48.	12.009	TRAY & RETAINER ASM.	3965143
49.	9.709	RETAINER	3710839
50.	RADIO SCREW		9416223
51.	RADIO SPEAKER ASM.		
52.	8.977	SCREW (#8—18 x 1/1)	
53.	8.977	SCREW	
54.	12.009	BUMPER	3948518
55.	10.263	BUMPER	3765243
56.	10.268	STRIKER	3984446
57.	8.977	SCREW ASM. (#10—16 x 5/8)	
58.	8.921	"U" NUT (#8—15)	
59.	10.260	COMPARTMENT ASM.	3939609

*Removed From Service

1965 PASSENGER INSTRUMENT PANEL—TYPICAL

1.	1.148	GAUGE
2.	9.761	HEAD ASSY.
3.	9.743	HOUSING
4.	10.230	PANEL
5.	10.266	LOCK ASSY.
6.	10.252	MOULDING
7.	10.261	DOOR
8.	10.252	PLATE ASSY.
9.	9.772	CLOCK
10.	8.852	CONTROL ASSY.
11.	9.650	RADIO
12.	12.009	TRAY ASSY.
13.	9.709	LIGHTER UNIT
14.	2.188	SWITCH
15.	2.820	CAP
16.	2.830	RING
17.	10.164	KNOB
18.	2.486	ROD ASSY.
19.	6.513	WHEEL ASSY.
20.	2.897	LEVER
21.	10.252	PANEL ASSY.
22.	10.261	MOULDING
23.	10.252	MOULDING
24.	9.743	CONSOLE ASSY.
25.	9.748	LENS

Chapter 16

Seats

Seat Adjuster Rail

Biggest factors to watch for are seat type, model usage, and position. Those outer rails from bucket seats on the driver's side and the passenger's side of the car will not interchange. However, in most cases the inner rails will. Bench seats and bucket seats each used a different set of rails and will not interchange. The good news is that rails are a GM part and can be found in a variety of GM makes and models.

On the charts, seats are manually adjusted unless otherwise noted. For example, "Bench" refers to the standard, manually adjusted seat, while "Bench, six-way power" refers to electrically-controlled seats.

Model Identification

Custom seat belt for 1968.

Standard seat belt for 1968.

Standard seat belt in 1970.

Interchange

Interchange Number: 1
Seat Type: Bench
Part Number(s): RH, 7666873; LH, 7666874
Usage: 1967 Camaro; 1967 Pontiac Firebird; both with manual seats
Notes: The right-hand side rail is the same unit in the 1968 Camaro and 1968 Pontiac Firebird.

Interchange Number: 2
Seat Type: Bucket (driver's)
Part Number(s): Inner, 7659752; outer, 7644518
Usage: 1967 Camaro; 1967 Pontiac Firebird
Notes: Inner rail also used on both driver's and passenger's side in the 1967–69 Camaro and Pontiac Firebird.

Interchange Number: 3
Seat Type: Bucket (passenger's)
Part Number(s): Inner, 7659752; outer, 7644519
Usage: 1967 Camaro; 1967 Pontiac Firebird
Notes: Inner rail also used on both driver's and passenger's side in 1967–69 Camaro and Pontiac Firebird.

Interchange Number: 4
Seat Type: Bench
Part Number(s): RH, 7666873; LH, 8727195
Usage: 1968 Camaro; 1968 Pontiac Firebird
Notes: Right-hand side rail also used in 1967 Camaro and Pontiac Firebird.

Custom seat belt in 1970.

Interchange Number: 5
Seat Type: Bucket (driver's)
Part Number(s): Inner, 7659752; outer, 8727193
Usage: 1968–69 Camaro; 1968–69 Pontiac Firebird
Notes: Inner rail also used on both driver's and passenger's side in 1967–69 Camaro and Pontiac Firebird.

Interchange Number: 6
Seat Type: Bucket (passenger's)
Part Number(s): Inner, 7659752; outer, 8727194
Usage: 1967 Camaro; 1967 Pontiac Firebird
Notes: Inner rail also used on both driver's and passenger's side in 1967–69 Camaro and Pontiac Firebird.

Interchange Number: 7
Seat Type: Bucket (driver')
Part Number(s): Inner, 9809496; outer, 9809495
Usage: 1970 Camaro; 1970 Pontiac Firebird
Notes: Inner rail also used on both driver's and passenger's side in 1970 Camaro and Pontiac Firebird.

Interchange Number: 8
Seat Type: Bench
Part Number(s): RH, 4411994; LH, 4411995
Usage: 1964–66 Chevelle (except El Camino or 1964–66 Chevelle SS); 1964–66 Buick Skylark; 1964–66 Olds Cutlass; 1964–66 Pontiac LeMans

Interchange Number: 9
Seat Type: Bucket (driver's)
Part Number(s): Inner, 4417896; outer, 7628330
Usage: 1964–65 Chevelle (except El Camino); 1964–65 Buick Skylark; 1964–65 Olds Cutlass; 1964–65 Pontiac LeMans
Notes: Inner rail also used on both driver's and passenger's side.

Interchange Number: 10
Seat Type: Bucket (passenger's)
Part Number(s): Inner, 4417896; outer, 7628329
Usage: 1964–65 Chevelle (except El Camino); 1964–65 Buick Skylark; 1964–65 Olds Cutlass; 1964–65 Pontiac LeMans
Notes: Inner rail also used on both driver's and passenger's side.

Interchange Number: 11
Seat Type: Bench
Part Number(s): RH, 4459308; LH, 7628331
Usage: 1964–66 El Camino
Notes: Left-hand rail was used on the outer rail of the driver's bucket seat in 1964–65 El Camino.

Interchange Number: 12
Seat Type: Bucket (driver's)
Part Number(s): Inner, 4459311; outer, 7628331
Usage: 1964–66 El Camino
Notes: Left-hand rail was used on the outer rail of the driver's side of the bench seat in 1964–66 El Camino. Inner rail was used on either driver's or passenger's side of 1964–66 El Camino with bucket seats.

Interchange Number: 13
Seat Type: Bucket (driver's)
Part Number(s): Inner, 4459311; outer, 4459310
Usage: 1964–66 El Camino
Notes: Inner rail was used on either driver's or passenger's side of 1964–66 El Camino with bucket seats.

Interchange Number: 14
Seat Type: Bench
Usage: 1967–72 Chevelle (except 1967 El Camino) 1967–72 Buick Skylark; 1967–72 Olds Cutlass; 1967–72 Pontiac LeMans
Notes: Two sets used. Early 1967 models used part numbers: RH, 7659761; LH, 7659762. Late 1967–72 models used RH, 7712007; and LH, 7779428. The difference is a stop screw in the upper channel of the early style.

Interchange Number: 15
Seat Type: Bucket (driver's)
Part Number(s): 4547730 Inner* 7779417 Outer
Usage: 1967–71 Chevelle (except 1967 El Camino) 1967–71 Buick Skylark; 1967–71 Olds Cutlass; 1967–71 Pontiac LeMans; 1968–72 El Camino.
Notes: Inner rail also used on passenger's side.

Interchange Number: 16
Seat Type: Bucket (passenger's)
Part Number(s): Inner, 4547730; outer, 8768007
Usage: 1967–71 Chevelle (except 1967 El Camino); 1967–71 Buick Skylark; 1967–71 Olds Cutlass; 1967–71 Pontiac LeMans; 1968–72 El Camino
Notes: Inner rail also used on passenger's side.

Interchange Number: 17
Seat Type: Bench
Part Number(s): RH, 4750795; LH, 4750796
Usage: 1959 to early 1960 full-size Chevrolet, Pontiac, or Oldsmobile
Notes: Use with assist spring.

Interchange Number: 18
Seat Type: Bench
Part Number(s): RH, 4803427; LH, 4803428
Usage: Late 1960 full-size Chevrolet, Pontiac, or Oldsmobile
Notes: Use without assist spring

Interchange Number: 19
Seat Type: Bench
Part Number(s): RH, 4810038; LH, 4810039
Usage: 1961–62 full-size Chevrolet
Notes: Other GM makes will not fit.

Interchange Number: 20
Seat Type: Bucket (driver's)
Part Number(s): Inner, 4846133; outer, 4810039
Usage: 1962–64 full-size Chevrolet

Interchange Number: 21
Seat Type: Bucket (passenger's)
Part Number(s): Inner, 4846132; outer, 4810034
Usage: 1962–64 full-size Chevrolet

Interchange Number: 22
Seat Type: Bench
Part Number(s): RH, 4880986; LH, 4880987
Usage: 1963–64 full-size Chevrolet

Interchange Number: 23
Seat Type: Bench seat
Part Number(s): RH, 7636704; LH, 4477531
Usage: 1965–66 full-size Chevrolet; 1965–66 full-size Oldsmobile (except Starfire); 1965–66 Pontiac Bonneville

Interchange Number: 24
Seat Type: Bucket (driver's)
Part Number(s): Inner, 4471364; outer, 4471362
Usage: 1965 full-size Chevrolet, Pontiac, Oldsmobile, or Buick
Notes: Inner rails also used on passenger's side.

Interchange Number: 25
Seat Type: Bucket (passenger's)
Part Number(s): Inner, 4471364; outer, 4471363
Usage: 1965 full-size Chevrolet, Pontiac, Oldsmobile, or Buick
Notes: Inner rails also used on passenger's side.

Interchange Number: 26
Seat Type: Bucket (driver's)
Part Number(s): Inner, 7659782; outer, 4541733
Usage: 1966 full-size Chevrolet, Pontiac, Oldsmobile, or Buick
Notes: Inner rail used on both driver's and passenger's side from 1966 to 1969 models.

Interchange Number: 27
Seat Type: Bucket (passenger's)
Part Number(s): Inner, 7659782; outer, 4541734
Usage: 1966 full-size Chevrolet, Pontiac, Oldsmobile, or Buick
Notes: Inner rail used on both driver's and passenger's side from 1966 to 1969 models.

Interchange Number: 28
Seat Type: Bench
Part Number(s): RH, 7659790; LH, 8768006
Usage: 1967–70 full-size Chevrolet, Pontiac, Oldsmobile, or Buick
Notes: Will not fit Strato back type bench seats.

Interchange Number: 29
Seat Type: Bucket (driver's)
Part Number(s): Inner, 7659780; outer, 7659779
Usage: 1967–69 full-size Chevrolet, Pontiac, Oldsmobile, or Buick

Interchange Number: 30
Seat Type: Bucket (passenger's)
Part Number(s): Inner, 7659781; outer, 7659782
Usage: 1967–69 full-size Chevrolet, Pontiac, Oldsmobile, or Buick

Interchange Number: 31
Seat Type: Bucket (driver's)
Part Number(s): Inner, 7659782; outer, 7779415
Usage: 1968–69 full-size Chevrolet, all except four-way seat models. Strato bucket seats.

Interchange Number: 32
Seat Type: Bucket (passenger's)
Part Number(s): Inner, 7659782; outer, 7779416
Usage: 1968–69 full-size Chevrolet, all except four-way seat models. Strato bucket seats.

Interchange Number: 33
Seat Type: Bucket (driver's)
Part Number(s): Inner, 7659782; outer, 7779228
Usage: 1967–69 full-size Chevrolet with four-way manual seats

Interchange Number: 34
Seat Type: Bucket (passenger's)
Part Number(s): Inner, 7659782; outer, 8768008
Usage: 1967–69 full-size Chevrolet with four-way manual seats

Interchange Number: 35
Seat Type: Bench
Part Number(s): RH, 7779422; LH, 7779423
Usage: 1968–69 full-size Chevrolet with 6-way manual seats.

Interchange Number: 36
Seat Type: Bench
Part Number(s): RH, 4866770; LH, 4452392
Usage: 1962–64 Chevy II, all except Nova SS or with four-speed
Notes: Right hand side rail also used in 1965 models.

Interchange Number: 37
Seat Type: Bench
Part Number(s): RH, 4866770; LH, 4487827
Usage: 1965 Chevy II, all except Nova SS or with four-speed
Notes: Right-hand side rail also used in 1962–64 models.

Interchange Number: 38
Seat Type: Bucket (driver's)
Part Number(s): Inner, 4881998; outer, 4881996
Usage: 1962–63 Chevy II

Interchange Number: 39
Seat Type: Bucket (passenger's)
Part Number(s): Inner, 4881997; outer, 4881995
Usage: 1962–63 Chevy II

Interchange Number: 40
Seat Type: Bucket (driver's)
Part Number(s): Inner, 4881998; outer, 4477185
Usage: 1964 Chevy II

Interchange Number: 41
Seat Type: Bucket (passenger)
Part Number(s): Inner, 4881997; outer, 4477184
Usage: 1964 Chevy II

Interchange Number: 42
Seat Type: Bucket (driver's)
Part Number(s): Inner, 4485918; outer, 4487831
Usage: 1965 Chevy II
Notes: Inner rail used on both driver's and passenger's side.

Interchange Number: 43

Seat Type: Bucket (passenger's)
Part Number(s): Inner, 4485918; outer, 4477184
Usage: 1965 Chevy II
Notes: Inner rail used on both driver's and passenger's side. Outer rail used on 1964–65 Chevy II.

Interchange Number: 44

Seat Type: Bench
Part Number(s): RH, 7582042; LH, 7582044
Usage: 1966 Chevy II

Interchange Number: 45

Seat Type: Bench
Part Number(s): RH, 7659753; LH, 7659754
Usage: 1967 Chevy II

Interchange Number: 46

Seat Type: Bucket (driver's)
Part Number(s): Inner, 7582811; outer, 7659783
Usage: 1966–67 Chevy II
Notes: Inner rail used on both driver's and passenger's side.

Interchange Number: 47

Seat Type: Bucket (passenger's)
Part Number(s): Inner, 7582811; outer, 7582810
Usage: 1966 Chevy II
Notes: Inner rail used on both driver's and passenger's side in 1966–67 models.

Interchange Number: 48

Seat Type: Bucket (passenger's)
Part Number(s): Inner, 7582811; outer, 7659784
Usage: 1967 Chevy II
Notes: Inner rail used on both driver's and passenger's side in 1966–67 models.

Interchange Number: 49

Seat Type: Bench
Part Number(s): RH, 7723851; LH, 7779402
Usage: 1968–72 Nova; 1971–72 Pontiac Ventura II

Interchange Number: 50

Seat Type: Bucket (driver's)
Part Number(s): Inner, 7735486; outer, 7779404
Usage: 1968–71 Nova; 1971 Pontiac Ventura II
Notes: Inner rail used on both driver's and passenger's side.

Interchange Number: 51

Seat Type: Bucket (passenger's)
Part Number(s): Inner, 7735486; outer, 8768012
Usage: 1968–71 Nova; 1971 Pontiac Ventura II
Notes: Inner rail used on both driver's and passenger's side.

Interchange Number: 52

Seat Type: Bucket (passenger's)
Part Number(s): Inner, 9809496; outer, 9809494
Usage: 1970 Camaro; 1970 Pontiac Firebird
Notes: Inner rail used on both driver's and passenger's side. 1971–75 rails will interchange if 1971–75 seats are used.

Seat type will affect headrest usage.

Interchange Number: 53

Seat Type: Bench
Part Number(s): RH, 7741305; LH, 7741306
Usage: 1968–70 full-size Chevrolet, Pontiac, Oldsmobile, or Buick; all with 6-way power seats

Front Seat Frame

The interchange for this component is the bare seat frame itself. Stripped of its upholstery and foam or cotton padding, the interchange is larger than you may think.

When buying a used seat, make sure the frame and springs are in good condition. Turn the seat over carefully and look for signs of heavy wear, such as drooping springs. The frame itself should be solid and not broken or repaired. Next, check the back hinges to make sure they are in good shape. Upholstery and stuffing should be the least of your concern, as these are easily replaced. Seats are sometimes sold with the adjustment rail, so you may want to cross-reference that section in this chapter.

Model Identification

Camaro	Interchange Number
1967–68	
Bench	
Cushion	1
Backrest	17
Bucket	
Cushion	2
Backrest	18
1969–70	
Bench (1969)	
Cushion	1
Backrest	17
Bucket	
Cushion	3
Backrest	19

Chevelle	Interchange Number
1964–66	
Bench	
Cushion	4
Backrest	20
Bucket	
Cushion	39
Backrest	21

Interchange

Interchange Number: 1
  Seat Type: Bench (cushion)
  Usage: 1967–68 Pontiac Firebird;
    1967–69 Camaro

Interchange Number: 2
  Seat Type: Bucket (cushion)
  Usage: 1967–68 Camaro; 1967–68 Pontiac Firebird

Interchange Number: 3
  Seat Type: Bucket (cushion)
  Usage: 1969–70 Camaro; 1969–70 Pontiac Firebird
  Notes: Low back style.

Interchange Number: 4
  Seat Type: Bench (cushion)
  Usage: 1964–67 Chevelle; 1964–67 Buick Skylark;
    1964–66 Olds Cutlass; 1964–67 Pontiac LeMans; all
    two-door

Interchange Number: 5
  Seat Type: Bucket (cushion)
  Part Number(s): 7788578
  Usage: 1967–68 Chevelle; 1967–68 Buick Skylark;
    1967–68 Olds Cutlass; 1967–68 Pontiac LeMans; all
    two-door

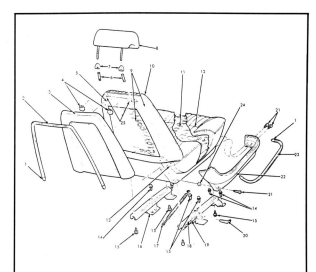

1966-68 ASTRO BUCKET SEAT AND HEAD RESTRAINT DETAILS

1. 14.818 CAP, Seat Side & Bk. Panel End
2. 13.818 MOLDING, Seat Back Panel Fnshg.
3. 11.358 PANEL, Seat Back Panel
4. 11.368 SUPPORT, Seat Back Panel Upper
5. 11.376 GUIDE ASSY., Seat Back Headrest Supt.
6. 11.376 TUBE, Seat Back Headrest Supt. Guide
7. 11.376 ESCN., Seat Back Headrest Pnl. Supt.
8. 14.924 HEADREST ASSY., Seat Back
9. 11.373 SPRING & FRAME, Seat Back
10. 14.800 COVER, Seat Back
11. 11.419 SPRING & FRAME, Seat Cushion
12. 14.880 COVER, Seat Cushion
13. 11.368 SUPPORT, Seat Side Pnl. Rear Outer
14. 11.561 BOLT, Seat Adjuster to Floor Pan
15. 11.561 BOLT, Seat Adjuster to Side Bar
16. 11.561 ADJUSTER ASSY., Seat Inner Manual
17. 11.581 SPRING, Seat Adjuster Assist
18. 11.561 ADJUSTER ASSY., Seat Outer Manual
19. 11.581 SPRING, Seat Outer Adjuster Lock Bar
20. 11.588 KNOB, Seat Adjuster
21. N.L. SCREW, Seat Side Panel
22. 11.362 PANEL, Seat Side
23. 14.818 MOLDING, Seat Side Panel Fnshg.
24. 11.362 SPACER, Seat Side Panel
25. 11.376 SPRING, Seat Back Headrest Stop

Interchange Number: 6
Seat Type: Bucket (cushion)
Part Number(s): 9865953
Usage: 1969 full-size Chevrolet; 1969–72 Chevelle; 1969–72 Buick Skylark; 1969–72 Olds Cutlass; 1969–72 Pontiac LeMans; 1969–72 Nova; 1971–72 Pontiac Ventura II; all two-door; 1969–72 El Camino; 1971–72 GMC Sprint

Interchange Number: 7
Seat Type: Bench (cushion)
Part Number(s): 9865955
Usage: 1969–72 Chevelle; 1969–72 Buick Skylark; 1969–72 Olds Cutlass; 1969–72 Pontiac LeMans; all two-door

Interchange Number: 8
Seat Type: Bench (cushion)
Usage: 1959–60 full-size Chevrolet, Pontiac, Oldsmobile, or Buick; all two-door

Interchange Number: 9
Seat Type: Bench (cushion)
Usage: 1961–62 full-size Chevrolet, Pontiac, Oldsmobile, or Buick; all two-door

Interchange Number: 10
Seat Type: Bench (cushion)
Usage: 1962–65 Chevy II; 1963–64 full-size Chevrolet, Pontiac, Oldsmobile, or Buick

Interchange Number: 11
Seat Type: Bucket (cushion)
Usage: 1962–64 full-size Chevrolet, Pontiac, Oldsmobile, or Buick; 1962–64 ; all two-door
Notes: Driver's and passenger's side do not interchange.

Interchange Number: 12
Seat Type: Bench (cushion)
Part Number(s): 9812274 and 9812275
Usage: 1965–70 full-size Chevrolet, Pontiac, Oldsmobile, or Buick; all two-door
Notes: Originally Biscayne and Bel Air used a width of 58 1/4 inches. The higher grade Impala used a 58 1/2 inch width. Impala cushion will fit Bel Air or Biscayne, but they will not fit Impala.

Interchange Number: 13
Seat Type: Bench (cushion and backrest)
Usage: 1962–65 Chevy II two-door

Interchange Number: 14
Seat Type: Bench (cushion and backrest)
Usage: 1966–67 Chevy II two-door

Interchange Number: 15
Seat Type: Bucket (cushion and backrest)
Usage: 1966–67 Chevy II two-door

Interchange Number: 16
Seat Type: Bench (cushion)
Part Number(s): 98070775
Usage: 1968–72 Nova; 1971–72 Pontiac Ventura II; both two-door

Interchange Number: 17
Seat Type: Bench (backrest)
Usage: 1967–69 Camaro; 1967–68 Pontiac Firebird

Interchange Number: 18
Seat Type: Bucket (backrest)
Usage: 1967–68 Camaro; 1967–68 Pontiac Firebird

Interchange Number: 19
Seat Type: Bucket (backrest)
Usage: 1969–70 Camaro; 1969–70 Pontiac Firebird
Notes: Low back type.

Interchange Number: 20
Seat Type: Bench (backrest)
Usage: 1964–67 Chevelle; 1964–67 Olds Cutlass; 1964–67 Pontiac LeMans; 1964–67 Buick Skylark; all two-door

Interchange Number: 21
Seat Type: Bucket (backrest)
Usage: 1964–66 Chevelle; 1964–66 Olds Cutlass; 1964–66 Pontiac LeMans; 1964–66 Buick Skylark; 1965–66 full-size Chevrolet; 1965–66 full-size Oldsmobile; 1965–66 full-size Pontiac; all two-door

Interchange Number: 22
Seat Type: Bench (backrest)
Usage: 1968 Chevelle; 1968 Olds Cutlass; 1968 Pontiac LeMans; 1968 Buick Skylark; all two-door
Notes: Two types of headrest, conventional and Strato. They will not interchange.

Interchange Number: 23
Seat Type: Bucket (backrest)
Part Number(s): Driver's, 7788605; passenger's, 7788601
Usage: 1968 Chevelle; 1968 Olds Cutlass; 1968 Pontiac LeMans; 1968 Buick Skylark; all two-door

Interchange Number: 24
Seat Type: Bench (backrest)
Part Number(s): Driver's, 9816999; passenger's, 9812322
Usage: 1969–70 Chevelle; 1969–70 Olds Cutlass; 1969–70 Pontiac LeMans; 1969–70 Buick Skylark; all two-door

Interchange Number: 25
Seat Type: Bucket (backrest)
Part Number(s): 9865958 (fits either side)
Usage: 1969–70 Chevelle; 1969–70 Olds Cutlass; 1969–70 Pontiac LeMans; 1969–70 Buick Skylark 1969–70 Nova; 1969 full-size Chevrolet; all two-door

Interchange Number: 26
Seat Type: Bench (backrest)
Usage: 1959–60 full-size Chevrolet, Pontiac, or Oldsmobile; all two-door

Interchange Number: 27
Seat Type: Bench (backrest)
Usage: 1961–62 full-size Chevrolet, Pontiac, or Oldsmobile; all two-door

Interchange Number: 28
Seat Type: Bench (backrest)
Usage: 1963–64 full-size Chevrolet, Pontiac, or Oldsmobile; all two-door

Interchange Number: 29
Seat Type: Bucket (backrest)
Usage: 1962–63 Chevy II; 1962–64 full-size Chevrolet, Pontiac, or Oldsmobile; all two-door

Interchange Number: 30
Seat Type: Bench (backrest)
Usage: 1965–66 full-size Chevrolet, Pontiac, or Oldsmobile; all two-door

Interchange Number: 31
Seat Type: Bench (backrest)
Part Number(s): Driver's, 7716543; passenger's, 7716542
Usage: 1967 full-size Chevrolet, Pontiac, or Oldsmobile; 1967 Chevelle

Interchange Number: 32
Seat Type: Bucket (backrest)
Part Number(s): Driver's, 7716543; passenger's, 7716542
Usage: 1967 full-size Chevrolet, Pontiac, or Oldsmobile; 1967 Chevelle; All two-door

Interchange Number: 33
Seat Type: Bench (backrest)
Part Number(s): Driver's, 7788649; passenger's, 7788648
Usage: 1968 full-size Chevrolet, Pontiac, or Oldsmobile; 1968 Chevelle; all two-door hardtop or sedan

Interchange Number: 34
Seat Type: Bench (backrest)
Part Number(s): Driver's, 8711181; passenger's, 8711180
Usage: 1968 full-size Chevrolet, Pontiac, or Oldsmobile; 1968 Chevelle; convertible only

Interchange Number: 35
Seat Type: Bucket (backrest)
Part Number(s): Driver's, 7788662; passenger's, 7788660
Usage: 1968 full-size Chevrolet, Pontiac, or Oldsmobile; all two-door

Interchange Number: 36
Seat Type: Bench (backrest)
Part Number(s): Driver's, 8777265; passenger's, 8777264
Usage: 1969 full-size Chevrolet, Pontiac, Oldsmobile, or Buick; all two-door

Interchange Number: 37
Seat Type: Bench (backrest)
Part Number(s): Driver's, 9812313; passenger's, 9812312
Usage: 1970 full-size Chevrolet, Pontiac, Oldsmobile, or Buick; all two-door

Interchange Number: 38
Seat Type: Bench (backrest)
Usage: 1968–72 Nova; 1971–72 Pontiac Ventura II; both two-door

Interchange Number: 39
Seat Type: Bucket (cushion)
Usage: 1964–66 Chevelle; 1964–66 Olds Cutlass; 1964–66 Pontiac LeMans; 1964–66 Buick Skylark; 1965–66 full-size Chevrolet; 1965–66 full-size Oldsmobile; 1965–66 full-size Pontiac; all two-door

Interchange Number: 40
Seat Type: Bucket (cushion)
Part Number(s): Driver's, 7788662; passenger's, 7788660
Usage: 1968 full-size Chevrolet, Pontiac, or Oldsmobile; all two-door

Rear Seat Frame

Again, the interchange involves the bare seat frame stripped of upholstery and stuffing. See the section on "Front Seat Frame" for suggestions when inspecting a used seat.

Interchange is for two-door models only. When swapping from another year or make, carefully measure the width and length of the frame and compare it to your car's interior to see if the interchange will properly fit. A frame that is 1/4 inch *too long* will fit, but one that is 1/4 inch *too short* should not be used.

Model Identification

Interchange

Interchange Number: 1
    Part Number(s): N/A (cushion)
    Usage: 1967–69 Camaro; 1967–69 Pontiac Firebird
    Notes: Hardtop and convertible differ. Convertible is narrower and won't fit a hardtop.

Interchange Number: 2
    Part Number(s): N/A (cushion)
    Usage: 1970–72 Camaro; 1970–72 Pontiac Firebird

Interchange Number: 3
    Part Number(s): N/A (cushion)
    Usage: 1964–67 Chevelle; 1964–67 Pontiac LeMans; 1964–67 Olds Cutlass; 1964–67 Buick Skylark
    Notes: Convertible differs; it is narrower than others.

Interchange Number: 4
    Part Number(s): 7788609 (cushion)
    Usage: 1968 Chevelle; 1968 Olds Cutlass; 1968 Buick Skylark; 1968 Pontiac LeMans; all two-door except convertible, or El Camino

Interchange Number: 5
    Part Number(s): 7788607 (cushion)
    Usage: 1968 Chevelle; 1968 Olds Cutlass; 1968 Buick Skylark; 1968 Pontiac LeMans; convertible only

Interchange Number: 6
Part Number(s): 9606478 (cushion)
Usage: 1969–72 Chevelle; 1969–72 Olds Cutlass; 1969–72 Buick Skylark; 1969–72 Pontiac LeMans; all two-door except convertible

Interchange Number: 7
Part Number(s): 9606479 (cushion)
Usage: 1969–72 Chevelle; 1969–72 Olds Cutlass; 1969–72 Buick Skylark; 1969–72 Pontiac LeMans; convertible only

Interchange Number: 8
Part Number(s): N/A (cushion)
Usage: 1959–60 full-size Chevrolet, Pontiac, or Oldsmobile; all two-door except convertible

Interchange Number: 9
Part Number(s): N/A (cushion)
Usage: 1959–60 full-size Chevrolet, Pontiac, or Oldsmobile; convertible only

Interchange Number: 10
Part Number(s): N/A (cushion)
Usage: 1961–62 full-size Chevrolet, Pontiac, or Oldsmobile; all two-door except convertible

Interchange Number: 11
Part Number(s): N/A (cushion)
Usage: 1961–62 full-size Chevrolet, Pontiac, or Oldsmobile; convertible only

Interchange Number: 12
Part Number(s): N/A (cushion)
Usage: 1963–64 full-size Chevrolet, Pontiac, or Oldsmobile; all two-door except convertible

Interchange Number: 13
Part Number(s): N/A (cushion)
Usage: 1963–64 full-size Chevrolet, Pontiac, or Oldsmobile; convertible only

Interchange Number: 14
Part Number(s): 7788663 (cushion)
Usage: 1965–68 full-size Chevrolet, Pontiac, or Oldsmobile; all two-door, including convertible

Interchange Number: 15
Part Number(s): 8777363 (cushion)
Usage: 1969–70 full-size Chevrolet, Pontiac, or Oldsmobile; all two-door including convertible
Notes: Impala Custom and Caprice used slightly different cushion. But Impala unit will fit. Caprice may fit Impala.

Interchange Number: 16
Part Number(s): N/A (cushion)
Usage: 1962–65 Chevy II two-door, except convertible

Interchange Number: 17
Part Number(s): N/A (cushion)
Usage: 1962–63 Chevy II convertible

Interchange Number: 18
Part Number N/A (cushion)
Usage: 1966–67 Chevy II two-door

Interchange Number: 19
Part Number(s): N/A (cushion)
Usage: 1968–69 Nova two-door
Notes: Interchange number 20 may fit.

Interchange Number: 20
Part Number(s): 9606477
Usage: 1970–72 Nova; 1971–72 Pontiac Ventura II; both two-door
Notes: May fit 1968–69 Nova.

Interchange Number: 21
Part Number(s): 8777334 (backrest)
Usage: 1967–69 Camaro with rear folding seat back; all bodystyles

Interchange Number: 22
Part Number(s): 8777298 (backrest)
Usage: 1967–69 Camaro without rear folding seat back; hardtop only

Interchange Number: 23
Part Number(s): 8777299 (backrest)
Usage: 1967–69 Camaro without rear folding seat back; convertible only

Interchange Number: 24
Part Number(s): 9865995 and 9865996
Usage: 1970 Camaro; 1970 Pontiac Firebird
Notes: Part number 9865996 used with Custom interior. Custom seat frame will fit cars without.

Interchange Number: 25
Part Number(s): N/A (backrest)
Usage: 1964–67 Chevelle; 1964–67 Pontiac LeMans; 1964–67 Olds Cutlass; 1964–67 Buick Skylark; convertible only

Interchange Number: 26
Part Number(s): N/A (backrest)
Usage: 1964–67 Chevelle; 1964–67 Pontiac LeMans; 1964–67 Olds Cutlass; 1964–67 Buick Skylark; all two-door, except convertible

Interchange Number: 27
Part Number(s): 7788613 (backrest)
Usage: 1968 Chevelle; 1968 Pontiac LeMans; 1968 Olds Cutlass; 1968 Buick Skylark; all two-door, except convertible

Interchange Number: 28
Part Number(s): 7788611 (backrest)
Usage: 1968 Chevelle; 1968 Pontiac LeMans; 1968 Olds Cutlass; 1968 Buick Skylark; convertible only

Interchange Number: 29
Part Number(s): 8777326 (backrest)
Usage: 1969 Chevelle; 1969 Pontiac LeMans; 1969 Olds Cutlass; 1969 Buick Skylark; all two-door, except convertible

Interchange Number: 30
Part Number(s): 8777312 (backrest)
Usage: 1969 Chevelle; 1969 Pontiac LeMans; 1969 Olds Cutlass; 1969 Buick Skylark; convertible only

Interchange Number: 31
Part Number(s): 9615771 (backrest)
Usage: 1970–72 Chevelle; 1970–72 Pontiac LeMans; 1970–72 Olds Cutlass; 1970–72 Buick Skylark; all two-door, except convertible

Interchange Number: 32
Part Number(s): 9865998 (backrest)
Usage: 1970–72 Chevelle; 1970–72 Pontiac LeMans; 1970–72 Olds Cutlass; 1970–72 Buick Skylark; convertible only

Interchange Number: 33
Part Number(s): N/A (backrest)
Usage: 1959–60 full-size Chevrolet, Pontiac, or Oldsmobile; all two-door, except convertible

Interchange Number: 34
Part Number(s): N/A (backrest)
Usage: 1959–60 full-size Chevrolet, Pontiac, or Oldsmobile; convertible only

Interchange Number: 35
Part Number(s): N/A (backrest)
Usage: 1961–62 full-size Chevrolet, Pontiac, or Oldsmobile; all two-door except convertible

Interchange Number: 36
Part Number(s): N/A (backrest)
Usage: 1961–62 full-size Chevrolet, Pontiac, or Oldsmobile; convertible only

Interchange Number: 37
Part Number(s): N/A (backrest)
Usage: 1963–64 full-size Chevrolet, Pontiac, or Oldsmobile; all two-door except convertible

Interchange Number: 38
Part Number(s): N/A (backrest)
Usage: 1963–64 full-size Chevrolet, Pontiac, or Oldsmobile; 1963–64 convertible only

Interchange Number: 39
Part Number(s): 7788671 (backrest)
Usage: 1965–68 full-size Chevrolet, Pontiac, or Oldsmobile; 1965–68 all two-door except convertible

Interchange Number: 40
Part Number(s): 7788673 (backrest)
Usage: 1965–67 full-size Chevrolet; 1965–68 full-size Oldsmobile; 1965–68 full-size Pontiac; convertible only

Interchange Number: 41
Part Number(s): 7788550 (backrest)
Usage: 1968 full-size Chevrolet convertible

Interchange Number: 42
Part Number(s): 8777294 (backrest)
Usage: 1969–70 full-size Chevrolet, Pontiac, or Oldsmobile; all two-door except convertible

Interchange Number: 43
Part Number(s): 8777323 (backrest)
Usage: 1969–70 full-size Chevrolet, Pontiac, or Oldsmobile; all two-door except convertible

Interchange Number: 44
Part Number(s): N/A (backrest)
Usage: 1962–65 Chevy II two-door, except convertible

Interchange Number: 45
Part Number(s): N/A (backrest)
Usage: 1962–63 Chevy II convertible

Interchange Number: 46
Part Number(s): N/A (backrest)
Usage: 1966–67 Chevy II two-door

Interchange Number: 47
Part Number(s): 9812432 (backrest)
Usage: 1968–72 Nova; 1971–72 Pontiac Ventura II; both two-door

Seatbelts

There is a large interchange for seatbelts, as they are a Fisher Body installed part and can be found in a variety of makes and models.

GM made two distinct types of seatbelts: the standard unit and the Custom belt, which usually has a bright buckle. Because the rear seat and front seats used two different sets of belts, they cannot be interchanged.

Seatbelts are color keyed to a car's interior. There is no color interchange in the charts, but you may use color as a guide to help you locate models and model years that used the same belts.

Model Identification

Interchange

Interchange Number: 1
Type: Standard
Usage: 1964–66 Chevelle; 1964–66 full-size Chevrolet, Pontiac, Oldsmobile, or Buick; 1964–66 Pontiac LeMans; 1964–66 Olds Cutlass; 1964–66 Buick Skylark; 1964–66 Chevy II

Interchange Number: 2
Type: Custom
Usage: 1965 Chevelle; 1965 full-size
Chevrolet, Pontiac, Oldsmobile, or Buick; 1965 Pontiac LeMans; 1965 Olds Cutlass; 1965 Buick Skylark; 1965 Chevy II

Interchange Number: 3
Type: Custom
Usage: 1966 Chevelle; 1966 full-size Chevrolet, Pontiac, Oldsmobile, or Buick; 1966 Pontiac LeMans; 1966 Olds Cutlass; 1966 Buick Skylark; 1965 Chevy II

Interchange Number: 4
Type: Standard
Usage: 1967 Chevelle; 1967 full-size Chevrolet, Pontiac, Oldsmobile, or Buick; 1967 Pontiac LeMans; 1967 Olds Cutlass; 1967 Buick Skylark; 1967 Chevy II

Interchange Number: 5
Type: Custom
Usage: 1967 Chevelle; 1967 full-size Chevrolet, Pontiac, Oldsmobile, or Buick; 1967 Pontiac LeMans; 1967 Olds Cutlass; 1967 Buick Skylark; 1967 Chevy II

Interchange Number: 6
Type: Standard
Usage: 1967 Camaro; 1967 Pontiac Firebird

Interchange Number: 7
Type: Custom
Usage: 1967 Camaro; 1967 Pontiac Firebird

Interchange Number: 8
Type: Standard
Usage: 1968 Chevelle; 1968 Pontiac LeMans; 1968 Olds Cutlass; 1968 Buick Skylark; 1968 Nova except Nova sedan

Interchange Number: 9
Type: Custom
Usage: 1968 Chevelle; 1968 Pontiac LeMans; 1968 Olds Cutlass; 1968 Buick Skylark; 1968 Nova except Nova sedan

Interchange Number: 10
Type: Standard
Usage: 1968 full-size Chevrolet, Pontiac, Oldsmobile, or Buick
Notes: Two-door hardtop and convertible each used a different set of belts. Two-door sedan used the same belts as the four-door sedan.

Interchange Number: 11
Type: Custom
Usage: 1968 full-size Chevrolet, Pontiac, Oldsmobile, or Buick
Notes: Two-door hardtop and convertible each used a different set of belts. Two-door sedan used the same belts as the four-door sedan.

Interchange Number: 12
Type: Standard
Usage: 1968 Camaro; 1968 Pontiac Firebird

Interchange Number: 13
Type: Custom
Usage: 1968 Camaro; 1968 Pontiac Firebird

Interchange Number: 14
Type: Standard
Usage: 1969 full-size Chevrolet, Pontiac, Oldsmobile, or Buick; 1969 Chevelle; 1969 Pontiac LeMans; 1969 Olds Cutlass; 1969 Buick Skylark

Interchange Number: 15
Type: Custom
full-size Oldsmobile; 1959–60 full-size Pontiac; convertible only

Interchange Number: 35
> Part Number(s): N/A (backrest)
> Usage: 1961–62 full-size Chevrolet, Pontiac, or Oldsmobile; all two-door except convertible

Interchange Number: 36
> Part Number(s): N/A (backrest)
> Usage: 1961–62 full-size Chevrolet, Pontiac, or Oldsmobile; convertible only

Interchange Number: 37
> Part Number(s): N/A (backrest)
> Usage: 1963–64 full-size Chevrolet, Pontiac, or Oldsmobile; all two-door except convertible

Interchange Number: 38
> Part Number(s): N/A (backrest)
> Usage: 1963–64 full-size Chevrolet, Pontiac, or Oldsmobile; convertible only

Interchange Number: 39
> Part Number(s): 7788671 (backrest)
> Usage: 1965–68 full-size Chevrolet, Pontiac, or Oldsmobile; all two-door except convertible

Interchange Number: 40
> Part Number(s): 7788673 (backrest)
> Usage: 1965–67 full-size Chevrolet; 1965–68 full-size Oldsmobile; 1965–68 full-size Pontiac; convertible only

Interchange Number: 41
> Part Number(s): 7788550 (backrest)
> Usage: 1968 full-size Chevrolet convertible

Interchange Number: 42
> Part Number(s): 8777294 (backrest)
> Usage: 1969–70 full-size Chevrolet, Pontiac, or Oldsmobile; all two-door except convertible

Interchange Number: 43
> Part Number(s): 8777323 (backrest)
> Usage: 1969–70 full-size Chevrolet, Pontiac, or Oldsmobile; all two-door convertibles

Interchange Number: 44
> Part Number(s): N/A (backrest)
> Usage: 1962–65 Chevy II two-door except convertible

Interchange Number: 45
> Part Number(s): N/A (backrest)
> Usage: 1962–63 Chevy II convertible

Interchange Number: 46
> Part Number(s): N/A (backrest)
> Usage: 1966–67 Chevy II two-door

Interchange Number: 47
> Part Number(s): 9812432 (backrest)
> Usage: 1968–72 Nova; 1971–72 Pontiac Ventura II two-door

Headrests

Headrests came in two basic styles, conventional and the Strato type. These styles are not interchangeable; however, each type is widely interchangeable with other makes since the headrests are used on GM lines. Also, for the most part, headrests interchange from side to side. That means those from a passenger's side will fit the driver's side.

Headrests came covered in colored vinyl to match the seats. But, as for a number of other components, no color is given in this interchange. Instead, the part number listed is for black. Headrests can be recovered in the correct color, though.

Model Identification

Camaro	*Interchange Number*
1967–68	9
1969	10
1970	11

Chevelle	*Interchange Number*
1966–67	
Conventional	1
Strato	5
1968	
Conventional	2
Strato	6
1969	
Conventional	3
Strato	7
1970	
Conventional	4
Strato	8

Impala	*Interchange Number*
1966–67	
Conventional	1
Strato	5
1968	
Conventional	2
Strato	6
1969	
Conventional	3
Strato	7
1970	
Conventional	4
Strato	8

Chevy II/Nova	*Interchange Number*
1966–67	
Conventional	1
Strato	5
1968	
Conventional	2
Strato	6
1969	
Conventional	3
Strato	7
1970	
Conventional	4
Strato	8

Interchange

Interchange Number: 1
> Part Number(s): 7709416
> Usage: 1967 Chevelle; 1967 Chevy II; 1967 Olds Cutlass; 1967 full-size Chevrolet, Oldsmobile, Pontiac, or Buick; 1967 Pontiac LeMans; 1967 Buick Skylark

Interchange Number: 2
Part Number(s): 7776767
Usage: 1968 Chevelle; 1968 full-size Chevrolet, Pontiac, Oldsmobile, or Buick; 1968 Chevy II; 1968 Olds Cutlass; 1968 Pontiac LeMans; 1968 Buick Skylark

Interchange Number: 3
Part Number(s): 8771007
Usage: 1969 Chevelle; 1969 full-size Chevrolet, Pontiac, Oldsmobile, or Buick; 1969 Chevy II; 1969 Olds Cutlass; 1969 Pontiac LeMans; 1969 Buick Skylark

Interchange Number: 4
Part Number(s): 9816284
Usage: 1970–71 Chevelle; 1970 full-size Chevrolet, Pontiac, Oldsmobile, or Buick; 1970 Chevy II; 1970–71 Olds Cutlass; 1970–71 Pontiac LeMans; 1970–71 Buick Skylark

Interchange Number: 5
Part Number(s): 7596335
Usage: 1966–67 Chevelle; 1966–67 full-size Chevrolet, Pontiac, Oldsmobile, or Buick; 1966–67 Chevy II; 1966–67 Olds Cutlass; 1966–67 Pontiac LeMans; 1966–67 Buick Skylark

Interchange Number: 6
Part Number(s): 7759740
Usage: 1968 Chevelle; 1968 full-size Chevrolet, Pontiac, Oldsmobile, or Buick; 1968 Chevy II; 1968 Olds Cutlass; 1968 Pontiac LeMans; 1968 Buick Skylark; 1968 Olds Toronado

Interchange Number: 7
Part Number(s): 8737463
Usage: 1969 Chevelle; 1969 full-size Chevrolet, Pontiac, Oldsmobile, or Buick; 1969 Chevy II; 1969 Olds Cutlass; 1969 Pontiac LeMans; 1969 Buick Skylark; 1969 Olds Toronado

Interchange Number: 8
Part Number(s): 8899215
Usage: 1970–71 Chevelle; 1970–72 Nova; 1970–72 Olds Cutlass; 1970–72 Pontiac LeMans; 1970–72 Buick Skylark; 1971–72 Pontiac Ventura II

Interchange Number: 9
Part Number(s): 7759726
Usage: 1967–68 Camaro; 1967–68 Pontiac Firebird

Interchange Number: 10
Part Number(s): Early, 8737455; late, 8787553
Usage: 1969 Camaro; 1969 Pontiac Firebird
Notes: Early models had straight post; late models had curved post. Change occurred around December 31, 1968.

Interchange Number: 11
Part Number(s): 9817854
Usage: 1970 Camaro; 1970 Pontiac Firebird

Index